FROM SHYLOCK TO SVENGALI

EDGAR ROSENBERG

From Shylock To Svengali

Jewish Stereotypes in English Fiction

STANFORD UNIVERSITY PRESS
STANFORD, CALIFORNIA
1960

STANFORD UNIVERSITY PRESS
STANFORD, CALIFORNIA

© 1960 BY THE BOARD OF TRUSTEES OF THE
LELAND STANFORD JUNIOR UNIVERSITY
ALL RIGHTS RESERVED

LIBRARY OF CONGRESS CATALOG CARD NUMBER: 60-8560
PRINTED IN THE UNITED STATES OF AMERICA

To My Parents

43956

Acknowledgments

I am chiefly indebted to Professor William Irvine, Stanford University, who saw this book through its preliminary drafts and without whose unfailing patience and sympathy I should hardly have gotten past the beginning of the job. At one stage or another, the manuscript has also been read, criticized, and marginally annotated by Professors Wallace Stegner, Richard Scowcroft, Wilfred Stone, David Levin, and Thomas Moser, all of Stanford, whose assistance I record with gratitude.

I have endeavored to indicate, in the text or the Notes, my principal creditors among earlier writers in the field. Anybody writing on the Jew in English literature must pay his respects to the late Montagu F. Modder, whose book remains much the most satisfactory full-length text on the subject. Since I split hairs with him in the introductory pages and elsewhere, I wish to acknowledge here my larger sense of indebtedness to him; his book not only helped me in getting started but provided essential bibliographical services. Since its publication more than twenty years ago, a dozen critical essays in *Commentary* and *Midstream* have kept the discussion from flagging. Of these I have availed myself throughout.

To Linda Brownrigg and the editors of the Stanford University Press I owe thanks for prodding me to keep deadlines which I habitually ignored; to the staff of Widener Library, Harvard University, for allowing me to keep books out of circulation beyond all limits of decency; and to Marvin Sadik and the staff of the Fogg Art Museum for steering me toward the illustrations which appear in the text.

Finally I record with pleasure two private debts: to Joseph and Lilly Kundmueller of Palo Alto for their kindness and hospitality to me during my last years of graduate study at Stanford, and to the Master of Leverett House, John Conway, who, for the past three years, has given me a desk, a shelter, a room with a view.

E. R.

Leverett House
Harvard University
May 1960

Contents

List of Plates

PART ONE

Prototypes

A type is like a neuralgic area. Some chronic ailment has created a zone of weakened resistance, and whenever an analogous phenomenon makes itself felt it immediately confines itself to this predisposed area, until the process becomes a matter of mechanical monotony.

MARIO PRAZ, *The Romantic Agony*

I

Introduction

These are some prolegomena to a study in the idea and uses of stereotype in literature. The types I have chosen for analysis are those of the Jewish criminal and the Jewish paragon as they appear in the English novel between 1795 and 1895. But I have used the word *fiction* in the subtitle of this essay in the widest sense, to allow me to relate the pertinent Jewish characters to their prototypes in some of the dramatic literature before the nineteenth century. It is difficult, in talking about Dickens's Jewish bogey, quite to ignore Shakespeare's; and an appreciation of George Eliot's Jewish apologists will not be crippled by an understanding of Cumberland's.

The novelists on whom I have drawn for the discussion are Maria Edgeworth, Walter Scott, Charles Dickens, Anthony Trollope, Edward Bulwer-Lytton, George Eliot, and George Du Maurier. The first and last of these are interesting minor novelists, the last-named hopelessly minor. But Edgeworth's *Harrington* is an important early milestone in the portrayal of civilized Jewish types: the first English novel to attempt anything like a meaningful social stratification of its Jewish personnel; the first to take its benevolent Jews seriously, without assuming them to be, for all their benevolent qualities, a collection of hyperborean oddities; the first to deal with anti-Semitism critically and problematically, as a destructive public force, not a whimsical form of muscular exercise. And in his portrayal of Svengali, at the opposite end of the study, Du Maurier has brought together so many of the themes which have been struck earlier that it would have been a shame not to hear what he has to say. Like Dracula and Frankenstein's monster, Svengali has been so vastly diffused and generalized by the public media that he has passed into the popular consciousness as something of a household name, with the result that one has difficulty in remembering his exact credentials. (Whoever remembers that Frankenstein's ogre is really a sentimental Outsider, a confirmed Godwinian, who is fond of lecturing the reader on the benefits of social and domestic coexistence and who goes into raptures over a good-looking piece of scenery?) Svengali has thus managed to horrify and amuse several million people who are apt to forget that the real Svengali is in the first instance a Jew, and that his Jewishness provides the source of all his horrific and comic endowments.

The novelists who are flanked by Edgeworth and Du Maurier are, except for Bulwer, the obvious ones. Scott's Isaac and Rebecca, Dickens's Fagin and Trollope's Melmotte, and the Jewish group in Eliot's *Daniel Deronda* remain, I imagine, the most distinguished Jewish names in the English novel to date. Among their creators, Scott's name leads all the rest. In the history of Jewish literary iconography, his importance is second only to Shakespeare's, and of a parallel nature. *Ivanhoe* to all intents made the Jews' fortune in the novel, in the sense in which Shakespeare's *Merchant of Venice* gave them a permanent place in the theater. And Scott was the first to make at least some attempt to repudiate a pre-logical cliché of the Jews by defining their conduct and motives in the light of their local habitation, their subservience to a specific time and place in history. If it is true that in describing Isaac, Scott still depends nine-tenths of the time on the stock-attributes of the old-fashioned Jewish curmudgeon (that compound of miser, coward, and sycophant, whose interests are vested about equally in his ducats and his daughter), it is also true that he endeavors to rationalize Isaac's conduct by relating it to the historical tensions that have depressed him into his ironic role and to view him as a member of a persecuted minority—an object of Scott's qualified sympathy in so far as he is persecuted, a source of unqualified interest in so far as he belongs to an exotic fringe group, on whom Scott the regional historian is free to lavish all the minute descriptive documentation that he elevated into a canon of art. In banishing Isaac and Rebecca from England at the end of the book, Scott recapitulates the dominant theme of the novel—the solemn theme of dispossession—and reaffirms its fundamental argument, its critique of superannuated feudal values and traditions whose maintenance is at best a gesture of frivolity and at worst a national disaster.

Dickens offers a simpler and more basic medieval grammar. In our search for the exemplary figure, the archetypal Jew, reptilian Fagin antedates the good dog Isaac and the bully Shylock, reverting past them both to the obscene stage-fiend of the Age of Belief, with its fierce academic respect for the categories of *ratio* and its automatic horror of that demon of *ultima ratio,* the God-killer and bogey who has in Satan's heart his hornet's nest. Though he has been divested of his theology and patched up for purposes of Victorian sensation-drama, the perspective has not significantly shifted, the conflict being what it is in the Dickens universe: between innocence and depravity, the boy-martyr and the tyrant-sadist with the knife, the princeling of orphans and the pedagogos of pickpockets. By using children as the interpreters of his world, Dickens achieves a simplicity of terror unimaginable except in a state of childlike incoherence: Fagin, seen through the eyes of a distraught little boy, becomes affectively a figure in a claustrophobic dream world, the great kidnapper, the child's vision of evil.

As a receiver of stolen goods, Fagin recalls the parasitic qualities which are traditionally associated with the Jew, and which, on the upper levels of commercial success, suggest the impersonal greed of Marlowe's Barabas, Shylock's cupidity, Isaac's already degenerate miserliness; he represents, too, the impoverished antitype of the aggressive Jewish monopolists and peculators who were becoming fashionable in the novels of Trollope and his contemporaries. To pass from *Oliver Twist* to *The Way We Live Now* is to move from the London underworld to the world of opulent and tasteless Anglo-Jewish homes and business offices, from the Jew who threatens the lives of young boys to the Jew who threatens the survival of the body politic, the vulgar parvenu and foreign swindler who is distinguished equally for his social undesirability and his commercial ruthlessness. In a novel like Trollope's, therefore, the Jew will no longer be placed in dramatic opposition to a basically healthy Christian community (as he had been in Shakespeare's play) nor will he be crowded out to the periphery of the active social world (as he had been in *Ivanhoe*); now we shall find him operating at dead center, symbol of a society (so runs the implication) that abandoned its native integrity when it admitted him into the drawing room, and that delivered itself into his hands when it allowed him to assume a financial power mandate. For the novelists of Trollope's generation, the criterion has become increasingly socio-economic, while the bogey side of the Jew has largely disappeared.

Dickens and Trollope, between them, saw the Jew in his two dominant criminal guises, in the twin roles of mutilator and usurer in which he had already been typecast in Chaucer's day—as something of a supervillain, whose criminality placed him beyond social and domestic commitments and underlined his basic isolation. He was quite *sui generis;* that was the point. Edgeworth and Scott saw his good as well as his bad sides, allowing him a large measure of sympathy whenever they looked on him as the member of a persecuted race, in the context of his group existence, and treating him with a corresponding degree of animosity or contempt whenever they focused on his personal identity, which was apt to be, on close examination, horrible or absurd. On the whole, he looked more impressive as villain than as victim. His wickedness and comicality had been his chief attributes on the stage down the centuries, and they continued to be presented by the novelist with the force and immediacy of drama and with the clarity of caricature, while his virtues remained, for the most part, the object of boring and tendentious conversation. And that, as we know, is the trouble with *Daniel Deronda,* George Eliot's panoramic social novel about a group of London Jews, in which the Jewish paragon achieves his apotheosis in English fiction. The convention on which Eliot drew for her Jewish characters was the moralistic, sentimental, and self-conscious convention of the impeccable Jew that writers like Lessing and Cumberland had, as it were, institutionalized a hundred years earlier in an attempt to drive Shylock off the stage by creating a satisfactory countermyth. Eliot differs from her eighteenth-century precursors chiefly in allowing her Jews more elbowroom to act in a public and political capacity (the novel owes much of its present-day fame, of course, to its alleged influence on

Zionism), but the rhetoric of motives is the same: to justify the Jews to the Gentiles and to reconcile them to each other. There are half a dozen important Jews in *Daniel Deronda,* important in so far as they allow Eliot to polemicize the "Jewish question," each of the characters contributing a particular Jewish viewpoint to a novel that is dialectic in structure and didactic in intention. The Jewish figures are thus the ones who are most heavily burdened with Eliot's philosophical messages (the Zionist, the positivist, the necessitarian), and it is not their fault if they collapse beneath the weight. They exhaust themselves in talk, and their talk is often theatrical without being dramatic. To understand their roles within the framework of this study, we shall need to know something of the whole pattern of apology and retraction that made the virtuous Jew possible, and condemned him to be dull.

The six novelists (an eminent Romantic, three eminent Victorians, a couple of lesser writers) comprise, I think, a fair cross section of what could be done in the way of stereotyping the Jew in fiction. Bulwer is evidently the maverick of the lot, and in admitting him to the discussion I confess to some high-handedness; almost any other novelist who has dealt with the Jew—William Ainsworth, Charles Reade, Mrs. Radcliffe, Mrs. Humphry Ward—might have done quite as well. It is difficult nowadays to find stimulating excuses for Bulwer. In the company of Scott, Dickens, Trollope, and Eliot he is clearly out of step; and Du Maurier has at least the excuse of supplying popular culture with a metaphor, whereas Bulwer merely supplied it with the vogue for black evening-wear. The most recent historian of the English novel has said of him that he is one of those novelists who may be very well for their own generation but "do nothing that has not been better done before"; instead of doing one thing well, and exploring, as did Conrad, "a few simple ideas," Bulwer does a dozen things badly.[1] The point for me is that he does those dozen things—practices them, moreover, with all the glibness of a cliché-expert. I claim for him therefore a certain strategic importance that none of the better novelists fulfill. Since he wrote about

[1] Superscript numbers refer to the Notes at the back of the book, pp. 341–79. Except for some explanatory asides which appear at the foot of the page, all aids to reflection (direct citations, supplementary evidence, and discursive matter) will be found in the Notes.

three quite different sorts of Jews, I have preferred not to give him a chapter all to himself but to parcel him out three ways, dealing with him as adjunct to Trollope, as continuator of the Wandering-Jew tradition, and as imitator of Scott.

I plead guilty to certain errors both of omission and of commission. The most glaring omission is that of Benjamin Disraeli. He wrote about Jews all the time, and in Sidonia he even created something of a suprapersonal literary symbol. But I can find no place for him in a study that deals with fixed and recurrent caricatures and their antipodes. Disraeli used all his major figures either as extensions of a rather marvelously inflated ego or as mouthpieces for his highly personal racial and political mystique, so that any discussion of his Jewish figures, instead of encouraging generalizations, leads straight back to Disraeli, who is a more or less interesting novelist, depending on one's view of him. Most readers are apt to find him rather deadly going, though F. R. Leavis, most distinguished among our current literary resurrection-men, has given him a new lease on life recently by underwriting him in one of his influential footnotes. Trollope's famous objection to his novels (that they smell of hair oil) is less likely to find support nowadays than very nearly the opposite one: that the novels are not "artificial" enough and that the polemical usefulness which Disraeli claimed for them in the preface to *Coningsby* prevents them from being very much more than polemic. Disraeli's Peel is simply Peel, instead of being Peel plus x: a passport-photographer's view of him, not a painter's. Any account of Disraeli's Jews that does not at once run aground on the topicality of the material, leads one sooner or later to the brink of his famous Asian Mystery, the answer to which Disraeli (or Tancred) kept to himself, so that once he has got there the reader has no choice except to retreat again. But whether one agrees with Trollope that he is a theatrical mountebank, or with Leavis that he is "so alive and intelligent," "so mature," or with the common reader that he belongs to history, he is not, in the framework of this essay, a useful writer.[2] In a number of places I have gone to him for incidental and corroborative evidence: in my remarks on George Eliot's view on race, in my concluding comments on the Jewish Merchant Prince, and again in my summary of the exotic novels that came out of *Ivanhoe*.

A somewhat similar obstacle—that of being stopped short by a particular biographical prototype, a "live" model, instead of being led back to an inherited literary type—has kept me from discussing at length a novel that at one time commanded a good deal of respect: Meredith's *Tragic Comedians.* In the 1880's it was fashionable to congratulate Meredith on having produced, in the hero of that novel, the most life-like portrait of a Jew in the whole of English fiction. Very likely he had, since he had taken him straight from life, took pains to say so, and so should not have been complimented on having created a character when he had merely written one up. *The Tragic Comedians* is fictionalized biography, the story of the German-Jewish socialist Ferdinand Lassalle, whose spectacular career and sensational death made their way into fiction elsewhere. Meredith used his material very much as he found it in the autobiographical memoir published by Lassalle's ex-fiancée a few months before his own hastily written novel came out. It is the history of a pampered young woman, brought up in a morbidly anti-Semitic household of petty Bavarian nobles, who scandalizes her family by falling in love with a Jewish labor agitator (i.e., Lassalle), is kept under lock and key to prevent her running off with him, and is browbeaten in other ways; eventually, a rival suitor who is more to the family's taste biologically and socially, a Roumanian Prince named Yanko von Racowitz, kills the Jewish lover in a duel and, half a year later, has the unique satisfaction of being accepted in marriage by the interesting girl whose fiancé he has shot.[3] Evidently the Princess von Racowitza had a good deal to explain in her memoir; Meredith, in the novel based on it, went her one better by seeing through her gushy rhetoric, providing his own dusty answer to her apologia, and showing her to be an essentially silly woman with a talent for self-dramatization. But he barely changed the details of a situation which, in actuality, contained all the elements of a tight novel (the elements, in effect, of a Meredith novel, if one considers the astounding stupidity, narcissism, vanity, and histrionics displayed by the principals in the affair), sticking closely to the facts of the case, and translating Lassalle's flamboyant language into his own turgid idiom. *The Tragic Comedians* is interesting minor Meredith, but the transparent presence of Lassalle places the book in a category of its own, relevant to the discussion incidentally, in so far as Meredith suggests, here and there, the general type behind the immediate impression.

The two chapters on the Wandering Jew that precede the discussion of Du Maurier are admittedly on the periphery of the thesis. The Wandering Jew is not, strictly speaking, a stereotype in the sense in which Shylock and Fagin are stereotypes—figures who conform to more or less identical patterns of behavior, resemble each other physically, and subscribe to a relatively fixed moral code; who react in predictable ways to similar stimuli; and who may exist independently of historical changes and often in the very teeth of historical change. Unlike the permanently conditioned Judases of Shakespeare, Scott, and Dickens, the Wandering Jew is a mythological figure with a tendency to change from generation to generation, and ideally he falls outside the framework of the discussion. I have, however, decided to include these chapters, and this for three reasons. First, the myth of Ahasuerus, though not really cognate to the more important Shylock story, has similar origins; both trace their histories to early Christian accounts of an offense against the Christian God—the treachery of Judas, the inhumanity of Cartaphilus—and every so often the two legends impinge on each other. Second, I believe that the Wandering-Jew tradition offers a fruitful alternative to the static conventions of the Jewish villain and his antipode, for the very reasons that each generation interprets it anew. It thus satisfies certain conditions that the Shylock story satisfies only accidentally: it reflects shifting ideologies and world views and provides a footnote to the history of ideas. In literature it is the Eternal Jew who periodically dies and is reborn, and the mortal Shylock who is eternally the same. And lastly I should have had difficulty in quite getting at Svengali without first taking stock of Ahasuerus and of his periodic costume changes on the long road from Rome.

So much by way of prospectus. The discussion comes in three parts. In Part One, I pay my respects to earlier critical literature on the subject, endeavor to establish a few uneasy dogmas of my own, and, in Chapters Two and Three, bring the stereotypes down to the beginning of the nineteenth century. In Part Two I deal with the major novelists: Scott, Dickens, Trollope, and Eliot. Part Three is given over to the development of the Wandering Jew and to some of the novelists who appropriated him: Monk Lewis, Godwin, Bulwer, and Du Maurier. In organizing my materials I have adopted the questionable method of classifying, by type, the fictional characters with whom I deal, assigning one or two of the more conspicuous functions of the stereotype to each of the writers who form the nucleus of the discussion—using Scott's Jew as a specimen of the old-fashioned comic miser, Dickens's as the archetypal bogey, Trollope's as the exemplary parasite, and so forth. In other words, the half-dozen novels that I include as self-evident are also those which present, in memorable ways, some of the dominant guises the Jew has assumed in literature and some of the prevailing metaphors that have been used to describe him: the familiar guises of the comic tightwad and the vulgar tycoon; the kidnapper and the Anti-Christ; the black magician and the esoteric sage; Old Testament warrior and New Testament samaritan; Judas Maccabaeus and Judas Iscariot. I admit at once that any such attempt to classify one's personnel may end in merely ossifying it, and that anybody who is familiar with Forster's proscription of the Nine Uses of Weather in the Novel ought to think twice before pinning labels on the Six (or Seven or Eight) Kinds of Jews in Fiction. I take it for granted that the functions, traits, images, overlap a good deal; it is one of my premises that they do. Still, the classification has its soundness, I think—always with the proviso that the types, so far from being isolable, have been chosen for their recurrence from one writer to the next, their inescapable resemblance, their sovereign position in literature, and their final imperturbability and resistance to fashionable winds of doctrine and changes in weather —all nine kinds of weather.

The minor nineteenth-century novelists who dealt with the Jew and whom I ignore in the body of the essay may be regarded (with similar qualifications) as grouping themselves around one of the five or six major novelists. Thus Scott may be thought of as setting the pace for all those lesser historical romancers (the Bulwer of *Leila* and the Disraeli of *David Alroy,* the Kingsley of *Hypatia,* and people like Hall Caine at the end of the century) who, like Scott, found the Jew interesting in proportion as they thought him picturesque, and edifying in proportion as he promoted the lavish expense of local color; who saw him as one of the instructive curiosities of literature, best exhibited at some period in the pluperfect past and in exotic Mediterranean circumstances, enveloped in costly wardrobes in which he might have been mistaken from a distance for a sheik, a khaffir, or one of the Magi—Moses as he appeared unto De Mille. Similarly, Dickens is empowered to speak for the half-dozen writers before and after him (Ainsworth most prominently, but also Mrs. Trollope and the early impenitent Edgeworth) who continued to treat their Jews as amoral sensation-figures, as poisoners, kidnappers, perjurers, hired assassins, and the like, creatures defined not by any one human frailty but by their criminality pure and simple, by their imperviousness to moral laws, and frequently to the laws of nature as well. Trollope's Jew, in turn, is intended to deputize that vast tribe of fictional Jews who are above anything else defined by their commitment to the Stock Exchange, who (though they often connect up with the sensation-Jew) are keener on getting their pounds sterling than their pound of flesh: the usurers and fences and old-clothes dealers who have walk-on parts in Mrs. Radcliffe's fiction and Captain Marryat's; the foreign swindlers and commercial Machiavels who appear in Thackeray's *Newcomes,* Bulwer's *My Novel,* and Trollope's *Eustace Diamonds;* the pathetic figures (both agents and victims of social bankruptcy) described by Charles Reade and Charles Lever and the Dickens of *Our Mutual Friend.* And George Eliot, finally, may be regarded as focal point for the novelists, most of them coming late in the century (Walter Besant, Hale White, Mrs. Humphry Ward, the Trollope of *Nina Balatka,* and Charles Kingsley when he is being serious), who stressed the Jew's domestic and civic performances and pictured him sympathetically in the roles of lover and husband, and who saw him (often with a sidelong squint at Spinoza) as profoundly introspective as well as vastly learned, endowed with sagacity, wit, bookishness, a high degree of verbal aptitude, and whatever stimuli would get him to discourse mellifluently and interminably on Jewish matters. Important as these lesser novels are, I have as a rule preferred not to weight down the discussion by parceling them out to the various chapters in which one might logically wish to see them discussed, but have kept a few of them in reserve for the Conclusion, where, taken together, they give promise of looking a little more formidable than if they were scattered over the essay as a whole.

Throughout the study I have sidestepped or ignored altogether the question of personal bias toward the Jews in the authors whose work I discuss, and though I have naturally had to pay some attention to historical currents, I have not stressed them. Instead, I have tried to relate the stereotypes and conventions to each other, to establish grounds for comparison and discrimination, and to investigate and explain the particular Jewish figure within the configuration of the novel in which it appears. This has led me at times into a good deal of plot-analysis, especially in the case of the lesser novels. But I hope that I have managed along the way to excavate and dust off half a dozen or so abandoned stories. I shall have relatively little to say about the difference between Shakespeare's world picture and Scott's, and, beyond the next few paragraphs, nothing whatever about Scott's opinion of the Jews. Lockhart's *Memoirs* suggest that he thought them a sorry and rascally lot, an opinion which may be of interest to Scott's biographers and of concern to anthropologists. It appears, however, not to have stood in the way of his presenting world literature with an almost distressingly fine Jewess, a touchstone of physical and moral good health, beside whom the Christians dwindle into a mass of sentimental clodhoppers, primitive fire-eaters, and decadent adventurers.

The relation of the Jewish types in literature either to a particular climate of opinion or to the private prejudice of the author is a problem which earlier writers on the subject have taken up at some length, and I shall say a word about it here to spare myself needless pains later on. Crudely stated, the argument from social change assumes that the treatment of the Jew in English drama and fiction became increasingly liberal in proportion as the governing bodies of England became increasingly liberal. This, for example, is the thesis of Montagu Modder's scholarly work on *The Jew in the Literature of England*: "It will be seen," he writes, "as the story unfolds itself, that invariably the poet, the novelist and the dramatist reflect the attitude of contemporary society in their presentation of the Jewish character, and that the portrayal changes with the economic and social changes of each decade."[4] Much may be said in favor of this approach, and though my own argument tends rather the other way, I reserve the right to trespass from time to time into the region of my own anathema. The principal objection to the historical rationale is that it is apt to slight the massive durability of a stereotype, which is almost by definition the least pliable of literary sorts, the one least sensitive to social vibrations. The historical argument can tell us a good deal: why Jews could not be presented sympathetically before the eighteenth century; why the typically bad Jew of the 1830's wore dirtier linen than the typically bad Jew of the 1870's; why the sentimentally good Jew of the 1780's differed from his near-relation a hundred years later in being older, more of a monkey, and less of a public figure.

On the other hand, the argument (which is most helpful when it pinpoints the accidental differences) is likely to leave unexplained some of the simple and obvious points of identity: the persistence of the Jew-villain in the popular novels that a supposedly enlightened constituency devoured in the palmy days of the Reform Bill; the depressingly uniform presentation of the Jewish paragon as a moralizing apologist, a tolerant and educated bore, long after the apologies had become supererogatory; the portrayal of the Jew as black priest centuries after the Jews stopped being suspected of poisoning the municipal water works and accused of cutting up babies for Passover. *Oliver Twist,* Bulwer's *Leila,* and Mrs. Trollope's *A Romance of Vienna* all appeared in 1838, but one would not necessarily guess at the publication date of these novels from the description of the Jews in them—infanticides, sexual ogres, magicians, fanatics, thieves, extortionists, and perjurers, who can hardly be said to reflect "the attitude of contemporary society." At most, they reflect the taste of the reading public, which is not quite the same thing. If the Judas of the old moralities has been secularized since his passage through the ghetto and the tycoon Barabas has been pauperized on his way from Malta to Houndsditch, the family resemblance is nonetheless patent for the migration; blood (so runs the formula) is thicker than water. No amount of political enfranchisement, then, can quite explain away the unflattering types, the cowards and murderers and human lice, who persist in the novels of Maria Edgeworth, Captain Marryat,

Charles Reade, and George Du Maurier; in the plays of Tom Taylor and Dion Boucicault, and who, for that matter, continue to be served up by Wyndham Lewis and Charles Williams, Evelyn Waugh and Graham Greene. To appreciate Shylock's persistent and international appeal, we shall have to observe him within a fairly static literary convention as well as the more flexible context of political and social history: this is where the argument tends.

The *ad hominem* argument, which makes a simple equation between the depravity of the subject and the bigotry (but we may as well call it the depravity) of the author, is no longer so fashionable as it once was, probably because the whole question of private race prejudice has come to be recognized as less and less of a socio-economic problem and is increasingly left in charge of the psychiatrists, who are sworn to professional secrecy. Still, if it has ceased to be of interest to literary historians, the question continues to be raised on nonacademic levels of conversation, and often with vehemence. Dickens introduced two Jews into his novels: Fagin, who is a villain, and Riah, who is a saint; admittedly Fagin is much the livelier of the two. *Was* Dickens anti-Semitic? Or was he not? We shall sample the available opinions. Hilaire Belloc thought he was. Dickens, he wrote, "disliked Jews instinctively; when he wrote of a Jew according to his inclination he made him out a criminal"; and the echo murmurs: "because he was really of the devil's party without knowing it"—the one inference being as legitimate as the other.[5] Edmund Wilson, whose opinion one should like to have above all others, is chiefly interested in Fagin and Riah as manifestations of "the two Scrooges" in Dickens, verbal translations (if the issue is pushed far enough) of Dickens's manic-depressive tendencies, by which "there has always to be a good and a bad of everything," a counterbalancing of opposites in each of the books; and beyond this constatation Wilson stays out of the controversy.[6] George Orwell thought Dickens unique among the novelists of his time in not being anti-Semitic, Orwell accepting *prima facie* Dickens's explanation (though he does not quote it) that he made Fagin a Jew "because it unfortunately was true of the time to which that story refers, that that class of criminal almost invariably *was* a Jew."[7]

Edgar Johnson, whose critical biography of Dickens has become the standard text since its publication eight years ago, also regards Dickens as philo-Semitic, and in an interesting article on the subject he has made out a strong case in favor of his view. In the course of the article, which is brief and, within its compass, definitive, Johnson necessarily sums up the episode—a little boring merely from having been told so often—about that pugnacious Mrs. Davis who, twenty-five years after *Oliver Twist* appeared, taxed Dickens with having "encouraged a vile prejudice against the despised Hebrew" and protested against the portrayal of Fagin as "a great wrong," which Dickens should be given the opportunity of redressing directly by donating a sum of money to the Lady Montefiore Memorial. Naturally the money was sent, but the imputation that he disliked Jews baffled Dickens—or at least he professed to be baffled by it. He said, in effect: some of my best friends are Jews—Mark Lemon, for example, the editor of *Punch* (a magazine, incidentally, which appears to be uncommonly fond of caricaturing our Jewish Prime Minister as Fagin, Richard Crookback, an Arab street-peddler, and the like) is a dear family friend; surely my children should be ill advised to let him read bedtime stories to them if they thought *him* the Anti-Christ. In so many words he told Mrs. Davis, "I have no feeling towards the Jewish people but a friendly one," "always speak well of them, whether in public or private, and bear my testimony (as I ought to do) to their perfect good faith in such transactions as I have ever had with them."[8]

On the face of it, certainly, Dickens's labors were all in the cause of light. Johnson reminds us that Dickens temperamentally opposed all signs of intolerance; that he found slavery, for example, an abominable testament to human idiocy; that he openly encouraged all sorts of libertarian movements (he supported the Swiss anticlericals in 1845, for instance, and the liberal revolutions elsewhere on the Continent three years later); and that his political affiliations were solidly those of a liberal: a disestablishmentarian in his religious ideology, a humanitarian moderate among the philosophical radicalists in his political theory. Little wonder that he found Mrs. Davis's charge of foul play against the Jews distressing and, to judge from the tone of his reply, tiresome. Had he not, in his *Child's History of England,* "expressed a strong abhorrence of their persecution in olden times?"

This is as far as his own evidence will take us. I add that I have not, myself, any idea whether Dickens was an anti-Semite, and I am not prepared to say that he had any idea; in public he denied being one, and with his own testimony on record, the subject may be dropped. For the rest, I suspect that the gulf which separates Fagin from Dickens's public professions of tolerance defines the difference between metaphor and statement, creation and criticism, and that one of the defects endemic to earlier studies on the Jew in literature lies in the general failure to distinguish the two. Since the authors are determined to come up with optimistic results, there is a tendency to slant the evidence by citing Macaulay's parliamentary performances and Dean Milman's sympathetic scholarship as potent antidotes to the disreputable characters in Dickens and Ainsworth. And naturally the scales dip in the desired way. But surely Edward Calisch ought not to lay to his soul the flattering unction that "the noble utterances of Macaulay, Hazlitt, Richard Grant, Lord John Russell, Gladstone, and Dr. Whateley in political matters" will dislodge Fagin by one inch, or that Gladstone or Dr. Whateley (in political matters) can contend in the dark places where the Muses are.[9] In *Nathan the Wise,* Lessing wrote: "We have not freed ourselves from superstition by detecting it."

It is convenient to indicate here one other doubtful critical assumption. None of the studies is quite exempt from it, but for a good example we may go to M. J. Landa's book on *The Jew in Drama.* Landa, who has been active in the theater, knows his subject intimately and thoroughly; his book teems with names and titles that often appear to exercise a charm of their own, independent of any real or fancied relevance; his work is encyclopedic and, like encyclopedias in general, frequently proves little except the unarguable presence of multiplicity. The author seems to be so much taken with the sheer number of playwrights who have introduced Jewish figures into their repertory that he feels urged from time to time to censure those who have *not* introduced them; and so, after pages and pages of positive entries, he pulls himself up short to remark, with an air of mild distress, that "T. W. Robertson managed without Jews." When he pauses for more extended comment, we are likely to get the following; the passage occurs in a chapter entitled "The Libel of the Lisp":

Charles Dickens, in addition to creating Fagin, must also bear the burden of blame for libelling the Jew with a lisp. . . . Jews are no more prone to lisping—after childhood—than are English, Scotch, or Irish people. There is no 'th,' no lisping sound, in either Hebrew or Yiddish. . . . Jews have never been different from other people in the matter of dialect. . . . Jewish dialects date from Biblical times. It is only necessary to mention the test of the pronunciation of 'shibboleth' (Judges xii, 6), a word with a special meaning in modern languages on that account. . . . Instead of any disability, most Jews are possessed of exceptional lingual capacity. One of the leading Scotch comedians of to-day, with a priceless Doric, is a Jew.[10]

"Now really, what a piece of extravagance all that is!"—Arnold's polite protest against Ruskin's Asiatic pedantries rises to one's lips. "It is to show in one's criticism, to the highest excess, the note of provinciality." The stereotype of the Jew was from the first anti-realistic; "observed inside literary tradition," as Louis Kronenberger reminds us, "Barabas and Fagin involve not how anti-Semitic but only how anti-realistic a Marlowe and a Dickens are." There is about most of the studies under discussion an oddly parochial (as well as unhistorical) sense of astonishment that the novelists and playwrights could have strayed so far, in their portrayal of Jews, from the biological or physiological or behavioral actuality. When Calisch complains that "no Jew would ever employ his child as Barabas did Abigail" or that Shylock "is not a true picture" because "vengefulness and thirst for blood are not characteristic qualities of the Jews," one has not the impression that issues are being met head-on: "the fitness, the measure, the centrality, which is the soul of all good criticism, is lost, and the note of provinciality shows itself." Hijman Michelson's monograph on *The Jew in Early English Literature* is spoiled everywhere by the mildly fantastic ill-humor with which the author flays each playwright as he catches him committing a "blunder" in his description—a blunder in the sense of his departing from the observed and experienced reality, whether the playwright experienced the reality or not. Since Michelson's study stops in the sixteenth century, his vehemence strikes one, as I say, as a little misplaced. In reading passages such as these, one is made to feel not merely that the authors are crusading against a purely abusive presentation of Jewish types, but that they would be happiest if all distinctions between Jews and other folk could be obscured or suppressed altogether. Whether the position is sound or not, it is certainly one which would have scandalized Disraeli and vexed George Eliot. "We shall aim to point out," writes David Philipson, "in how far the presentation [of the Jews] is correct, where the writer was actuated by prejudice, and where the Jewish character has been misunderstood either for good or ill."[11] But were it not to consider too curiously to consider so? In the long run, the argument that "Jews are not like that" confuses life and art, experience and literature; it ignores the possibility that a fiction may be all the more convincing and durable for being a basic distortion, with deep-seated attractions for the superstitious mass of men.

The remarks which follow are thus intended to complement and correct similar works undertaken in the last fifty years or so. A study such as this has got to justify itself in one of two ways: it has either to bring light into the dark spaces or to adjust the prevailing angle of vision. I hope to do a little of both. I shall expect to observe the fictional image of the Jew inside literary convention: to explain the image by referring it to the special aesthetic canons of the writer who has used it, and by relating it to an ulterior tradition on which the writer was free to draw. It is thus equally relevant, from my point of view, to recognize in Scott's Jews the presence of certain devices and themes peculiar to Scott the novelist, and to recognize the indebtedness of Isaac and Rebecca to their literary prototypes in Marlowe and Shakespeare. The important thing, it seems to me, is to note the operation of both these impulses and to discriminate between them: between the Jew as stereotype and the Jew as product of a particular literary bias; between the Jew of tradition and the Jew as he emerges in the single work. I am aware, all the same, that literary conventions can tell us only so much about a subject which is, at bottom, impenetrable. At the heart of a superstition lies a mystery. It is relatively easy to see what a writer like George Eliot is about with her Jews, or a writer like Lessing, since they tell us what to see and tell us, moreover, what to think. Their motives are accessible to us in proportion as everything is verbalized and out in the open. But how *can* one account for Fagin? At age twelve Dickens suffered some spasms in a blacking factory; there young Bob Fagin "recalled him to life" by giving him rub-downs and walked him to a place which Dickens pretended was his home, lest his escort discover his home to be a debtor's prison. One should have to command some ultimate psychology to track down the curious processes by which the fine lad who walked young Dickens to his imaginary dwelling place burst forth, fifteen years afterwards, as the hideous bogeyman with the red hair, and the hooked nose, and the devilish leer.

Oh! my eyes and limbs! Oh! my lungs and liver! Oh! goroo! goroo! . . . You dear simple-minded Britisher, and bucolic, I love you, but I don't love your Lombard Street Jews who rule you. . . . What with your Jew crusade for gold, and your hopeless subservience to the speculative interests of the city of London, we were drifting very far apart.

HENRY ADAMS, letter to Sir Robert Cunliffe (1898)

Have we ever stopped to consider the intolerable situation of men condemned to live in a society that adores the God they killed?

SARTRE, *Anti-Semite and Jew* (1948)

II

The Rise of the Jew-Villain

The myth of the Jew as villain has been with us long enough to have passed into a literary stereotype centuries ago. It dates back at least to Herod, the slayer of children and aspiring Christ-killer in disguise ("and when you have found him, bring me word, that I may also come and worship him"); to Judas, the original businessman with the contract in the pocket; and to the anonymous vulgar Jewish farceur who, in answer to Christ's "eli, eli," forced a reed filled with vinegar between His lips. Even the physical characteristics of the stereotype are already provided for in the Biblical descriptions: Herod's frenzy on being mocked by the wise men foreshadows the violent gestures with which subsequent caricatures have been afflicted; and the group of Jewish elders who come to watch the Crucifixion are already pictured as wagging their heads in the immemorial fashion that Shylock re-enacts when "they" spit at him. Saint Paul, the popularizer of the new religion, has provided the necessary program note. In his correspondence with the Romans, Paul does, in fact, lump Gentiles and Jews together as standing equally in need of righteousness;

but the specific counts of his indictment were afterwards found to tally very neatly with the crimes chargeable to the Jews alone. With characteristic vehemence Paul denounces them as "filled with all unrighteousness, wickedness, covetousness, maliciousness, envy, murder, strife, deceit, malignity; whisperers, backbiters; haters of God; insolent, haughty, boastful; inventors of evil things; covenant-breakers; without natural affection, unmerciful."*

The Jewish criminal in a variety of masks—as Christ-killer, traitor, financial hog—thus had Scriptural sanction from the first. At a time when literature flourished under clerical auspices and when nine-tenths of the *corpus poeticum* derived from Biblical paraphrases and martyrologies, the image of the Jew was everywhere linked with the event of the Passion and Crucifixion. To appreciate the "tone" of the medieval attitude toward the Jews, one has to go to the religious drama of the period. Since the subjects of the mystery plays performed at York, Coventry, Chester, and Towneley were largely taken from the New Testament, the Jew appears generally in the guise of Judas, fitted out with a large nose, red hair, and a red beard. But other roles were available. In a spectacle like the "Play of Corpus Christi," for

* Rom. 1:29–32. With Paul's description compare the following prolix paraphrase fabricated in 1753, at a time when the passage of the Jewish Naturalization Bill aroused a stream of abuse. "The Jews are a people of whom God has given the following most shocking description and character, even at the time when they were accounted His peculiar, chosen people. He complains that they were a most rebellious, disobedient, gainsaying, stiff-necked, impenitent, incorrigible, adulterous, whorish, impudent, forward, shameless, perverse, treacherous, revolting, backsliding, idolatrous, wicked, sinful, stubborn, untoward, hard-hearted, hypocritical, foolish, sottish, brutish, stupid, ungrateful, Covenant-breaking nation of people; a set of evil-doers, a generation of vipers, doing evil greedily with both hands, according to all the nations that were round about them; as bad, nay worse, than Sodom and Gomorrah, casting all God's laws and ordinances behind them, trampling them under their feet, rejecting, forsaking, and despising God Himself; provoking Him continually to His face, grieving Him to His heart, forgetting Him days without number, always erring in their hearts and disobeying His voice, etc. etc. And shall it be recorded that Britannia, the first amongst the Christian states, ever admitted such a nation or people as this to become one people, and to enjoy the privileges of a true born Englishman?" *Vide* "An Appeal to the Throne against the Naturalization of the Jewish Nation: in which are exposed the Practices for which the Jews were expelled out of England" (1753); as quoted in Calisch, *The Jew in English Literature,* p. 42.

A Jewish Broker

"Fagin's Political School"

example, which was performed in 1415, more than fifty Jew-parts appear; and what they were like may be gathered from the Order of the Pageants:

Pilate, Caiaphas, two soldiers, three Jews, Judas selling Jesus. . . . Jesus, and Judas kissing and betraying Him.

. . . and four Jews persecuting and scourging Jesus.

. . . and four Jews accusing Christ.

Jesus, covered with blood, bearing His cross to Calvary; Simon of Cyrene, Jews compelling Him to bear the cross. . . .

The Cross, Jesus stretched upon it on the earth, four Jews scourging and dragging Him with ropes.[1]

In the moralities, finally, the Iscariot role devolved on an unmistakably Semitic Satan, accompanied by the quasi-comic servant Vice, a generalized prototype of Marlowe's Ithamore and Shakespeare's Launcelot Gobbo. Elsewhere—in the morality *Respublica,* for example—the Jew appears as one of the seven deadly sins, preferably as Avaritia. From Avaritia he passed, by way of Usury and the Usurer, into the figures of Barabas and Shylock—to be played in the make-up which, as late as 1664, is still described in a contemporary jingle as the make-up appropriate to the stage-Jew:

His beard was red; his face was made
Not much unlike a witches;
His habit was a Jewish gown,
That would defend all weather;
His chin turned up, his nose hung down,
And both ends met together.[2]

Mutilation

In the writers anterior to the Norman Conquest, the Jew preserved something of the one-dimensional purity that is naturally conferred on one about whom nothing is known except that the devil had commissioned him to kill God. Since the image of the Jew until 1066 was a strictly traditional one, unobstructed by personal contact with the race, it was possible to regard the Jew with a certain metaphysical awe.[3] But in the two centuries between the Conquest and their expulsion under Edward I, the Jews were installed as the chief engines of finance; and so one was bound to run into them.

One might expect that their physical presence would suffice to explode some of the superstitions which clung to them and that their bogey qualities would cease to be credible once the visible reality could be compared with the historical fiction. Demonstrably the Jewish residents of London, York, and Norwich had not horns. On the other hand, it has always been one of the prerogatives of the devil to take on human shape; and besides, the Jews' traditional renown as physicians made them doubly vulnerable to the charge of witchcraft. It is difficult to be surprised at the persistent terror among the multitude when one learns that Richard surnamed the Lion-Heart so dreaded the Jews that he forbade them to be present at his coronation lest they bewitch him—a coronation of which the historian John Speed complacently remarks that, in spite of Richard's precaution, it was "auspicated" by the massacre of hundreds of Jews "who in a tumult raised by the Ocean [mob] were furiously murthered."[4]

Indeed, not only did the medieval Jew, as contemporary literature reflects him, fail to shed any part of his satanism; but, besides retaining his reputation of slaughterer, he consolidated his reputation of parasite. The accusation of commercial villainy had already been associated with Judas and his thirty pieces of silver; it was now given credence by the overt practice of high finance. In Chaucer, for example, the attributes of murderer and parasite, devil and usurer, already flourish side by side. In the Prioress's pathetic tale about the "litel clergeon," the Jews are the "cursed folk of Herodes," hateful to Christ whose "blood out-crieth on youre cursed dede," and the consorts of the devil,

> Our firste foo, the serpent Sathanas
> That hath in Jewes herte his waspes nest.

At the same time, the association with usury is pointedly made in the passage describing the *locus delicti:*

> . . . a Jewerye,
> Sustened by a lord of that contree,
> For foule usure, and lucre of vilanye,
> Hateful to Crist and to his companye.[5]

By the time Chaucer wrote his *Tales* the murder of Hugh of Lincoln was already a hundred and thirty years in the past (though he alludes to the event as having occurred "but a litel whyle ago"), and the Jews had been banished from England for almost a century. The transference of the story to Asia suggests that the Jews had already become strangers to the English scene. Their absence may well have fostered rather than obscured their evil reputation; the Jews once more receded into the distorted past of legend and history. But more likely their sojourn in England did not materially affect the traditional view of them one way or another, except to confirm the universal rumors. The point is that Chaucer was working with very familiar materials, used by writers equally during the settlement of the Jews in England and after their expulsion. The crime at the heart of Chaucer's story is one of blood sacrifice and mutilation with a knife, a staple of medieval balladry. The charges of kidnapping and the ritual murder of Christian children had been current for some two and a half centuries before Chaucer fictionalized them. How deeply the crime of *Kinderschaendung* was identified with the Crucifixion can be judged from our first extant account of ritual murder, to be found in the Saxon Chronicle for 1137:

> Nu we will saegen sumdel waet belaemp on Stephnes Kinges time. On this time the Judeus of Noruuic bohton an cristen cild before Estren pineden him alle the ilce pining that ure Drihten was pined on lang fridaei him on rode hengen for ure Drihtines luve sythen byrieden him. Wenden they it sculde ben forholen or ure Drythin atywede that he was hali martyr to munckes him namen bebyried him heglice in the minstre he maked thur ure Drihten wunderlice manifaeldlice miracles hatte he S'Willem.[6]

By the time Marlowe and Shakespeare appeared on the scene, at all events, the relatively—but only relatively—secular crime of money-lending had come to claim about as much attention as the ritual murders and physical mutilations. The one crime, of course, did not exclude the other: the Jew's knife was now poised for purposes of extortion. In the well-known ballad of Gernutus, for example, distinguished as a close analogue and possible source of Shakespeare's *Merchant of Venice,* the two crimes of mutilation and usury are as fully assimilated to each other as they are in Chaucer's tale.[7] From cutting out the Christian's heart, it was only a step to feeding on it; and occasionally the charge of mutilation carried with it obscure implications of cannibalism. Such hints are at the root of the whole flesh-bond story that Shakespeare inherited; and the threat of cannibalism persists explicitly in plays like Robert Daborne's *A Christian Turn'd Turk,* composed as late as 1612.[8]

When the medieval and Renaissance Jew does not pose as crucifier or mutilator, he frequently appears as poisoner. The whole of Marlowe's *Jew of Malta* is presumably an echo of the accusation, widely circulated in the fourteenth century, that the Jews had caused the Black Plague by poisoning the wells, though doubtless the old superstition of the Jewish witch-doctor contributed to his being cast in this role. Barabas, the exemplar of the type, has mastered every trick in the manual: he kills with a poisoned nosegay, feigns death with "poppy and cold mandrake juice," and the broth he administers to the nuns, and allegedly brewed according to the recipes of the Borgias, is seasoned with "all the poisons of the Stygian pool."[9] In Marston's *The Malcontent,* Mendoza's question "Canst thou empoison?" provokes from Malevole the answer, "Excellently; no Jew, pothecary, or politician better," a parallel the more interesting when it is remembered that the word *policy,* with its implications of Machiavellian cunning, occurs no fewer than a dozen times in reference to Marlowe's Jew.[10] In Webster's *Devil's Law-Case,* in which a Christian disguises himself as a Jew in order to expedite his schemes, Romelio suggests that among other homicidal techniques he might

> poyson a friend
> With pulling but a loose haire from's beard,
> or give a drench
> He should linger of't nine years, and ne'er complaine
> But in the Spring and Fall, and so the cause
> Imported to the disease naturall.[11]

It is often difficult, in retrospect, to determine precisely in how far the Jew, in passages like these, is still being stigmatized on religious grounds, and in how far the theological odium has been generalized to the point at which he can be incriminated on almost any charge. By 1633 someone like James Howell, Charles the Second's official historiographer, could make it a point to deny that the Jews had been expelled for their religion, "but for villainies and cheatings, for clipping coins, poisoning of waters, and counterfeiting of seals."[12]

But the religious stigma, no doubt, remains at the bottom of all other charges; the original superstition of the Christ-killer could easily give rise to the universal belief in other Jewish villainies, only less serious than the Ur-crime of the Crucifixion in proportion as the victims were less consequential.

Usury

In Act II of *The Jew of Malta,* Barabas treats his ghoulish slave, the Turk Ithamore, to a recital of his crimes. Whether Barabas is merely boasting or telling the truth is not the issue here; what matters is that his catalogue pretty well exhausts the Jewish capacity for criminal variety in the sixteenth century. Having killed sick people groaning under walls, poisoned wells, practiced physic upon the Italian, played off both sides against each other in the wars between France and Germany, Barabas has successfully run the gamut of professions open to enterprising Jews, except one:

> Then, after that, was I an usurer,
> And with extorting, cozening, forfeiting,
> And tricks belonging unto brokery,
> I filled the gaols with bankrouts in a year,
> And with young orphans planted hospitals;
> And every moon made some or other mad.
> And now and then one hang himself for grief,
> Pinning on his breast a long great scroll
> How I with interest tormented him.[13]

"Etre juif," said Casanova, "c'est être usurier." By the end of the sixteenth century, the presentation of the Jew as money-lender had become a dramatic cliché. In the ninety years between 1553 and the outbreak of the Civil War, the usurer appeared in over sixty plays, each revealing "an analogous similarity of the very devices used by the dramatists to bring about the desired conclusion."[14] Although the stage-usurers were not necessarily Jewish—so that the correspondence was not an absolute one—the stage-Jews were almost presumptively and uniformly extortionists.[15] Even though money-lending had been legalized in England in 1571 and was openly practiced by Christians, at bottom it continued to be regarded as a Jewish profession. "For a play treating of usury," writes Pettet, "a Jew had two particular points of significance: in the first place, Jews were certainly prominent in the business abroad, and in the second, it is possible that Shylock symbolizes the feeling, shared by Shakespeare, that usury is something alien to the national and traditional way of life."[16] It is not surprising to discover that, despite the occasional presence of Jews in sixteenth-century England, the Jewish usurers in Tudor and Stuart drama are hardly ever to be found in London, but continue to ply their trade in Turkey, Italy, Portugal, and the Near East.

Besides, the odium in which the Middle Ages had held usury, for being economically unsound and religiously damnable, still clung to the profession. Lactantius had labeled its practice outright robbery; Ambrose had called it murder; and the Church, supported by the patristic doctrines, condemned it in decrees of twenty-eight councils. Wilson, in his *Discourse upon Usury,* quotes Saint Jerome to the effect that "there is no difference betwixt usury, fraud, and violent robbing, as who should say, he that is a usurer is a deceitful false man, an errant thief, and an extreme extortioner." Benevenuto a Imola, writing in the fourteenth century, declared that "he who practiseth usury goeth to hell"; and by then Dante had already provided the demonstration by thrusting usurers into the seventh circle of his Inferno. Dante, like the Elizabethans afterwards, also contributed to the familiar presentation of the money-lender in the context of canine imagery: his usurers, sitting on the burning sands with pouches hanging from their necks, are doomed to scratch their bodies in the manner of flea-bitten dogs.[17]

The economic situation in the latter part of the sixteenth century merely reinforced the religiously based prejudice against money-lending. The popular nobility were constantly and deeply in debt—some, like the Earl of Leicester, by as much as 60,000 pounds, "while Shakespeare's own patron, the Earl of Southampton who, at one time, had surrendered his estates to creditors . . . 'scarce knows what course to take to live.'"[18] In the eyes of the conservative majority, the usurer was therefore regarded as a disagreeable and dangerous parvenu, a threat to the continuance of the old order. And in any contest between the tight-fisted money-lender and the irresponsibly lavish nobility, the money-lender was bound to get the worst of it.

It is not by chance that the regulation costume of the stage-usurer should display a rather overbearing amount of fur, the traditional uniform of the medieval money-lender, "shocking in the upstart who had seized on the lands of the gentry."[19]

In its more general ramifications, the struggle between the liberality of the old order and the threatening values of the new provides *The Merchant of Venice* with one of its main themes. Though Antonio, from the commercial point of view, is committed to the ambitions of the new class of burghers, in his ethical context he represents the old traditions: for example, he takes it for granted that he should freely share what wealth he has with a friend whom he knows perfectly well to be a spendthrift, and that he should persistently disparage Bassanio's reminders of the commercial risk involved in signing the bond. Within this frame of reference, Bassanio himself, whose prodigality has always furnished the nineteenth-century school of Shakespearean character interpreters with pretexts to whitewash Shylock, falls naturally into the role of morally unimpeachable protagonist. In the trial scene, the conflict literally "at heart" of the play is still the conflict between the ethics of liberality and the ethics of rapacity, but the terms of the antithesis have been stretched to the point at which the issue finally resolves itself into a dialectic of human justice.[20] "Antonio's objection to usury," writes Pettet,

> and in particular his practice of granting free loans, raises him to the level of a symbol of the whole medieval attitude, for the positive core of traditional teaching on the usury question was precisely that loans ought to be a pure act of Christian charity, without interest. . . . While Shylock reveals himself more and more as the child of the "cash-nexus," the idealized relationships of friendship and mutual service embodied in the Antonio-Bassanio world meet and ultimately overcome the challenge to them.[21]

The upshot of the usurer's ethics is that he comes to regard the amassing of money as a gigantically distorted substitute for all other human activities and that gold itself takes on the powers of a totem. For Barabas the augmentation of his fortune is sanctified by divine benediction: "these are the blessings of the Jews / And therein was old Abraham's happiness." From one point of view, Barabas's "O girl! O gold! O beauty! O my bliss!" and Shylock's famous echo, as Salanio parrots it, "My daughter! O my ducats! O my daughter!"[22]

represent obvious examples of comic juxtaposition; but from another point of view they also indicate a deadly confusion in values. By both Barabas and Shylock property is regarded as the very source of their vitality. In the speech to Ferneze beginning, "You have my goods, my money and my wealth," Barabas goes on to suggest that the Governor may as well take his life, too. The suggestion is picked up by Shylock after the Duke has confiscated his property:

> Nay take my life and all, pardon not that,—
> You take my house, when you do take the prop
> That doth sustain my house: you take my life
> When you do take the means whereby I live.

How totally Shylock has perverted the vital values in identifying them with material wealth becomes evident when his lines are read in juxtaposition with an earlier scene: in choosing the golden casket above the others, Portia's first suitor is mocked, on unlocking the chest, by the picture of a death's head and a scroll bearing the message that "gilded tombs do worms infold."[23]

When at the beginning of the Fourth Act of *The Merchant of Venice,* the Duke describes Shylock as

> A stony adversary, an inhuman wretch
> Uncapable of pity, void, and empty
> From any dram of mercy,[24]

his judgment may be provisionally taken at face value as coming from the highest arbiter of order in the play and the party least affected by Shylock's stratagems. If Shylock's villainy admits of immediate historical explanations, it needs secondarily to be explained in the wider context of literary convention; and if the usurer's social and religious disesteem partly accounts for his success on the Tudor and Stuart stage, the universal unpopularity of his profession accounts for the rest. In his *Defence of Usury,* Jeremy Bentham admirably formulates the money-lender's special qualification for playing the villain:

> Those who have the resolution to sacrifice the present to the future, are natural objects of envy to those who have sacrificed the future to the pres-

ent. The children who have eaten their cake, are the natural enemies of the children who have theirs. . . . Now I question whether, among all the instances in which a borrower and a lender have been brought together upon the stage, from the days of Thespis to the present, there ever was one, in which the former was not recommended to favour in some shape or other—either to admiration, or to love, or to pity, or to all three;—and the other, the man of thrift, consigned to infamy.[25]

Bentham's explanation suggests, among other things, why the usurer is likely to flourish in comedy above any other genre. The money-lender's villainy is of the kind that naturally arouses the scorn of the audience, and it requires the type of foil with whom the audience is disposed to sympathize romantically. Moreover, the profession of extortionist—and the cognate professions of miser and cheat—lend themselves ideally to the classic comic situation of the wit outwitted by which Molière made his living. If one catalogues, as Celeste Wright has done, the personal traits and habits of the Elizabethan stage-usurer, one comes up with a complex of attributes that sounds like a perfect syndrome of villainous comicality. The usurer is almost always old and physically repulsive. As a rule, he suffers from dropsy or the gout, dropsy symbolizing the miser's insatiable thirst for gold, while gout "naturally accompanies the high living of parvenu aldermen." In the matter of the gout, however, Wright discovers that "there is some confusion in the tradition, since the typical usurer is a half-starved miser."[26] Even the relatively munificent Barabas, in bargaining for Ithamore, prefers to hold out for a slave "that's sickly, and be but for sparing vittles"; Launcelot Gobbo absconds for being "famished in [his] master's service"; and in Jonson's *Staple of News,* Pennyboy lectures the porter for wasting sixpence on alcohol which, in seventy years, will cost him twenty-five pounds.[27] Occasionally, the role of money-lender was combined with the role of procurer: both Barabas and Sir Giles Overreach, for example, build on their daughters' sexual desirability to gain their ends. After Marlowe's introduction of the money-lender's daughter, the usury play had found its "typical and excellent comic situation";[28] and Wright's dossier of the usurer's psychological components may be supplemented briefly by a glance at the plot conventions compiled by Stonex.

The manner in which the tables are turned on the usurer involves typically one or more of three chief agents. Most common is the situation by which a young prodigal, heavily in debt to the usurer, comes into his own, or into the usurer's property, elopes with the usurer's daughter, and—legitimately or not, but always with the approval of the playwright and the audience—absconds with the usurer's money, jewelry, and whatever else he and the daughter can lay their hands on. A second device, introduced at a somewhat later stage and reminiscent of French classical comedy, calls for the rivalry between usurer and spendthrift for the hand of an heiress, whom the spendthrift inevitably wins. Finally, the usurer may be ignominiously defeated either in failing to win a rich widow or by being cuckolded. It can be seen that the last two situations are difficult to apply to the Jewish usurer, who is on prior grounds ineligible as husband and unthinkable as competing for the hand of a Gentile. There remains therefore the popular plot involving the Jew's disobedient daughter of which Marlowe melodramatically and Shakespeare comedically avail themselves. Although *The Merchant* antedates most of the plays that rely on the intervention of the usurer's daughter, it is easy to see how Shakespeare manipulated and jumbled the various agents of Shylock's comeuppance. From the point of view of the standard usury play the essential characters, of course, are represented by Bassanio, Jessica, and Shylock; if Bassanio had borrowed directly from Shylock without the intervention of Antonio, and if he, rather than Lorenzo, had abducted Jessica, "the first type of the usurer-prodigal plot would have been evolved as early as 1594 or 1595."[29] The Lorenzo-Jessica relationship itself, by which a young Christian is permitted to woo a fair Jewess, derives, like almost everything else in the play, from medieval sources, the prototypes figuring both in medieval exampla and cognate romances.[30]

The mythical pattern is completed when the usurer has paid his penalty, which is more or less made to fit his crime, or his criminality. In comedy the issue, if he is a Jew, may be conversion—granting one can always argue that conversion, even when regarded by the culprit as a dreadful punishment, turns out, *sub specie aeternitatis,* to be the greatest possible compliment and reward which the Christain can pay the Jew. Indeed it has been convincingly argued[31] that Shylock's enforced conversion is to be interpreted as the final gesture of magnanimity that the forces of Belmont extend toward the forces of the Rialto. The ethical implications of forcing salvation down the Jew's throat would seem not to have bothered the Elizabethan audience: if the Jew could be redeemed, so much the better for him. But as a rule, the usurer, Gentile or Jew, does not get off so lightly. The Mammon of *Jacke Drum's Entertainment* and Sir Giles Overreach succumb to their gold fever by going mad; Pertenas, in Francis Quarles's *The Virgin Widow,* is poisoned; Barabas is cast into a boiling cauldron; the villain in a pamphlet of 1606 is devoured by "an innumerable sort of rats."[32] The most frequent punishment of all, however, according to Wright, is the penalty that Launcelot Gobbo and Gratiano demand for Shylock, "a halter gratis." Wright alleges some fifteen plays in which death by hanging is either suggested as the usurer's appropriate end, or in which the money-lender himself contemplates hanging after his schemes have miscarried.[33] In recording as much we are brought back at this juncture in our inquiry to its starting point: "In view of the close connection between Avarice and Usury the idea [of hanging] may reasonably be traced back to the story of Judas. [Thomas] Wilson's Ockerfoe reminds us: 'Iudas had the rewards of his covetousness, for he hanging him selfe did brast in the middest.' "[34] And although Barabas ends not on a rope but in a cauldron, his name itself tells us plainly whither Marlowe wants to direct our attention. It is no coincidence that Ithamore remarks of him at one point that "The hat he wears, Judas left under the Elder when he hanged himself."[35]

The Composite Portrait

By the time Shakespeare gave classic expression to the myth of the Jew-villain, he was in possession of all the facts; the type was fully constituted as he found it, and it had been for centuries. In one manifestation or another, the Jew-villain had passed into countless folk ballads and dramatic pageants. The components and functions ascribed to him were thereafter available to playwrights and fictionists alike: Scott, Dickens, Trollope, might strike variations on the type but they could not dislodge it. Certain specific attributes of the myth might be attenuated or discarded from time to time as literature increasingly divorced itself from its theological connections, but the basic image of the Jew as usurer and mutilator was far too deeply embedded in the popular consciousness not to survive the divorce. Other attributes were added in process of time. It became customary after Marlowe to invest the Jew with a daughter, a girl sufficiently good and beautiful to serve as foil to the wicked father. Where the Jew had all along been an object of hate, the Jewess, within the context of the myth, became an object of lust, who could be stolen from under her father's nose all the more readily because her seduction by the Gentile automatically conferred upon her the patent of salvation. The type, which reaches its apotheosis in Jessica and, with some significant historic hindsight, in Scott's Rebecca, may be literally prostituted: at a fairly late stage in the history of the myth she reappears, without benefit of clergy and stripped of all religious excuses, as the type of *la belle juive,* the exotic (or patriotic) whore, a stock-figure in the stories of Balzac, Maupassant, Huysmans, Zola, and Proust.[36] (I have sometimes thought that Nancy in *Oliver Twist* fills somewhat the same role: that of the melodramatically good prostitute functioning as daughter-surrogate to Fagin and, like her counterpart, betraying the Jew to the lily-white Christians on the other side of the fence. In George Eliot, the clash between the grasping Jew and the pure daughter is retained, and so, essentially, is their ethical relationship; Mirah runs away and finds refuge in a Gentile family who think her quite good enough to wish to marry her to the son of the house. But the issue is no longer conversion; Mirah, like Rebecca, ends by affirming her ties to Judaism.)

On the other hand, though the Jew may be permitted a daughter, he must on no account be shown in the presence of a wife. To present him affectively in the role of paterfamilias would destroy the illusion of unrelieved villainy. It is imperative that in his function of *eiron,* of dog, he shall act and suffer by himself, apart from the Catholic majority, insulated while he sniffs at his "infinite riches in a little room," and that, at the conclusion of the pattern, the beast shall be domesticated (i.e., tamed) from without: by forcible conversion in comedy, by violent death in melodrama. The daughter offers no threat to his insulation, since she will run off to Belmont anyway, but the Jew's wife would be too old to serve the desired sexual purpose. The Jew-villain must therefore be in effect unmarried, though nominally a widower. In exceptional cases he may be, like Fagin, a bachelor; but, as a rule, the presence of the daughter within the myth requires at least the patent, if not the reality, of the wife. Since she is out of the way to begin with and thus remains without dramatic effectiveness, she cannot jeopardize the villain's comic immobility by an appeal to pathos. When Shylock alludes to his dead wife Leah, the audience is intended to howl him down with laughter. For the rest, the Jew frequently retains enough of his early bogey qualities to preclude the possibility of marrying. Except in a handful of fairy tales (and, by extension, fairy-novels like Dickens's *Old Curiosity Shop*), an ogre cannot very well keep a wife, without considerable loss of face.

By the time Scott wrote, then, certain things could be predicted about the Jew. He was a fairly thoroughgoing materialist, a physical coward, an opportunist in money matters, a bit of a wizard in peddling his pharmaceutica; queer in his religious observances in so far as he still paid attention to them, clannish in his loyalties, secretive in his living habits, servile in his relations with Christians, whom he abominated; for physical signposts he had an outlandish nose, an unpleasant odor, and frequently a speech impediment also. (The red hair was no longer essential; black had the advantage of suggesting an excess of hair oil.) Though a widower, he had the comfort of an attractive daughter; Gentiles wooed her, and sometimes won her. A literalist and stickler in debate and a trained Talmudist in his logic, he was bound to be defeated in all fundamental contests by the other party. His conversation was attended by much frenzied gesticulating, and when he did not have his way he resorted to a disgusting display of self-indulgence. His affections were unevenly divided between his ducats and his daughter. As a rule, he was permitted one confidant, a business friend, Jewish, male. He himself sat, spider-like, in the center of an impressive commercial network. Other animal metaphors which described him were the hog, the dog, the rat, the vulture, the weasel, the fox, the toad, the serpent, and the wasp. As a creature less sinned against than sinning, he hardly qualified for tragedy; on the other hand, his repulsive physiognomy, his eccentric habits, and his hostile motives conspired to suit him ideally for purposes of the comic and the horrific.

From the Anglo-Saxon point of view, he combined all the odious traits that are, on other occasions, parceled out separately to the hated nationalities: he was greedy like the Scotch, effeminate like the French, treacherous like the Italians, vulgar like the Germans. His isolation was a source of strength to him only in so far as it allowed him to concentrate on his business; beyond this point, his exclusiveness merely went to reveal his nuisance value, demonstrate his expendability, and dictate his ostracism. He was old, and born old. He had neither youth nor middle age; and his after-dinner sleep was ruined by his obsessive fear of thieves. He came to no good end. In Chaucer he was torn by wild horses and hanged also. In Gower a lion tears him to death. Marlowe has him burned in a cauldron. Shylock, the fox at bay, loses both daughter and ducats, as well as his religion. Fagin, too, gets his halter gratis; these are his final investitures: "the black stage, the cross-beam, the rope, and all the hideous apparatus of death."[37]

Such, roughly, are the components of the image as it devolved on Shakespeare, Scott, and Dickens. The type was there, and they needed only to avail themselves of it. Myths such as these are pervasive and persistent; and perhaps they will never die. Sporadic attempts may be made to correct them and to deny their validity; and such attempts, as will be seen in the next chapter, were introduced toward the end of the eighteenth and throughout the nineteenth century, often in a spirit of apology and recantation by the very writers who had helped to keep the stereotype in circulation.

There remains one other alternative. That is to erect a countermyth, go into competition against the original myth, and hope that the newly discovered type will obscure and eventually supersede the old. An effort in this direction has been operating in a good deal of recent literature. The Jew has come to typify more and more the outsider, the alien pure and simple, without the concomitant attributes of criminality implicit in the old convention. Thus it is possible nowadays to have Proust's sensitive dilettante, Joyce's Jew-in-Dublin, Mann's Biblical dreamer, the pariah figures in the nightmare world of Kafka. If there has been any general tendency toward the evolution of a new stereotype, it has been along these lines. The result has been to fairify the Jew out of all proportions; the comic eiron of old has been translated into the irresolute, pathetic, ultimately self-destroying man. To some extent Shylock already anticipates the modern hypochondriac Jew. "I am not well," reads his exit line; and the audience is assumed to jeer at his adolescent refusal to take his comeuppance like a man.[38] "Just like a dog," reads the exit line of Joseph K, the protagonist of a more fashionable trial than Shylock's, as he is being stabbed to death by the unknown tormentors: just like an eiron. The metaphor remains the same: the dog is a dog still. Only the knife has changed hands.

The countermyth of the Jew as Ironic Man is a latecomer in the history of the stereotype. The nineteenth century had nothing like it to offer; and even while the countermyth has been gaining sufficient ground to attract the most distinguished novelists of our time, the original myth of the Jew-villain, as we have seen, has kept right on flourishing in the productions of Waugh, Greene, and Lewis. To note as much is merely to note the astounding tenacity of the Jew-villain as a poetic convention. Scott and Dickens found the type made to order. That it was a fundamentally antirealistic type was nothing against it; Dickens found it congenial on that very account. That it dealt with an isolated minority did not lessen its appeal to the reading public; Scott made a living by depicting clannishness in remote corners. That it precluded the reader's sympathetic participation commended it to the satirical bias of Trollope. But, like other marginal types, the Jew was also capable of arousing one's scientific curiosity; it was this aspect of him which the French naturalists brought into focus. The point to be insisted on is that there was fundamentally nothing to invent. To someone like Dickens it was axiomatic that Fagin was typically Jewish; in no other way could he have justified him morally. Dickens thought that he needed only to assure readers like Mrs. Davis of Fagin's typicalness to be in the clear.

The popularity and artistic success of the stereotype were largely ensured by its very antiquity. It had always been there. It had tradition to recommend it; more important, it had the spontaneous endorsement of the playgoer and the reading public. The writers who appropriated the type did so because, for one reason or another, they found it naturally congenial to their temperaments, and there were no taboos to prevent them from cashing in on the convention. No doubt there were more deep-seated reasons for the success of the type. The Jew-villain fulfilled all the qualifications of the societal scapegoat; he lent himself beautifully to the important tribal function of being laughed or whipped out of existence. The general failure to find a substitute for the image of the Jew-villain merely confirmed the success of the type. Conversely, its success placed special difficulties in the way of those writers who endeavored to amend or counteract it.

To those writers I must turn in the following chapter.

dem Menschen ist
Ein Mensch noch immer lieber als ein Engel.

LESSING, *Nathan the Wise* (1779)

"No, boy, we must not"—so began
My Uncle (he's with God long since)
A-petting me, the good old man!
"We must not"—and he seemed to wince,
And lost that laugh whereto had grown
His chuckle at my piece of news,
How cleverly I aimed my stone—
"I fear we must not pelt the Jews!"

BROWNING, *Filippo Baldinucci on the Privilege of Burial* (1876)

III The Advent of the Saintly Jew: Cumberland and Edgeworth

If one cannot find an adequate substitute for the myth and dislikes the content of the myth as it stands, one tries to disprove its reality by an appeal to reason and hopes to argue it out of existence. Something very like this happened toward the close of the eighteenth century and kept happening throughout the nineteenth, and this brings us to the emergence of the "good" Jew in literature and the reason for his failure in art.

Unlike the Jew-villain, the good Jew is of relatively recent origin. His foundations are not religious; no mean mass superstitions cling to him, and he cannot be explained in terms of profound collective motives and neuroses. He emerged in the drama of the Enlightenment, brought forth in a spirit of tolerance tempered by sentimentality. His first full-length avatar in English literature is to be found in the title figure of Cumberland's *The Jew,* Sheva, a kind of professional do-gooder whose animating principle reads to the effect that "he builds his hospital in the human heart," and whose good deeds shine the more brightly in a naughty world because he commits them by stealth.[1] The generic title of Cumberland's play is itself of some significance—Lessing likewise had given the title *Die Juden* to his early one-acter, an obvious *Vorstudie* to *Nathan the Wise.*[2] These writers wanted to get something said about the Jew as a separate and socially viable organism. Such an attempt in itself was something quite new in the treatment of the Jew. Hitherto the creators of the Jew-villain had been in the habit of presenting the Jew as an inflated individual, and though his qualities were manifestly stereotypical—so that one Jew could be assumed to look and behave pretty much like every other—it was customary to dramatize him as a solitary, without emphatic reference to his tribal membership.* After Cumberland and Lessing it became possible to treat the Jew didactically as a member of a persecuted group. But from this point on also the Jew, in so far as he was to be good, surrendered his effective identity for the purposes of drama and ceased to be very much more than an agent of benevolent propaganda, a mouthpiece for the author's high principles. Since Cumberland initiated this mode in a major way in the literature of England, it will be useful to summarize his dramaturgy in so far as it affected his presentation of the Jew.

* Some qualification is necessary here. It is true that Marlowe had also entitled his play *The Jew of Malta* and that Stephen Gosson recorded the performance of a lost drama *The Jew* that has sometimes been thought the missing link between the Italian sources and *The Merchant of Venice.* Moreover, it may be argued that Shylock and Barabas naturally identify themselves throughout with their abominated religion. But at the same time the conventions required the Jew to be sufficiently super-villainous to obscure his communal associations. As stated earlier, it is essential to the psychological make-up of the Jew-villain that he should be a solitary. Shakespeare may have introduced the dramatically superfluous figure of Tubal on the same grounds that Goethe (in *Wilhelm Meister*) alleges for the presence of both Rosencrantz and Guildenstern in *Hamlet:* the two serve to suggest the threat of a hostile *society* rather than a hostile individual. But Tubal remains as shadowy as Barabas's three Jewish cronies; though Tubal and Shylock talk about going to synagogue and thus point up the presence of a Semitic community, Shylock remains, within the conventions of the stereotype, a dreadful individualist.

Cumberland's Friendly Hebrews

Cumberland's dramatic principles are set forth, broadly and honestly, in his *Memoirs,* written at a time when his career as a playwright was very nearly over. "I hold it matter of conscience and duty in the dramatic poet," he writes,

> to reserve his brightest colouring for the best characters, to give no false attractions to vice and immorality, but to endeavour, as far as is consistent with that contrast, which is the very essence of art, to turn the fairer side of human nature to the public, and, as much as in him lies, to contrive so as to put men into good humour with one another.

In the same breath he objects to the Restoration playwrights for their prurience and dismisses Shadwell's comedy as "little better than a brothel."[3]

So described, Cumberland's credo merely recapitulates, though in a neat and useful way, the position of the sentimental school. That he should define *contrast* as "the very essence of art" shows that he had grasped the principles of melodrama as well; and it may be noted in passing that the sensation-novelists who grouped themselves around Dickens in mid-century subscribed to identical principles, in theory no less than practice. For them, as for Cumberland, "contrast" constituted the alpha and omega of their art.[4]

What actually distinguished Cumberland from his fellow writers of sentimental comedy and gave him his claim to originality was chiefly his subject matter. Cumberland appears to have felt that playwrights like Steele and Goldsmith had not "carried their idealization of life far enough."[5] By exalting characters of an anyhow romantic and heroic timbre, these writers were engaged merely in ennobling the conventionally noble, romanticizing the inherently romantic, and idealizing the obvious. Unlike them, Cumberland thought that "the goodness of human nature should henceforth be illustrated, not only by those types of character which had been repeatedly exalted, but also by those which had been disregarded or treated in comic and disdainful fashion."[6] The passage in the *Memoirs* in which Cumberland explains what he himself knew to be his most marked contribution to sentimental comedy throws a good deal of light on his conception of the good Jew Sheva. He writes:

> I perceived that I had fallen upon a time when great eccentricity of character was pretty nearly gone by, but still I fancied there was an opening for some originality, and an opportunity for showing at least my good-will to mankind, if I introduced the characters of persons who had been usually exhibited on the stage, as the butts for ridicule and abuse, and endeavoured to present them in such lights as might tend to reconcile the world to them, and them to the world. I thereupon looked into society for the purpose of discovering such as were the victims of its national, professional, or religious prejudices; in short, for those suffering characters which stood in need of an advocate, and out of these I meditated to select and form heroes for my future dramas, of which I would study to make such favourable and reconciliatory delineations, as might incline the spectators to look upon them with pity, and receive them into their good opinion and esteem.[7]

Cumberland carried these principles into effect primarily in three of his comedies, not counting the unsuccessful opera *The Jew of Mogadore,* a product of his old age. His procedure in each case was to pick one or two national stock-figures which, he thought, had been undeservedly pilloried by the dramatists of the day, and to give them at least semiserious status in his own productions. "With this project in my mind and nothing but the turf-stack to call off my attention, I took the characters of an Irishman and a West Indian for the heroes of my plot." Irishmen and West Indians had been traditional objects of contempt. Among Cumberland's precursors and contemporaries, Farquhar, Murphy, and Colman had portrayed the Irish as unfailingly absurd stock-figures; and the colonials from the West Indies had been famously lampooned by Foote some eight years before Cumberland came to their rescue. By Cumberland's own account, the convention of the ostentatious and loud-mouthed colonial was so firmly established in the minds of the spectators that when his play was announced it was taken for granted that he, too, would follow in the predictable "Footesteps"—so much so, that a number of West Indians went to the theater on purpose "to chastise the author."[8]

The following year, having found a good thing in the advocacy of the despised minorities, Cumberland bethought himself of redeeming the Scotch. The result was *The Fashionable Lover,* which Cumberland ranked among his best work and which he later described as "a drama of moral, grave, and tender cast, inasmuch as I discover in it sentiments laudably directed against national prejudice, breach of trust, seduction, gaming, and the general dissipation of the time then present."[9] *The Fashionable Lover* has considerable claim on our attention. For one thing, Cumberland's treatment of Colin Macleod, the Scottish servant to the extravagant Lord Abberville, foreshadows in its ethical implications his treatment of the Jew Sheva twenty-two years later. Just as Macleod's proverbial Scottish niggardliness is explained away as selfless and commonsensical economy, Sheva's miserly habits are shown to be rooted in his desire to do good to others. Even more revealing—in the opposite direction—is Cumberland's presentation, in the same play, of his first stage-Jew. Napthali, a relatively incidental figure, is a typical scoundrel of the old school, an ugly little monkey with a broken accent, who subscribes to the ethics of the profiteer: "Ay, ay, a charming stroke: war is a var goot thing; and then the plague; a blessed circumstance, tank Heaven; a blessed circumstance, coot 7 *per cent.*"[10] It is decidedly to Macleod's credit that he pushes the Jew around, throws him out of the house, beats him up, and boasts of his beating to his betters. Clearly, while Cumberland was willing to combat the English prejudice against the North Briton, his sense of tolerance was easily exhausted. The *Memoirs,* significantly, are silent on the subject of Napthali.

When Cumberland put Sheva on the boards in 1794, he thus already had a Jew-villain on his conscience. Sheva accordingly entered the picture with an air of apology and self-justification. Between the composition of *The Fashionable Lover* in 1772 and of *The Jew* two decades later, Cumberland had, in 1779, paid a visit to Spain as secretary to the Board of Trade, a journey that he describes in fulsome detail in Chapters VI to IX of the *Memoirs.* While in Spain he seems to have gathered a good deal of information about the Marranos, whose Italian and Portuguese coreligionists had already been active in the London of Shakespeare's day. A direct result of his Spanish travels were a series of papers in his periodical, *The Observer* (Nos. 89–90), in which he describes one of these crypto-Jews, one Nicolas Pedrosa, who escapes from the Inquisition and settles as a doctor in London.[11] Nicolas retains some of the comic elements of his prototype; he is decidedly "the little Jew," whose cunning could easily, one feels, degenerate into rascality; he does not so much circumvent the Inquisition as outsmart it. Cumberland indeed treats him with a mixture of slick sympathy and contempt that is cloyingly present from the opening sentence about the "busy little being" on his mule in Madrid to the closing description of Nicolas in London:

> As for little Nicolas, whose prize-money has set him up in a comfortable little shop in Duke's-place, where he breathes the veins and cleanses the bowels of his Israelitish brethren, in a land of freedom and toleration, his merry heart is at rest, save only when with fire in his eyes, and vengeance on his tongue, he anathematizes the inquisition, and struts into synagogue every sabbath with as bold a step and as erect a look, as if he was himself High Priest of the Temple, going to perform sacrifice upon the reassembling of the scattered tribes.

From about the middle of the 1780's Cumberland repeatedly constituted himself the champion of the Jews, sometimes *in propria persona,* more often through the device of a (transparent) prolocutor.* Even before he published the Pedrosa numbers, he had devoted a series of articles in *The Observer* (Nos. 41–46) to the depiction of a naturalized London Jew who was to serve, in all essentials, as a model for Sheva.[12] Abraham Abrahams, like his later dramatic avatar, is all benevolence and hospitality; he rescues a poor widow and her daughter from destitution, pays their debts, and puts them up at his house. To describe him, Cumberland resorts to tags that ought to be read in juxtaposition with, say, Defoe's metaphors for the Jew in *Roxana.* Gone out of the window are devil and dog, hog and vulture; all is now domestic affability and mutual endearment; Abraham Abra-

* This summary does not take into account Cumberland's participation, in 1787, in a theological dispute involving the Jewish deist David Levi and Dr. Joseph Priestley, the well-known dissenting minister. Cumberland here takes issue with the deistical position that right reason prevailed in the world before the coming of Jesus. In his controversial ire Cumberland gives a fairly prejudiced (as well as prejudicial) coloring to his vade mecum against Levi, whom he variously alludes to as "the modern caviller," "our Jew who tauntingly asserts," etc. "Is this a man to confute the Holy Scriptures? Weak champion of an unworthy cause!" *Vide* Nos. 61–66, *British Essayists,* XXXIX, 65–102; Newman, *Richard Cumberland,* pp. 12–15. But see also *The Jew of Mogadore,* in which Cumberland's philosophical premises approach Levi's more closely.

hams is variously denominated "the humble Israelite," "the worthy Hebrew," "the honest Jew," "the friendly Israelite," "the compassionate Israelite," and the like.

In No. 38 of *The Observer* Cumberland came firmly to grips with the whole problem of the wicked stage-Jew, to which he had himself contributed his share in the plays of the 'seventies. Writing under the *nom de plume* of Abraham Abrahams[13] (whose story he was yet to tell in subsequent papers), he protests the presentation of the fashionable stage-Jew as a rogue, usurer, or buffoon. Abrahams begins by airing his grievances as a theatergoer:

> I no sooner put my head into an obscure corner of the gallery, than some fellow roars out to his comrades—*Smoke the Jew!—Smoke the cunning little Isaac!—Throw him over,* says another, *hand over the smoutch!—Out with Shylock,* cries a third, *out with the pound of man's flesh—Buckles and buttons! Spectacles!* bawls out a fourth—and so on through the whole gallery, till I am forced to retire out of the theatre, amongst hootings and hissings, with a shower of rotten apples and chewed oranges vollied at my head, when all the offense I have given is an humble offer to be a peaceable spectator.

Nor are the playwrights of any help in stemming the tide of buoyant anti-Semitism: "I observe with much concern that you great writers of plays take delight in hanging us out to public ridicule and contempt on all occasions: if ever they are in search of a rogue, an usurer, or a buffoon, they are sure to make the Jew serve the turn." And in a postscript, he adds that "if you could persuade one of the gentlemen or ladies who write plays . . . to give us poor Jews a kind lift in a new comedy, I am bold to promise we should not prove ungrateful on a third night." This, of course, is precisely Sheva's historic complaint in the opening scene of *The Jew:* "If your playwriters want a butt or a buffoon or a knave to make sport of, out comes a Jew to be baited and buffetted through five long acts for the amusement of all good Christians." In the prologue of the play, in words more or less indistinguishable from Sheva's or Abrahams's, Cumberland directly appoints himself appellant

> For a poor client, for a luckless wight,
> Whom Bard ne'er favoured, whose sad fate has been
> Never to share in one applauding scene.

The Jew was produced at Drury Lane on May 8, 1794. Its plot is soon told. Sheva, an elderly Jewish money-lender and something of a skinflint, comes to the aid of Frederic Bertram who has been expelled and disinherited by his father, choleric Sir Stephen, for marrying an apparently penniless girl, Eliza Ratcliffe. The young lady's brother, Charles, an employee of Sir Stephen's, by a series of transparent contrivances adds to the familial sorrows by misconstruing Frederic's good nature and laudable conduct. The misconstruction leads to a quarrel, the quarrel to a duel, the duel to the inevitable reconciliation. Through all these sorrowful and recriminatory activities, the honest Sheva, the friendly Israelite, the worthy Hebrew, moves with an air of sad and serious affability. Let anyone who will call him a miser, a bloodsucker, a muckworm, a Jewish dog, a baboon, an imp of Beelzebub—Sheva goes right on relieving the impoverished Gentile majority. He lends money to Frederic; he settles ten thousand pounds on the pauperized Eliza; he discovers in plenty of time for the fifth act that the hot-headed young Charles rescued him once from a brutal anti-Jewish mob, that Charles's father (deceased) saved his life when it was threatened by the Inquisitors of Cadiz; hence now he appoints Charles heir to that portion of his fortune which he has not already squandered philanthropically in other places.[14]

Why is Sheva being so good? Sheva himself provides a variety of answers, all tending to the same construction: "thou [speaking of himself] dost stint thine appetites to pamper thine affections; thou dost make thyself to live in poverty, that the poor may live in plenty"; "I love my monies, I do love them dearly; but I love my fellow-creatures a little better"; "I did see your son struck down to the ground with sorrow, cut to the heart: I did not stop to ask whose hand had laid him low; I gave him mine, and raised him up; . . . I do not talk of [charity]; I feel it." At the same time, there is the self-righteous identification with the persecuted minority, already made by Abraham Abrahams and soon to become part and parcel of the new convention:

> We have no abiding place on earth, no country, no home; every body rails at us, every body flouts us, every body points us out for their may-game and their mockery. . . . Cruel sport, merciless amusement! hard dealings for

a poor stray sheep of the scatter'd flock of Abraham! How can you expect us to shew kindness, when we receive none?

The question, so put, loses some of its persuasiveness when everything in the play goes to prove that Sheva shows kindness in superabundance, whether he receives any in return or no. A rather more difficult question, never really resolved by Cumberland except on generally sentimental assumptions, is why Sheva, apart from his occasional semipublic lectures on the advantages of human decency, prefers to remain incognito while going about his charitable errands. The simplest answer, no doubt, would be to say that it is all part of his quintessential goodness, his modesty, his unwillingness to inflict upon his beneficiaries a sense of their indebtedness. But then again why does he act the philanthropist toward abusive strangers while practically starving his own servant? Or again, how is so much inward nobility of soul to be reconciled with such an unkempt, even repellent exterior? The fact seems to be that Cumberland, in spite of his explicit intentions to the contrary, is still not a little faithful to the comic possibilities of the Shylock-type—if only in order to explain them away. Not only does Sheva preserve part of the ludicrous stage-accent brought into fashion after Cibber; his miserliness at home runs altogether true to type. "Heigho," soliloquizes Sheva:

I cannot chuse but weep . . . Three hundred pounds by the way; how much is that in the year?—Oh dear, oh dear! I shall be ruin'd, starv'd, wasted to a watchlight. Bowels, you shall pinch for this: I'll not eat flesh this fortnight; I'll suck the air for nourishment; I'll feed upon the steam of an alderman's kitchen, as I put my nose down his area.

Visitors, unless they come to borrow money—which they may have in plenty and at a paltry enough rate—are not likely to return to Sheva's for dinner; hear with what an odd mellifluence he promotes the excellence of water and anathematizes the disadvantages of wine: "No, no, it is goot water, it is better than wine: wine is heating, water is cooling; wine costs monies, water comes for nothing—Your good health, Sir—Oh! 'tis delicious, it is satisfying: I was very empty before, my stomach was craving, now I am quite content."[15]

Yet another relic of the old stereotype is preserved in the role of the grumbling servant, descendant of Vice, Ithamore, and Launcelot, who goes hungry with his master. "Oh! what a starving star was I born under," complains Jabal, "to be the rich Jew's poor servant. . . . If it is charity to keep an empty cupboard, he has that to boast of; the very rats wou'd run away from such a caterer." At the same time, as Van der Veen has pointed out, Jabal differs from his prototypes perhaps as markedly as he resembles them: the fact that the servant is himself a Jew is decisive in his relationship with the Jewish master. The discontent is largely externalized; Jabal, unlike Gobbo, would never dream of leaving has master in the lurch but will, on the contrary, brave considerable risks to protect Sheva's safety.[16] In *The Jew of Mogadore* an identical relationship is presented between Hebrew master and Hebrew man; indeed, Nadab, the title figure in the opera, is Sheva all over again, set to music.[17]

Yet it would be wrong, I think, to consider Sheva as very much more than a simple one-dimensional type. In spite of his affinities with Shylock (which are ultimately illusory) he is clearly intended to be a fundamental antipode. Van der Veen thought that Cumberland was unfortunate in merely building on Shylock's character in order to present anti-Shylock; but there may have been a sound pedagogic instinct behind this procedure—as though Cumberland wanted to demonstrate how good the Jew could be even while he looked to the outside world preternaturally like the wicked Jew.[18] Behind Shylock's mask lies the reality of Sheva. It was no doubt in the same associative context that Abraham Abrahams, in his letter in the *Observer,* asked his correspondent as a special favor to discover whether Shylock was really a Jew at all.

As I am interested to know if this blood-thirsty villain really existed in nature, and have no means to satisfy my curiosity but your favour, I take the liberty humbly to request that you will tell me how the case truly stands, and whether we must of necessity own this Shylock; also I should be glad to know of which tribe this fellow was, for if such a monster did exist, I have strong suspicion he will turn out a Samaritan. . . . and pray be particular as to the tribe of Judah, for if nothing less than half my fortune could oust him there, I would pay it down to be rid of such a rascal.

Looking back on the success of *The Jew,* Cumberland wrote in the *Memoirs:*

The benevolence of the audience assisted me in rescuing a forlorn and persecuted character, which till then had only been brought upon the stage for the unmanly purpose of being made a spectacle of contempt, and a butt for ridicule. In the success of this comedy I felt of course a greater gratification than I had ever felt before upon a like occasion.

In view of Cumberland's instructive biases as a playwright generally, we need not, then, be surprised by the papier-mâché figure that Sheva is made to cut. He is plainly little more than a pawn—not in the plot, but of the message behind the plot. "I take credit to myself," Cumberland writes elsewhere, "for the character of Abraham Abrahams. I wrote it upon principle, thinking it high time that something should be done for a persecuted race. I seconded my appeal to the charity of mankind by the character of Sheva, which I copied from this of Abrahams."[19] The phrase *upon principle* goes a long way toward explaining not only Sheva's general dramatic insufficiencies, but the collapse of subsequent attempts to redeem the Jew for literature. It may always be objected, of course, that the pallor of Cumberland's Jews proves nothing about the success or failure of the good Jew in literary art; it merely proves that Cumberland was a mediocre playwright. But Lessing was quite a good playwright; Maria Edgeworth was an occasionally fine novelist, and George Eliot and Charles Dickens were great novelists. I have dwelt on Cumberland not merely because he fathered the first important good Jew in literature, but because, in a broader sense, he fathered all the rest of them as well.

Maria Edgeworth: Early Tales

Cumberland anticipated fairly well what was going to happen to the type throughout the nineteenth century. After him the figure of the good Jew, presented as a bloodless abstraction, gained almost as much currency as the Jew-villain. The good Jew is always there on principle, a product at once of the author's didactic energy and dramatic impotence. He is hardly ever more than the representative member of a maligned race; and in this capacity he has himself a number of set speeches, or else the author makes them for him; for the difference between the two is purely nominal. Dickens's Riah, for example, insists on his representative qualifications with the same cheap obviousness as Sheva:

> For it is not in Christian countries with the Jews as with other peoples. Men say, "This is a bad Greek, but there are good Greeks. This is a bad Turk, but there are good Turks." Not so with Jews. Men find the bad among us easily enough—among what peoples are the bad not easily found?—but they take the worst of us as samples of the best; they take the lowest of us as presentations of the highest; and they say "All Jews are alike."[20]

There is an appalling obtrusiveness in editorial flourishes such as this. "Whenever Riah evinces a trait especially beautiful," Philipson accurately notes, "we are told that this is characteristic of his people, as though the novelist wished to say: 'The Jews are not as black as I painted Fagin.' "[21] Occasionally this split between the dramatically convincing Jew-villain and the rhetorically good Jew, who is good chiefly by virtue of his delegating a minority, operates rather curiously in one and the same figure. Whenever Scott, for example, talks about Isaac of York in terms of his persecuted group life, the treatment is entirely and tediously sympathetic; one feels that Scott is playing the patron to the unhappy few.[22] When, by contrast, he presents Isaac with any sort of immediacy, as an achieved dramatic character, Isaac automatically falls back into the traditional roles of the fox, the vulture, and the funny dog, who hoards his shekels, tries to outsmart the Christians, indulges himself in his stigmata if you prick him, and, as eiron, is fair game in gratifying the sanguinary humor of the Norman aristocracy.

It is probably no coincidence that the pattern of apology and vindication established by Cumberland (the pattern by which the impeccable Sheva was intended to atone for the wicked Napthali) kept repeating itself among the nineteenth-century novelists. Maria Edgeworth, at the threshold of the century, exemplifies the pattern as well as anybody. Edgeworth peopled story after story with Jewish criminal types, until she published a full and explicit recantation in *Harrington*—like Dickens, she wrote in response to a letter of remonstrance from a disgruntled reader, and avowedly as an apology to the Jews. Since she is the first important English novelist before Scott to come within the compass of this study, the remainder of this chapter will be devoted to the five or six works in which she deals with Jews. It is useful to treat her together with Cumberland, for it must be remembered that when *The Jew of Mogadore* was written, Edgeworth had already done half of her best work. *Castle Rackrent* and *Belinda* are chronologically far closer to Cumberland's *Jew* than they are to *Ivanhoe*; *The Absentee* was published a year after Cumberland's death.

Moreover, Edgeworth began her career as a writer in a tradition as solidly moralistic as the tradition in which Cumberland wrote. Byron found the didactic strain in her work exasperating enough to volunteer the opinion that surely "Miss Edgeworth's Cupid must be a Presbyterian."[23] Madame de Staël, while conceding that "Miss Edgeworth est digne de l'enthousiasme," was careful to qualify her own enthusiasm by adding the reservation "mais elle se perd dans votre triste utilité." How unabashedly moral the tone of literature became in the hands of the earnest bluestockings toward the end of the century can be illustrated by a characteristic remark of one of them. "The great and important duty of a writer," said Clara Reeve, "is to point out the difference between virtue and vice, to show one as rewarded and the other as punished."[24] To such a literary code Edgeworth assented in principle. If anything, she gave to her early stories a more narrowly pragmatic and utilitarian basis than her contemporaries were able to give to theirs. Her father, Richard Lovell Edgeworth, was a dedicated and rather eccentric educationist, a disciple of Bentham and lifelong friend of Thomas Day, the bizarre author of *Sandford and Merton;* and it was her father who stood over her while she wrote her books, and who kept tampering with their endings whenever these threatened to upset the moral balance as he conceived it. He provided her novels with prefaces, ludicrous and overbearing promotional appendages; he provided his daughter with her golden theme. "It has been my daughter's aim," he announced in the Preface to *Tales of Fashionable Life,* "to promote, by all her writings, the progress of education from the cradle to the grave."[25] Maria's literary judgments up to a point were thus strictly utilitarian. In one of her early *Moral Tales,* the youthful protagonist presides at the auction of his aunt's library. "Mrs. Howard selected a few [books] for her own use, and she allowed her nephew to select as many for himself as she had done. He observed that there was a beautiful edition of Shakespeare, which he knew his aunt liked particularly, but which she did not keep, reserving instead of it Smith's *Wealth of Nations,* which would, in a few years, she said, be very useful to him."[26] One can see what it was Dickens crusaded against in *Hard Times.*

Edgeworth's maiden efforts in the field of fiction were thus entirely ancillary to her filial efforts in the field of Hard Facts. Her early stories were intended chiefly as illustrative material to the treatise on *Practical Education* that she had helped her father grind out in 1798. There were didactic nursery tales to be written, didactic storiettes for the juvenile market, with improving titles like *Forgive and Forget; Waste not, Want not.* As Lady Ritchie once pointed out, Edgeworth's tales may be lacking in witches, ogres, castles, and fairy princesses, but then "philanthropic manufacturers, liberal noblemen, and benevolent ladies in travelling carriages do as well."[27] It is with this evident didactic intention in mind, then, that one has to approach the rather innocuous *Moral Tales* and *Popular Tales,* which contain her earliest portraits of Jews.

In reading Edgeworth's early novels and stories, one gets a fairly thorough cross section of the conventional variants of the Jew-villain. The volume entitled *Moral Tales* (1801) contains several such tales in which wicked Jews help Miss Edgeworth to point the intended moral. "The Prussian Vase" will do as exemplum.[28] The ulterior purpose of the story is to eulogize the English method of trial by jury, in contrast to the arbitrary judicial practices among European despots. The scene is the court of Frederick the Great at Potsdam. The Count Laniska, a young nobleman of good fame and family, is accused of having burned into a porcelain vase the inflammatory message that Frederick the Great is a tyrant. So he is; and at his royal pleasure Laniska is convicted, without trial, of treasonable activities and dispatched to the Fortress of Spandau. An English observer at Potsdam, the bearer of Miss Edgeworth's libertarian tidings, prevails upon Frederick to grant the young firebrand a hearing *à l'anglais,* by summoning a jury; and Frederick, rather from motives of eccentricity than good will, allows Laniska his public trial. Witnesses are examined, among them an individual named Solomon.

> In the midst of the general indignation, Mr. Warendorff [for the prosecution] called upon the Jew to come forward and give his evidence. This Jew was an old man, and there was something remarkable in his looks. His head was still; his neck was stiff; but his eyes moved with incessant celerity from side to side, and he seemed uneasy at not being able to see what was passing behind him. There was a certain firmness in his attitude; but his voice trembled when he attempted to speak.

The upshot is that "the Jew did it," with the intention of framing Laniska, whom he has his own good reasons for hating. Amidst the general jubilation the Jew is sentenced, "not to a year's imprisonment in the castle of Spandau, but to sweep the streets of Potzdam (including the court in front of count Laniska's palace) for a twelvemonth." In Modder's quite accurate reading, "the object of the sentence . . . is not so much to punish the offender, as to humiliate the Jew."[29] Had he been a Christian traitor, Solomon would have been sentenced to prison. There is no indication that Edgeworth questions the sentence, any more than Shakespeare questions the degrading punishment of Shylock. The point is that Solomon is only a Jew. When Solomon is asked the reasons of his hatred in the course of the trial, a modern reader may feel that his motives warrant a measure of sympathy, but Edgeworth's laughter is all on the side of the Gentiles. Her attitude at the end of the trial very neatly recalls Shakespeare's attitude toward Shylock:

> Witness: . . . I asked [Solomon] why he hated the Count. The Jew replied, "Because the christian dog has made [Frederick's military] corps of Jews his laughing stock. This day, when my son was going through his manual exercises before the king, count Laniska was holding his sides with laughter. I'll be revenged on him some time or other."

The Jew is led away on the dual counts of being a traitor and a Jew, and Edgeworth steps from behind the curtain to speak the epilogue and point the moral. "You will observe, that this trial by jury, which is a matter of favour to you Prussians, is a matter of right to us Englishmen. Much as I admire your king of Prussia, I admire our English constitution more." Ironically enough the Jew in English literature frequently persists as the archenemy in works aimed at toleration and moral reform.[30]

Far longer and correspondingly more tedious than "The Prussian Vase" is the novella which immediately follows it in the same collection, "The Good Aunt." The point of that tale is rather more elusive than the point of "The Prussian Vase"; according to one of Edgeworth's standard biographer-critics, Helen Zimmern, " 'The Good Aunt' insists upon the necessity of home example and instruction, the lack of which no school training can supply."[31] The domestic exemplar is represented by the title figure, the sagacious lady who, like Count Tolstoi, would rather read Adam Smith than Shakespeare. The novella rather strikingly foreshadows *Harrington* in its character casting. Both novels postulate, in addition to the public-school hero (Charles Howard, Harrington), a brutal young swell who is the hero's schoolmate and foil (Holloway, Lord Mowbray), a defenseless member of a minority group who is bullied by the dandy and rescued by the hero, whom he slavishly adulates thereafter (Oliver, Jacob the Pedlar), and finally the adult moral agent who enunciates the lecture (Mrs. Howard, Montenero). The secondary villain in "The Good Aunt" (and this, of course, is where the two stories part company) is a Semitic jeweller named Carat who conducts a fraudulent lottery and cheats English schoolboys, a theme that harks back to the medieval children-slayers and looks forward to Fagin. Van der Veen has noted some more definite parallels between "The Good Aunt" and *Oliver Twist* and has drawn the interesting inference that Dickens may have had Edgeworth's story in the back of his mind.[32] In both fictions we have a pleasant, much-abused young lad named Oliver who ultimately causes the exposure of a Jewish receiver of stolen goods. Carat, though belonging to a more genteel income group than Fagin, retains the traditional ethos of the Jew as well as his mercurial excitability:

The Jew, all this time, stood in the greatest trepidation; he trembled lest the alderman should have him taken up and committed to gaol for his illegal, unlicensed lottery. He poured forth as many protestations as his knowledge of the English language could afford of the purity of his intentions; and, to demonstrate his disinterestedness, began to display the trinkets in his prize-box, with a panegyric upon each. . . . The word *illegal,* pronounced in a tremendous tone, operated instantaneously upon the Jew; his hand, which had closed upon Holloway's guineas, opened; he laid the money down upon the table; but mechanically seized his box of trinkets, which he seemed to fear would be the next seized, as forfeits. No persons are so apprehensive of injustice and fraud as those who are themselves dishonest.

The weakest and most childish of the three early tales involving Jews is "Murad the Unlucky," which appeared in the volume of *Popular Tales* issued in 1804.[33] The story takes place in the Orient but, as the opening paragraph demonstrates, the moral is strictly English, and for all time. The problem comes down to this:

"I am inclined, please your majesty," replied the vizier, "to think that success in the world depends more upon prudence than upon what is called luck, or fortune."

"And I," said the sultan, "am persuaded that fortune does more for men than prudence."

To show which of them is right, Edgeworth tells an unnecessarily elongated tale about two brothers, Saladin the Lucky and Murad the Unlucky—or, as the story goes to prove, Saladin the Prudent and Murad the Imprudent—both of whom are exposed to identical adventures, trials, temptations; Murad reacts to them without taking thought and therefore invites mischance upon mischance, whereas Saladin, as it were, counts to ten each time and succeeds to health, wealth, and happiness. By page fifty-one, the Sultan has heard all he needs and wishes to hear; "I acknowledge," he concedes to the vizier, "that prudence has more influence than chance."

One of the major adventures that helps to convince the Sultan involves the Jew Rachub of El Arish, a money-lender who attempts to kill his enemies by spreading plague germs in old clothes—an interesting juxtaposition of the medieval poisoner and the modern impoverished, "old-clothes" Jew who figures as a recurrent type in the nineteenth-century novel.* In order to disseminate his poisoned

* The figure of the old-clothes man was a familiar one in nineteenth-century England. Coleridge, in particular, seems to have found the type unpleasantly tantalizing. In *Table Talk,* August 14, 1833, he notes: "The two images farthest removed from each other which can be comprehended under one term are, I think, Isaiah,—'Hear O heavens, and give ear, O earth!' and Levi of Holywell-street—'Old clothes'—both of them Jews, you'll observe. *Immane quantum*

vestments and have the blame fall on other heads than his, Rachub persuades the gullible Murad to buy the clothes at a suspiciously advantageous rate. Murad purchases them, congratulates himself on having struck a fine bargain, and resells the clothes to some Damascene merchants. "What was my terror and remorse, the next day, when one of them came to inform me that plague-boils had broken out under the arms of all the slaves who had worn this pestilential apparel." But hear now of the prudence of Saladin when confronted by the same Jew with the same offer. Instead of taking him up on it, Saladin asks himself all the questions Edgeworth would have us ask ourselves under such circumstances. Is it likely, says Saladin, that a Jew, notorious for being an insolent dog and exorbitant usurer, will get rid of such fine clothing for a pittance? It is *not likely.* Saladin suspects; pursues the dark business; discovers the plot; saves dozens of lives; *de te fabula.* But the Jew escapes. "In these stories," Modder writes, "Miss Edgeworth has not presented one honest Jew to redeem the race. . . . it is obvious that the author has simply taken over the old stock figure of the wicked Jew, placed him in a modern setting, and there left him to do his worst."[34]

---

discrepant." Under the date of July 8, 1830, he records two anecdotes involving the ubiquitous Jewish ragman, neither of which positively redounds to Coleridge's credit. "I have had a good deal to do with Jews in the course of my life, although I never borrowed any money from them. Once I sat in a coach opposite a Jew—a symbol of old clothes' bag—an Isaiah of Holywell Street. He would close the window; I opened it. He closed it again; upon which, in a very solemn tone, I said to him: 'Son of Abraham! thou smellest; son of Isaac! thou art offensive; son of Jacob! thou stinkest foully. See the man in the moon! He is holding his nose at thee in the distance; dost thou think that I, sitting here, can endure it any longer?' My Jew was astounded, opened the window forthwith himself, and said he was sorry, he did not know before I was so great a gentleman." Coleridge reveals the same insensitivity on a similar occasion: "The other day I was *floored* by a Jew. He passed me several times, crying for old clothes, in the most nasal and extraordinary tone I ever heard. At last, I was so provoked that I said to him, 'Pray, why can't you say "old clothes" in a plain way, as I do now?' The Jew stopped, and looking very gravely at me, said in a clear and even fine accent, 'Sir, I can say "old clothes" as well as you can; but if you had to say it ten times a minute, for an hour together, you would say *ogh clo* as I do now'; and so he marched off. I was so confounded with the justice of his retort, that I followed and gave him a shilling, the only one I had." *The Complete Works of Samuel Taylor Coleridge,* ed. W. G. T. Shedd (New York, 1884), VI, 474, 338.

Two of Edgeworth's distinguished Irish novels remain to be mentioned briefly in relation to her Jewish figures before the obverse side of the picture becomes apparent. *The Absentee*[35] has often been thought her masterpiece, as it is certainly the masterpiece of her middle years; but her conception of the evil Jew who appears briefly in the book is no more sophisticated than her conception of Solomon, Carat, or Rachub. Mr. Mordicai, the London coachmaker with the sinister wooden face, is the time-honored extortioner who is pitted against the defenseless spendthrift. The identification with Shylock is pointedly made. While the lavish absentee landlord, Sir John Berryl, lies on his deathbed, Mordicai attempts to extort from his son an exorbitant bond. When young Berryl refuses, the Jew threatens to arrest Sir John: "The bond or the body, before I quit this house." The alternative is Shylock's still. We are told that

> the coachmaker appeared at this time the foremost and the most inexorable of their creditors. Conscious that the charges in his account were exorbitant, and that they would not be allowed if examined by a court of justice; that it was a debt which only ignorance and extravagance could have in the first instance incurred, swelled afterwards to an amazing amount by interest, and interest upon interest; Mordicai was impatient to obtain legal security for the whole sum from the heir. Mr. Berryl offered his bond for the amount of the reasonable charges in his account; but this Mordicai absolutely refused, declaring that now he had the power in his own hands, he would use it to obtain the utmost penny of his debt . . . that a debtor never yet escaped him, and never should; that a man's lying upon his deathbed was no excuse to a creditor; that he was not a whiffler to stand upon ceremony about disturbing a gentleman in his last moment" etc., etc.

It will be noticed that all Edgeworth's Jew-villains who have been considered thus far have certain types of dishonesty in common. All of them, for example, conduct practices which are in the strictest sense punishable by law. Solomon is guilty of both treason and perjury, Mordicai of extortion, Carat of fraudulence; and Rachub is an old-fashioned murderer. All except the first are animated by the profit motive, pure and simple; Rachub and Mordicai are money-lenders. Rachub has a straight, if mordant answer to Murad's grievances: you like opium, I like money; I've supplied you with your favorite commodity, now supply me with mine. At the same time, it may be noted that all these Jews, with the exception of the coachmaker, are characterized very largely by their underhandedness. Barabas and Shylock used not to be, conspicuously, liars—at worst, they hid their monies where nobody could get at them. But Solomon, Carat, and Rachub (when he is being a salesman) are distinguished for their cowardly and sly indirectness: Solomon and Rachub blame their own crimes on an innocent third. Each of them is also without a shred of pity, abusing children and moribundi both; but that is an old story.

A good deal more interesting as well as original are the allusions to the Jewess in *Castle Rackrent*.[36] The vogue of the wholly wicked Jewess was never, perhaps, more than an accidental and singular one; to all intents it exhausted itself with the balladry of the Jew's Daughter in the Middle Ages. Occasionally the vulgar Jewish wife, essentially a reflection of the husband's vulgarity, is to be met with; for example, she occupies a prominent place in *The Way We Live Now*. But it is not safe to generalize about the Jew's wife in literature. Within the strict convention of the stereotype, as I have indicated, she does not function at all. In *Daniel Deronda* and Du Maurier's *The Martian,* neither of which is concerned with types of Jewish criminality, her chief business is to be a good housewife. In *Castle Rackrent* Sir Kit's Jewish wife is a thoroughly disagreeable lady; but, except in the one respect to be mentioned, it would be difficult to refer her to any significant prototype.

In dealing with Edgeworth's Jewish characters up to this point, I have disregarded the chronology in order to group the more obvious stereotypes together. Actually, *Castle Rackrent* precedes the *Moral Tales* by a year and *The Absentee* by more than a decade, and it also takes precedence over Edgeworth's other compositions in point of literary excellence. The book has been called "the most influential narrative between the death of Smollett and the publication of *Waverley*," and it is generally considered the great ancestor of the regional novel.[37] It has other claims to originality. For one, it represents the first attempt in English fiction to do on a modest scale what, on a monumental scale, became standard practice among the Victorian and Edwardian novelists, as well as their contemporaries on the continent: to pursue the fortunes and misfortunes of a single family through several generations. *Castle Rackrent* appeared in 1800; *Bud-*

denbrooks in 1900. Like Mann, Edgeworth might have subtitled her novel *Verfall einer Familie*. In the Jewish wife of Sir Kit, the third-generation master of Rackrent, the Jews are indirectly blamed for contributing to the deterioration of the Irish nobility; drink, temper tantrums, and Irish prodigality do the rest. "But from first to last she brought nothing but misfortune amongst us; and if it had not been all along with her, his honour, Sir Kit, would have been now alive in all appearances."

The story of Sir Patrick, Sir Murtagh, Sir Kit, and Sir Condy is told by Thady Quirk, the almost fanatically devoted servant at Rackrent. It is Thady's narrative that provides the novel with still another technical point of interest and that determines the portrayal of the Jewess. In presenting her material through the eyes of a nominally detached observer, whose narrative takes on the color of his personality, Edgeworth achieved for the first time the kind of oblique point of view that James raised into a canon of art. At that Thady's prose is so flexible and full of astonishing nuances that one may reasonably extend to it the compliment T. S. Eliot paid to the style of *Huckleberry Finn* when he described it as one of the miracles of the nineteenth century.

What keeps Sir Kit's wife from being simply another unpleasant Jew, therefore, is Thady's highly original view of the lady. Seen through the medium of his peasant superstitiousness and misplaced sense of family loyalty, she is, among Jews, comfortably *sui generis*. Thady's first communiqué about her reads to the effect "that she spoke a strange kind of English of her own, that she could not abide pork or sausages, and went neither to church or mass."

> Mercy upon his honour's poor soul, thought I; what will become of him or his, and all of us, with his heretic blackamoor at the head of the Castle Rackrent estate! I never slept a wink all night for thinking of it: but before the servants I put my pipe in my mouth, and kept my mind to myself; for I had a great regard for the family; and after this, when strange gentlemen's servants came to the house, and would begin to talk about the bride, I took care to put the best foot foremost, and passed her for a nabob in the kitchen, which accounted for her dark complexion and everything.

Within the context of the stereotype, however, the lady, whom Sir Kit indifferently treasures as "my pretty Jessica" and curses for a "stiff-necked Israelite," suffers from the proverbial Jewish sin of avarice. Thady's chief complaint about her is that "she gave no vails to the servants of Castle Rackrent at parting, nothwithstanding the old proverb of *'as rich as a Jew'* which she being a Jewish, they built upon with reason," and that once she became mistress of the estate, "there were no balls, no dinners, no doings." Then, to point up her miserliness, there is the fatal business of the diamond cross, which drives Sir Kit fairly to distraction: "she has thousands of English pounds concealed in diamonds about her, which she as good as promised to give up to my master before he married, but now she won't part with any of them, and she must take the consequences." Sir Kit's revenge is not without its macabre touches:

> My master made it a principle to have the sausages, and swore at her for a Jew herself, till he drove her out of the kitchen; . . . and from that day forward always sausages, or bacon, or pig meat in some shape or other, went up to the table; upon which my lady shut herself up in her own room, and my master said she might stay there, with an oath: and to make sure of her, he turned the key in the door, and kept it ever after in his pocket. We none of us ever saw or heard her speak for seven year after that.

Maria Edgeworth: Harrington

Having impressed her readers with her ability to manipulate the stereotype of the Jew-villain and having informed them some six times over that Jews were frauds, usurers, poisoners, perjurers, traitors, parasites on the national economy, threats to the body politic, and violators of young boys, Edgeworth decided to take it all back and wrote *Harrington*.[38] The decision was not entirely hers. In the last of his awful prefaces, Richard Lovell Edgeworth noted that "*Harrington* was occasioned by an extremely well written letter, which Miss Edgeworth received from America, from a Jewess, complaining of the illiberality with which the Jewish nation had been treated in some of Miss Edgeworth's works."[39] The main character of the novel trots out the same formula of which Cumberland and, later on, Scott and Dickens availed themselves, Edgeworth being a little more candid in her *mea culpa* than the others, in that she specifically draws attention, by title, to her past errors.

> And here I must observe [says Harrington], that not only in the old story books, where the Jews are as well fixed to be wicked as the bad fairies,

or bad genii, or allegorical personifications of the devils and the vices in the old emblems, mysteries, moralities &c., but in almost every work of fiction I found them represented as hateful beings; nay, even in modern tales of very late years. Since I have come to man's estate, I have met with books by authors professing candour and toleration—books written expressly for the rising generation, called, if I mistake not, *Moral Tales for Young People;* and even in these, whenever the Jews are introduced, I find that they are invariably represented as beings of a mean, avaricious, unprincipled, treacherous character.

Modder rightly remarks of the Jewish characters in *Harrington* that Edgeworth created them too plainly "out of her moral consciousness," and that, in consequence, "her delineations are superficial." The remark, as I have said, may be generalized to include most writers who have dealt with the good Jew in a spirit of apology and hindsight, through whose character, in Modder's good phrase, "an amnesty is to be effected."[40] In the case of *Harrington,* though critics have condemned the book with astonishing unanimity, the pallor of the Jewish characters does not prevent the novel, in its general outlines, from being an interesting one, not least for the ethical fingernail-biting with which it concludes. Technically *Harrington* is old-fashioned stuff compared with *Castle Rackrent.* The novel is a first-person *Erziehungsroman* that purports to describe a sympathetic young man's education in anti-Semitism and his reaction against it. The book gains a good deal of initial momentum by being set against the background of the Jewish Naturalization Bill of 1753, which evoked such a storm of protest that it had to be repealed the following year. Its other strictly historical interest derives from its exciting as well as authoritative description of the Gordon Riots twenty-seven years later, which Dickens treated rather less reliably than Edgeworth in *Barnaby Rudge.*[41]

One of the outspoken opponents to the Naturalization Bill is young Harrington's father, a blustering if gentlemanly anti-Semite who indoctrinates his son in the axiom that "when a man once goes to the Jews, he soon goes to the devil." The boy's early antipathy toward Jews has deeper roots than any which propaganda can strike, however. As a baby Harrington is prey to terrifying bogey neuroses, which his governess fosters by telling him bedtime stories about Jews who have been known to abduct and crucify other little boys, using them hideously at midnight orgies.

> Above all others, there was one story, horrible! most horrible! which she used to tell at midnight, about a Jew who lived in Paris in a dark alley, and who professed to sell pork pies; but it was found out at last, that the pies were not pork,—they were made of the flesh of little children. His wife used to stand at the door of her den to watch for little children, and, as they were passing, would tempt them in with sweetmeats. There was a trap-door in the cellar, and the children were dragged down; and—Oh! how my blood ran cold when we came to the terrible trap-door. Were there, I asked, such things in London now?

The governess assures him that indeed there are, ready to catch just such saucy little boys as he. An old-clothes Jew, Simon by name, who passes the Harrington mansion at night, calling out his wares, turns into the boy's nightmare image; and what now follows is worthy of Dickens:

> Every night, the moment she and the candle left the room, I lay in an indescribable agony of terror; my head under the bed-clothes, my knees drawn up, in a cold perspiration. I saw faces around me grinning, glaring, receding, advancing, all turning at last into one and the same face of the Jew with the long beard, and the terrible eyes; and that bag in which I fancied were mangled limbs of children—it opened to receive me, or fell upon my bed, and lay heavy on my breast, so that I could neither stir nor scream.

It is a rather sad comment on Edgeworth's inability to depict decent Jewish types that when she does finally pull them out of her hat, they turn out to be scarcely more credible than the fantastic ghouls of little Harrington's imaginative world. But in the meantime Harrington grows up a bit; his spontaneous superstitious fear of Jews gives way to a prematurely intellectual acceptance of the superstition: he comes to recognize that his childish anti-Semitism confers certain definite social advantages.

> I soon grew vain of my fears. My antipathy, my *natural,* positively natural antipathy to the sight or bare idea of a Jew, was talked of by ladies and by gentlemen, it was exhibited to all my mother's acquaintances, learned and unlearned, it was a medical, it was a metaphysical wonder, it was an *idiosyncracy,* corporeal, or mental, or both—it was—in short, more nonsense was talked about it than I will repeat.

The age of six finds Harrington, absurdly, offering his views on the Naturalization issue. Why should not the Jews be naturalized? "I, with all the pertness of ignorance, replied, 'Why, ma'am, because the Jews are naturally an unnatural pack of people, and you can't naturalize what's naturally unnatural.'" These paradoxes, at age six, do not promise well for Harrington; still, he grows into a normally anti-Semitic youth; eventually he is sent off to school, to discover in his schoolmates the same antipathy toward Jews that he himself has been taught to entertain. While at school, he is thrown into contact with a destitute Jewish peddler named Jacob, a figure outrageously victimized, whose helplessness arouses the hero to a sense of the injustice and inhumanity under which Jews are smarting. Of Jacob we are pointedly informed that

> he was as unlike to Shylock as it is possible to conceive. Without one thought or look of malice or revenge, he stood before us Thursday after Thursday, enduring all that our barbarity was pleased to inflict; he stood patient and long-suffering, and even of this patience and resignation we made a jest.

Once he has made Jacob's acquaintance, Harrington shakes off his anti-Semitism with the ease of one who has never devoutly believed in the thing to begin with. He appoints himself Jacob's champion against a brutal young dandy, Lord Mowbray, whose own anti-Judaism is merely a form of extroverted sportiveness and therefore no more beyond apostasy than Harrington's. On page seventy, Jacob confronts Harrington with the awful truth: "My father," he announces with the éclat of Lohengrin acknowledging the paternity of Parzifal, "was Simon, the old clothes man." Considering the Jewish population figures in the 1760's, Jacob's disclosure is not perhaps so indefensible technically as it might sound today.

Harrington graduates into the world. At a performance of Macklin's *Jew of Venice* he beholds among the spectators Berenice Montenero, a raven-haired beauty, pale and very agitated. To all appearances the girl is Jewish, for during Macklin's "hath not a Jew eyes" speech she displays symptoms of hysteria, and it is remarked by her escorts that of all plays this about Jessica is least calculated to entertain her.[42] As a fictional character, Berenice embodies all the dull attributes of her statuesque type; she is even a little less interesting than Scott's Rebecca, who has at least her medical accomplishments to justify her. But Harrington, to everyone's consternation, has already fallen in love with her, and the remainder of the novel deals with the obstacles he must overcome in order to marry her.

There are quite a number of such obstacles. Harrington's parents, for one, of course. Surprisingly, Lord Mowbray presents another, for despite his blatant dislike of Jews he has taken it into his head to compete with Harrington for Berenice's hand. When the girl rejects him for the anti-Semitic cad he is, he slanders his rival and produces the old governess to testify that her erstwhile charge suffers from fits of insanity, with periodic outbursts against Jews. Most mystifying of all about his objection to the match is Mr. Montenero, Berenice's father. For some 150 pages he puts off Harrington and tells him that he cannot be sure whether he will sanction the marriage or no; the young man must season his admiration for a year or so. Montenero himself is a banker and philanthropist, a wholly good, patient, and sage individual who eventually rescues Harrington's father from the threat of bankruptcy. Prototypes for such bankers were not lacking in the eighteenth century; Abraham Goldsmid has already been cited in connection with Cumberland; Sir Sampson Gideon, too, moved easily among the Gentile aristocracy, and by the time Disraeli picked up the type, he had also the Rothschilds and the Montefiores to choose from. As a character in fiction, Montenero is of very considerable historical importance. He represents the first full-length portrayal of a sympathetic Jew in the whole of the English novel. Smollett's Joshua Manasseh, the first benevolent Jew to be found in English fiction, and the last before Montenero, had been a rather incidental figure in the novel. And it is an awe-inspiring fact that more than sixty years had to pass after Smollett before another good Jew appeared. Between 1753, the publication date of *Ferdinand Count Fathom,* and 1817, when *Harrington* appeared, the English novel is littered with Jewish comic villains; such few good Jews as found their way into literature during those years entered via the stage-door.[43]

The second half of *Harrington,* then, is taken up with the hero's pursuit, the heroine's availability, and the father's hanging fire. The latter part of the novel introduces us to all sorts and conditions of

Jews and anti-Semites alike. It will be noticed again when we come to George Eliot that the creators of the good Jew tend toward a panoramic view of their subject: a variety of opinions is brought to bear on the Jewish issue. Such a structure has its rightness, perhaps its indispensability, when it is remembered once again that the good Jew is almost always treated sociologically, within the context of a persecuted group. There can be only one opinion about Shylock and Fagin; so their authors need not sample public opinion. But Edgeworth and Eliot derive half their effects from the way in which they intellectualize the whole problem by deploying a number of its contributory issues and aspects over as many characters. In Edgeworth this method is essential to the very conception of the pedagogic novel, which assumes that the young man not only is to be exposed to a variety of physical trials but must choose from among a number of accessible moral problems. Thus in *Harrington* we have the politically based anti-Semitism of the hero's father; the inherited family prejudice of Lord Mowbray's mother, who keeps reminding her children, with a considerable insistence on the tradition involved, that their ancestors used to help John Lackland torture the Jews when they did not pay up; the "gentleman's agreement" kind of anti-Semitism typified by Harrington's mother, whose attitude is the fashionable one, that one does not associate with such people. Mowbray, apart from his sheer effervescence, represents the type of anti-Jewish feeling that is likely to be found among the officers' set, the Grand Illusionists. Finally, there are the superstitious, pure and simple, as represented by the governess. Among the Jews, the stratifications in *Harrington* tend to be professional rather than ethical; for, as we have seen, the Jews are all, in a moral way, perfect. At the bottom of the commercial ladder we have old Simon, the old-clothes peddler, with whom the novel begins; at the top we have Mr. Montenero, the banker with whom the novel ends. Jacob works his way up to a respectable middle-class position as assistant to a diamond merchant. The prosperous mercantile class itself is represented by the Manessas, Jacob's benefactors. In Israel Lyons we have an early portrait of the Anglo-Jewish intellectual; in Berenice, finally, the beautiful Jewess.

But Berenice is not a Jewess at all, although from Harrington's own point of view, she might as well be. He has long ago conquered all his prejudices; he no longer regards Jews either as maleficent spooks or as undesirable commercial contacts; allowing for the family scandal, there is nothing against his marrying the girl. Indeed, Harrington's blustering old father has been all but brought to his knees by Montenero's financial generosity toward him:

"Can you conceive, Mr. Montenero," cried my father, "that after all I have seen of you! all you have done for me—can you conceive me to be such an obstinately prejudiced brute?—My prejudices against the Jews I give up—you have conquered them—all, all. But a difference of religion—between man and wife—"

Edgeworth herself cannot after all bring herself to condone such a union. As Modder ruefully remarks, "the novelist doubtless holds that she has done enough for Jewish emancipation."[44] So, before the curtain falls, Miss Montenero, having been permitted to masquerade as an Israelite sufficiently long, is discovered to harbor a Christian mother; she herself has been cleansed at the baptismal font; and the day is saved for intradenominational felicity and the confirmation of the Gentleman's Agreement. A difference of religion—between man and wife—

"Is a serious objection indeed," said Mr. Montenero, "but if that be the only objection left in your mind, I have the pleasure to tell you, Mr. Harrington," addressing himself to me, "that your love and duty are not at variance—I have tried you to the utmost, and am satisfied both of the steadiness of your principles and of the strength of your attachment to my daughter. Berenice is not a Jewess. . . . according to my promise to Mrs. Montenero, Berenice has been bred in her faith—a Christian—a Protestant.

"An *English* Protestant!" the elder Harringtons outdo each other in exclaiming. For it would not be a good idea to do things by halves, and if you are to have a Protestant daughter-in-law where you merely expected a Sephardic one, only an English Protestant can fill the measure of familial happiness. But now the groom wants to know why Mr. Montenero withheld that vital information from him. The respondent, in his curtain speech, makes it amply clear that the intelligence that guided Saladin the Lucky directed Mr. Montenero as well: "Had I spared you the pain, you would never have enjoyed the delight—had I spared you the trial, you would never have had the triumph."

The neat syntactic balancing of uncomplicated opposites reveals the whole animating motive: the contrast between Saladin and Murad; between the little girl in "The Birthday Present" who spends her half-guinea on a useless gift and the little girl who gives her half-guinea to a poor child; between the little boy in "Waste not, Want not" who cuts his piece of cord and trips over it, and the little boy who providently unties his piece of cord and saves it.[45]

"The triumph, did I say? Better than all triumph, this sober certainty of your own integrity. . . . My daughter was determined never to marry any man, who could be induced to sacrifice religion and principle to interest or to passion. She was equally determined never to marry any man, whose want of the spirit of toleration, whose prejudices against the Jews, might interfere with the filial affection she feels for her father—though he be a Jew."

It is not a pleasant ending. Winding up her plots was not Edgeworth's forte. One can see why. Her perceptions of human motives and relationships were subtle and intelligent enough to enable her to set the complications into motion. But her morality, which was at bottom sentimental, led her to pair off her characters in simple antitheses, as if there were only two sides to each question, the prudent and the imprudent; and so, instead of resolving her complications honestly and inevitably, she stuck on whatever ending happened to suit her notions of theodicy. For complex problems and potentially profound relationships she found rather superficial solutions. Scott, writing *Ivanhoe* three years later, dealt with the issue more honestly; and in *Deronda,* as was said, the *Harrington* situation is exactly inverted. The Gentile is free to marry the Jewess only when he can bring her evidence that he is, after all, himself a Jew.

The Pattern of Apology

Over and above whatever intrinsic interest it possesses, *Harrington* has the documentary value predicated for it: it confirms the pattern of self-conscious retraction by a novelist who feels that she has to make up for earlier slips-of-the-pen. In reading *Harrington* one is uncomfortably aware that what the author is saying between the lines all along is, "I know that the Jews in my earlier stories were unforgivable; I know there are good Jews; here is one to prove it." No wonder that *Harrington* "dragged with her as she wrote it, and dragged with the public."[46] The identical *raison d'être* for Dickens's Riah has already been alleged. "The whole atmosphere of [*Our Mutual Friend*]," Calisch remarks, "seems to justify the supposition that Dickens is trying to repair the wrong as far as he may." And Philipson likens the presentation of Riah to "some sweets that are given a patient after he has swallowed a very bitter dose." The same may be said of Leah Gibson, the Jewish heroine of George Du Maurier's *The Martian*.[47] Apparently Du Maurier felt that the presentation of the terrible Svengali called for some official act of recantation.[48] The result is that while Svengali, like Shylock (or Frankenstein) has passed into popular parlance, Leah, a product of Du Maurier's second thoughts, does not even begin to rate. Like Edgeworth's Berenice and Scott's Rebecca, she accounts for merely another idealized portrait in the gallery of beautiful Jewesses.

Among the apologists there is also Trollope, who is said to have "expressed regret" for his presentation of Melmotte, the bloated and sadistic Jewish plutocrat whose activities are intended to symbolize *The Way We Live Now*.[49] Unlike his confreres, Trollope confined himself to an extra-literary expression of regret, without bothering to offset the horrible Melmotte clan with the customary good Jew. In *Nina Balatka,* however, written some years earlier, Trollope did make an attempt to deal impartially with the problem of interracial marriage, interestingly inverting the traditional religious attributions of the lovers by making the hero, rather than the heroine, the Jewish party. It is a pity that Trendelssohn, Nina's Jewish lover, though a far cry from Riah and his type, is still addicted to making speeches and holding protracted interior monologues in defense of his race. Compared with *The Way We Live Now, Nina Balatka* is feeble stuff; and Trendelssohn is only less obnoxious than are Sheva, Riah, and Leah, in proportion as he is less the paragon.

The reasons for the failure of the good Jew in literature should by now be fairly clear. The chief reason, I think, is that he has been almost consistently a product of far too obvious and explicit ulterior motives. He bore from the first the pale cast of afterthought. Given the convention, the authors who kept the Jew-villain in circulation created their man with a good deal of spontaneity. The Jew-villain might not be a realistic figure; but within the canons of comedy and melodrama he could give the illusory appearance of being a creature of flesh and blood. The purveyors of the immaculate Jew, on the other hand, produced not so much a character as a formula. Riah and his type will not bleed if you prick them.

The result is that although the Jewish criminal can at least be described on his own terms (as resembling such and such a man, behaving in such and such a way, propelled by such and such impulses), the good Jew cannot be described at all except in terms of the author's intention. He remains a blank in the memory—vapid, depersonalized, a disembodied Voice, testifying to the author's high principles. Since the speeches are all alike and the voices are indistinguishable, the good Jews end by being basically undifferentiated. And this voice, blandly and monotonously, assures us that the Jew is misunderstood, maligned, victimized; he is selfless and self-sacrificing; *edel, hilfreich, und gut.* And though all this may be true, one would like to see the truth a little more compellingly acted out; after so much exordium one pines for the illustrative text. Naturally, somebody like George Eliot is no longer quite so simple-minded about the matter as Cumberland, and one can begin to picture characters like Daniel and Mordecai; but they, too, are all talk, good advice, earnest remonstrance. All of Mordecai's long-winded lucubrations taken together do not add up, in dramatic effectiveness, to the brief and sporadic appearances of Mordecai's felonious father, and Mirah is only the beautiful Jewess all over again, invested with a missionary purpose.

I suppose that the difference between the wicked Jew and the good Jew in English literature reflects finally the difference between an imaginative figure and a name in an editorial—the difference between art and polemic, metaphor and literalism. Shylock's "ducats and daughter" cry is at least a form of dramatic art; Sheva's "Jews are outcasts" is a platform speech. As such, it may have virtue, but, as Willa Cather has said of the novel, literature cannot be at once a form of imaginative art and a brilliant form of journalism. Fagin is the villain of the piece; hence he is, if nothing else, an essential agent in the plot. Riah is an apologetic supernumerary, whose editorial *nota bene* might as easily be Dickens's own.[50]

I turn now to Walter Scott, whose debts to *The Merchant of Venice* and *The Jew of Malta* have been repeatedly acknowledged. If Edgeworth was the first novelist of the nineteenth century to make room for the Jews in her novels, Scott was the first to give them an abiding place in English fiction. He knew Cumberland's *Jew* and criticized it. Between Scott and Edgeworth there existed a bond of mutual admiration; but unlike Miss Edgeworth, Scott dealt with Jews in only a single major work, so that it is idle to endow him with precisely the same motives that resulted in the writing of *Harrington*. Edgeworth first presented some overwhelmingly bad Jews, and then some overwhelmingly good ones in order to achieve an artificial balance. Although Scott has only one Jew and one Jewess apiece, he points up, in the single figure of Isaac, the two extremes that Edgeworth manipulated in separate novels. Isaac is Shylock rationalized into Sheva.

PART TWO

Stereotypes

There is in the words "a beautiful Jewess" a very special sexual signification, one quite different from that contained in the words "beautiful Rumanian," "beautiful Greek," or "beautiful American," for example. This phrase carries an aura of rape and massacre. The "beautiful Jewess" is she whom the Cossacks under the czars dragged by her hair through the streets of her burning village. And the special works which are given over to accounts of flagellation reserve a place of honor for the Jewess. . . . From the Rebecca of *Ivanhoe* . . . the Jewess has a well-defined function in even the most serious novels. Frequently violated or beaten, she sometimes succeeds in escaping dishonor by means of death, but that is a form of justice; and those who keep their virtue are docile servants or humiliated women in love with indifferent Christians who marry Aryan women.

SARTRE, *Anti-Semite and Jew* (1948)

IV

The Jew as Clown and the Jew's Daughter: Scott

Among the nineteenth-century novelists who contributed conspicuously to the mythology of the Jew, Scott represents perhaps a larger number of available attitudes than any of the novelists who followed him. Unlike Dickens and Eliot, who continued to reflect the extreme positions encouraged by Shylock and Sheva, Scott in the pages of a single novel cuts across a variety of traditional moods. In *Ivanhoe* he regards the Jews from at least three kinds of perspective.

In his dramatic portrayal of Isaac of York, Scott updated the tradition of the comic miser; indeed, he may be said to have given Shylock his first eminent place in the English novel. It may be well to insist on this point at once, if only to correct the fashionable tendency to stress Scott's tolerance toward Isaac at the expense of some other things in his portrayal. Instead of Isaac's being viewed, as I think he should be viewed, as Shylock's historical ancestor and fictional heir, it has too often been taken for granted that Scott meant him to be Shylock's antipode. Thus we find a reasonably modern scholar, whose entire text is given over to tracing Shakespeare's influence on Scott, basking in the comfortable faith that "Shylock is petty, spiteful and materialistic; Isaac is high-principled, generous and brave," when nine-tenths of Scott's text goes to demonstrate that Isaac is unprincipled, grasping, and cowardly.[1] Francis Jeffrey, writing up *Ivanhoe* in the *Edinburgh Review* a hundred years before Mr. Brewer began to think wishfully, saw Isaac more clearly for what he was: "but a milder Shylock, and by no means more natural than his original."[2]

At the same time, Scott—and this is where he parts company from the purveyors of the Jew-villain pure and simple—grants Isaac a considerable measure of absolution by establishing the historical basis for his cupidity. Here, Scott says in effect, are the historical motives as they operate in 1194; such and such are the social forces that have propelled Isaac into a state of abject terror, unrestrained avarice, and canine submissiveness. By explaining the historical and environmental facts that have molded Isaac's character and hardened his ruling vices, Scott goes a long way toward explaining the vices themselves away. The difference between Isaac and a character like Fagin is not really accounted for by assigning the two figures to different traditions and modes of thinking: the elements of the medieval Judas-type determine the portrayals of both. But where Fagin's wickedness is presented as a gratuitous perversion, Isaac's displays of moral turpitude are the result of his social and historical conditioning. Unlike Fagin, he has always the pretext and consolation of his enemies.

Isaac thus not only retains on the one hand all the features of the traditional Jewish miser; he is also the pathetic victim of inimical historical pressures, and perhaps the worst that can be said of him is that he reacts as badly as possible under pressure. Every so often Scott explicitly enlists the reader's sympathy for Isaac's marginal position and in so many words rationalizes his conduct. If Isaac's dramatic appearances confirm his resemblance to the Jew-dog and the Jew-fox, Scott's purely verbal excuses for him sound indistinguishably like

Sheva's jeremiads—or Señor Montenero's, or Mordecai's, or Riah's. Where Isaac's individual behavior speaks against him, Scott speaks, not positively for him, but for the whole tribe of Isaacs instead. "It is not [Isaac] that enlists sympathy," Philipson well notes; "it is the occasional descriptions and explanations of the lot of the Jews."[3] Scott can have it both ways: he can show the reader with his right hand what a disagreeable Jew looks like, while his left scribbles away about the persecution of the Jews under Richard Lion-Heart. Scott's plea from history, his insistence that Isaac is not the master of his fate, has, I think, unwarrantably obscured Isaac's link with the Shylock tradition; and any theory that seeks to make him over into a relatively decent character has to assume an indecently high degree of relativity.

Still another perspective is provided by the portrayal of Isaac's daughter Rebecca, the Noble Jewess. Where Isaac is nine-tenths of the time the conventional scoundrel of the old school for whom Scott has to make face-saving speeches, Rebecca, of course, is the Jewish paragon in word and deed. Frequently, as a matter of dramatic convenience and heroic routine, Scott allows her to take his wholesale lament over the Jews out of his own mouth and to deliver it, *in loco parentis,* in the high astounding terms of Wardour Street. Since her business in the novel is to fall in love with the hero, it is only to be expected that in portraying her Scott should be animated by the principle that handsome does and handsome speaks as handsome is. Rebecca's artistic supremacy over everybody else in the novel has been conceded her so consistently and loquaciously in the century and a quarter since she took her seat at Ashby-de-la-Zouche, that it seems hardly worth the effort to begin questioning the consensus so late in the day.

I add at once that Scott's importance in the framework of this study lies only secondarily in the relative complexity, the shifting allegiances, the many points of view that he succeeded in bringing to bear on his portrayal of the Jews. His real significance here, as in more general matters, is chiefly historical; he was the first to give the Jews any kind of popular prominence in the English novel. As we know, the mere presence of Jewish personnel in English fiction does not date from the publication of *Ivanhoe*. Two years earlier

Maria Edgeworth had assigned a prominent role to a civilized Jewish businessman in the pages of *Harrington,* and had centered the romantic interest in a crypto-Jewess whose last-minute redemption for Protestantism hinges on a shallow and dishonest formality. More than half a century before Edgeworth, Smollett had in a minor way introduced the first good Jew into English fiction; and before Smollett all the major eighteenth-century novelists—Defoe, Fielding, and Richardson—had peopled at least the margins of their stories with the fashionable Jewish criminal types. And behind these peripheral figures one can still glimpse the Jewish villains whom Jack Wilton encounters on his unsentimental journey through Italy. Then, too, there had been in the twenty-five years or so before Scott a sudden recrudescence of interest in that sad and fabulous mythological oddity the Wandering Jew. By 1820, that antique dromomaniac, hateful to Christ and marvelous to men, had been appropriated for fiction by Monk Lewis, Godwin, and Shelley, glossing the past and future; conjuring up the blood-stained ghosts of Bavarian Catholics and then putting them back into their graves; tantalizing the gullible and the banal with his evil eye; not merely hoarding gold in the dead of night but manufacturing it by some secret Arabian patent, some dark and dismal abracadabra; living forever and dying very rich and very repentant.

If Scott was thus verifiably not the first to place his Jews on the fiction market, he was almost as verifiably the first to make them an immensely marketable commodity.[4] Nothing comparable had been offered since Shakespeare. From the point of view of chronology, therefore, Scott's importance is very great. His use of Jews ensured their instant éclat, as well as their survival in the nineteenth-century novel.

The Ivanhoe Strategy: Saxons and Normans

To appreciate the strategic importance of the Jewish group in *Ivanhoe,* something needs to be said about the historical problems Scott has raised in the novel, and about the way in which he has worked them out in terms of theme and conflict.

With the composition of *Ivanhoe* Scott abandoned the series of

Hibernian novels on which his modern critical reputation rests, and branched out into a field in which he allegedly had no business. The consensus among critics is that Scott did not really understand the Middle Ages and that he had only the vaguest and most fitful notions of the Catholic Church, with the result that he drifted into insincerity and a rather tawdry sensationalism.[5] Walter Bagehot's damaging opinion that Scott "describes the middle ages as we should have wished them to have been" has become accepted doctrine.[6] To run down the A B C of modern Scott criticism is to come up with uniformly hostile comments on *Ivanhoe,* always based on the assumption that Scott is being trivial. "I have made my peace with *Quentin Durward,*" Walter Allen writes, "but I am still unable to read *Ivanhoe* and *The Talisman*; when I pick them up ennui still rises like a soporific dust from their pages." John Buchan, the author of one of the standard biographies, discovers in *Ivanhoe* specifically the fault that nineteenth-century critics like Carlyle, Bagehot, and Leslie Stephen attributed to the whole of Scott: "The real blemish is that this romance is concerned only with externals." David Cecil notes that "though like everything [Scott] wrote, [the medieval romances] have vivid scenes and a fine narrative gusto, as serious novels *Ivanhoe* and the rest of them are failures"; and on similar grounds David Daiches opines that "a novel like *Ivanhoe,* though it has qualities of its own, is much more superficial than any of the Scottish novels, and is written throughout on a much lower plane."[7] Bagehot's sentiment that "the charm of *Ivanhoe* is addressed . . . to that kind of boyish fancy which idolises medieval society as the 'fighting time,'" has been echoed in our own day by two of Scott's biographers, Sir Herbert Grierson, who considers the novel "mainly a good story of adventure for boys," and Una Pope-Hennessy, who calls it "first and last a boy's book, opening up exciting horizons for the young."[8]

Such unanimity cripples dissent. But, contrary to what has generally been alleged against *Ivanhoe,* I believe that Scott, working all the time with traditional romantic materials, used these materials in order to compose an epitaph on some of the romantic follies and excesses which, in *Ivanhoe,* he specifically associated with medieval chivalry. In speaking of the early Scottish books, David Daiches has remarked that

> Scott's first and characteristic novels . . . might with justice be called "anti-romantic" fiction. They attempt to show that heroic action, as the typical romantic writer would like to think of it, is, in the last analysis, neither heroic nor useful, and that man's destiny, at least in the modern world, is to find his testing time not amid the sound of trumpets but in the daily struggles and recurring crises of personal life.

In the same article Daiches defines Scott's dominant theme as reflecting "the tragic sense that romantic man must compromise with his heroic ideals if he is to survive in the modern world."[9] It seems to me that the same meaning may be found in *Ivanhoe,* and that the novel has in fact been consistently underrated because of the critics' refusal to see in it an extension, rather than a repudiation, of Scott's early novels. Granting provisionally that by Scott's own definition *Ivanhoe* may contain most of the elements of romance rather than those of a novel[10] (which I take to be a critique of romance), it should nevertheless be possible to regard *Ivanhoe* as a reasonably responsible, rather disillusioned, essentially antiromantic work, in which many of the structural patterns of the early novels are repeated and extended instead of being replaced by flamboyant claptrap. It is the point of the following remarks that *Ivanhoe* is a more serious "criticism" than has been generally recognized, and that the Jewish characters not only occupy highly strategic positions in the novel, but contribute significantly to the comprehensiveness of Scott's critique.[11]

The flamboyant claptrap, no doubt, is all one remembers of the novel—the flashy tournaments; the rather dilatory collapse of Torquilstone Castle; the sanguinary crone Ulrica and her Anglo-Saxon screams; the Good King and the Wicked Pretender; the lymphatic Heroine with the blond hair and the quivering Heroine with the raven hair; the appearance of the Hero just as the raven-haired Heroine is about to be burned; the collapse of the Villain, *idem*; the bewildering preponderance of leafy matter and arborial backdrops, with the robber-philanthropist whistling in the sunlight between some tree stumps; the very funny business about Athelstane coming to life in the middle of the funeral banquet in his behalf; the apparent affability with which people slaughter and propose to ravish each other; the ways in which the heroes disclose their identities by whispering something into somebody's ear—very unpromising, very sensational, an insult to the austere and the discriminating. "Yesterday," Balzac wrote to Madame Hanska, "I spent the whole day in reading *Peveril of the Peak*, lest I should be forced to think."[12]

How is one to salvage any half-way serious material from a mass of such exorbitant climaxes, rescues, deaths, transfigurations? One way to begin is by stating at once the chief thematic conflict in the novel, which takes place between two historic forces, both clinging to outmoded heroic ideals and weakened by their allegiance to them. "Four generations," says Scott, "had not sufficed to blend the hostile blood of the Normans and Anglo-Saxons, or to unite by common language and mutual interests, two hostile races, one of which still felt the elation of triumph, while the other groaned under the consequences of defeat."[13] And again: "The great national distinction betwixt [the Saxons] and their conquerors, the recollection of what they had formerly been, and to what they were new reduced, continued down to the reign of Edward the Third, to keep open the wounds which the Conquest had inflicted, and to maintain a line of separation betwixt the descendants of the victor Normans and the vanquished Saxons." Scott does not conceal his regret at the passing of the old native tradition, and he pays the Saxons some handsome compliments that he withholds from the Normans; but it becomes increasingly clear that there is not very much to choose between the contestants. On both sides the governing bodies attach themselves to ideals that have outlived their practical usefulness.

The conflict formulated, the sun is permitted to set on "the rich grassy glades" of a forest that has already been wheeled onstage in the opening scene, and the plot begins to take, if not shape, at least an optical illusion of shape. Two Saxon hirelings are discovered: Gurth the swineherd and Wamba the jester. These two are ushered into the novel, like every subsequent personage, with a view toward impressing upon the reader a strong sense of the importance of wardrobe; and then Wamba strikes up the theme of civil discord, in a very minor key, by engaging the swineherd in a few philological pleasantries, the point of the joke being that the Saxon *sow, ox, calf,* are no sooner slaughtered for the gratification of the Norman parasites than they turn into *pork, beef,* and *veal*—it is very instructive to watch Scott as he serves up his popular linguistics. And then the two Normans appear on horseback, the Templar Brian de Bois-Guilbert, who is Scott's "heavy emotional" man, and the fat monk, who is comic relief, followed by their attendants. More wardrobe. Descriptions of the escorts. Description of the horses. A great deal of armor described. Then Brian and the monk fall in with a stranger; "here," says Brian, "is some one either asleep or lying dead at the foot of this cross." The person so designated, who gives himself out to be a Palmer but is really Ivanhoe, volunteers to direct the Normans to Rotherwood Hall, the seat of the Saxon party, where they expect to put up for the night. Chapter III and a thunderstorm.

"The plot now thickens," says Jeffrey, "and assumes a complication which would be a little perplexing to vulgar makers of abstracts."[14] With the arrival of the Templar at Rotherwood the chief antagonists are brought face to face; the ideological battle is joined; and from here on in it is possible to see very clearly how Scott stigmatizes the major parties to the quarrel.

The chief spokesman for the Saxons is Cedric of Rotherwood, the hero's father, and thus one of Scott's recurrent types.[15] Cedric is consistently drawn as a romantic illusionist, nostalgically committed to a dead-letter cause, talking in his cups of the days when the Saxon will reign again in his land and the Norman be booted back to Normandy. Meanwhile his preadamite loyalty has led him into certain barbaric excesses in his own family; for example, he has expelled and disinherited his only son for following Richard Lion-Heart to the Middle East and for casting eyes on his cousin Rowena, whom Cedric has already settled on the hereditary Saxon chieftain, Athelstane, an imbecile thirty years her senior.[16] Athelstane's fitness to meet the national emergency is described by his tag-name, "The Unready"; and Scott's respect for him may be measured by the degree of seriousness with which he treats him: he portrays him throughout as a caricature. Like most caricatures, he has his emblematic speech, a series of variations on the proposition: "No matter what Front-de-Boeuf will do, we must have dinner." Scott describes him as "dull eyed, heavy-browed, inactive and sluggish," and by Chapter XXII even the devout Cedric is forced to admit that "he hath no pleasure save to fill, to swill, and to call for more."

"Alas! [says Cedric] that so dull a spirit should be lodged in so good a form! Alas! that such an enterprise as the regeneration of England should turn on a hinge so imperfect! Wedded to Rowena, indeed, her nobler and more generous soul may yet awake the better nature which is torpid within him. Yet how should this be, while Rowena, Athelstane, and I myself, remain the prisoners of this brutal marauder, and have been made so perhaps from a sense of the dangers which our liberty might bring to the usurped power of his nation?"

The prison alluded to in the foregoing reverie is the Fortress of Torquilstone, Front-de-Boeuf's Castle and the stronghold of the Norman nobility. Its presiding spirit is a Saxon aboriginal named Ulrica, who has been a silent party to Front-de-Boeuf's crimes and has been kept incommunicado by him in a remote sector of the fortress. According to Duncan, this *locum tenens* represents "the most ancient and barbarous elements in the Saxon culture."[17] Old age, and a consciousness of having someone to talk to at long last, have powerfully stimulated Ulrica's loquacity, if not her verbal aptitude. In her final appearance on the roof of the fortress that she has set on fire, Scott describes her as "yelling forth a war song, such as was of yore raised on the field of battle by the scald and yet heathen Saxons"; and in a note, defending the anachronism implied in her character, he subjoins that "she may be supposed to return to the wild strains which animated her forefathers during the time of paganism and unrestrained ferocity."

A minister and aspiring king-maker who is an impractical sentimentalist; a presiding chief of state who is a fool and a glutton; a primitive culture figure who is a concatenation of horrific absurdities: nothing very heroic in these. The Normans, who are more properly associated with the forms and the spirit of chivalry, are no better served by their leaders. The government is presided over by an absentee king who, in playing the truant abroad, encourages dissension at home. The leader of the rival faction, Prince John, is a depraved and cowardly playboy. John's followers, the flowers of the feudal aristocracy, pass across the stage like so many allegorical Vices.

The most brutal of the lot, Front-de-Boeuf, has killed his father at lunch. Malvoisin prepares to practice larceny on a grand scale. De Bracy is a purely frivolous adventurer. Bois-Guilbert is an unprincipled cynic, with intervals of remorse, who thinks nothing of violating his clerical vows by losing his head over a Jewess and, when the Jewess declines to lose hers, underwrites her death as a witch. The Norman clergy are represented either by debonaire hedonists like the Prior, who have severed all ties with orthodox belief, or by despots like Beaumanoir, who enforce the ordinances of the church by a fanatic and superstitious formalism.

There remains King Richard himself. Together with Ivanhoe Richard symbolizes the means by which internal discord is to be quelled and the basis for a peaceful coexistence may be provided. Richard alone among the Normans goes out of his way to establish rapport with the diverse Saxon elements. He champions Ivanhoe against the Normans at Ashby; he fraternizes with Robin Hood and his tribe, the most patently indigenous segment of the Saxon culture; he even fights on the Saxon side in the assault on Torquilstone. When, toward the end of the novel, he decides to abandon his masquerade as Black Knight and revert to the role of king, his first gesture is to repudiate Cedric's address to "Richard of Anjou" and insist on being recognized as "Richard of England," "whose deepest interest . . . is to see her sons united with each other."

Yet Richard is in a sense the most "deeply wounded" victim of Scott's antiromantic mood. Scott calls him, in effect, "brilliant but useless." His picture of Richard is that of a ruler who is gallivanting abroad, doing high deeds in Palestine, while the peers of the realm plunder the country, ruin the economy, quarrel among themselves, and plan to install a brutal weakling on the throne. Richard's Middle Eastern policy, meanwhile, has been a costly debacle. His "repeated victories had been rendered fruitless, his romantic attempts to besiege Jerusalem disappointed, and the fruit of all the glory which he had acquired had dwindled into an uncertain truce." He no sooner returns home than he panders to the public amusement by performing gymnastic feats and takes part in skirmishes worthy of an adventurer. " 'Your kingdom [Ivanhoe lectures him] is threatened with dissolution and civil war—your subjects menaced with every species of evil, if deprived of their sovereign in some of those dangers which it is your daily pleasure to incur.'" Scott's point, of course, is that Richard is just as reprehensible a magistrate as Cedric: the one in his irresponsible knight-errantry and blindness to the needs of the country, the other in his delusion that the existing order of things can be dreamed away. Both are inspired by a fraudulent attachment to ways of life that have ceased to make sense. For it is the onus of Scott's critique that Richard's kind of chivalry belongs as clearly to a bygone tradition as Cedric's adherence to a pre-Norman code.

> In the lion-hearted King, the brilliant, but useless character of a knight of romance, was in a great measure realized and revived; and the personal glory which he acquired by his own deeds of arms, was far more dear to his excited imagination, than that which a course of policy and wisdom would have spread around his government. Accordingly, his reign was like the course of a brilliant and rapid meteor . . . which is instantly swallowed up by universal darkness; his feats of chivalry furnishing themes for bards and minstrels, but affording none of those solid benefits to his country on which history loves to pause, and hold up as an example to posterity.[18]

Ivanhoe's role, finally, the pivotal role in the novel, is interestingly juxtaposed with Richard's. A Saxon noble by birth and a Norman crusader by profession, Ivanhoe straddles both positions and is capable of loyalty to both sides. He has successfully assimilated to the Norman way of life, but he marries the descendant of King Alfred. He is wounded in fighting for the Saxon cause, but he is fighting in the train of the Norman ruler. He can explain Richard to Cedric, and the reverse. As "symbolic observer"[19] he is detached enough to size up and criticize the positions of both parties. He can dissociate himself from his father when Cedric's Francophobia becomes intolerable; he can read Richard a homily when Richard's quixoticism strikes him as inept. When touring the country, he is flanked by a Saxon swineherd and a Norman sovereign.

If Ivanhoe's role as mediator does not really come up to the mark, it is because his neutrality, like Richard's tolerance toward the Saxons, is at bottom defective. Ivanhoe is very much the knight-errant himself—so that his criticism of Richard at the end of the book rings a little hollow. He has a way of turning up in the same hippodromes as his master, whispering the same plot contrivances into the ears of startled subalterns; and in one exciting place in the novel it is Ivanhoe rather than Richard who delivers the most impassioned defense of Horseback Hall to be found in the entire book.

Who, then, shall guard the guardians? Who shall speak for Heartbreak House? Rebecca, of course.

In *Ivanhoe,* Duncan writes, "the Hebraic culture is a kind of touchstone by which both Normans and Saxons may be judged."[20] More specifically it can be said, I think, that Scott uses the Jewish group as exponents of that critical, basically antisentimental attitude toward chivalry which gives the novel its essential content.

Rebecca: Romance and Critique

No matter what we may think of Ivanhoe, there can be only one opinion of Rebecca. She seems to be one of those literary creations who assume a sort of suprapersonal significance the moment the book is out on the market. "The true interest of this romance," the reviewer in *Blackwood's* declared, "is placed . . . in the still, devoted, sad and unrequited tenderness of a Jewish damsel—by far the most romantic creation of female character the author has ever formed—and second we suspect, to no creature of female character whatever that is to be found in the whole annals either of poetry or of romance."[21] Jeffrey availed himself of reasonably identical superlatives, proclaiming that Rebecca "is from the beginning the most angelic character in the story, and ends with engrossing its chief interest. . . . A being of more 'nymph-like form or goddess-like deport,' never has been represented in the fictions of painting or poetry." Since then we have had G. H. Maynadier's testimony to "the truly great character of Rebecca," and Thomas Seccombe's very high rating, which ranks her with Scott's two or three most successful females; we have Grierson leaving her on top of the heap, "Scott's finest creation of a woman, not only of high principles and steadfast character like Jeannie Deans, but also refined, cultured, and beautiful."[22]

Rebecca does not come into the novel until everybody else has already been seated, which is to say that, in order of appearance, hers is roughly the thirtieth speaking part in *Ivanhoe.* In presenting her, Scott dozies the arithmetic of the readership by dividing her inventorially, descending from the millinery aspect of her appearance to the hosiery, pausing along the way to contemplate her bosom. Her credentials are as follows:

Her form was exquisitely symmetrical, and was shown to advantage by a sort of Eastern dress, which she wore according to the fashion of the females of her nation. Her turban of yellow silk suited well with the darkness of her complexion. The brilliancy of her eyes, the superb arch of her eyebrows, her well-formed aquiline nose, her teeth as white as pearl, and the profusion of her sable tresses, which, each arranged in its own little spiral of twisted curls, fell down upon as much of a lovely neck and bosom as a simarre of the richest Persian silk, exhibiting flowers in their natural colours embossed upon a purple ground, permitted to be visible—all these constituted a combination of loveliness, which yielded not to the most beautiful of the maidens who surrounded her. It is true, that of the golden and pearl-studded clasps, which closed her vest from the throat to the waist, the three uppermost were left unfastened on account of the heat, which something enlarged the prospect to which we allude. A diamond necklace, with pendants of inestimable value, were by this means also made more conspicuous. The feather of an ostrich, fastened in her turban by an agraffe set with brilliants, was another distinction of the beautiful Jewess, etc. etc.[23]

So much for her external attractions; but as for her spiritual ones, these appear to most marked advantage whenever she is allowed to improvise a speech on the proposition that in all circumstances death is preferable to a fate worse than death.

While Rebecca spoke thus, her high and firm resolve [not to yield to the Templar] . . . gave to her looks, air, and manner, a dignity that seemed more than mortal. Her glance quailed not, her cheek blanched not, for the fear of a fate so instant and so horrible; on the contrary, the thought that she had her fate at her command, and could escape at will from infamy to death, gave a yet deeper colour of carnation to her complexion, and a yet more brilliant fire to her eye.[24]

We are in the presence once more of the Jew's Daughter, Shylock's better part; and if she is no longer quite what one looks for in a plausible dramatic character, the fault lies no doubt largely with Scott's raw materials.[25] Rebecca's historical significance as one of the major specimen of the Idealized Jewess is at all events very considerable, though it may have been somewhat exaggerated along with the general praise that she has inspired on other grounds.[26] It may be as well to qualify at once Rebecca's debts to some of the Jews'

Daughters who came before. Her resemblance to Jessica, for one, is almost wholly meretricious. It begins and ends with the fact that both are good-looking daughters of an ill-looking Jew. "The contrast between Jessica and Rebecca," as one commentator puts it, "is best expressed by trying to attribute to Jessica the Hymn of Rebecca."[27] With Marlowe's Abigail she has much more in common. The similarities have been traced by Isaac Abrahams, who has convincingly argued that Scott's sources for the Jewish group as a whole are Marlovian rather than Shakespearean.[28] On the other hand, it has repeatedly been pointed out that Rebecca owes as much to Clarissa Harlowe as she owes to any of the specifically Jewish prototypes. It was Balzac's complaint that Scott's women all come out of Clarissa; and in the case of Rebecca the debt seems irrefutable.[29] Scott himself, in that curious literary performance of his, the anonymous review of his own novels in the *Quarterly,* drew attention to his source: "We have little doubt that the mode in which Rebecca repels the Templar is borrowed from the celebrated scene in which Clarissa awes Lovelace by a similar menace of suicide."[30] The more general parallel of Richardson's heroine with Scott's—both forced to endure the relentless attentions of a libertine, both kidnapped by their suitor, both inclined to prefer death to seduction—loses perhaps some of its force if we consider Clarissa's polyprogenetive effects on the nineteenth-century novel as a whole. In Rebecca's frustrated passion for Ivanhoe, a German scholar notes a parallel with yet another Richardsonian heroine.[31]

It can be seen that Scott takes his source material where he finds it; and Abrahams has therefore argued Rebecca's originality, quite rightly, I think, from the consistency with which she affirms her Jewishness. She is the first, that is, in an already impressive line of Jewesses, who does not repudiate her religion. Rebecca, of course, remains a Jewess to the end, forgoes a heroic and desirable marriage with an eligible dragon-slayer, and condemns herself to a life of celibacy, filial devotion, and social work among the Spanish. Scott's ostensible reasons for withholding Rebecca from Ivanhoe are well known:

> Not to mention that the prejudice of the age rendered such a union almost impossible [he notes in his Introduction], the author may, in passing, observe, that he thinks a character of a highly virtuous and

"Ivanhoe Ransoms a Jew's Grinders"

Rebecca

" 'Back dog!' said the Grand Master. 'I touch not misbelievers save with the sword—Comrade, take thou the letter from the Jew, and give it to me.' "

lofty stamp, is degraded rather than exalted by an attempt to reward virtue with temporal prosperity. Such is not the recompense which Providence has deemed worthy of suffering merit, and it is a dangerous and fatal doctrine to teach young persons, the most common readers of romance, that rectitude of conduct and of principle are either naturally allied with, or adequately rewarded by, the gratification of our passions, or attainment of our wishes.

The question of historical fitness, the hopelessness of intermarriage in the thirteenth century, naturally counts for a good deal with a scholarly intelligence like Scott's, but it is not really the decisive issue. From the historical point of view, the whole relationship between Rebecca and Wilfred is, of course, a transparent poetic license. The very rapprochement of the two is almost as absurd historically as their marriage would have been. The anachronism involved in the portrayal of the lovers was already manifest to the critic of the *British Review* who objected to the "awkward episode of a rich merchant Jew and his paragon of a daughter" as "not very probably or congruously blended with the story, or much corresponding with the state of society, if society it could be called, in the period selected for the date of these imaginary transactions."[32]

In his treatment of the lovers, Scott the historian is, in fact, constantly running up against Scott the romancer, and half the time the collision issues in the triumph of romance over history. The historian holds his own admirably whenever Scott depicts the feelings of the Christian hero toward the Jewish heroine as reflecting "the universal prejudice of his age and religion." "[Rebecca] could but sigh internally when the glance of respectful admiration, not altogether unmixed with tenderness, with which Ivanhoe had hitherto regarded his unknown benefactress was exchanged at once for a manner cold, composed, and collected, and fraught with no deeper feeling than that which expressed a grateful sense of courtesy received from an unexpected quarter, and from one of an inferior race." "Ivanhoe was too good a Catholic to retain [chivalrous] feelings towards a Jewess," and so forth. Scott displays a similar honesty in allowing Ivanhoe a mild share in the general Jew-baiting directed against Isaac. All the more illogical then are Rebecca's amorous gestures. "Had [Scott] truly portrayed Jewish feeling of the time," Philipson notes, "not even by a syllable would he have indicated that any passion had sprung up. . . . Prejudice on the one hand, bitter wrong on the other . . . should have taught the absurdity of the entertainment of such a notion."[33] For the rest, any overt romance between a Norman Crusader and a Jewess accused of sorcery "in the period selected for the date of these imaginary transactions" remains, flagrantly and ostentatiously, a romance.

Scott's historical piety is thus perhaps somewhat too tinged with marketable heresies to establish convincing grounds for separating the lovers at the end of the novel. They ought never to have met. As Scott himself acknowledges, he was less concerned with the historical than the ethical implications of their rupture; and there are compelling structural advantages in keeping the lovers apart as well. Rebecca's role is didactic and elucidative; and here I must revert to the problem of theme I left dangling at the end of the last section.

When Abigail and Jessica leave their fathers in the lurch and run off with the Christians, the intention is not merely to initiate that slow turning of the tables on the villain which is completed either by the villain's violent death or by his comic disgrace: the intention is also to insulate him completely from the possibility of any sympathetic human involvement, deprive him of his last domestic ties, and leave him free to engage in his diabolic activities unhampered by human commitments and restrictions. A devil, so long as he keeps the homefires burning, is necessarily defective as devil. At the same time, the daughter's desertion measures the very depth of the father's criminality. Barabas, so runs the inference, must be profoundly depraved to rouse Abigail, that most devoted of daughters and household spirits, to defection and apostasy. For Marlowe and Shakespeare the desertion of the Jewess is the final judgment upon the villainy of the Jew, and such a judgment becomes all the more incisive and awful when we remember that a Jew's daughter constitutes, after his ducats, his most prized portable property.

To separate Rebecca from her father in the time-honored tradition would defeat Scott's very purpose in *Ivanhoe,* which—times having changed—is no longer to degrade the Jews summarily but to justify their ways to Christian man. All the old dramatic conventions and hoary prejudices, as we shall see, still cling to Isaac himself; but the implications of his personal avarice are no longer, for the Jews as a body, intended to be damaging. At worst, the Jews are, in Rebecca's grandiose phrase, "the blind instruments of some irresistible fatality"; at best, they are justified in their practices by the conduct of their persecutors. "Heaven in his ire has driven [the Jew] from his country" says Rebecca, giving what has become the fashionable explanation since Cumberland's day, "but industry has opened to him the only road to power and to influence which oppression has left unbarred." And the moment Scott begins to define his Jewish personnel critically, in context, in their historical perspective, the Jews themselves become the accusers of the society that rejects them. To inculcate Scott's historical lesson, the Jew's daughter is much better suited than Isaac, who is constantly depressed into his disagreeable role by the very conditions Scott is endeavoring to depict. If Isaac were not the miser and worm he is, Scott's plaidoyer from history would be considerably weakened; and it is precisely because Isaac is such a worm that he cannot articulate any halfway dignified defense. At most Scott can point to Isaac as acting out all the fears and terrors that a persecuted Hebrew is likely to endure under pressure; but the role of interpreter can only devolve on a figure who experiences the persecution less keenly than the paterfamilias. In the one passage in the novel in which Scott explicitly compares the two, he notes that Rebecca is incapable of imitating Isaac's "excess of subservience" not only because she is temperamentally more shock resistant than he is but because she is "a stranger . . . to the constant state of timid apprehension, by which [Isaac's meanness] was dictated."

The Jewish group stands naturally apart from the Anglo-Norman conflict that provides Scott's major theme. At the same time, since they are equally at the mercy of all comers, Saxon and Norman alike, they emerge for that very reason as a kind of critical norm, the yardstick by which Scott can measure the abnormities and abnormalities of their oppressors. "Upon the slightest and most unreasonable practices," he notes in one place, "as well as upon accusations the most absurd and groundless, their persons and property were exposed to every turn of popular fury; for Norman, Saxon, Dane and Briton, however adverse these races were to each other, contended which should look with greatest detestation upon a people, whom it was accounted a point of religion to hate, to revile, to despise, to plunder, and to persecute." For the first time in English literature, the Jews alone are right and everybody else is wrong. The outcast defines the community; the scapegoat indicts the king. And Scott never lets the reader forget this. When, for example, in his one admirable moment in the novel, Isaac forgets his ducats long enough to agonize over Rebecca's abduction, the point is that Scott can use such an incident to contrast Isaac's basic loyalty to his daughter with the familial disaffections that prevail among the Saxons, whose leader has banished his son, and among the Normans, whose leaders are would-be fratricides. It is no longer the Jew's daughter who runs away from home, but the Christian's eldest son. There are many such contrasts deployed throughout the novel.

Rebecca is thus qualified not only to rationalize the conduct of the Jews but, conversely, to comment upon the way of life that characterizes their persecutors. That way of life, as I have suggested, is intimately associated by Scott with the follies and vices inherent in the chivalric code; and in the scene which represents, I think, the moral center of the novel, Scott gives Rebecca full power of attorney to articulate his critique. "In the meeting of Ivanhoe with Rebecca," writes Duncan, "there is an encounter of the highest ideals of the chivalric tradition with those of the Hebraic-Christian tradition"; and it is certain that in the critical agon of the book the Jewess carries the day. Where Ivanhoe "champions a chivalry, which he ironically associates with Christianity" and "which rates life far beneath the pitch of honor," Rebecca insists on the idleness of a code that makes a virtue of bloodshed and glorifies violence.[34] The debate not only illuminates Scott's skepticism of antiquated ideologies but supplies the structural function of the Jew's Daughter as she appears two and a half centuries after her novitiate in Marlowe. Ivanhoe is speaking:

> "Rebecca," he replied, "thou knowest not how impossible it is for one trained to actions of chivalry to remain passive as a priest, or a woman, when they are acting deeds of honour around him. The love of battle is the food upon which we live—the dust of the *melee* is the breath of our nostrils! We live not—we wish not to live—longer than while we

are victorious and renowned—Such, maiden, are the laws of chivalry to which we are sworn, and to which we offer all that we hold dear."

"Alas!" said the fair Jewess, "and what is it, valiant knight, save an offering of sacrifice to a demon of vain glory, and a passing through the fire to Moloch!—What remains to you as the prize of all the blood you have spilled—of all the travail and pain you have endured—of all the tears which your deeds have caused, when death hath broken the strong man's spear, and overtaken the speed of his war-horse?"

"What remains?" cried Ivanhoe. "Glory, maiden, glory! which gilds our sepulchre and embalms our name."

"Glory?" continued Rebecca; "alas, is the rusted mail which hangs as a hatchment over the champion's dim and mouldering tomb—is the defaced sculpture of the inscription which the ignorant monk can hardly read to the enquiring pilgrim—are these sufficient rewards for the sacrifice of every kindly affection, for a life spent miserably that ye may make others miserable? Or is there such virtue in the rude rhymes of a wandering bard, that domestic love, kindly affection, peace and happiness, are so wildly bartered, to become the hero of those ballads which vagabond minstrels sing to drunken churls over their evening ale?"

"By the soul of Hereward!" replied the knight impatiently, "thou speakest, maiden, of thou knowest not what. Thou wouldst quench the pure light of chivalry, which alone distinguishes the noble from the base, the gentle knight from the churl and the savage; which rates our life far, far beneath the pitch of our honour; raises us victorious over pain, toil, and suffering, and teaches us to fear no evil but disgrace. Thou art no Christian, Rebecca; and to thee are unknown those high feelings which swell the bosom of a noble maiden when her lover hath done some deed of emprize which sanctions his flame. Chivalry!—why, maiden, she is the nurse of pure and high affection—the stay of the oppressed, the redresser of grievances, the curb of the power of the tyrant—Nobility were but an empty name without her, and liberty finds the best protection in her lance and her sword."[35]

Rebecca, of course, need only point to herself and her father to refute Ivanhoe's definition of knight-errantry as "the stay of the oppressed, the redresser of grievances, the curb of the power of the tyrant"; and, inferentially, she does. "The high-minded maiden concluded the argument in a tone of sorrow, which deeply expressed her sense of the degradation of her people." In the long run, she has the last word. The chaos inspired by the chivalric mentality, the tyranny it cannot curb, the grievances it does not choose to redress, the oppression it runs away from, drag on and on. The coffers are depleted by usurer and king; the Jews' departure for Spain turns into a symbolic admission that England, "the hospitable, the generous, the free," is a long way from evolving a decent national existence.

As for Ivanhoe, he settles down and becomes domesticated, for he cannot, after all, remain a bohemian-in-armor all his life. The mail, as Rebecca foresaw, does grow rusty; the thing ceases to be interesting. Eventually he turns up in a tired burlesque.[36] Any permanent alliance between him and Rebecca was foredoomed from the start; and anyhow it would have turned Scott's novel into the sheerest humbug. Historically the marital problem could have been solved in the way Scott's predecessors solved it, and as Thackeray solved it in parody, by allowing Rebecca to submit to baptism. In that case she would have compounded the venial sin of bombast with the mortal sin of hypocrisy, and her function in the novel would have lost what meaning it has. She has to stick it out with her father, if only to make good her protests and act out her creeds. The only way in which Scott could have eaten his cake and had it too would have been to recruit Ivanhoe for the synagogue.[37]

Isaac: Dog and Desdichado

One is rather astonished, in reading Scott's "Life of Cumberland," to run across a passage in which he criticized Cumberland for his unflattering portrayal of Sheva. Speaking of Cumberland's chagrin at getting no thanks from the Jews for making them a present of Sheva and Abraham Abrahams, Scott notes: "We cannot be surprised that the people in question felt a portrait in which they are made ludicrous as well as interesting to be something between an affront and a compliment. Few of the better class of the Jewish persuasion would, we believe, be disposed to admit either Abrahams or Sheva as fitting representatives of their tribe."[38] Scott could hardly have failed to see that his portrayal of Isaac—committed shortly before he wrote the sketch on Cumberland—flattered the Jews much less than Cumberland's risible paragons. Possibly he thought that Cumberland's offense lay in describing a contemporary Jew, whose propinquity was more likely to displease the London congregation at the turn of the century than a conventional medieval miser who could be in part historically rationalized and who had moreover passed so firmly into an accepted literary stock-type that the implications of verisimilitude and the danger of identification were extremely remote.[39]

Isaac serves a less important function in the book than Rebecca and is a much less original creation. He is one of those characters who "move in an aura of the author's pleasure," with whom Scott can afford to relax, whom he can use for both comic relief and as a means of casting light on the sensibilities of his major figures. Scott takes him fairly straight as he found him in Shakespeare, with some important qualifications to be noted, and puts him through the regulation motions through which Shakespeare puts Shylock.

In his admirable study of Dickens, Julian Symons defines Dickens's art as establishing "a framework in which a puppet reenacts over and over again with lunatic fervour a single activity."[40] The definition may be extended to Isaac as well as Fagin. Since Isaac is not really necessary to the plot at all, in the sense that both Fagin and Shylock are, Scott can keep him entirely static on the periphery of the story. Shakespeare traces, step by step, Shylock's deepening bestiality as the plot advances, so that Shylock actually becomes increasingly depraved by the concatenation of dramatic circumstances; and Fagin, though a fully constituted character from the beginning, communicates to the reader a growing sense of his depravity by the sheer momentum of the story, which sweeps him to his ruin. Isaac can do neither. From the moment he appears at Rotherwood in Chapter V until he leaves England at the close of the novel, he is arrested in a single motive that he obsessively reiterates, but which he neither significantly modifies nor accelerates. The motive can be defined as a ludicrously dreadful suspicion that somebody or other is after his moneybags and a ludicrously vehement denial (or deprecation) of his wealth. Beyond this single gesture, Isaac has for the moment no substantial life in the novel. It defines him completely. He re-enacts it with the startling predictability of a robot.

It would be idle to trace this purely iterative pattern through the whole novel; to do so would be to account for nearly every scene in which Isaac appears. To illustrate the way his ritual works we need look only at the twenty pages or so that follow his entrance. The method is transparent and easily exhausted. Scott predicates Isaac in a few fine and sharp strokes; sketches his physiognomy; hurries over the wardrobe with admirable self-restraint; does not hurry quite fast enough to elude an anachronism in the description of his cap;[41] and catches Isaac's *Gestalt* in a metaphor worth two pages of haberdasher's inventory: "Had there been painters in those days capable to execute such a subject, the Jew, as he bent his withered form, and expanded his chilled and trembling hands over the fire, would have formed no bad emblematical personification of the Winter season."[42] There are some other characters to be ushered in and seated; Scott has his hands full with the Templar, the Prior, Rowena; the conflict between Cedric and the Norman guests at his board has to be initiated; the mysterious Palmer must be obtruded on our notice every so often lest we forget to be mystified.[43] But no sooner has Isaac made his first move than the mechanism is already fully in operation: "I warrant thee store of shekels in thy Jewish scrip," the Templar provokes him:

"Not a shekel, not a silver penny, not a halfling—so help me the God of Abraham!" said the Jew, clasping his hands; "I go but to seek the assistance of some brother of my tribe to aid me to pay the fine which the Exchequer of the Jews have imposed upon me—Father Jacob be my speed! I am an impoverished wretch—the very gaberdine I wear is borrowed from Reuben of Tadcaster."

Eight pages afterward the Jew is again the center of attention, and so the motion is repeated. This time Isaac is asleep beside the swineherd and the ritual recurs on a traumatic plane; it is the old song of the Jew who "dreamt of money-bags tonight."

His hands and arms moved convulsively, as if struggling with the nightmare; and beside several ejaculations in Hebrew, the following were distinctly heard in the Norman-English, or mixed language of the country: "For the sake of the God of Abraham, spare an unhappy old man! I am poor, I am penniless—should your irons wrench my limbs asunder, I could not gratify you!"

Five pages further:

No sooner had they reached the mules, than the Jew, with hasty and trembling hands, secured behind the saddle a small bag of blue buckram, which he took from under his cloak, containing as he muttered, "a change of raiment—only a change of raiment." Then getting upon the animal with more alacrity and haste than could have been anticipated from his years, he lost no time in so disposing of the skirts of his gaberdine as to conceal completely from observation the burden which he had thus deposited en croupe.

"It is a convenience for an author when he can strike with his full force at once, and flat characters are very useful to him, since they never need reintroducing, never run away, have not to be watched for development, and provide their own atmosphere—little luminous disks of a pre-arranged size, pushed hither and thither like counters across the void or between the stars; most satisfactory."[44] Lest the mechanical laughter give way to satiety, Scott naturally has to introduce slight variations on the basic formula; for example, the greed and cowardice that are the conditions of Isaac's character and very nearly exhaust it, may be supported by ancillary gestures of terror, submission, and the like. That Isaac should remain a laughable figure even in a context which presents him as the poor persecuted Jew indicates pretty clearly how much Scott borrowed, consciously or unconsciously, from the stereotype. Isaac's sense of terror under circumstances which would terrify the most stouthearted is tinged with laughter; the fool is always before us. We can be certain that in any contest between the professional fool and the Jew, the Jew should get the worst of the bargain. "Finding the abomination of his tribe opposed to his very nose, while the Jester at the same time flourished his wooden sword above his head, the Jew recoiled, missed his footing, and rolled down the steps." To note as much is merely to note that Isaac is consistently the comic butt provided by the prototype, the difference between him and Shylock being that Shylock suffers the classic change from top dog to underdog, whereas Isaac has already been bullied into submission, dog-tagged, and chained, before the curtain goes up.

Even if Scott had not bothered to decorate four chapters in the novel with mottoes taken from *The Merchant of Venice* and *The Jew of Malta,* all but the first inimical to the Jew's character, it would be quite plain that in portraying Isaac Scott was working, though with a certain freedom, within the established mythology.[45] Some of the parallels with Shylock are transparent, and they include a number of inescapable verbal echoes. Most obvious, perhaps, is Scott's recurrent use of the ducats-daughter theme. The motif is anticipated, by way of direct citation, in the epigraph to Chapter XXIII, which introduces the scene in which Isaac expresses simultaneously his fear that Front-de-Boeuf may extort his money and that Bois-Guilbert may ravish his daughter. The same theme is elaborated, much more seriously to Isaac's detriment, in his encounter with Locksley, whose services he would like to enlist in liberating Rebecca, were he not checked by the dreadful possibility that Locksley will overcharge him. "Isaac, recalled to think of his worldly goods, the love of which, by dint of inveterate habit, contended even with his parental affection, grew pale, stammered, and could not deny there might be some small surplus." Isaac's equivocating and haggling while Rebecca is in the process of being abducted, gives added piquancy to Locksley's rather appalled reaction to the Jew's "ill-timed avarice." "'Good Jew—good beast—good earthworm!' said the yeoman, losing patience; 'an thou dost go on to put thy filthy lucre in the balance with thy daughter's life and honour, by Heaven, I will strip thee of every maravedi thou hast in the world, before three days are out.'" It is significant that even in his sympathetic moments Isaac should resort to Shylock's verbal stratagems. When, for example, Isaac taxes the Christians with duplicity in their negotiations with the Jews, he frames his reproach exactly in the terms employed by Shylock:

> "Hold, father," said the Jew, "mitigate and assuage your choler. I pray of your reverence that I force my monies upon no one. But when churchman and layman, prince and prior, knight and priest, come knocking to Isaac's door, they borrow not his shekels with these uncivil terms. It is then, Friend Isaac, will you pleasure us in this matter, and our day shall be truly kept, so God sa' me?—and Kind Isaac, if ever you served man, show yourself a friend in this need! And when the day comes, and I ask my own, then what hear I but Damned Jew, and The Curse of Egypt on your tribe, and all that may stir up the rude and uncivil populace against poor strangers!"

Fundamental to Isaac's ethos, similarly, is the belief, formulated by both Shylock and Barabas, that "it's no sin to deceive a Christian," with its underlying assumption that the Jew's extortionist practices are automatically sanctioned by the relentless Jew-baiting of the Christians. Like his Marlovian and Shakespearean models, Isaac is largely motivated by the feeling that Sartre defines as "the hostile consciousness of others." Isaac is as persuaded as Shylock that if the impoverished aristocracy are outraged by the rates of usance, the fault is theirs.[46]

But here some important qualifications must be made and some basic distinctions begin to emerge. The principal one of these is that Scott himself tends to agree with Isaac's defense of usury, though he regrets the necessity for agreeing with him and deplores the conditions which compel his assent. For Shakespeare, reflecting the post-medieval nostalgia for the openhanded ways of the old gentry, any taint of usury was, as we have seen, a positive stigma of corruption, whereas a spendthrift like Bassanio came off very well. Bassanio's expensive party-going argued, on the whole, a fundamentally honest heart and decent disposition; and Antonio's willingness to endorse his carnivals argued a positively Christian forbearance. There is no suggestion that Antonio is threatening the economy of Venice, though there is every suggestion that Shylock, abetted by Tubal, is personally ruining it. For an Elizabethan looking back on the Middle Ages for his moral guidance and golden standards, an illiberal canniness was not, as a rule, so safe a passport to felicity as a liberal irresponsibility. Creditors were a great nuisance; they all the time wanted a pound of flesh, when all the debtor wanted was Mercy. Judas, the apostle of the cash nexus, stands rebuked forever by the hospitable Christ. Shylock's road leads to the elder tree; Antonio's to Rome. Between the miser and the prodigal the choice was a foregone conclusion.

Scott is no longer so sure. What for Shakespeare meant all the difference between a hero and a villain becomes for Scott something of Hobson's choice. For Scott the reckless extravagance of the Norman nobles is really no more defensible than the Jew's sordid venality. Richard's expensive pursuit of idleness, his conduct of a war that has degenerated into a costly and ostentatious one-man parade, the thriftlessness of the Norman way of life, are hardly less vicious a drain on the treasury than Isaac's relatively genteel rapacity. The point is that the one vice creates, at best, a market and, at worst, a necessity for the other; and Scott has his historical facts to back him up.[47] "To maintain these retainers," he notes with his customary disregard for euphony, "and to support the extravagance and magnificence which their pride induced them to affect, the nobility borrowed sums of money from the Jews at the most usurious interest, which gnawed into their estates like consuming cankers, scarce to be cured unless when circumstances gave them an opportunity of getting free, by exercising upon their creditors some act of unprincipled violence." Naturally Jews like Isaac are severe in enforcing their usance rates as long as nobles like John and Richard ignore the most elementary principles of economics and squander their entire capital on the maintenance and expansion of Horseback Hall.

The result is a conscious attempt to understand Isaac's profit motives and to examine them in the light of Scott's more general critique. If Isaac is thus, on one level of perception, the conventional money-grubbing codger, "a Jew" in the vulgar acceptance of the term, he is also, like his daughter, the touchstone by which Scott can judge the degree of Norman malversation and misrule. Rebecca has already been heard on the subject; and elsewhere Scott elaborates her rationale with admirable objectivity:

> The obstinacy and avarice of the Jews being . . . in a measure placed in opposition to the fanaticism and tyranny of those under whom they lived, seemed to increase in proportion to the persecution with which they were visited; and the immense wealth they usually acquired in commerce, while it frequently placed them in danger, was at other times used to extend their influence and to secure to them a certain degree of protection. On these terms they lived; and their character influenced accordingly, was watchful, suspicious, and timid—yet obstinate, uncomplying, and skillful in evading the dangers to which they were exposed.

The difference between Shakespeare's perception of Shylock as an essentially *oblivious* Jew-miser—separated from the community life of Venice, partly conditioned by his separateness, but at heart animated by a diabolic energy which is instinct, illogical and gratuitous—and Scott's perception of Isaac as a critical locus of the social chaos all about him, defines itself in other ways; it defines itself, for example, on the purely verbal level of invective. In *The Merchant,* as I noted earlier, the Jew-baiting in which all the characters are engaged can be taken on face value, if only because the Duke himself, the definitive interpreter, takes part in it. In *Ivanhoe* name-calling is much more likely to stigmatize the speaker than the nominee, and the implications are not complimentary to the Jew-baiters. It is a presumption in favor of Scott's more relaxed and generous attitude toward Isaac that the characters who publicly deprecate him are on the whole a good deal blacker than he is. At the same time, Scott is honest enough to recognize that each one of the Anglo-Norman figures, including decent characters like Wilfred, Robin Hood, and Gurth, automatically joins in the game of Jew-baiting; and the unanimity with which the game is being played becomes not, as in Shakespeare, a way of ascertaining the character of the Jew, but a way of measuring the conduct of his maligners.

The terms of the insult, too, have shifted since Shakespeare's day. In Shylock the devil and the dog enjoyed roughly equal status. But not even the most fanatic of the barons in *Ivanhoe* can flatter himself that in kicking Isaac downstairs he is casting Satan out of Ashby. Isaac, more consistently the eiron than Shylock, is treated pretty uniformly to the canine ascription.* When he is not being labeled a dog, he is generally described in the context of vulnerable rather than predatory animals; Robin Hood calls him "good earthworm"; and Isaac refers to himself as "the hunted fox, the tortured wildcat," which love their young just as "the despised and persecuted race of Abraham love their children." One can no more imagine Antonio describing Shylock as "good-dog—good earthworm," than one can imagine Locksley shrinking from Isaac's lupine and satanic aspects; and between these extremes the differences pretty well define themselves.

And there are others, dictated by the shifting creeds and changing climates of opinion. Nothing, for example, reflects so nicely the historic transmutations, the diversity of attitudes assumed and stated, between Shakespeare's day and Scott's, than the way in which the two

* The Templar calls him "dog Jew" and "unbelieving dog"; John calls him "infidel dog" and, himself the prince of prodigals, hails him as "prince of usurers"; Front-de-Boeuf degrades him to "the most accursed dog of an accursed race"; the Prior calls him "Hound of a Jew"; etc. The supernumerary Jacques Fitzdotterel alone alludes to him as a "usurious bloodsucker," and *that* epithet apparently entitles Isaac to institute proceedings for slander.

writers regard their Jews in the light of religious deviants. For Shakespeare, there is so much of the depraved individualist in Shylock that Shakespeare pays relatively little attention to his congregational status. Still he makes it plain that when Shylock and Tubal go off to synagogue together, they go there to hatch plots against the Gentiles. It must be remembered that in the post-medieval consciousness, the synagogue lingered on as the domicile of Satan; Luther thought of it as "ein Teuffels Nest." For Scott the Jew's religious habits have already become "quaint." Scott is interested in them only in so far as they are picturesque, stage properties of the historic muse. A general impression of costly and bizarre accoutrements, Oriental objets d'art, queer bric-a-brac out of the Semitic Museum, is all one brings away from Isaac's household. Isaac's private religious fervor is chiefly reflected in a strong disposition to swear by Abraham, Jacob, and Moses, and to call upon the patriarchs for succor in time of stress. Naturally Scott takes it for granted that, *qua* religion, the Jewish is hopelessly confused, and occasionally he recalls the general Christian readership to a sense of their manifest primacy. Once or twice he politely submits that Rebecca, splendid girl though she is, was not on the whole well advised to be born into the synagogue. If her Jewishness is the source of her heroism as well as of her heroics, she is not to be positively congratulated on waiting upon the false Messiah. In one place he notes that she was "erroneously taught to interpret the promises of Scripture to the chosen people"; and in another he suggests that Judaism will not broaden the mind. "When [Rebecca] entered the turret-chamber, her first duty was to return thanks to the God of Jacob. . . . Another name glided into her petition—it was that of the wounded Christian . . . a Nazarene, and an enemy of her faith. But the petition was already breathed, nor could all the narrow prejudices of her sect wish it recalled."

But misguided though the Jews may be, dangerous they are not. There is not in the whole of *Ivanhoe* a single Christian ecclesiastic who is not considerably more detestable than Isaac. The general idea is that Judaism may be heresy but Catholicism is humbug. The tyrant Beaumanoir has much to learn from the martyr Rebecca. Isaac's country house, it will be remembered, instead of serving as devil's nest where the Jews conspire to cut up the Christians is the place where Rebecca nurses Ivanhoe back to life.[48] In Scott's day Jews no longer eat Christians but dress their wounds.

Isaac's role is thus in some ways as significant as his daughter's, though his purely comedic attributes tend to disguise the fact. Presented as Marginal Man, he illuminates the figures in the center of the World Picture—the clergy, pleasure-loving and bigoted; the Saxon chieftains, sustained by empty ceremonials; the Norman nobles, seeking the bubble reputation in a game of darts. Looking at the picture in retrospect one understands Bagehot's praise of Scott for capturing "the undulations and diversified composition of human society"; and one understands, too, his explanation for Scott's distrust of the egalitarian mind: "that it would sweep away this entire picture, level prince and peasant in a common égalité—substitute a scientific rigidity for the irregular and picturesque growth of centuries,—replace an abounding and genial life for a symmetrical but lifeless mechanism."[49] In such a picture the Jewish group, with their picturesque customs and irregular lives, have a very definite place.

Nor is this, I think, the whole story. For over and above their dramatic function—to observe the major conflict between Saxons and Normans and, from the detached position of the *tertium quid,* to interpret the depths and follies of that conflict—the Jews are in a sense also symbolically identified with their persecutors. Isaac and Rebecca are the ultimately outcast, the finally disinherited; and as I look back on *Ivanhoe* it seems to me that the entire novel, for all its idle extravagances, its summer slaughters and sunshine jousts, is shot through with the themes of estrangement and dispossession. In the center, of course, there is Ivanhoe himself, the literally *desdichado,* the Disinherited Knight, disowned by his father and forced to assume a false identity to enter the parental house. There are the Saxons who are gathered around the person of Cedric, strangers in their own land in which their ancestors "had been extirpated and disinherited, with few or no exceptions; nor were the numbers great who possessed land in the country of their fathers, even as proprietors of the second, or of yet inferior classes." The Normans themselves have scarcely struck root deeply enough to be thought much more than an occupationary force, maintaining separatist policies and speaking an alien tongue. There are, on the periphery of our picture, the figures of the romantic outlaw-by-choice and his tribe, deliberate deviants from the body politic, forming their own independent marginal community, demonstrating the possibility of a utopia only by existing outside the social limits.[50] "Nor could [Richard]," Scott sardonically observes, "avoid expressing his surprise at having witnessed so much of civil policy amongst persons cast out from all the ordinary protection and influence of the laws." The truth is that any other effective civil policy has been suspended and the law is left to take care of itself. Among such a diversity of Ishmaelites, Isaac and Rebecca point the final moral. There is no room for them in the kind of England Scott has painted. "The people of England," Rebecca serves notice in the last scene of the book, "are a fierce race, quarrelling ever with their neighbors or among themselves, and ready to plunge the sword into the bowels of each other. . . . Not in a land of war and blood, surrounded by hostile neighbors and distracted by internal factions" can the Jew find rest.[51]

The novel thus ends on a very pessimistic note. In leaving England, the Jewish group affirm for the last time their role of critical observers and touchstones of social integrity. No one may be very sorry to see Isaac leave. When all is said and done he remains "but a milder Shylock," though a very much milder one. He is Shylock after the trial, Shylock without his fangs, Shylock depressive. In drawing his character Scott obviously stuck very closely to the stereotype whose latter-day history is being here set down. Those who like to exalt Isaac into a figure "high-principled, generous and brave," will do well to remember that the man who howls with pain at the news of his daughter's abduction also haggles interminably over her ransom, and that the same man who is willing to save Ivanhoe's life acts solely in the consciousness of instant reward and future protection. But every one will regret Rebecca's departure. While among us, though given to cosmic rhetoric and planetary music, she held her own very well. It was she who bore the burden of Scott's message:

Allez, stériles ritournelles:
La vie est vraie et criminelle.

Rebecca with Child (Half-Aryan): The Surgeon's Daughter

Literary historians, who know all about Rebecca, have little or nothing to say about a handsome Jewish woman who appears in one of Scott's last and least novels, *The Surgeon's Daughter* (1827), in which she figures in the interesting guise of Jew's Daughter as unwed mother.[52] Her last name is variously given as Moncada, Tresham, Witherington, and Middlemas, a confusion occasioned both by her father's intricate lineage and her common-law husband's urge to conceal himself from the British police under a variety of aliases. Her first name is undeviatingly Zilia. The milieu of the book is nineteenth-century Scotland[53] rather than medieval York, so that the issues it raises and (fitfully) resolves cannot really bear comparison with the historical issues raised in *Ivanhoe*. But as a racial type, Zilia sufficiently conforms to Rebecca's measurements to provide literature with another, minor example of the exotic Jewess, who is, in a family way, a few steps ahead of Rebecca.

> Zilia Moncada was the only child of a Portuguese Jew of great wealth, who had come to London, in prosecution of his commerce. Among the few Christians who frequented his house, and occasionally his table, was Richard Tresham, a gentleman of a high Northumbrian family, deeply engaged in the service of Charles Edward during his short invasion, and though holding a commission in the Portuguese service, still an object of suspicion to the British government, on account of his well-known courage and Jacobitical principles. The high-bred elegance of this gentleman, together with his complete acquaintance with the Portuguese language and manners, had won the intimacy of old Moncada, and, alas! the heart of the inexperienced Zilia, who, beautiful as an angel, had as little knowledge of the world and its wickedness as the lamb that is but a week old. . . . Tresham made a dishonourable use of the opportunities which the poor Zilia so incautiously afforded, and the consequence was her ruin.

Her ruin brings on the event with which the novel gets under way, the birth of a bastard son, who takes the name of Richard Middlemas from the Scottish town in which Zilia stopped off for her confinement. It is here that the first half of the novel takes place. Since Zilia is made to wear a black mask during most of the Middlemas proceedings, it is difficult to describe her. In giving us our first glimpse of her, Scott interestingly invests her with the same descriptive phrase with which he took leave of Rebecca eight years before: her "deep sorrow," he says, "seemed to indicate an unhappy creature, who had lost the protection of parents, without acquiring a legitimate right to that of husband." For Scott, as for Marlowe, Bulwer, and some others, the exotic Jewess is plainly doomed to a variety of frustrations. The husband absconds just in time to avoid a head-on collision with old Moncada, who arrives with much clatter, fury, and flinging of coins, to unmask his daughter. He whisks her off in his chariot, depositing "the miserable being which has been the seal of her dishonour" with the good-natured local doctor who brought him into the world.

If Isaac of York has exemplified the "typical" full Jew who is half bad, Middlemas comes to us in the singular guise of a half-Jew who is all bad. He begins well enough. Brought up, in ignorance of his origins, by the kindly Dr. Gray, he gives rise to the fondest hopes as a child at once clever and beautiful, who talks like a book, and who promises to make an excellent match some day for Menie Gray, the daughter of the house, for whom the novel is—misleadingly—named. Menie, surrounded and courted by the local Hibernian philistia, is easily swept off her feet by this eccentric half-Hebrew who, by the time he comes into his teens, is described as looking "dark, like his father and mother, with high features, beautifully formed, but exhibiting something of a foreign character," and whose manners, moreover "were, in elegance and ease, far beyond any example to be found in his native burgh." It is clear from the description that up to a point Richard is treated much like a male counterpart to the exotic Jewess, whose consuming interest for Christians derives chiefly from her foreign complexion: the type of exotic young Jew that looks forward, with essential reservations, to Deronda, Disraeli's heroes, and the spiritualized Raphael of Kingsley's *Hypatia.*

Like Daniel Deronda, too, and like Disraeli's rising young men, Richard passes his childhood in dreaming of his mysterious paternity and the hidden conditions of his birth—those oddly persistent themes that are so inseparably linked up with the literature about the Jew. "It is not, perhaps, a very favourable point in your horoscope," his guardian remarks at one point, "that everything connected with you is a secret." Dr. Gray's astute remark has a far broader application than he intends it to have. Meantime Nurse Jamieson, the gullible domestic, has been heating the boy's imagination with stories of "what she called the awful scene of his coming into the world"—

> the personal appearance of his father, a grand gentleman, who looked as if the whole world lay at his feet—the beauty of his mother, and the terrible black mask which she wore, her een that glanced like diamonds, and the diamonds she wore on her fingers, that could be compared to nothing but her own een, the fairness of her skin, and the colour of her silk rokelay, with much proper stuff to the same purpose. . . .
>
> To hear all this did Richard seriously incline, and still more was he interested with the idea of his valiant father coming for him unexpectedly at the head of a gallant regiment, with music playing and colours flying, and carrying his son away on the most beautiful pony eyes ever beheld: or his mother, bright as the day, might suddenly appear in her coach-and-six, to reclaim her beloved child; or his repentant grandfather, with his pockets stuffed out with bank-notes, would come to atone for his past cruelty, by heaping his neglected grandchild with unexpected wealth.

These stories are bound, sooner or later, to affect Richard's moral welfare: "Nurse Jamieson's history of the past, and prospects of the future, were too flattering not to excite the most ambitious visions in the mind of a boy who naturally felt a strong desire of rising in the world, and was conscious of possessing the powers necessary to his advancement." He feels himself increasingly stifled among the Scottish hinterlanders; a great deal of "flashing fire" in his dark eyes, and much flushing of his "broad and well-formed forehead" are on view; a boy who, at fourteen, is capable of saying, "Oh Doctor! The Scots are too moral, and too prudent, and too robust," is not, at twenty-one, to be trusted with one's daughter. Menie Gray, it is felt, would be much better off marrying Richard's foil, the surgeon's apprentice Adam Hartley, "the son of a respectable farmer on the English side of the border," who excels in all the solid middle-class virtues and who combines those very qualities of morality, prudence, and robustness which Richard has publicly deprecated. But it is clear that Menie prefers the dark Israelite, just as Ivanhoe, if pressed for an answer, would probably admit to a preference for Rebecca over Rowena.

Richard's degeneration proceeds apace. Violent quarrels break out between Adam Hartley, who has handsomely renounced his claims on Menie, and Richard, who has no intention of marrying her. The dual traits with which Scott taxes Richard from here on in are those of "ambition and avarice." Indeed, in Scott's mind these two stigmas function almost in the sense of an idea-cluster, the one word automatically suggesting the other. "The demons of Ambition and Avarice would return after the exorciser Love had exhausted the force of his spells." "Surely the demons of Ambition and Avarice will unclose the talons which they have fixed upon this man." "Heaven," the prudential Adam Hartley lectures him, "Heaven has placed happiness, competence, and content within your power, and you are willing to cast them away, to gratify ambition and avarice." And he enjoins Richard "to lay aside the sneer, which is designed to be a sarcastic smile. . . . So saying, he turned contemptuously from the youthful votary of ambition, and left the garden." The avarice of the Jew, of course, is old hat; and occasionally Richard is made to assume a pose that strikingly recalls the traditional pose of the money-grubbing hypocrite. For example, just as Barabas, Shylock, and Isaac find it difficult not to confuse the principles of ducats and daughters in their vocabulary, Richard, after the death of the long-lost Zilia, rakes in his legacy with one hand while with the other he wipes away the tears he sheds for the testator, with a painstaking sense that the gain of the one easily compensates for the loss of the other.

Middlemas took the bills which his mother had bequeathed him. As he raised his head, Hartley could observe that his face was stained with tears. Yet he counted over the money with mercantile accuracy; and though he assumed the pen for the purpose of writing a discharge with an air of inconsolable dejection, yet he drew it up in good set terms, like one who had his senses much at his command.

Pursuant to his ambition and avarice, then, Middlemas abandons his native Scotland to enroll "as a candidate for glory in the service of the Honourable East India Company"; and the novel declines into a series of sorry sensational clichés. As long as Scott kept his leading man north of the border, the familiar milieu itself acted as a restraint on Scott's cloak-and-dagger tendencies, with the result that Richard himself has, up to this point, absorbed some of the sympathy and good humor which Scott has shed over the story as a whole. For example, there is the fine and funny scene, early in the novel, in which Scott shows you how his provincial folk react to those alarming oddities the Jews—a reaction not very far different from the confusion into which the Meyrincks are plunged by the prospect of entertaining Daniel Deronda's Hebrew protégés.

"I should not be surprised [says the local clerk about Zilia and her father] that he took her abroad, and shut her up in a convent."

"Hardly," replied Dr. Gray, "if it be true, as I suspect, that both the father and daughter are of the Jewish persuasion."

"A Jew!" said Mrs. Gray; "and have I been taking a' this fyke about a Jew?—I thought she seemed to gie a scunner at the eggs and bacon that Nurse Simpson spoke about to her. But I thought Jews had aye had lang beards, and yon man's face is just like one of our ain folks—I have seen the Doctor with a langer beard himsell, when he has not had leisure to shave."

"That might have been Mr. Moncada's case," said Lawford, "for he seemed to have had a hard journey. But the Jews are often very respectable people, Mrs. Gray—they have no territorial property, because the law is against them there, but they have a good hank in the money market—plenty of stock in the funds, Mrs. Gray, and, indeed, I think this poor young woman is better with her ain father, though he be a Jew and a dour chield into the bargain, than she would have been with the loon that wranged her, who is, by your account, Dr. Gray, baith a papist and a rebel. The Jews are well attached to government; they hate the Pope, the Devil, and the Pretender as much as any honest man among ourselves."[54]

Once this sustaining viewpoint is withdrawn, Scott is left with little except a silly plot.[55] Accordingly, the novel now goes to pieces as swiftly as its hero, and I must hurry to Richard's death by elephant-heel. Seduced by visions of some Oriental El Dorado, Richard is lured into the East India Company by a villain-friend, robbed of his patrimony, drugged en route to England, and left to crepitate in a lazar-house on the Isle of Wight, which is teeming with the dead and dying victims of similar piratical practices. To this pestilential atmosphere he would be certain to succumb at once, were it not for a recognition scene, conducted in the Latin language for maximum secrecy, between Richard and the sympathetic medical officer, who turns out to be our old friend Adam Hartley, in a condition to shake hands and let bygones be bygones. Richard naturally desires to be released from service in a company into which he has been impressed on false allegations, but the company, as naturally, refuses to sanction requests which, were they honored, would deprive it of half its recruits. Under the circumstances, Adam Hartley is to be congratulated on enjoying limitless influence with the Commanding General of the place, whose children he has, only a month ago, snatched from the grave by a species of radical treatment upon which he has staked his entire medical reputation. He intercedes in Richard's behalf; Richard is given a respectable lieutenant's commission to Madras; and, the day before he sails, he presents himself at the home of his benefactor, the Commanding General. But now the General, wonderful to relate, turns out to be Richard's renegade father, the erstwhile seducer with the Jacobitical principles; and the General's lady, at long last lawfully united to him, turns out to be Zilia Moncada; and the little children, "yonder sickly brats," whose lives Adam Hartley has so opportunely saved, are Richard's new step-siblings, about to cheat him out of the Moncada legacy. The idea is that the elder Moncada, remarking his daughter's tendency to waste away under the persistent strains of unwed motherhood, has finally consented to her marrying the Jacobitical seducer, provided that the "seal of her dishonor" be permanently kept out of sight and out of mind.

Out of sight, perhaps; out of mind, never. While Richard has grown into a nasty lad on Dr. Gray's bounty, his mother has been filled with distress at having abandoned in his infancy the overbearing person whom she continues in secret to lament as her *benoni,* her son of pain.[56] Her looks have suffered in consequence. A beautiful woman she still appears to be, but very tired. "On a heap of cushions, wrapped in a glittering drapery of gold and silver muslins, mingled with shawls, a luxury which was then a novelty in Europe, sate, or rather reclined, a lady, who, past the full meridian of beauty, retained charms enough to distinguish her as one who had been formerly a very fine woman, though her mind seemed occupied by the deepest emotion." The miscellaneous identities are established, and as a result Zilia Moncada dies of shock. Like Tosca, Trilby, and Hoffmann's third sweetheart, she dies chromatically; Scott—like Disraeli, Eliot, and Du Maurier—regards music as a Jewish monopoly.

She flew to a harpsichord which stood in the room, and, while the servant and master gazed on each other, as if doubting whether her senses were about to leave her entirely, she wandered over the keys, producing a wilderness of harmony, composed of passages recalled by memory, or combined by her own musical talent, until at length her voice and instrument united in one of those magnificent hymns in which her youth had praised her Maker, with voice and harp, like the Royal Hebrew who composed it. The tear ebbed insensibly from the eyes which she turned upwards—her vocal tones, combining with those of the instrument, rose to a pitch of brilliancy seldom attained by the most distinguished performers, and then sank into a dying cadence, which fell, never again to rise—for the songstress had died with her strain.

The rest is pure stage-work, not to be read but declaimed, early-nineteenth-century Sudermann. "Come hither," says the father in the confrontation scene:

"Come hither . . . thou for whom a life of lowest obscurity was too mean a fate—come hither, and look on the parents whom thou hast so much envied—whom thou hast so often cursed. Look at that pale emaciated form, a figure of wax, rather than flesh and blood—that is thy mother—that is the unhappy Zilia Moncada, to whom thy birth was the source of shame and misery, and to whom thy ill-omened presence has now brought death itself. And behold me!"—he pushed the lad from him, and stood up erect, looking well-nigh in gesture and figure the apostate spirit he described—"Behold me"—he said; "see you not my hair streaming with sulphur, my brow scathed with lightning?—I am the Arch-Fiend—I am the father whom you seek—I am the accursed Richard Tresham, the seducer of Zilia, and the father of her murderer!"

Richard timidly advances his claims on the paternal favor and purse strings, but the Arch-Fiend is not to be put off by such trifles: " 'Wretch!' exclaimed the maniac father, 'canst thou think of thine own sordid rights in the midst of death and frenzy? My son!—thou art the fiend who hast occasioned my wretchedness in this world, and who will share my eternal misery in the next. Hence from my sight, and my curse go with thee!' "

"Three years," says Scott, "passed away after the fatal rencounter mentioned in the last chapter"; and Richard next shows up in Mysore, intriguing by turns against the British government and the government of Hyder Ali, spying and counter-spying, now appearing in the disguise of a charcoal-faced Indian domestic, now relapsing into a whiteness scarcely more reassuring. By the time he arrives in India, he "had been guilty of mutiny, murder, desertion, and the serving of the enemy against his countrymen"; and to these the charges of procuring and white-slave trading are presently to be added. Scott is not at his best in coping with the East.* The difference in quality between the Scottish half of the novel and the Indian half may be measured in part by the characters of Richard's respective female companions in the Western and the Eastern worlds. His Mysore phase finds him conniving with a woman named Adela de Montreville, who is as implausibly sinister as Menie Gray back in Scotland used to be believably humdrum. It is plain from the way Scott describes her that Mme de Montreville is to be classed as one of those monumental superwomen who figure recurrently in Scott's novels, and whom he venerates for their virile intelligence as well as their superior muscular control.[57] In speaking about her, Scott accordingly outdoes himself in exotic allusions, parading her in short order as "a Semiramis-looking person," "yon Queen of Sheba," "a Zenobia," "this same Boadicea," "the Amazon," "the female tyrant," and so on. Middlemas's relations with the Semiramis-person, though they are evenly sinister and tend toward the general annihilation, are of two sorts: when he is not conspiring with her, he is conspiring against her. The attendant complications, as they affect the increasingly wavering plot-line, may be given in her own mantic words to Middlemas: "Thou wilt be a double-traitor, forsooth—betray thy betrothed

* For one thing, the language presents difficulties. "Let me see thee flinch," says one character, "when we are beyond the Ghauts, and the Nawaub shall know thy intrigues with the Nizam and the Mahrattas, and thy resolution to deliver up Bangalore to the English, when the imprudence of Tippoo shall have made thee Killedar." This is not clear, though it sounds well-informed. Elsewhere Scott writes: "These facts ascertained, the Sirdar of the Nawaub took up his own encampment within sight of that of the Begum . . . despatching to the city a messenger to announce to the Prince Tippoo, so soon as he should arrive, that he had come hither with the English Vakeel." When one character ("the counterfeit Sadoc") addresses his lady as "my Nourjehan, my light of the world, my Mootee Mohul," one feels that the resources of language are being strained, and that clarity is being sacrificed to a perverse regionalism.

to the Prince, in order to obtain the means of betraying the Prince to the English, and thus gain thy pardon from thy countrymen. But me thou shalt not betray." "Peace, screech-owl," says Middlemas, and he makes up his mind to betray her at once.

The end is now in sight. A miniature portrait of Menie Gray has found its way into the hands of Hyder Ali's son, the profligate Tippoo, who forthwith expresses his intention of adding the portrait's original to his harem. Menie, accordingly, is procured by Richard, under the pretext that their long-deferred marriage is at last to take place. Instead of being married, Menie, upon arrival, finds herself impressed into Mme de Montreville's esoteric household, pending her secret transfer to Tippoo's seraglio. But now the peripatetic Adam Hartley—or, as Scott foolishly hails him from afar, "this eager vindicator of betrayed innocence"—also turns up again; he arrives, fresh from another one of his auspicious life-saving jobs, which has gained him indirect access to Hyder Ali himself, with full powers of vindication. By way of unclogging the bureaucratic pipelines to Hyder's palace, Hartley next closets himself in secret confabulation with an influential elderly Indian religious, whose favorable intercession he compels by providentially recalling one of those cryptic and cosmically adaptable storiettes that seem to yield less and less meaning the more one looks into them, but in which influential Mussulmen appear to take infinite satisfaction, and which, if uttered at the seasonable moment, have the power of conferring upon the recitalist every imaginable boon. The rest of the novel turns on the fundamental question: who will get to Bangalore first? Hartley, to secure justice for Menie Gray from Hyder Ali, or the Middlemas-Montreville transport, to deliver her up to the pleasures of Tippoo? Accordingly, Scott presents us next with a chase, this issuing in a draw. The parties reach Bangalore in time for a royal reception at which both Hyder Ali and Tippoo preside. As he draws closer to this heart of darkness, Scott is everywhere ambushed by appositives.

> [The messenger] presented the *nuzzur* (a tribute consisting of three, five, or seven gold mohurs, always an odd number), and received in exchange a Khelaut, or dress of honour. The messenger, in return, was eloquent in describing . . . the pleasure which the Begum experienced on the prospect of their motakul, or meeting. . . . He then departed; and orders were given that on the next day all should be in readiness for the *Sowarree,*

a grand procession . . . [The procession follows.] The solemn and deep sound of the naggra, or state drum . . . was then heard. . . . The howdah, or seat, which the Prince occupied, was silver, embossed and gilt, having behind a place for a confidential servant, who waved the great chowry, or cow-tail, to keep off the flies. . . . This splendid procession having entered the royal gardens, approached . . . a chabootra, or platform of white marble. . . . In the center of the platform was the musnud, or state cushion of the Prince.

In the course of the *durbar,* or official reception, the disputants air their grievances. Hartley (we may as well call him "the *hakim*" or "the Feringi Sahib"), the respectable farmer's son, triumphs over the hyperborean half-Jew, Mme de Montreville having meantime got one point ahead of the double traiter and informed against him. While Hartley conducts Menie from out the presence of musnud, chowry, and chabootra, and Mme de Montreville is dismissed to die of poison in the sequel, Middlemas is being detained for the spectacular climax: "As he spoke, [Hyder Ali] signed with his finger; and the driver of the elephant instantly conveyed to the animal the pleasure of the Nawaub. Curling his long trunk around the neck of the ill-fated European, the monster suddenly threw the wretch prostrate before him, and, stamping his huge shapeless foot upon his breast, put an end at once to his life and to his crimes."

Although it has been suggested that "Scott goes out of his way to make [Middlemas] Jewish,"[58] it seems to me clear that by the end of the novel whatever distinctively Jewish features he may have possessed originally have been sacrified wholesale to the demands of a purely sensational story-line. One is therefore apt to remember Middlemas less as a Jewish villain than as an undiscriminated species of depravity, without affective racial, religious, or inherited literary qualities. It is reasonable to assume, that his Jewishness, like almost everything else in the novel, is a sop to the public: Scott, willing to profit by Rebecca's spectacular box-office appeal, found himself with another Jewish Daughter in his repertoire, whose story automatically called for the presence—and eventual dominance—of the half-Jewish son. But the fact that he was thus stuck with him does not mean that Scott knew how to draw out the implications of Middlemas's half-Jewishness except in incidental and frequently immaterial ways. One is reminded all along the line that while he had plenty of precedents for Isaac and Rebecca, he lacked literary models for Middlemas.

The situation, and Scott's failure to cope with it, suggests rather dramatically the hopeless difficulty of breaking through the accepted convention without in the process surrendering all semblance of psychological definition and ignoring even the substratum of accuracy that underlies the stereotype and helps to perpetuate and petrify it in the imagination. If, therefore, we note that Richard's avarice recalls every caricature in the book, we are forced to add at once that there is nothing in the book about miserly Jews who are young, handsome, and unfunny; and the notation, conversely, that Richard's youth and good looks point forward to the type of immaculate Jew popular later in the century dwindles to insignificance in the face of Richard's wickedness. It seems at times as though Scott had taken the two types and gotten their properties mixed up, revealing the devilry of Shylock underneath the photogenic features of the young exotic. There is no apparent reason why this should not work; but it is a pity that in Scott's case the result turns out to be a defective person, who appears, moreover, perversely nondenominational, or else interdenominational: a nominal Catholic who assimilates to a Presbyterian community that persists in regarding him as a Jew.* In reading *The Surgeon's Daughter,* one is led to conclude that the seducer's son is in more ways than one a bastard production.

The Jewish mother with whom Scott began is much more of a piece, and her story recapitulates all the essential features of her legendary prototype. That she is no longer the "high-minded maiden" of *Ivanhoe* hardly matters: the Jewess's celibacy is the least durable element in her composition. What does matter is that she should be rich, beautiful, extraordinary, defenseless, and good, the sole surviving daughter of a widower who is rich, vindictive, and easily

* Before he runs out on his family, his father insists on Richard's being received into the Catholic Church, in deference to his own Jacobitical principles and as a stratagem directed against the Sephardic grandfather. But Richard's Catholicism is even more gratuitous than his Jewishness: it exists as an isolated datum, without echoes or consequences, while his half-Jewishness at least reveals itself in his "flair" and some incidental motifs in the book.

duped. Preferably she should be submissive under adversity. The legend, as we know, does not prescribe her conduct toward her father, in so far as she may scheme against him in overt complicity with the spoliators of his wealth and of her chastity. Shylock loses both ducats and daughter; Isaac keeps both; old Moncada keeps the one but not the other. It can be seen that Zilia comes up to the mark. She is rich and beautiful. She hides beneath a black mask in order to diffuse the desirable quantum of secrecy, but there would be no need for the mask had she not incautiously exposed herself on a previous occasion. Gentiles have loved her and kidnapped her against the better judgment of her father, the scrupulous, unbending, and narrowly pious Jew, who henceforth spurns her as a thing twice violated, in point of religion and in point of sex. Lacking Rebecca's firm will and Jessica's frivolity, she eats out her heart in perpetual remorse and dies of grief. On her tombstone she will be recorded as a dedicated mother, devoted wife, loving daughter, and accomplished harpsichordist. If she sinned against the faith of the Jews, at least she bore her defection from the synagogue with Christian meekness.

Since the myth does not really make provision for the Jewish son, it is difficult to generalize about him. One is free to detect symbolism in his conduct. For example, Middlemas's projected outrage on a decent Christian girl, who loves him for his Jewishness, may be seen as a symbolic attempt to avenge the Jewish mother's seduction by the Gentile father. Middlemas completes the pattern by allying himself later in the novel with a woman whose tall, exotic, and matriarchal features confirm in a general way the qualities Scott associates with the Rebecca-type. Candor compels me to add that I can think of few novels so little responsive to the critical scalpel as *The Surgeon's Daughter*. For the rest, Richard's interest as a Jew depends on a number of motifs which are often extrinsic to his character but which will be sounded again later on: the motif of the ambitious young Jew whose world is his oyster; the song of the handsome Jewish lad with the alien complexion; the sad old tune of the lost and outlawed child, of the orphan whose father is slain at the crossroads or simply goes under, leaving behind him a legacy of confusion, terror, and hope, leaving the child to encounter in single combat the Prince of Darkness. When in London, the Prince has his passport made out in the name of Fagin. The powers of the air build their nest in a Houndsditch attic. For there is also the Jew as bogeyman.

From the sterile sunshine world of Ashby and of Bangalore we descend to the real, the criminal life of the very young in *Oliver Twist;* we pass from Isaac the diffident country-mouse to the city-rat Fagin, from the funny dog to the very merry devil. It is but exchanging the Middle Ages for the Middle Ages.

Now there is a certain class of human beings upon whom not a god, indeed, but a stern goddess—Necessity—has laid the task of giving an account of what they suffer and what they enjoy. . . . Take the case of a poor orphan lad, to whom you have given the address of some employer where he may perhaps get work. On the way there he falls into a day-dream suitable to the situation from which it springs. The content of the phantasy will be somewhat as follows . . .

FREUD, "The Relation of the Poet to Day-Dreaming" (1908)

V

The Jew as Bogey: Dickens

There is a sense in which Fagin, crouching over the fire, crawling forth at night "in search of some rich offal," performing grotesque jigs in the underworld, is a more nearly archetypal Jew-villain than any of the literary Jews who have come up for study so far. Compared with him there is something fine and civilized even in characters like Barabas and Shylock. For with Fagin we are in a way thrown back to that anonymous crowd of grinning devils who, in the religious drama of the fourteenth century, danced foully around the Cross and who, in mythology, functioned as bugaboos to frighten little boys. One imagines again young Harrington being lulled into his nightmares by the stories told him by his nurse; one remembers the song of the Jew's Daughter and the story of Hugh of Lincoln.[1]

If Fagin strikes us as so much more atavistic than any of his precursors, the chief reason, so it seems to me, lies in Dickens's removing him altogether from the social sphere. Barabas, Shylock,

Isaac, are all figures dramatically at odds with the culture in which they operate; they can be appreciated against a particular historical backdrop and defined within an historical context. They are all to a greater or lesser extent defined by their "hostile consciousness of others" and—to a greater or lesser extent—vindicated by it. Scott's vindication of Isaac, as we have seen, depended completely on his ability to depict the depth of Isaac's oppression. Marlowe and Shakespeare obviously will not go so far; but if a character like Barabas impresses us as a motiveless barbarian compared with Isaac, one need only compare him on the other hand with Fagin to get back into perspective. From the beginning of the plays Barabas and Shylock are much abused men; and both are saved from deteriorating into melodramatic figures by the presence of an inimical majority. Marlowe's and Shakespeare's Jews assert themselves actively against their persecution and regard it as a source of terror. The point is that none of them can be sensibly appreciated without an awareness of the restrictions which prevent them from participating fully in the social world. There comes a point at which Barabas, the professional poisoner, ceases to be a satanic figure and can lecture Ferneze on the conditions of injustice without immediately sounding ludicrously hypocritical.

Dickens works differently. Fagin enjoys only the barest status as *homo Europaeus.* There is scarcely anything which ties him to the nineteenth century. His profession of fence may partly identify him with the early decades of the century, but even so his thievery is less important for its documentary relevance than as a basic function of his type: the Jewish criminal is always a thief, whether he operates at Houndsditch or entertains in Bruton Street. Even his Judaism is defective. For the abandonment of all civilized qualities in Fagin involves also his withdrawal from any communal kinship with other Jews. Barabas and Shylock at least were Jews in a specific social and religious sense, and though their religion was not a point in their favor, it defined their bearings and so automatically qualified their villainy. Fagin, we know, falls completely outside of any religious framework; indeed Dickens could use this deficiency when defending himself against the charges of anti-Semitism.[2] Shylock strictly observes the dietary laws and disdains to eat or drink with Christians; Fagin gobbles up pork sausages and ham, not because he is emancipated from religious practices, but because the whole issue of religion is irrelevant.[3] Significantly, the one detail in the entire novel that relates Fagin to Judaism comes at a moment when, as a number of scholars have noted,[4] Dickens has adopted a radically altered viewpoint toward his villain: on the eve of his execution Fagin is visited by some rabbis and drives them out of his cell. At that Dickens dismisses the rabbis as perfunctorily as possible: "Venerable men of his own persuasion had come to pray beside him, but he had driven them away with curses. They renewed their charitable efforts, and he beat them off."[5]

Fagin is also a murderer. Since he is much too old and cowardly to plunge the knife into the victim's breast himself, he resorts to subtler means; for example, he informs against his burglar friends once they have outlasted their usefulness and watches them hang. There is no implication of revenge in this, as there used to be in Shylock's day, but merely a diabolical cupidity. Yet even Fagin's cupidity, though it provides the shadow of a motive, is not stressed; Fagin is having fun; and afterward he talks about his victims with a certain sense of melancholy, as though he himself were a purely impersonal agent of their going to the gallows. Nor are these idle murders directed against the Christians as Christians; it might be the funny Jew Barney's turn next.

Dickens, in short, has "de-historicized" his man and come up with some prehistoric fiend, an aging Lucifer whose depravity explains him wholly. The knife he raises is not raised against the Gentile defaulter but against the angelically innocent, the pure in heart, who may be tempted but cannot be corrupted; for around the corner there is always Brownlow, who is rich the honest way, who smothers the child with tears, and who four hundred pages after the encounter holds up to the audience the placard which reads: This portrait on the wall is your grandmother's sister's portrait; I was your grandfather's best friend. And of course everyone knows that Brownlow is powerless against Fagin; it is absurd to think that an eccentric do-gooder is a match for the devil. One need not believe, with Graham Greene, that the novel is tainted with "the eternal and alluring taint of the Manichee," but his presumption is right, that in the Dickens world "we can believe in evil-doing, while goodness wilts into philanthropy, kindness, and those strange vague sicknesses into which Dickens's young women so frequently fall and which seem in his eyes a kind of badge of virtue, as though there were a merit in death."[6]

Characters like Fagin who are without grace, who terrify the very young and murder the innocent, exist in two worlds and operate on two levels of reality. They can dance about on the Victorian stage, making the theatrical noises of their forefathers who danced around the cross; or they can be interpreted as distorted dream-figures, the grotesquely magnified bogeys out of a fairy tale. In either case their source is in a past other than the historical. There is Dickens the sensation-novelist and there is the Dickens of whom Edmund Wilson has said that his whole career was an attempt to digest and assimilate his early shocks.[7] In a piece written for *All the Year Around,* Dickens asked: "Are not the sane and insane equal at night as the sane lie a dreaming?" and in *The Chimes* he wrote:

> Black are the brooding clouds and troubled the deep waters, when the Sea of Thought, first heaving from a calm, gives up its Dead. Monsters uncouth and wild, arise in premature, imperfect resurrection; the several parts and shapes of different things are joined and mixed by chance; and when, and how, and by what wonderful degrees, each separate from each, and every sense and object of the mind resumes its usual form and lives again, no man—though every man is every day the casket of this type of the Great Mystery—can tell.[8]

Dislocation: The Waifs

Wilson subtitled his essay on Dickens "The Two Scrooges." There are also two Fagins and two corresponding prototypes.

In the autobiographical fragment written for Forster, Dickens recaptured some of the early traumatic experiences he suffered when, as a boy of twelve, he found himself pasting labels on the bottleware of Warren's Blacking, 30, Strand, "a crazy, tumbledown old house, abutting of course on the river, and literally overrun with rats. Its wainscotted rooms and its rotten floors and staircase, and the old grey rats swarming down in the cellars, and the sounds of their squeaking and scuffling coming up the stairs at all times, and the dirt and decay of the place, rise up visible before me as if I were there again." Among his fellows one stood out in Dickens's memory afterward, a pedagogic friend, who "came up, in a ragged apron and a paper cap, on the first Monday morning, to show me the trick of using the string and tying the knot. His name was Bob Fagin; and," Dickens adds very coolly, "I took the liberty of using his name, long afterwards, in *Oliver Twist*." While at Warren's Blacking, Dickens seems to have displayed for the first time the symptoms of hysteria which became pronounced in later life, and during one such spasm young Fagin revealed himself in a light which lends to Dickens's "liberty" a touch of existential absurdity.

Bob Fagin was very good to me on the occasion of a bad attack of my old disorder. I suffered such excrutiating pain at that time, that they made a temporary bed of straw in my old recess in the counting-house, and I rolled about on the floor, and Bob filled empty blacking-bottles with hot water, and applied relays of them to my side, half the day. I got better and quite easy towards evening; but Bob (who was much bigger and older than I) did not like the idea of my going home alone, and took me under his protection. I was too proud to let him know about the prison; and after making several efforts to get rid of him, to all of which Bob Fagin in his goodness was deaf, shook hands with him on the steps of a house near Southward-bridge on the Surreyside, making believe that I lived there. As a finishing piece of reality in case of his looking back, I knocked at the door, I recollect, and asked, when the woman opened it, if that was Mr. Robert Fagin's house.[9]

Although Dickens refers his liberty of using Fagin's name to a period "long afterwards," he wrote *Oliver Twist* at an age when, as a psychoanalytic interpreter of the novel has noted, he "was still young enough to re-imagine the despairing hours in his boyhood with an intensity that made them seem a long nightmare, and that turned his success in manhood into a dreamlike miracle. . . . The more sharply Dickens realized his still recent victory, the more horrible appeared the despair he had overcome."[10] Dickens wrote about frightened little boys in an important way three times in his life, once as a young man, once on the threshold of middle age, and again nine years before his death. The three books—*Twist, Copperfield,* and *Great Expectations*—mark three fairly distinct stages in Dickens's development as a craftsman and reflect an increasingly serious and pessimistic interpretation of life, of the social world, and of the sources of well-being. In spite of its underlying horror, *Twist* is plainly the work of a young man who is still writing the inflated language of the eighteenth-century comic epic, who, instead of saying "he beamed from ear to ear" would rather say that "his grin agitated his countenance from one auricular organ to another." The heroes of these early novels, all of them orphans—whether they are juveniles like Oliver and Little Nell or romantic young men like Nicholas Nickleby—are all alike at the mercy of some impossibly benevolent machinery, of fortuitous encounters with amiable gentlemen who are willing to part with their wealth at short notice and who hold the clue to all mysteries, the key to all safe-deposits.[11]

In *Copperfield* the facile solutions of the early books have been largely discarded. Though David, as Julian Symons has noted, "is granted at least the formal satisfaction of becoming a famous author and making a happy marriage," Dickens can no longer afford to keep up the pretense that Pickwick helps those who cannot help themselves: David has to make his own way by hard work and self-discipline. Moreover, there are genuinely dark touches deployed throughout the novel; for example, David's breakdown, after the death of his first wife, is treated much more responsibly by Dickens than the chills and fevers with which his terrified little boys are recurrently afflicted. In these novels of the 'fifties the eleventh-hour rescues recede in importance, while the role of the professional do-gooder is likely to devolve on a disillusioned figure like Jarndyce in *Bleak House.*

Of *Great Expectations* Shaw has said that "its beginning is unhappy; its middle is unhappy; and the conventional happy ending [inflicted at Bulwer's suggestion] is an outrage on it."[12] By the close of the novel Pip has been, from the point of view of conventional happiness, totally depressed: the mortifying basis of his wealth has been revealed to him; he has lost Estella; in the final chapters it is no longer the hero who gets married but everybody except the hero. As though to leave no doubt about the terrible instability of the World We Live In, Dickens surrounds Pip with a group of marionettes, all of whose great expectations have turned to ashes in the course of the book. Characteristically, the key to the mysteries and the dispensation of fortunes is no longer in the hands of a harmless lunatic like Pickwick or an affable pensioner like Brownlow, but a distempered lawyer who patronizes the criminal classes and manipulates acquittals for them by hiring perjurers, not because he loves humanity in the Pickwickian sense, but because he sees through the rotten conditions of the prevailing jury methods. But the real measure of Dickens's increased pessimism lies in that he is forced to abandon the sentimental illusion that buoyed him up through the 'forties: that the fundamental moral tensions presume a wholly innocent party to the dispute who may, like Oliver, triumph over the forces of darkness, or, like Nell, go under, but whose very existence argues the possibility of goodness and joy. It is no coincidence that *Great Expectations* contains no major villains, for it has no genuine hero either. When Pip capitulates to the hypocrites' party, he provides his own foil; the conflict which, in the earlier novels, had to be supplied by strict improbable antithesis rages here in the soul of a waif who has betrayed the conditions of waifdom.[14]

In *Oliver Twist* the antithesis is still absolute: the little Christian chorister against the serpent-Jew, the fairy princeling setting out to come into his principalities and meeting the child-devouring ogre on the way.

By the time Oliver arrives in Fagin's lair he has already endured a staggering series of collisions with lesser tormentors, disreputable oddities who have none of Fagin's ghoulish qualities but who abuse the boy in a stupid and infantile way—fat and alcoholic vulgarians like Bumble, whose epicene gluttony Dickens tirelessly contrasts with the starved faces of the workhouse orphans. Taine pointed out in his pioneering study that Dickens's great hypocrites, his pedagogues and disciplinarians, can be recognized by their fondness for moralizing over food; and certainly Oliver's initial contacts in life are uniformly with the florid, the well-fed, and the drunken.[15] These characters are all in one way or another fools, whose brutalities are inspired by spasms of whimsy rather than a sense of calculated malice; when they administer earcuffs and kicks one is made to feel that they act from a superabundance of misdirected humor.[16] They can present no final threat to the child, who is stronger than they are and in comparison with whom they dwindle into contemptible figures of infantile lunacy. For in this topsy-turvy world the children and grown-ups have exchanged their roles: while characters like Bumble are given over to the irrational outbursts of a child howling for attention, undernourished children like Oliver's friend Dick take on the stunted, wizened, terribly serious features of premature old age. Dickens achieves some of his best effects in the novel by this relentless juxtaposition of the superannuated child, dying of starvation, and the babyish adult, in fair round belly with good capon lin'd. "The child was pale and thin; his cheeks were sunken; and his eyes large and bright. The scanty parish dress, the livery of his misery, hung loosely on his feeble body; and his young limbs had wasted away, like those of an old man." "Having disposed of these evil-minded persons for the night, Mr. Bumble sat himself down . . . and took a temperate dinner of steaks, oyster-sauce and porter. Putting a glass of hot gin-and-water on the chimney-piece, he drew his chair to the fire; and, with sundry moral reflections on the too-prevalent sin of discontent and complaining, composed himself to read the paper."[17] At one point in the book the topsy-turviness and frightening dislocation are obtruded on Oliver's notice in one of those passages which no amount of cheap rhetoric can really damage.

As Oliver accompanied his master in most of his adult expeditions, too, in order that he might acquire that equanimity of demeanour and full command of nerve which are essential to a finished undertaker, he had many opportunities of observing the beautiful resignation and fortitude with which some strong-minded people bear their trials and losses.

For instance; when Sowerberry had an order for the burial of some rich old lady or gentleman, who was surrounded by a great number of nephews and nieces, who had been perfectly inconsolable during the previous illness, and whose grief had been wholly irrepressible even on the most public occasions, they would be as happy among themselves as need be—quite cheerful and contented—conversing together with as much freedom and gaiety, as if nothing whatever had happened to disturb them. Husbands, too, bore the loss of their wives with the most heroic calmness. Wives, again, put on weeds for their husbands, as if, so far from grieving in the garb of sorrow, they had made up their minds to render it as becoming and attractive as possible. It was observable, too, that ladies and gentlemen who were in passions of anguish during the ceremony of interment, recovered almost as soon as they reached home, and became quite composed before the tea-drinking was over. All this was very pleasant and improving to see; and Oliver beheld it with great admiration.

It is little wonder that in such a world the orphan who is too young to fight back and too fine to grow old overnight is reduced to a condition of permanent hysteria. In the first forty pages or so of the novel Oliver suffers from weeping fits so intense and so relentless as to be almost programmatic. "It was no very difficult matter for the boy to call tears into his eyes." "A sense of his loneliness in the great wide world, sank into the child's heart." "Oliver bowed low by the direction of the beadle, and was then hurried away to a large ward: where, on a rough, hard bed, he sobbed himself to sleep." "He . . . cried bitterly all day, and when the long dismal night came on, spread his little hands before his eyes to shut out the darkness, and crouching in the corner, tried to sleep: ever and anon waking with a start and tremble, and drawing himself closer and closer to the wall, as if to feel even its cold hard surface were a protection in the gloom and loneliness which surrounded him." By the time he arrives at Sowerberry's, Oliver has given way to complete despair; he has reached a point where, in a Dostoyevski novel, the child would now hang himself. "He wished, as he crept into his narrow bed, that that were his coffin, and that he could be lain in a calm and lasting sleep in the church-yard ground, with the tall grass waving gently above his head."

But of course Dickens's children do not hang themselves; at the breaking point they either die (or, as Dickens foolishly says, "the cart is shaken all to pieces and the rugged road is very near its end") or else run away. For there comes a moment in Dickens's fiction where the gloomiest contingencies are overnight translated into a picaresque walking tour; and Oliver, having washed the tears out of his system, journeys to London, there to fall from the fire into the frying pan. The frying pan is the first thing he sees.

Distortion: Fagin

In a frying-pan, which was on the fire, and which was secured to the mantelshelf by a string, some sausages were cooking; and standing over them, with a toasting-fork in his hand, was a very old shrivelled Jew, whose villainous-looking and repulsive face was obscured by a quantity of matted red hair. He was dressed in a greasy flannel gown, with his throat bare; and seemed to be dividing his attention between the frying-pan and the clotheshorse, over which a great number of silk handkerchiefs were hanging.[18]

Just as Oliver is Dickens's first and prototypical all-Britannic waif, Fagin is Dickens's first substantial villain, and his villainy must be commensurate with Oliver's goodness. In Dickens's early novels the criminals all tend to be sensationally evil; it is only in the novels of the 'forties that the great comic hypocrites really come into their own. The antagonists in the first half-dozen books are not noticeably funny; they are either old-fashioned theatrical types like Ralph Nickleby, Gride, Chester, and Jonas Chuzzlewit, or superhuman ogres like Fagin and Quilp.[19] What buoys up a character like Fagin and makes him somehow accessible to humor is, I suppose, what Edgar Johnson calls his "sinister hilarity." "Fagin is one of those nightmare images, often recurrent in his creator's mind, that Dickens regarded with a loathing so fascinated as to be half horrible enjoyment: an image of hilarious evil delighted in cunning self-applause. Daniel Quilp . . . in whom malice boils up into an atrocious playfulness, is a grotesque mutation of the image." Edwin Pugh similarly ranks Fagin not with Dickens's sensational types but his great comic villains: "Throughout the book, until the final catastrophe, Fagin . . . is like some frowsy, obscene bird that seems to chuckle and mock in a secret language of its own. He shares with the rest of Dickens's really great villains that saving grace of humour, that grace which saves them from . . . utter unreality."[20]

To be merry in the way indicated is, of course, one of the devil's privileges; the epithet "merry old gentleman," which is repeatedly applied to Fagin, is still a well-known euphemism for the devil. At one point Dickens speaks of "the old gentleman's merry heart"; and one of the critical moments in the novel, just when the Tempter seems on the point of having "instilled into [Oliver's] soul the poison which he hoped would blacken it," is marked by Fagin's great good humor: "At other times the old man would tell them stories of robberies he had committed in his younger days: mixed up with so much that was droll and curious, that Oliver could not help laughing heartily, and showing that he was amused in spite of his better feelings. In short, the wily old Jew had the boy in his toils."

Deprived of his affability, Fagin is a wholly sinister demon. "Fagin, the arch-devil," writes Pugh, "though he is limned in the fewest possible words, stands forth lurid and malignant as the figure of Satan in medieval pageantry. He appears like that typical mythical Satan, with his toasting fork, and the firelight playing over him."[21] The typical mood in which Dickens likes to catch him is one in which the Jew broods over his stolen silverware or hatches his plots, "plunged in deep thought, with his face wrinkled into an expression of villainy perfectly demoniacal." In moments of repose he strikes the attitude of the mythical medieval monster whom some anonymous scribe sketched a thousand years ago:

> The dragon sits on his mound, old and exultant in treasure.

To Sikes Fagin in his long kaftan looks preternaturally like "the devil when he's got a great-coat on"; Nancy describes him to Brownlow as "devil and worse than devil"; occasionally, too, Sikes, himself the most sensational of criminals, pays Fagin the tribute of his superstitious awe:

> "I don't feel like myself when you lay that withered old claw on my shoulder, so take it away," said Sikes, casting off the Jew's hand.
>
> "It makes you nervous, Bill—reminds you of being nabbed, does it?" said Fagin, determined not to be offended.

If a brutal burglar and murderer confesses to feelings of discomfort "to see his lean old carcase shivering in that way, like a ugly ghost just rose from the grave," a child of nine who has been battered, not into apathy, but into acute *Angst,* cannot be expected to regard Fagin with equanimity. What lends Fagin his terrifying air of unreality is not only that he seems always to be alone and is always seen crouching in the dark, but that Dickens's level of perception—the child's—brings out Fagin's nightmarish qualities with unforgettable immediacy and vividness. Compared with him, not only is Shylock a daylight creature, sunning himself on the Rialto; he is also viewed and judged by an adult society, and so he remains relatively in focus. The same is true of Isaac, whose character is kept at a certain remove by Scott's own patient definitions and analyses, and whose conduct is judged in the clarifying light of historical perspective. For young Oliver, on the other hand, gazing on the bogey-Jew, all leveling processes of custom and routine have been suspended; he contemplates the Jew with the fantastic directness of the child who has not yet learned to see with the simplifying eye of habit. Even when Oliver's gaze is actually withdrawn, the viewpoint continues to be that of a boy frightened into the hysterical conviction that he has seen a ghost. Since Fagin is the more ghastly for his total dissociation from human traffic, Dickens naturally prefers to dwell on his figure as it appears in solitude, but it is all the time Oliver who catches him out of the corner.

"The shadow of Fagin," says Chesterton, "falls everywhere";[22] and it is his shadow as he crawls forth at night that stays in the memory. "As he glided stealthily along, creeping beneath the shelter of the walls and doorways, the hideous old man seemed like some loathsome reptile, engendered in the slime and darkness through which he moved: crawling forth, by night, in search of some rich offal for a meal."

"In the Fagin darkness, Dickens's hand seldom fumbles."[23] In the white world of the Maylies, it loses control. While Satan is battling for Oliver's soul, the forces of supreme goodness consolidate their strength: the tearful, the virtuously ill, the not-of-this-earth. Adult tears, like the tears of children, betray a whole syndrome of natural pieties in the Dickens universe: Mrs. Bedwin sheds them, Brownlow sheds them; and these manly lachrymosities lead Dickens to posture sickeningly: "Mr. Brownlow's heart, being large enough for any six ordinary gentlemen of humane disposition, forced a supply of tears into his eyes, by some hydraulic process which we are not sufficiently philosophical to be in a condition to explain." No six ordinary gentlemen of humane disposition, however, are a match for Satan; to lead the sanctimonious myrmidons one wants an angel, and so the curtain rises to reveal, very pale and beautiful, dress-rehearsing a death-bed scene which is subject to being called off any moment, the cloying figure of Rose Fleming, the Mary Hogarth who is destined not to die, Little Nell, *aet.* 17, betrothed to a Protestant divine. That, by a series of bewildering genealogical complexities, she turns out to be Oliver's mother's younger sister is nothing to the purpose, for we are not meant to believe that such supernal creatures can harbor blood-connections any more than Fagin can. Dickens views her consistently in her unearthly possibilities: "Cast in so slight and exquisite a mould," he says, lulling himself to sleep with the cheap pentameter which adumbrates Nell's transfiguration in the cottage, "so mild and gentle; so pure and beautiful; that earth seemed not her element, nor its rough creatures her fit companions. The very intelligence that shone in her deep blue eye . . . seemed scarcely of her age, or of the world." "She playfully put back her hair . . . and threw into her beaming look, such an expression of affection and artless loveliness, that blessed spirits might have smiled to look upon her." As her tears touch his forehead, Oliver, dying of exhaustion after the mangled burglary attempt, is insensibly recalled to life: "the younger lady *glided* softly past"—and there is something idiotic in applying the same verb of motion to the angel and the reptile in search of offal—"and seating herself in a chair by the bedside, gathered Oliver's hair from his face. As she stooped over him, her tears fell upon his forehead. . . . Oliver's pillow was smoothed by gentle hands that night; and loveliness and virtue watched him as he slept. He felt calm and happy and could have died without a murmur."

Before the devil is finally caught, Dickens has still to engineer, as a gratuitous present to the upright and the sensation-seeking, that cliché of the sentimental stage, the confrontation of the pure angel and the fallen angel; we have our last view of Fagin at home, and what we see urges the conclusion that Brownlow is a profoundly self-deluded fool for thinking that he can get through to him.

> It was nearly two hours before day-break, that time which in the autumn of the year, may be truly called the dead of night; when the streets are silent and deserted; when even sounds appear to slumber, and profligacy and riot have staggered home to dream; it was at this still and silent hour, that Fagin sat watching in his old lair, with face so distorted and pale, and eyes so red and blood-shot, that he looked less like a man, than like some hideous phantom, moist from the grave, and worried by an evil spirit.
>
> He sat crouching over a cold hearth, wrapped in an old torn coverlet, with his face turned towards a wasting candle that stood upon a table by his side. His right hand was raised to his lips, and as, absorbed in thought, he bit his long black nails, he disclosed among his toothless gums a few such fangs as should have been a dog's or rat's.

It is perhaps just as well that Fagin's capture, since it mocks the higher probabilities, is not directly described but reported at second hand by the loquacious Chitling. When next we see Fagin he is already as good as dead in the flesh; and as a devil he has quite given up the ghost. "There is a passion for *hunting something* deeply implanted in the human breast," says Dickens, speaking of Oliver's pursuers in the early part of the book; ". . . and as they follow on his track, and gain upon him every instant, they hail his decreasing strength with still louder shouts, and whoop and scream with joy." Fagin can no more be left at large than Shylock can; the passion for hunting something is being gratified; and Fagin swings within the week.

But first Dickens decides to civilize him.

Two recent articles have offered some admirable insights into the psychology of Dickens's moribund villains; taken together, they throw a good deal of light on the remarkable change which comes over Fagin in the famous chapter entitled "Fagin's Last Night Alive."

We have first Warrington Winters's extremely interesting study,[24] in which he discusses Dickens's obsessive curiosity about dream-psychology and alights on the interesting fact that not only do nightmares play a very considerable role in Dickens's books but only the good people are made to suffer them. Copperfield, Stephen Blackpool, Esther Summerson, Pip, Barnaby Rudge, Dick Swiveller, are all afflicted with oppressive dreams, all of them characterized by sensations described as "horrible fear," "horrible dread," "mortal fear," "hopeless labor," "carking care," "inexplicable agony and misery"— I am citing the phrases as Winters gives them. When we come to the criminals, we find that they enjoy the sleep of the just and the pure in heart. The reason for this is very plain: the villains pay for their sins by suffering in their waking hours substantially the same traumas which the innocent figures suffer in their sleep: "their waking terror and remorse so closely resembles the dreams of the 'good' characters that if Dickens had described their sleeping experiences as well, his efforts would have been not only meaningless but also repetitious." Chesterton used to declare that Dickens's villains were so wholly depraved as to be incapable of remorse; Winters's article endeavors to amend this view. Thus he reminds us that a distinction needs to be made between a handful of unregenerate criminals—Quilp, Riderhood, Blandois—whom Dickens destroys without first making them mad, and others in whom "the qualms of conscience are described at great length. One has only to remember Fagin's last night, the flight of Bill Sikes, Ralph Nickleby's suicide, Carker's flight . . . and the remorse of Jonas Chuzzlewit."

We have secondly an article by Fred W. Boege.[25] The article, which takes some of Winters's conclusions into account, is an attempt to correct the general assumption that Dickens could only portray his characters from the outside, looking at them either from the objective-dramatic or from the omniscient viewpoint, and that he eschewed the introspective point of view. Now admittedly, as Boege grants, the few scattered remarks on the craft of fiction which Dickens has left us—most of them in the form of editorial suggestions to contributing authors—all tend to stress Dickens's preference for a limited dramatic viewpoint to one strictly omniscient or introspective: "The people do not sufficiently work out their own purposes in dialogue and dramatic action," reads one of his editorial *obiter dicta* which Boege quotes. "You are too much their exponent; what you do for them, they ought to do themselves."[26] This is, of course, the sort of formulation that we might expect from a novelist who fetches his aesthetics from repeated analogies to the stage. Still every novelist at one moment or another resorts automatically to introspective writing, especially a novelist like Dickens who is capable of pouring out pages and pages of hysterical clap-trap from sheer uncontrolled *Einfuehlung*; and it is this truism which casts over Boege's thesis—but only his thesis—a certain tautological quality. The value of his study lies in his singling out the passages in which Dickens falls back on the limited introspective view and in his pulling them together in an interesting way. He notes first that Dickens himself occasionally came out with critical observations on the uses of viewpoint (he cites five such comments) and so cheated Percy Lubbock out of his copyright; and he goes on to remark:

Among the hundreds of Dickensian characters there exists a small diverse group whose members have but two things in common. They are all about to die and they all, for a brief time before their deaths, become the subjects of the limited point of view. With them there is no doubt about the effect. Even the most casual reader must forcibly realize that the drama has been transferred from the external world where Dickens usually moves to the realm of the mind and the soul. . . . Two motives can be distinguished for this practice. Certain of the characters are in those abnormal states of mind which Dickens was as fond of investigating in real life as in fiction; and all of them, by the mere fact of approaching death, offer rich possibilities for dramatic treatment. . . . We have hitherto seen little or nothing of the minds of these people; now the conscious (or the subconscious) becomes the protagonist and plays the role con spirito.[27]

If we put the above studies together, it becomes fairly evident that Dickens, consciously or not, endeavored to penetrate the minds of those of his villains who, he felt, deserved some saving touches before he sent them off to the gallows.[28] The procedure in Chapter III of *Oliver Twist* is startling and in some ways productive of more real terror than anything that has gone before. In front of our eyes the devil now dwindles into a poor, frightened, conscience-stricken Jew. What has happened is simply that Dickens has withdrawn the sustaining point of view, Olivers's, and substituted alternately his own and Fagin's: what the child saw as a monster collapses, from any other vantage point, into a silly old man with a minimal claim on one's pity.

He looked up into the gallery again. Some of the people were eating, and some fanning themselves with handkerchiefs; for the crowded place was very hot. There was one young man sketching his face in a little notebook. He wondered whether it was like, and looked on when the artist broke his pencil-point, and made another with his knife, as any idle spectator might have done. . . .

Not that, all this time, his mind was, for an instant free from one oppressive overwhelming sense of the grave that opened at his feet; it was ever present to him, but in a vague and general way, and he could not fix his thoughts upon it. Thus, even while he trembled, and turned burning hot at the idea of speedy death, he fell to counting the iron spikes before him, and wondering how the head of one had been broken off, and whether they would mend it, or leave it as it was. Then, he thought of all the horrors of the gallows and the scaffold—and stopped to watch a man sprinkling the floor to cool it—and then went on to think again.

The verdict of Guilty is pronounced; general jubilation in the court and among the hunting parties outside.

The noise subsided, and he was asked if he had anything to say why sentence of death should not be passed upon him. He had resumed his listening attitude, and looked intently at his questioner while the demand was made; but it was twice repeated before he seemed to hear it, and then he only muttered that he was an old man—an old man—an old man—and so, dropping into a whisper, was silent again.

We have come back after all to Shylock's "I am not well," Isaac's "do not harm the poor Jew." Shakespeare paid Shylock the ambiguous compliment of driving him to the baptismal font; Dickens pays Fagin the ambiguous tribute of withholding the damning epithet Jew during his last appearance and calling him by his proper name. It is one way of stressing the human element; another is to bring on the rabbis and impress upon the reader the condition that Fagin *could* have friends.

And last of all young Oliver himself arrives, his purebred Lord Fauntleroy speech habits quite intact, thank Heaven, as though he had never been born in a workhouse, bred on the Poor Law, starved in an undertaker's cellarage, and drilled in a thieves' lair; he arrives, the young hero, and pays Fagin a kind of "get-saved" visit in the condemned cell. The tamed monster and the domesticated orphan enjoy a final tête-à-tête. It is the crowning indignity committed upon both of them; for there is something positively staggering in bringing the child to see the devil brought low. And Oliver actually invites Fagin to get down on his knees and join him in prayer. Naturally Fagin has no idea what he is talking about. "Oh! God forgive this wretched man!" Oliver cries, bursting into tears for the last time. Afterwards—only an hour or so is wanting to Fagin's execution and Dickens has already laid out the "dark cluster of objects in the centre of all—the black stage, the cross-beam, the rope, and all the hideous apparatus of death"—we are told that "Oliver nearly swooned" and "was so weak that for an hour or more, he had not the strength to walk." One remembers Dickens's neuritic foot, his spasms at the warehouse, and the other Fagin, the Fagin who recalled him to life.

Sensation: The Fence

"It has been the peculiarity and the marvel of this man's power," Trollope wrote of Dickens in his *Autobiography,* "that he invested his puppets with a charm that enabled him to dispense with human nature."[29] Trollope is expressing the resentment and the grudging admiration which the realist harbors toward the writer of the sensation-novel.

In addition to Fagin as Satan, there is Fagin the theatrical villain, the Barney Fence character. "Ha! Ha! The man against the child, for a bag of gold!" Fagin says at one point, having himself one of his spectacular leers, and reminding the audience that if he is the Jew-murderer, the medieval Anti-Christ, he is also the melodramatic Jew-thief, Arthur Gride with a hooked nose and red hair, Shylock Houndsditched. *Homo moralis,* the killer, yields to *homo economicus,* the receiver of stolen goods. Fagin's cupidity, of course, is seen in the light of his bloodier activities, and so it cannot really bear comparison with the tame avarice of Isaac, except on the general proposition already alleged, that to cry thief after the Jew is to engage in redundancy. How inseparably Shylock's dual functions of economic parasitism and would-be cannibalism have come down to Dickens's day is revealed in a dramatic way in the single most extended scene in which Dickens lingers over Fagin's thievery. Like Shakespeare, Dickens juxtaposes the symbols of the jewel casket and the knife.

> After satisfying himself upon this head, the Jew stepped gently to the door: which he fastened. He then drew forth: as it seemed to Oliver, from some trap in the floor: a small box, which he placed carefully on the table. His eyes glistened as he raised the lid, and looked in. Dragging an old chair to the table, he sat down; and took from it a magnificent gold watch, sparkling with jewels. . . .
>
> "What a fine thing capital punishment is! Dead men never repent; dead men never bring awkward stories to light. Ah, it's a fine thing for the trade! Five of 'em strung up in a row, and none left to play booty, or turn white-livered!"
>
> As the Jew uttered these words, his bright dark eyes, which had been staring vacantly before him, fell on Oliver's face; the boy's eyes were fixed on his in mute curiosity; and although the recognition was only for an instant . . . it was enough to show the old man that he had been observed. He closed the lid of the box with a loud crash; and laying his hand on his bread knife which was on the table, started furiously up. He trembled very much though; for, even in his terror, Oliver could see that the knife quivered in the air.

Fagin's economic rascality suggests an immediate link with the Victorian stage and brings into the picture the more verifiable of the two Fagins, the dramatic and historical prototype as distinguished from the psychical.[30] Of Ikey Solomons, the world's great fence, Edwin Pugh has presented the following *vita*:

He began as an itinerant street vendor at eight, at ten he passed bad money, at fourteen he was a pickpocket and a "duffer," or a seller of sham goods. He early saw the profits to be made out of purchasing stolen goods, but could not embark in it at first for want of capital. He was taken up when still in his teens for stealing a pocketbook and was sentenced to transportation, but did not get beyond the hulks at Chatham. On his release an uncle, a slop seller in Chatham, gave him a situation as "barker," or salesman, in which he realized £150 within a couple of years. With this capital he returned to London and set up as a fence. He had such great aptitude for business and such a thorough knowledge of the real value of goods, that he was soon admitted to be one of the best judges known of all kinds of property, from a glass bottle to a five hundred guinea chronometer.[31]

In 1830 Solomons was tried at the Old Bailey before Mr. Serjeant Arabin and sentenced to seven years' transportation to Van Diemen's Land. Solomons's trial seems to have alerted the writer and his audience to the existence and publicity value of fences in general. His transportation proved to be a particular windfall for the hack W. T. Moncrief, who had just written to order a melodrama entitled *Van Diemen's Land*—"a jumble of bush-rangers, exciting episodes, songs and a panorama."[32] One of Moncrief's episodes had to do with a convict plantation scene into which he had introduced a Jew by name of Barney Fence. The Solomons trial induced Moncrief to change the character's name from Barney Fence to Ikey Solomons. By the time Dickens wrote *Oliver Twist* the trial was already seven years out of date and the scandal surrounding his figure might easily have been forgotten. This time gap has now led Landa to conjecture with some plausibility that Ikey must have passed into Fagin via Moncrief's play, which enjoyed such enduring popularity that Dickens no doubt saw or read it. The identification, loosely, of Fagin and Ikey is also taken for granted by Pugh, allowing for the glaring differences between a "loathsome reptile crawling forth by night in search of some rich offal" and an enterprising and resourceful capitalist with a twenty-thousand-pound establishment in Rosemary Lane.

Of course Dickens need not have had Ikey specifically in mind. As Pugh admits (and as Dickens himself noted in his letter of apology

Fagin's Last Night Alive

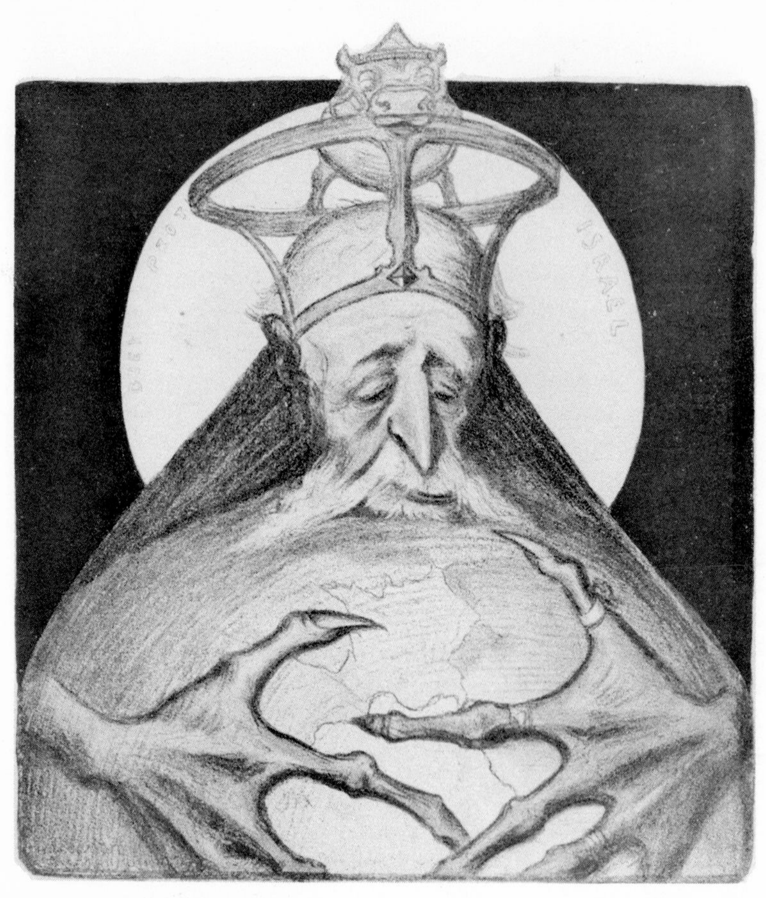

Rothschild: Dieu Protège Israel

to Mrs. Davis), it happened to be true that at the beginning of the nineteenth century the profession of fence was largely a Jewish one. Ikey was merely kingpin of the lot. "There was another Solomons who was not above reproach, and an Abrahams, and Money Moses, a publican, who kept the Black Lion in Vinegar Yard, Drury Lane." Moreover, a good many of these fences trained children to steal their glass-bottles and chronometers for them. The early decades of the nineteenth century were anyhow a time when juvenile delinquency had become alarmingly widespread; according to Pugh the London prisons sometimes contained as many as three thousand inmates under twenty years of age during any one year, nearly half of these again under seventeen. There were thus ample precedents for the Artful Dodgers and the Charlie Bateses as well as for the Fagins and Barneys. "Some were barely nine or ten. Children began to steal when they could scarcely crawl. Cases were known of infants of barely six charged at the courts with crime."[33]

Fagin's economic qualifications could thus have been borrowed from any number of live models. But the indebtedness to Moncrief's sensation-piece, whether real or spurious, appears singularly appropriate to a novelist who wrote an elaborate parody of melodrama into Chapter XVII of *Oliver Twist* and delivered himself of the genuine article in the remaining fifty-two chapters. "Wolves tear your throat," cries Bill Sikes idiotically; and elsewhere he alludes to a bungling murderer-friend as a "screeching hell babe"—a phrase of which Gissing remarks that it sounds "natural enough on the boards of the Adelphi Theatre but incongruous in a London slum."[34] Fagin the stage-Jew needs therefore to be appreciated largely in the light of that marketable credo which Wilkie Collins articulated when he laid down the principle by which he and his mentor were actuated, that "the Novel and the Play are twin sisters in the family of Fiction; and that the one is a drama narrated as the other is a drama acted." Since Dickens and Collins programmatically ignored the difference between drama and melodrama, and perhaps lacked the means for distinguishing between them, it followed that "all the strong and deep emotions which the Play-writer is privileged to excite, the Novel-writer is privileged to excite also" and that "those extraordinary accidents and events which happen to few men, seem . . . to be as legitimate materials for fiction to work with . . . as the ordinary accidents and events which may, and do, happen to us all."[35]

Naturally Dickens clamored for stage adaptations of *Oliver Twist* before the final installment of the novel appeared in *Bentley's;* it is to his credit that he seems to have been revolted by some of the things he saw.[36] Dickens's fiction is not really translatable to the stage at all. In the novel *Oliver Twist* the spectacular coincidences may, retrospectively, look outrageous; but Dickens's genius for concealment, which is practicable in the novel medium, was so surpassing that one does not mind them in the reading; one permits oneself to be drawn, unresisting, into the deepening mysteries that surround his hero, and resists only the discovery. This secrecy, which is at the bottom of Dickens's genius, can no more be transferred to the stage than the hideous decor, the framework in which his characters tantalize each other and act out their strident lunacies. Dickens had an extraordinary talent and patience for histrionics, and during one of the early stage-performances of *Oliver Twist* he stretched out on the floor of his box in protest and did not get up again until the play was over. To see what can happen when Dickens's secrets are broadcast, one need only quote the concluding speeches of the play, in which Oliver is absolutely made to *say* the nonsense lines about his dead mother.

Mr. Brownlow. And what is now wanted to complete the happiness of Oliver Twist?

Oliver. First that you will erect a small white tablet in the church near which my poor mother died, and on it grave the name of Agnes. There might be no coffin in that tomb; but if the spirits of the dead ever come back to earth to visit spots hallowed by their love, I do believe that the shade of my poor mother will often hover about this solemn nook, though it is a church, and she was weak and erring.

Mr. Brownlow. The next request I will make for you, dear Oliver, myself, and will make it here—to you (to audience). Our hero is but young; but if his simple progress has beguiled you of a smile, or his sorrows of a tear, forgive the errors of the orphan boy, Oliver Twist.[37]

Toward the end of his life, against doctor's orders and against his better judgment, Dickens added "The Murder of Nancy" to his repertory of public recitals. Thanks to an article in *Tinsley's Magazine* for February 1869 we have a good idea of what Dickens looked like when he tried to look like Fagin.

There is nothing comic about him, there is nothing grand or tragic, as in Shylock; he is sordid, mean, avaricious, and revengeful, and Mr. Dickens shows him to you in every phrase. You read it in his rounded shoulders, in his sunken chin, in his pinched cheeks and hanging brow, in his gleaming eyes, and quivering, clutching hands, in the lithe shiftiness of his movements, and the intense earnestness of his attitudes. The voice is husky and with a slight lisp, but there is no nasal intonation; a bent back, but no shoulder-shrug: the conventional attributes are omitted, the conventional words are never spoken; and the Jew fence, crafty and cunning in his bitter vengeance, is here before us.[38]

The child in Dickens must have enjoyed himself vastly; but the elder Dickens ran up a pulse of 114. It is now generally agreed that he killed himself in this way. "The murder of Nancy," says one of his recent biographers, "indeed, did more than anything else to sap his waning powers of resistance. Moreover, seeing the effect it was having upon his audience, he deliberately set out to increase its horrors, and, closing his eyes to the additional risks he was running, persisted in reading it night after night."[39] Is it fanciful to imagine that in some obscure way Dickens was exploding his vital superstitions, that "the Sea of Thought, first heaving from a calm, was giving up its Dead"? As he stepped onstage for his final impersonation of Fagin he remarked to an acquaintance in a half-whisper, "I shall tear myself to pieces"—one wonders what debts were being paid here, and to whom.

Mark my words, Mr. Dedalus [Deasy] said, England is in the hands of the jews. In all the highest places: her finance, her press. And they are the signs of a nation's decay. Wherever they gather, they eat up the nation's vital strength. I have seen it coming these years. As sure as we are standing here the jew merchants are already at their work of destruction. Old England is dying. . . .

A merchant, Stephen said, is one who buys cheap and sells dear, jew or gentile, is he not?

They sinned against the light, Mr. Deasy said gravely. And you can see the darkness in their eyes. And that is why they are wanderers on the earth to this day.

JOYCE, *Ulysses* (1922)

VI

The Jew as Parasite: Trollope and Bulwer

Fagin represents the most nearly archetypal Jew which the nineteenth century had to offer; the Jewish group in *Deronda* were to represent the most self-conscious corrective to Fagin. Dickens had resurrected the medieval idea of the Jewish bogey as nearly as an early Victorian sensation-novelist is capable of resurrecting that ghastly caricature. As the century wore on, some fairly subtle variations and modifications of the criminal stereotype became possible—innovations just perceptible enough to keep Fagin from being an entirely representative nineteenth-century Jew-villain. If we borrow Modder's valid discrimination between earlier and later nineteenth-century criminal types, Fagin has to be assigned quite clearly to the same class of early, comparatively crude bogey types to be found in Maria Edgeworth's tales and in Ainsworth's *Jack Sheppard,* as distinct from the more realistic portrayals of itinerant peddlers, dishonest old-clothes men, small-time thieves, and big-time monopolists that became increasingly prominent after the 1830's.[1]

Here statistics offer at least a provisional clue. In 1800, when Miss Edgeworth committed her old-fashioned Jewish poisoners to paper, Jews were still something of an exotic minority in England, and so it was easy to vilify them beyond recognition. The situation was crudely analogous to the situation in Shakespeare's day, when the scarcity of first-hand knowledge about Jews encouraged unbridled superstitions about them. At the beginning of the nineteenth century the Jewish population in England numbered no more than 8,000; by the end of the century it had swelled to 250,000, some two-thirds of whom were accredited residents of London; and naturally the observed reality spoke against the assumption that there were a quarter million gargoyles loose in England. Once the Jews got to be an accessible, neighborly, domesticated actuality, it became increasingly difficult to credit them with wholesale slaughter and cannibalism. The restrictive legislation against Jews had been relaxed materially. In 1858 Lionel Rothschild took his seat in Parliament as Member for London; by 1880 a Jew had been Lord Mayor and Disraeli had been twice Prime Minister. As I suggested earlier, population figures and philo-Semitic legislation do not, I suppose, permanently affect a stereotype, whose property is precisely its tendency toward stability; and with changing literary fashions and conventions Fagin can again be summoned from the deep in all his subliminal horror. But it is nevertheless true that among the more realistic novelists during the second half of the century the criminal stereotype was subtly modified and brought a little more in line with the experienced actuality than it had been at any earlier period in its history.

To accomplish this, it was not really necessary to deviate very far from the existing stereotype, which had always admitted at least a realistic substratum by regarding the Jew in the light of the cash-nexus. The Jew as money-lender, if not the Jew as murderer, was a fact of experience, and had been from the first. Novelists like Trollope, Marryat, and Bulwer found it convenient therefore simply to eliminate the bogey element, which had lost much of its force anyhow once the fundamental religious sanctions were no longer in force, and stressed instead the motif of economic cupidity which had co-existed with the bogey motif from Biblical times. On the principle that profiteering, malversation, and petty larceny are more plausible activities in the modern world than kidnapping and cannibalism, the latter half of the nineteenth century celebrates the Jew as social parasite. Half the time novelists chose to go no further for their originals than to some much-maligned member of the Rothschild family, who seem to have sat for an endless number of scurrilous portraits and supplied an inexhaustible fund of prototypes.[2]

The Way We Live Now

Much the most interesting specimen of the Jewish criminal to be furnished by the domestic realists in the latter half of the century is Augustus Melmotte, the massive swindler in Trollope's *The Way We Live Now*.[3] Trollope's novel appeared one year before *Daniel Deronda*; Walter Allen has called it "one of the remarkable novels of the language" and "the only other novel in English of the century that, as a study of the role of money in society, can stand with *Our Mutual Friend*."[4] Melmotte emerges in the novel at first as a somewhat shadowy figure, of rather mixed nationality and indeterminate origins, of whom scarcely anything is known beyond the fact of his immense gusto for vast, and vastly suspicious financial transactions, and who turns up in London, attended by a vulgar wife and comely daughter, to play the English market after apparently losing his millions on the Continent.

> It was at any rate an established fact that Mr. Melmotte had made his wealth in France. He no doubt had had enormous dealings in other countries, as to which stories were told which must surely have been exaggerated. It was said that he had made a railway across Russia, that he provisioned the Southern army in the American civil war, that he had supplied Austria with arms, and had at one time bought up all the iron in England. He could make or mar any company by buying or selling stock, and could make money dear or cheap as he pleased. All this was said of him in his praise,—but it was also said that he was regarded in Paris as the most gigantic swindler that had ever lived; that he had made that city too hot to hold him; that he had endeavoured to establish himself in Vienna, but had been warned away by the police; and that he had at length found that British freedom would alone allow him to enjoy, without persecution, the fruits of his industry. He was now established pri-

vately in Grosvenor Square and officially in Abchurch Lane; and it was known to all the world that a Royal Prince, a Cabinet Minister, and the very cream of duchesses were going to his wife's ball. All this had been done within twelve months.

The novel—which is extremely long, even for Trollope—describes Melmotte's last and English phase: his meteoric rise to wealth as chairman of the board (with dictatorial powers) of a stock company which amasses a fortune by issuing fraudulent stock on a spurious American railway network. Melmotte's grand ambition is to be a bigwig in Parliament; and toward the end of the novel he is seated, like Lionel Rothschild, as Member for London.[5] His triumph is short-lived; the election victory is no sooner his to enjoy than the swindle is discovered and Melmotte commits suicide. His swift fall from power is handled by Trollope with a degree of mordant artistry that has hardly been surpassed in English fiction: Melmotte entertaining the Emperor of China at a dinner which half the guests decline to attend; Melmotte stumbling into a half-drunken utterance at the House of Commons before he goes home to kill himself—these are unforgettable scenes in what has increasingly come to be recognized as Trollope's masterpiece.

Though the story of Melmotte's malfeasances is central to *The Way We Live Now,* it is by no means coextensive with it. Trollope's novel, which is panoramic in scope, constitutes a large-scale attack on the whole of the Victorian *haut monde,* and Melmotte is not so much the dramatic villain of the piece as he is Trollope's focal point for the vulgarity and cupidity which are defined in the title of the book. If Trollope regards the upstart Jew as representing The Way We Live Now, his indictment is far too comprehensive to alight on Melmotte alone.[6] Dissolute spendthrifts like Felix Carbury, pretentious bigots like the Longestaffes, unprincipled hangers-on like the Nidderdales and their set, and idiotically envious social climbers like Ladies Monogram and Triplex are only less repulsive than the Jew in proportion as they are sillier and less dangerous. "As I had ventured to take the whip of the satirist into my hand," Trollope notes in defining the impulse behind *The Way We Live Now,* "I went beyond the iniquities of the great speculator who robs everybody, and made an onslaught also on other vices,—on the intrigues of girls who want to get married, on the luxury of young men who prefer to remain single, and on the puffing propensities of authors who desire to cheat the public into buying their volumes."[7] The legendary conflict, we see, is in process of shifting: Trollope is no longer under the illusion that the Jews are to blame for all social ills and that everybody else is blameless. But he makes it painfully clear all the same that he means Melmotte's conquest of London to point up the fatal corruption of a society which tolerates and makes common cause with Jewish opportunists on the order of Melmotte; in a way, the terms are as insulting as they have ever been. Trollope's spokesman in the novel, and one of his two or three decent figures, is a conservative gentleman-farmer, Roger Carbury, a terribly disillusioned *Laudator temporis acti,* who detests the fashionable cash-nexus and dissociates himself from a society compounded of lickspittles to a Jew-swindler.

> Men say openly that he is an adventurer and a swindler. No one pretends to think that he is a gentleman. There is a consciousness among all who speak of him that he amasses his money not by honest trade, but by unknown tricks,—as does a card sharper. He is one whom we would not admit into our kitchens, much less to our tables, on the score of his own merits. But because he has learned the art of making money, we not only put up with him, but settle upon his carcase as so many birds of prey.

Melmotte himself is perhaps too much the symbolic type to be conceived on anything like a thoroughly realistic plane.[8] Trollope, as though to set him apart deliberately from the contemptible figures who hang on to his coattails, repeatedly stresses his gigantic amorality and detachment from human concerns. Even his foolish prattle in Parliament and his inarticulate gropings take on, like Mynheer Peeperkorn's, a certain grandeur and depth; and in his one gesture of defeat, his suicide, he is more like an antique Roman than a Jew. "Such a man rises above honesty," comments one of the few characters in the novel who stands to gain nothing from Melmotte, "as a great general rises above humanity when he sacrifices an army to conquer a nation. Such greatness is incompatible with small scruples. A pigmy man is stopped by a little ditch, but a giant stalks over the rivers." Even when Melmotte's transactions remain vague, Trollope at least assures us that they are incalculably vast.

People said that Mr. Melmotte had a reputation throughout Europe as a gigantic swindler,—as one who in the dishonest and successful pursuit of wealth had stopped at nothing. People said of him that he had framed and carried out long premeditated and deeply laid schemes for the ruin of those who had trusted him, that he had swallowed up the property of all who had come in contact with him, that he was fed with the blood of widows and children.

The phrase about the widows and children reminds us that no matter how far we have traveled from the archetype, somewhere along the line we are bound to be pulled up short by the specter of Barabas; and every so often Trollope treats Melmotte and his Hebrew associates to the conventional old-fashioned epithets: "the horrid, big, rich scoundrel"; "the bloated swindler"; "the vile city ruffian"; "the horrid Jew"; and so forth. Trollope's portrayal of the Jewish vulgarian Brehgert, for example, suggests a good many of the old clichés, though the impulse behind them is a new one.

As soon as [Brehgert] was gone Mr. Longestaffe opened the door and walked about the room and blew out long puffs of breath, as though to cleanse himself from the impurities of his late contact. He told himself that he could not touch pitch and not be defiled! How vulgar had the man been, how indelicate, how regardless of all feeling, how little grateful for the honour which Mr. Longestaffe had conferred upon him by asking him to dinner! Yes;—yes! A horrid Jew! Were not all Jews necessarily an abomination? Yet Mr. Longestaffe was aware that in the present crisis of his fortunes he could not afford to quarrel with Mr. Brehgert.

Such a passage may not cast much credit on the abominated Jew; but it incriminates the speaker a great deal more. The point, of course, is that Longestaffe ought not to do business with these people. As Roger Carbury puts it, "a social connection with the first crossing-sweeper would be less objectionable." Indeed Trollope, even when he speaks through the fundamentally anti-Semitic Roger, has a good deal of grim fun at the expense of his Jew-baiting Christians. Here Brehgert's position in the novel is relevant. Brehgert figures in one of the more caustic sub-plots in the book, the episode involving the Longestaffe daughter who, condemned to a prospect of spinsterhood and genteel poverty, determines, after months of agonizing reappraisal, to accept Brehgert's offer of marriage, only to see him renege on it after she imposes some absurd ultimata. The situation is repulsive to Trollope and ludicrously exemplifies The Way We Live Now: Georgiana, all other prospects having failed, is ready to throw herself at a Jewish arriviste whose presence would not be tolerated in her family; a Jew, moreover, whose instinctive decency cannot conceal the fact that he is "a fat, greasy man," with dyed hair and purple mustaches, the charm of whose face "consisted in a pair of very bright black eyes, which were, however, set too near together in his face for the general delight of Christians. He was stout;—fat all over rather than corpulent,—and had that look of command in his face which has become common to master-butchers, probably by long intercourse with sheep and oxen." What mortifies Georgiana—and what gives the episode its acid power—is the certainty that she is committing an irreparable social blunder and can count on violent scenes with her father—who has no scruples about doing business with one Jew and is dependent on the villainies of another. Georgiana's reflections on the subject of her marriage are a source of rather uncomfortable humor—uncomfortable since they must be read in the light of Roger Carbury's—and Trollope's—equivocal assent to Georgiana's ideas about Jews in society.

Poor Miss Longestaffe! Although she had acknowledged the fact [of her engagement to Brehgert] to Lady Monogram in her desire to pave the way for the reception of herself into society as a married woman, she had not as yet found courage to tell her family. The man was absolutely a Jew;—not a Jew that had been, as to whom there might possibly be a doubt whether he or his father or his grandfather had been the last Jew of the family; but a Jew that was. So was Goldsheiner a Jew, whom Lady Julia Start had married,—or at any rate had been one a short time before he ran away with that lady. She counted up ever so many instances on her fingers of "decent people" who had married Jews or Jewesses. Lord Frederic Framlinghame had married a girl of the Berrenhoffers; and Mr. Hart had married a Miss Chute. She did not know much of Miss Chute, but was certain that she was a Christian. Lord Frederic's wife and Lady Julia Goldsheiner were seen everywhere. Though she hardly knew how to explain the matter even to herself, she was sure that there was at present a general heaving-up of society on this matter, and a change in progress which would soon make it a matter of indifference whether anybody was Jew or Christian. . . .

Had she been alone in the world she thought that she could have looked forward to her destiny with complacency; but she was afraid of her father and mother. . . . And . . . her father,—if he had ever earned for himself the right to be called a Conservative politician by holding a real opinion of his own,—it had been on that matter of admitting the Jews into parliament. When that had been done he was certain that the glory of England was sunk for ever. . . . How could she tell parents such as these that she was engaged to marry a man who at the present moment went to synagogue on a Saturday and carried out every other filthy abomination common to the despised people?

Who is the *bête noire* here? Since Trollope introduces as specimens of their race three Jewish businessmen of whom one is physically odious, another a swindler in the grand manner of a Balzacian monomaniac, and a third—the detestable Cohenlupe—a cowardly sneak, the novel can hardly be said to flatter the Jews. But in reading a passage such as the foregoing we are, of course, expected to remember also that old Longestaffe, who tirelessly denounces the Jews, finds it expedient to enrich himself with their help, and that Georgiana herself has been in the habit of making the fashionably anti-Semitic noises until her engagement to a Jew made that practice inadvisable.

If Trollope's Jews are thus not very much better than the criminal prototypes we have encountered in earlier writers, they are not appreciably worse than the Gentiles either; they are part and parcel of the general corruption. Naturally one does not like to be told that the Jews are symbols of social depravity; such a position, in so far as it is shared by Trollope, is much more explicitly anti-Semitic than the position taken by Dickens in his fairy tale about a dream boy and a traumatic ogre. But for the purpose of this study it is perhaps more pertinent to observe that Trollope has really quite broken with the simplistic tradition that opposes the Jew to the rest of the world. *The Way We Live Now* is much too sophisticated and angry a novel to perpetrate the glib assumptions and melodramatic conflicts which informed the earlier stereotypes. "Almost every character in *The Way We Live Now*," says Michael Sadleir, "is in one way or another a sham. . . . Trollope was angry when he wrote it; and the anger burns through its four hundred thousand words, until one fancies that the whole jerry-built society of scheming women, money-grubbing aristocrats and blatant millionaires must needs go up in the fierce flame of the old novelist's disgusted rage."[9]

The very sweep of Trollope's attack on society-at-large gives to his anathemas a certain democratic quality; and it keeps Melmotte from degenerating into the crude old-fashioned type. True, Brehgert and Cohenlupe, who are kept on the periphery of the story, retain some of the external traits of the stereotype with their greasy hair and fat stomachs; but though Melmotte is also subjected occasionally to the customary invectives, there is a general attempt, if not quite to humanize him, at least to individualize him. Trollope accomplishes this in a number of ways. Melmotte's purely physical features, for example, though not prepossessing, are no longer the familiar distorted features of the caricature in which the nose proclaims the usurer, but are treated with an attempt at something like photographic realism. A family portrait of the Melmottes reveals that

> Melmotte himself was a large man, with bushy whiskers and rough thick hair, with heavy eyebrows, and a wonderful look of power about his mouth and chin. This was so strong as to redeem his face from vulgarity; but the countenance and appearance of the man were on the whole unpleasant, and, I may say, untrustworthy. He looked as though he were purse-proud and a bully. She was fat and fair,—unlike in colour to our traditional Jewesses; but she had the Jewish nose and the Jewish contraction of the eyes. There was certainly very little in Madame Melmotte to recommend her, unless it was a readiness to spend money on any object that might be suggested to her by her new acquaintances.

The Jew-villain, we see, is now allowed to harbor a wife. Though there is every suggestion that Melmotte beats her and has reduced her to a condition of permanent terror and awe, there she is, an unusual figure in the history of the legend, showing up the Jew in the role of husband—a very bad husband, a wife-beating husband, but nevertheless one who keeps the family together and has been to that extent civilized and domesticated. For figures like Shylock and Fagin, as we saw, a wife would have been totally out of place, for it is one of the conditions of their personalities that they shall nurse their grievances, hatch their plots, and shoulder their responsibilities quite by themselves; there must be no suggestion of a home to come back to, of a society to appeal to. Melmotte, on the other hand, for all his Napoleonic aloofness, defines himself by the degree to which he reflects the prevailing social climate; and as member in good standing it is quite proper for him to lord it over a tightly knit, if unhappy, household. Madame Melmotte's position in the context of this study is the more exceptional when it is remembered that by and large the good Jews in literature are no more permitted to play the husband than the wicked ones, if only because their widowerhood is productive of the desired sentimentality. Nathan the Wise, Sheva, Isaac, Lever's Oppovich, Reade's Levi, Trollope's Father Trendelssohn, have all buried their wives by the time we make their acquaintance, and the author takes care to make some pathetic allusion to their dead Rebeccas, Rachels, and Leahs. Indeed Jewish family life, apart from the legendary father-daughter relationship, seems to have been, except for Trollope and George Eliot, something of an unfamiliar area to English novelists, explored chiefly—from the inside—by a number of such minor Jewish writers as Benjamin Farjeon, Amy Levy, and Israel Zangwill. In the history of the stereotype, Madame Melmotte is thus very much of a *rara avis.*

The Melmottes have a daughter, Marie, who is, like her mother, a congenitally speechless female—but now there seems to be considerable doubt whether Marie is the daughter of "that Jewish-looking woman" at all. It is odd how family dislocations and mystifications get themselves written into novels about Jews: heroes who have been disinherited or disowned or whose parents have willfully misplaced them are rampant in *Deronda, Ivanhoe, Oliver Twist, Coningsby,* Levin's *That Boy of Norcott's,* Bulwer's *My Novel,* and Marryat's *Japhet in Search of a Father*—as though there existed in the writer's mind some profound inner tension between the ideas of the Jew and the orphan. So far as Marie is concerned, "Enquiries had been made, but not successfully, as to the date of the Melmotte marriage. There was an idea abroad that Melmotte had got his first money with his wife, and had gotten it not very long ago. Then other people said that Marie was not his daughter at all. Altogether the mystery was rather pleasant as the money was certain." Whether her birth has been properly legitimated or not, Marie is at all events an interesting and by no means disagreeable variation on the Beautiful Jewess. Beautiful she is not. She does not positively look like a Jewess. Moreover, "she was not clever, and she was not a saint. But then neither was she plain, nor stupid, nor, especially, a sinner. She was a little thing, hardly over twenty years of age . . . who seemed to be overwhelmed by the sense of her own position."

Marie's desertion of her father and her attempt to turn away with the Christian lover becomes, in Trollope's hand, almost a parody of the Jessica story. The Lorenzo of the novel is Felix Carbury, a dissipated playboy, gambler, and drunkard, who is dependent for his penny antes on the prostituted literary labors of his widowed mother—the relationship suggests Henry James's "Greville Fane."[10] Marie's relationship with Felix gains added piquancy by being juxtaposed with the story of Brehgert and Georgiana Longestaffe, in which the roles are reversed, the girl being a Gentile and the suitor being a Jew. Up to a point Trollope sticks to the traditional story pretty closely; for example, Marie, in league with a confidante, schemes to steal her father's jewelry and money and hand it over to her lover preparatory to their flight. But what chiefly interests Trollope about the courtship are the reactions it arouses not only in the parties to the engagement but in the members of their families. Roger Carbury, the normative character in the book, is revolted by the idea of intermarrying with Jews and pleads to keep the family name free of any taint of Melmottery. On the Jewish side, Melmotte himself has no intention of allowing his daughter to squander the Melmotte millions on a spendthrift with streaks of imbecility. Madame Melmotte, in her turn, contemplates Marie's engagement with the frightened listlessness of one who abandoned all powers of positive thinking when she herself married Melmotte. Most eloquently in favor of the marriage is the groom's mother, Lady Carbury, the Ouida of fiction, who is as dishonest in her way as Melmotte is in his, and who desperately puffs the alliance for the same reason that Melmotte opposes it: the Carburies stand to enrich themselves at Melmotte's expense; the marriage will free her from writing unhistorical books on historical subjects, will keep honest critics at arm's length and the bookshelves from groaning under the heavy load of light literature.

There remains the Jew's Daughter herself. In sharp contrast to all the others, Marie Melmotte alone grows in stature during the marital crisis. While Felix weakens steadily throughout the novel, Marie turns from a silly goose into a strong-willed young woman; and in view of her anserine beginnings, even her thefts and underhanded stratagems become signs of fortitude and character. Here is Trollope's portrait of Lorenzo and Jessica, the way they look now:

It was evident that she did not care to what extent she braved her father on behalf of her lover, and now she coolly proposed to rob him. But Sir Felix saw no reason why he should not take advantage of the money made over to the girl's name, if he could lay his hands on it. He did not know much of such transactions, but he knew more than Marie Melmotte, and could understand that a man in Melmotte's position should want to secure a portion of his fortune against accidents, by settling it on his daughter. . . . Marie, who had no doubt been regarded as an absolutely passive instrument when the thing was done, was now quite alive to the benefit which she might possibly derive from it. Her proposition, put into plain English, amounted to this: "Take me and marry me without my father's consent,—and then you and I together can rob my father of the money which for his own purposes he has settled upon me." He had looked upon the lady of his choice as a poor, weak thing, without any special character of her own, who was made worthy of consideration only by the fact that she was a rich man's daughter; but now she began to loom before his eyes as something bigger than that. She had not been afraid of her brutal father when he, Sir Felix, had trembled before him. She had offered to be beaten, and killed, and chopped to pieces on behalf of her lover. There could be no doubt about her running away if she were asked.[11]

There is, as we can see, a good deal of the traditional Jessica in Marie's relation to Melmotte. The analogy breaks down, totally and ruthlessly, with the figure of the lover, whose character suggests in a flash the difference between the way we lived then and the way we live now: Trollope's Lorenzo is as horrible a creature in his fashion as Trollope's Shylock is in his. This time there is no escape to Belmont and nobody lives happily ever after. The morning of the lovers' flight finds Felix bedridden with a hangover, having the night before gambled away the fare to America that Marie stole for him. Marie, who is to meet her lover en route, is seized by the police, thanks to her father's effective vigilance. The triumph, in so far as it is anybody's, is Shylock's. After the great man's suicide, the lovers are free to marry; but Marie has been permanently soured on Felix by his final act of disloyalty; by degrees she hardens into a penny-wise and pound-conscious spinster; at the end of the novel she emigrates to the States with the timid Madame who may or may not be her mother, there to pursue the portion of, perhaps, a Jamesian heiress,

The foregoing account of Trollope's novel not only has neglected some of its most impressive general qualities but has necessarily ignored a number of those details about the Jewish monopolist which relate *The Way We Live Now* to the rest of this study. It is extremely difficult, in excerpt or paraphrase, to suggest Trollope's masterful presentation of Melmotte in his commercial capacity: presiding at staff meetings, conniving at fraud with Jews and Americans, parceling out favors to his useful associates and withholding them from useless ones. Trollope, when he is not being a somewhat self-conscious buffoon, brings to bear on his portrait of Melmotte a vast amount of inside information; and it is by the sheer mass of such accumulated detail that Melmotte lives in the memory as a considerably more realistic Jew-villain than most of his precursors.

In the history of the stereotype Melmotte stands out as a fitting complement to Fagin: the one a receiver of stolen goods, operating at the lowest level of economic malpractice; the other an influential speculator, operating at the highest. Fagin reflects the stereotype in its older and cruder form as it devolved on the greatest of the sensation-novelists; Melmotte suggests a partial corrective to the superannuated bogey type and reflects the interests of the domestic realists who lined up behind Thackeray and George Eliot. Comparing Melmotte and Fagin, one can see why Trollope enjoyed the support of literary critics, and why Dickens could count on the adulation of the public. Dickens had an instinctive sense for popular superstitions and archetypal fears. *Oliver Twist* is not nearly so good a novel as Trollope's, but Fagin has the advantage of appealing to elements that are not satisfied by a critical exposé of The Way We Live Now.

My Novel

"It is perhaps improper to class all his novels together," Trollope wrote of Bulwer-Lytton's fiction, "as he wrote in varied manners . . . but from all of them there comes the same flavour of an effort to produce effect. The effects are produced, but it would have been better if the flavour had not been there."[12]

The dishonest Jewish tycoon, with residence in Bruton Street, had appeared before Melmotte in the Baron Levy who figures in Bulwer's

My Novel. Levy's entrances and exits are not nearly so important as Melmotte's, either for literature or for the book in which he appears; and *My Novel* is a much less impressive work than *The Way We Live Now,* though it is quite as long, and though Bulwer's critics think highly of it.[13] Nowadays it is no longer easy to see *My Novel* as very much more than a rather incoherent, at times insufferably whimsical study of mid-century English politics, with a great deal of taffeta and Axminster on display for the gratification of the reading public.[14] Like most of Bulwer's stories, *My Novel* is vastly overfurnished with intrigues and intrigants, and it teams with grandiose articles of faith on every page. In the Bulwer canon, *My Novel* follows *The Caxtons,* the story with which Bulwer embarked on his studies of contemporary *mœurs.* Nominally the narrator of *My Novel* is Pisistratus Caxton, Bulwer's idea of a nineteenth-century Trismegistus Shandy.[15] Why a study of English politics should be written after the model of Sterne is not clear. But there is in all of Bulwer so much of the crank that it is pointless to look for explanations; one takes him as he comes and hopes for the best.

For all the elaborate interweavings of plots and sub-plots, *My Novel* is a rather episodic affair. Baron Levy, unlike Melmotte, is not central to the story but figures on the periphery in half a dozen political and domestic conspiracies. At that he does not enter the picture until about page 700, when Bulwer introduces him with an air of having forgotten all about *him.* "Mr. Levy," to give his credentials,

> had been a solicitor by profession. He had of late years relinquished his ostensible calling: and not long since, in consequence of some services towards the negotiations of a loan, had been created a baron by one of the German kings. The wealth of Mr. Levy was said to be only equalled by his good-nature to all who were in want of a temporary loan, and with sound expectations of repaying it some day or other.

For the next five hundred pages or so the Baron walks in and out of salons redolent of *Codlingsby,* moving—one is made to feel—pretty much at Bulwer's pleasure, plotting ruin with volubility and savoir-faire. To give an idea of the antecedents seems a hopeless task, but T. H. S. Escott's plot-synopsis will serve as a short cut. Anybody embarking on *My Novel* needs to be cautioned, however, that Escott's account acutely streamlines Bulwer's plots and does not really do justice to their remarkable complexity.

The two chief personages on whom the action mainly turns are Audley Egerton and Harley L'Estrange. These have been chums at Eton and friends in after-life. The mutual attraction of each to the other arises not from likeness of character, but from dissimilarity. Egerton, the older, the stronger and the more energetic, furnishes a complete contrast to the shy dreamy L'Estrange. L'Estrange is in love with Norah Avenel [*sic*], who is much beneath him and who has been sent by his mother, Norah's patroness, on a visit to be out of his way. Egerton, commissioned by L'Estrange to plead his cause with the young lady, falls in love with her himself. To provide himself with a counter attraction and so to prevent the betrayal of his friend, Egerton rushes into politics. He does, however, after all betray that friend and at the same time undoes himself. Here the chief moral interest of the plot begins. The rest is occupied with gathering up the story's different threads, averting the final blow, and turning revenge to pity. Egerton, humbled and dying, comes out at last as the real hero of *My Novel*.[16]

This is not all there is to the novel, but it is quite enough.[17] It is in connection with Audley Egerton's ministerial phase, which occupies the second half of *My Novel,* that Baron Levy spins his plots. Levy's origins, like Melmotte's, are confused. His ancestry is just exotic enough to give him a touch of the Italianate villain; and though a similar strain of exoticism could be used by novelists like Disraeli and George Eliot to point up the romantic qualities of their Jews, it is plain that a good deal of anti-Jewish prejudice in the nineteenth century continues to be directed against the Jew as alien, whose alienation is underlined by his suspect parentage.

You seldom saw a finer-looking man than Baron Levy . . . so well-preserved—such magnificent black whiskers—such superb teeth! Despite his name and his dark complexion, he did not, however, resemble a Jew—at least externally; and, in fact, he was not a Jew on the father's side, but the natural son of a rich English *grand seigneur,* by a Hebrew lady of distinction—in the opera. After his birth this lady had married a German trader of her own persuasion, and her husband had been prevailed upon, for the convenience of all parties, to adopt his wife's son, and accord to him his own Hebrew name. Mr. Levy, senior, was soon left a widower, and then the real father, though never actually owning the boy, had shown him great attention—had him frequently at his house—initiated him betimes into his own high-born society, for which the boy showed great taste. . . . Indeed he was so useful, so pleasant, so much a man of the world, that he grew intimate with his clients—chiefly young men of rank; was on good terms with both Jews and Christian; and being neither one nor the other, resembled (to use Sheridan's incomparable simile) the blank page between the Old and the New Testament.

Levy's position in the novel turns on his efforts to annihilate Audley Egerton as a public figure and to interfere with Egerton's private enjoyment of Nora Avenel, the girl whom Egerton has lured away from his friend L'Estrange. As a high-powered money-lender Levy has financed Egerton's rise to political office, and, from personal motives which Bulwer keeps heavily concealed lest he have no aces left to play by page 1200, the Baron plots Egerton's fall in hopes of sending him to jail as a defaulter. The motif is a familiar one, though later on Bulwer is going to give it a particularly silly and exasperating twist. To turn Egerton out of office Levy secures the aid of one Leslie Randal, himself a ruthless young Turk in Egerton's own party, Levy forcing Randal's collaboration by threatening to foreclose on his heavily mortgaged family estate. In the light of Randal's own unsavory qualities, it is interesting to note that his one saving grace lies in his attachment to the traditionary values represented by the ancestral home which the Jew is on the verge of appropriating.

If there was one ambitious scheme in [Randal's] calculation which, though not absolutely generous and heroic, still might win its way to a certain sympathy in the undebased human mind, it was the hope to restore the fallen fortunes of his ancient house, and repossess himself of the long alienated lands that surrounded the dismal wastes of the mouldering hall. And now to hear that those lands were getting into the inexorable grip of Levy—tears of bitterness stood in his eyes.[18]

The viewpoint is very close here to Trollope's; and it anticipates the famous complaint in T. S. Eliot's "Gerontion":

My house is a decayed house,
And the jew squats on the window sill, the owner,
Spawned in some estaminet of Antwerp,
Blistered in Brussels, patched and peeled in London.

Though Levy scarcely originates in the Belgian sewer, Bulwer repeatedly stresses the qualities of the cosmopolitan upstart suggested in Eliot's lines. Like Melmotte, Levy foreshadows the stereotype of the internationally potent, vulgarly aggressive parvenu whom we meet, in our own day, in the fiction of Graham Greene.

Vulgar, some might call Mr. Levy, from his assurance, but it was not the vulgarity of a man accustomed to low and coarse society—rather the *mauvais ton* of a person not sure of his own position, but who has resolved to swagger into the best one he can get.

The Baron's style of living was of that character especially affected both by the most acknowledged exquisites of that day, and, it must be owned, also, by the most egregious *parvenus*. For it is noticeable that it is your *parvenu* who always comes nearest in fashion (so far as externals are concerned) to your genuine exquisite.

Elsewhere Levy himself, addressing Randal with some of Shylock's bitterness against the ingrate Christian, who depends on the Jew's capital while disparaging his status, defines the difference between the old aristocracy and the *nouveau riche*:

"Well," said Levy, with great kindness of manner, "I see I pain you; and though I am what my very pleasant guests would call a *parvenu,* I comprehend your natural feelings as a gentleman of ancient birth. *Parvenu!* Ah! is it not strange . . . that no wealth, no fashion, no fame can wipe out that blot. They call me a *parvenu* and borrow my money. They call our friend the wit, a *parvenu,* and submit to all his insolence —if they condescend to regard his birth at all—provided they can but get him to dinner. They call the best debater in the Parliament of England a *parvenu,* and will entreat him, some day or other, to be prime minister, and ask him for stars and garters. A droll world, and no wonder the *parvenus* want to upset it."

If the grievance sounds familiar by now, suggestive of the good rather than the wicked side of the Jew, it loses most of its sympathetic force in the light of Levy's Machiavellian tendency to candid and lucid self-analysis. Indeed Bulwer endows his man with a good deal of the dandy's glib charm as well as an infinite capacity for voluble self-enjoyment. Like the traditional Machiavel, Levy is fond of patting himself on the back, and so he is quite explicit about the sources of his material well-being. "I am now a very rich man. How have I become so? Through attaching myself from the first to persons of expectations, whether from fortune or talent. I have made connections in society, and society has enriched me. I have still a passion for making money. *Que voulez-vous?* It is my profession, my hobby." Bulwer calls him at one point "that cynical impersonation of Gold" and has Levy compare himself "to the Magnetic Rock in the Arabian tale, to which the nails in every ship that approaches the influence of the loadstone fly from the planks, and a shipwreck per day adds its waifs to the Rock." The simile fits Melmotte even more neatly than it fits Levy, but it is difficult to imagine Melmotte applying the conceit to himself in so many words. Between the two of them Melmotte and Levy suggest alternative means toward the same end, the misuse of power; and thus the two complement each other admirably. Melmotte's appropriate habitat is his executive suite; Levy's is a fashionable London salon. Melmotte tantalizes his colleagues because no one really knows what the great man is up to; Levy compels discipleship from his hirelings because he tells them precisely what he is up to.

It is in the privacy of his thoughts that a Machiavel needs to be watched; and it is in the soliloquy that he traditionally reveals himself in his most odious colors. Levy *chez soi* degenerates from a halfway realistic latter-day monopolist to the crude melodramatic Jew-villain, the "sleek destroyer" with his "hard and sinister eyes" thirsting for revenge in words which might be prosaic transcriptions of some boast by Barabas.

> The Baron sate thoughtful. ". . . *this* man! . . . I shall have *him* for life. And should he fail in this project, and have but this encumbered property—a landed proprietor mortgaged up to his ears—why, he is my slave. . . . And . . . if I lost ten thousand pounds—what then? I can afford it for revenge!—afford it for the luxury of leaving Audley Egerton alone with penury and ruin, deserted, in his hour of need, by the pensioner of his bounty—as he will be by the last friend of his youth—when it so pleases me—me whom he has called 'scoundrel!' And whom he—" Levy's soliloquy halted there, for the servant entered to announce the carriage. And the Baron hurried his hand over his features, as if to sweep away all trace of the passions that distorted their smiling effrontery.

As a matter of fact, Levy's soliloquy halts where it halts and the servant enters when he enters because Levy has been on the point of giving away Bulwer's cherished secret three hundred pages too soon; and the secret brings us round to Levy's private life and resentments. For while Levy has been busy with his political stratagems against Egerton, Levy the homebreaker has not been idle. The disposition of the parties is as follows. Egerton, having married Nora Avenel over his friend L'Estrange's objection, has begun to neglect his wife, though she is about to bear his child and both she and Egerton continue to be much devoted to each other. At this point Levy reappears. "His crowning hour," Bulwer says grandly, "was ripe." He insinuates himself into Nora's confidence, offers to bring Egerton round to the fulfillment of his marital duties, and in the same breath darkly hints that Nora is *enceinte* without benefit of clergy:

> He used ambiguous phrases, that shocked her ear and tortured her heart, and thus provoked her to demand him to explain; and then, throwing her into a wild state of indefinite alarm . . . he said, with villainous hypocrisy of reluctant shame, "that her marriage was not strictly legal; that the forms required by law had not been complied with; that Audley, unintentionally or purposely, had left himself free to disown the rite and desert the bride."

Nora, naturally appalled by Levy's news, which, "with lawyer-like show, he contrived to make truth-like to her inexperience," leaves London for the country, where she dies in childbirth under circumstances which seduce Bulwer into much that is lachrymose and declamatory. In situations that call for silence Bulwer can usually be trusted to make a maximum of noise.

Nora's death brings on a scene in which the rival claimants outdo each other in responsive self-recriminations, Egerton assuring L'Estrange that, since Nora never loved him in the first place, L'Estrange has nothing with which to reproach himself. The assurance, though intended to quiet L'Estrange, produces an effect so far the opposite that he bursts a blood-vessel. The scene may be quoted, not only because it hails Egerton's moral regeneration, as Escott views the matter, but because it demonstrates the appalling glibness with which Bulwer makes free with his heroes' blood-vessels.

> "Hold!" exclaimed Harley, with a terrible burst of passion—"you kill her twice to me if you say that! I can still feel that she lives—lives here, in my heart—while I dream that she loved me—or, at least, that no other lip ever knew the kiss that was denied to mine! But if you tell me to doubt *that*;—you—you—" The boy's anguish was too great for his frame; he fell suddenly back into Audley's arms; he had broken a blood-vessel. For several days he was in great danger; but his eyes were constantly fixed on Audley's, with wistful intense gaze. "Tell me," he mut-

tered, at the risk of re-opening the ruptured veins, and of the instant loss of life—"tell me—you did not mean *that*!" . . .

"Hush, hush—no cause—none—none. I meant but to comfort you, as I thought—fool that I was—that is all!" cried the miserable friend. And from that hour Audley gave up the idea of righting himself in his own eyes, and submitted still to be the living lie—he, the haughty gentleman!

Toward the end of the novel, L'Estrange asks Levy the question which the reader has been intermittently asking himself for six hundred pages: what is it Levy has against Egerton that he keeps scheming against him? Bulwer has supplied stop-gap motives from time to time by suggesting, tenuously enough, that Egerton has insulted Levy in the time-honored tradition of Antonio, and that Levy, in the time-honored tradition of Shylock, has been lying in ambush, waiting to catch him once upon the hip. One might wish that Bulwer had worked out the conflict along these lines; but the answer, when we finally get to it, shows in a flash the whole flimsy pretexts by which Levy has been kept going.

"My lord, my lord," faltered Baron Levy, "I, too, wooed Nora Avenel as my wife; I, too, had a happier rival in the haughty worldling who did not appreciate his own felicity; I too—in a word, some women inspire an affection that mingles with the entire being of a man, and is fused with all the currents of his life-blood. Nora Avenel was one of those women."

"Harley," says Bulwer, "was startled." He may well be. To see "the sleek destroyer" unmask himself as a frustrated lover turns out, after all, to be an unforgivably theatrical *coup*. One may argue that within the compass of six hundred pages all kinds of moral metamorphoses and somersaults are possible; and there seems to be no reason why Levy's romantic despair should not serve as a plausible incentive for criminal action. But as Bulwer manipulates him, Levy deteriorates in the final pages into the worst sort of melodramatic creature, who rushes onstage just before the curtain falls to cry: my heart bleeds. Compared with Levy's feeble cues for passion, there is something fine and civilized in Melmotte's impervious silence; and beside Levy's slickly sentimental curtain-speech Melmotte's suicide takes on a degree of pathos which falls just short of having tragic possibilities. "In all that he did," Trollope wrote of Bulwer, "affectation was his fault."[19]

Levy's profession of love is not quite his last say; at the conclusion of his interview with L'Estrange he reverts to the old formula of the insulted and the injured Jew.

"No, my lord, I cannot forgive [Egerton]. You he has never humiliated—you he has never employed for his wants, and scorned as his companion. You have never known what it is to start in life with one whose fortunes were equal to your own, whose talents were not superior. Look you, Lord L'Estrange—in spite of this difference between me and Egerton, that he has squandered the wealth that he gained without effort, while I have converted the follies of others into my own ample revenues—the spendthrift in his penury has the respect and position which millions cannot bestow upon me. You would say that I am an usurer, and he is a statesman. But do you know what I should have been, had I not been born the natural son of a peer? . . . The blot on my birth, and the blight on my youth—and the knowledge that he who was rising every year into the rank which entitled him to reject me as a guest at his table . . . all this made me look on the world with contempt; and, despising Audley Egerton, I yet hated him and envied."

Though Levy falls back on the standard excuses and phraseology of the bad Jew in his defensive moments, we may detect behind his complaint a significantly new note: Levy's vindictiveness is no longer really aimed against the Gentile's Jew-baiting but against social prejudices in a much wider sense. Levy resents not so much the stain on his Jewishness but the stain on his equivocal status as a *nouveau riche*. The Victorian novelists were not, on the whole, kindly disposed toward the rising aristocracy of Croesuses. Dickens bitterly lampooned them in *Our Mutual Friend*; for Trollope, as we saw, the plutocracy represented some of the worst features of the Victorian upper crust. Similarly in *My Novel* Bulwer attacks Levy chiefly in terms of a socio-economic and political position that Bulwer feels to be an undesirable one. The Baron's Judaism becomes finally irrelevant except in so far as being a Jew implies the maintenance of material values which Bulwer detests. The capitalist's creed seems to bother Bulwer as much as it bothers Trollope, and in a fine expository passage he describes Levy's grounds of political action:

Randal had hitherto supposed that this notorious tuft-hunter—this dandy capitalist—this money-lender, whose whole fortune had been wrung from the wants and follies of an aristocracy, was naturally a firm supporter of things as they are—how could things be better for men like Baron Levy? But the usurer's burst of democratic spleen did not surprise his precocious and acute faculty of observation. He had before remarked, that it is the persons who fawn most upon an aristocracy, and profit the most by the fawning, who are ever at heart its bitterest disparagers. Why is this? Because one full half of democratic opinion is made up of envy.

Levy defends his status, as we have seen, by a reference to values which are, in a curious way, reminiscent of the values suggested in *Ivanhoe*: between the spendthrift and the usurer commend me to the usurer. But Levy no longer sees himself maligned primarily for being a Jew, though he plies a traditionally Jewish trade and is fitted out with most of the accoutrements of the type—with his duplicity, his fawning, his obsessive appetite for vengeance. He thinks of himself as an Englishman, with a dash of the foreigner in him. In a recent book about a family of wealthy London Jews, the English novelist C. P. Snow has amusingly described the viewpoint of an Anglicized Jewess who, as early as 1816, takes her national commitments sufficiently for granted to allow herself the following complacent remark: "It must be admitted that in the arts of the toilette and the cuisine France excels our country: but we hearten ourselves as English people that in *everything* essential we are infinitely superior to a country which shows so many profligacies that it is charitable to attribute them to their infamous revolution."[20] Baron Levy, though he would not be likely to underwrite the political sentiments suggested in this passage, considers himself as much a full-fledged citizen of London as Snow's character. He merely dislikes being cut and undercut for being a parvenu. The issue is no longer one of strictly Jewish disability.

Moreover, by the second half of the century, intermarriage between Christians and Jews needed no longer to be regarded as a case of extravagant miscegenation; and this enabled novelists to create fringe characters like Levy, whose ancestry does not, on both sides of the family tree, point back either to the ghetto or to the Diaspora. It is not by chance that the problem of intermarriage comes up in a good many Victorian novels. In one way or another intermarriage takes place or is contemplated in Trollope's *Nina Balatka* and *The Way We Live Now,* Lever's *That Boy of Norcott's,* Eliot's *Deronda,* Disraeli's *Tancred,* Besant's *Rebel Queen,* Bulwer's *Leila,* Du Maurier's

The Martian. The old story of the Gentile who loved a Jewish girl still exerts its spell, either as a romance or as a vehicle for serious discussion.

Melmotte and Levy fairly represent, I think, the stereotype as he looked to the mid-Victorians. What generalizations can we make about him? He has at least an even chance of being tremendously rich and bears a certain unflattering resemblance to Lionel Rothschild. On the stock exchange he has recouped most of Shylock's losses and recaptured some of the grandiose mercantile success of the Marlovian Jew. He is still a money-lender or peculator, and as unscrupulous as ever. He tends to be rather more cynical and amoral than his forbears used to be; for example, he no longer practices extortion because he hates Christians, but because he likes to enrich himself. If he continues to be a "jew" in the vulgar acceptance of the term, in his commercial ethics, he has come a long way toward being politically assimilated. He not only walks and talks with Christians nowadays, but eats and drinks with them. Conservative England continues to distrust him as an arriviste and upstart. To himself a cunning and successful citizen, he remains to others something of a rare Italianated Jew, the Hebrew charlatan from the South, Disraeli the way Carlyle saw him. He has quite ceased to be a bogey.

Deprived of his crudely traumatic qualities, the Jew has dwindled into a quite secular Shylock. He was allowed to keep a wife or adore a mistress. If his daughter ran off with a Christian, the novelist no longer needed to insist on her conversion, though the elopement was likely to create a family scandal. On the whole, it was fashionable to contemplate the Jew from a perspective that passed for realism. Beside the sensational gargoyles—the kidnappers and poisoners and cannibals—promoted by the Age of Belief, the Victorian Jew no doubt looks comparatively sane and domesticated. Even so, his realistic qualities are all too often exhausted by the novelist's attention to his exquisite furniture and incriminating finances. By 1870 no English novelist had really improved much, if at all, on Balzac's Baron de Nucingen. Realism consisted not in seeing the Jew steadily and whole, but in treating the English reading public to the edifying and detailed scandals of the very rich.

Constantius. . . . Little by little I began to feel that I cared less for certain notes than for others. I say it under my breath—I began to feel an occasional temptation to skip. Roughly speaking, all the Jewish burden of the story tended to weary me.

Theodora. . . . As for the Jewish element in *Deronda,* I think it a very fine idea; it's a noble subject. Wilkie Collins and Miss Braddon would not have thought of it, but that does not condemn it. It shows a large conception of what one may do in a novel.

Pulcheria. . . . You cannot persuade me that *Deronda* is not a very ponderous and ill-made story. It has nothing that one can call a subject. A silly young girl and a solemn, sapient young man who doesn't fall in love with her! That is the *donnée* of eight monthly volumes.

HENRY JAMES, "Daniel Deronda: A Conversation" (1876)

VII

The Jew as Hero and Isaiah Reborn: Eliot

More important perhaps than the attempt to humanize the Jew-villain within the prescribed conventions of the day was the revival, on an unprecedented scale, of the impeccable Jew fostered by Lessing and Cumberland. When we get to George Eliot, for example, we find that the whole problem of the Jew in literature has undergone some notable changes since the days of Scott and Dickens. The transition from Dickens to Eliot is evident in writers like Trollope and Bulwer, whose efforts to strip the Jew of his most egregious criminal qualities encouraged them to stress his domestic and realistic vices. It is evident, in a singularly revealing way, in someone like Charles Reade, whose Isaac Levi, one of the fringe characters in *It Is Never Too Late to Mend,* plays the roles of Shylock and Sheva about equally. As an instance in literary schizophrenia, Levi points the interesting moral that between Shylock and Sheva the Jew exhausted most of his literary possibilities.

In Eliot, finally, the Shylock-side of Jewry has almost entirely disappeared and the Sheva-side is distressingly uppermost—distressingly because the picture remains, when all is said and done, almost as one-sided as ever. Eliot's place in this study, if it harks back on the one hand to Cumberland, on the other may be thought of as completing the semi-revolution begun with *Oliver Twist*: Dickens pictured the Jew's sensational vices; Trollope pictured his domestic and credible sins; Eliot celebrates his domestic virtues—and there is an element of the sensationally virtuous in her characters as well.

Although Eliot had, as we know, a number of fairly distinguished late-eighteenth-century precedents for her Jewish paragons, the overall picture had changed very little by the time she picked up the type. It must be remembered that characters on the order of Nathan and Sheva were, in their own day, fairly isolated and exceptional figures, hopelessly outnumbered by the wicked stage-Jews whom they were originally intended to supplant. And whereas by 1876, when *Daniel Deronda*[1] was published, the good Jew was as comfortably installed in English literature as the criminal Jew, he had precious little to show for the hundred years which separated *Deronda* from *Nathan the Wise*. He had grown somewhat in public stature; he could propagate political doctrines tending to Zionism; like his antipode, he had kept pace with his time far enough to control international finances. For if Rothschilds sat for the portraits of Melmotte and Levy, they were also accessible to the flattering brushstrokes of Disraeli. But, looking at the lot of them, one would not really guess from their speech habits that a century had passed since Sheva made his original plea for tolerance. The voice is still the voice of the humiliated and oppressed Jew, the victim of irrational prejudices, who freely extends to his Christian neighbors the charity which they insist on withholding from him; it is still the author talking, making generalized assumptions in defense of Jews, the voice of the ventriloquist audible behind the dummy.

Purpose

In the eighty years since Henry James, speaking through the mouth of Constantius, professed to be wearied by "all the Jewish burden of the story," the "Jewish half" of *Daniel Deronda* has been so roundly condemned by all subsequent critics that it is difficult to say anything fresh on the subject. "The conception of Daniel's character and story arises out of a conscious—almost a propagandist—intention," Joan Bennett writes in her admirable study of Eliot. "One is tempted to assert that the part of the book concerning Gwendolen is a success and the part concerning Daniel a failure." Gerald Bullett, identically, records that "a great part of *Daniel Deronda* [he means the Jewish part] . . . illustrate[s] with painful force the thesis which so persistently crops up in our study of her art and gives a title to the present chapter ['Intention vs. Inspiration']." Eliot's recent biographers, the Hansons, note that "Mordecai, Mirah and Daniel . . . fail because they are not genuine imaginative creations, but puppets of the mind, put where they are and saying what they say merely to advance the cause which the book advocates." F. R. Leavis, in his famous critique of *Deronda* in *The Great Tradition,* the most elaborate study of Eliot's novel to be undertaken in recent years, would like to see the "bad half," the half "represented by Deronda himself, and what may be called in general the Zionist inspiration" detached from the novel altogether and the good half preserved independently under the title *Gwendolen Harleth.*[2] Finally we may cite Robert Speaight's blunt opinion that *Daniel Deronda,* "smothered by its title," "is remembered as a humorless essay in Jewish national uplift."[3]

Unfortunately the case is unarguable. One may as well listen at once to Eliot in her most didactic mood. The conversation takes place between Mirah and Daniel in Chapter XVII, shortly after he has all but fished her out of the Thames, and represents the first generalized statement in the novel having to do with Jews in the mass.

> ". . . I will tell you" [Mirah is speaking], "I am English-born. But I am a Jewess."
>
> Deronda was silent, inwardly wondering that he had not said this to himself before, though any one who had seen delicate-faced Spanish girls might simply have guessed her to be Spanish.
>
> "Do you despise me for it?" she said presently in low tones, which had a sadness that pierced like a cry from a small dumb creature in fear.

"Why should I?" said Deronda. "I am not so foolish."

"I know many Jews are bad."

"So are many Christians. But I should not think it fair for you to despise me because of that."

One is not to suppose that such complacent disputes are likely to occur between two characters one of whom has been on the point of drowning herself two minutes earlier, while the other has been busy with the customary rescue attempts. It is clear that Eliot is all the time putting her own humanitarian dogmas into the mouths of her characters, even in dramatic contingencies which peculiarly illuminate the vanity of dogmatizing. The situation, as I have said, is not new: Rebecca, in the throes of passion and the depths of danger, will stop long enough to lecture Ivanhoe on the scandalous treatment of medieval Jewry; Reade's Levi, on the point of being evicted and sent packing, straightway translates his present grievance into a platform speech. Eliot's characters in *Daniel Deronda* talk unceasingly in this way; it is what has so consistently been held against a book which demonstrates too ostentatiously that it was written, in Eliot's own words, "on purpose to ennoble Judaism."[4] Sheva, we recall, was similarly engineered "on principle"; so was Harrington. "Instead of feeling life itself," James was to write, "it is 'views' upon life that she tries to feel."[5]

It is a pity that all Eliot's Jewish characters tend to polemicize "the Jewish problem" quite so blatantly and thus deteriorate into talking puppets. It is doubly distressing in the case of Mordecai, not only because he talks more lugubriously than anybody else in the book but because his portrayal comes closest to what it is customary to designate "an ambitious failure." In Mordecai Eliot had it almost in her to create something like a new myth, a myth which Disraeli had rather ineptly anticipated in *David Alroy* as early as 1833 and which Meredith picked up more effectively four years after *Deronda* in the hero of his *Tragic Comedians*: the myth of the Jew as political man, as social prophet and Isaiah reborn, who takes Sheva's grievances as a point of departure for political action, and who translates Sheva's defensive plea for greater tolerance into a positive plea for greater national or racial or territorial recognition. Hitherto the good Jew had been too far depressed into his isolated social role to voice anything stronger than a purely private protest against being cheated out of his ordinary deserts as a human being. Why, so ran the standard complaint, are Christians so hateful to us; why do they refuse to recognize our decent qualities and prevent us from going about our businesses? Mordecai takes this complaint and raises it to the level of a public program. In a perceptive short tribute to *Daniel Deronda,* written to celebrate the seventy-fifth anniversary of its publication, Sol Liptzin admirably formulated this attempt of Eliot's to introduce a fundamentally original type; and his formulation is the more serviceable in that it defines the differences between the earlier Jewish paragon as Cumberland conceived him and his descendant as he comes up in Eliot, Disraeli, and Meredith.

> The most important layers that made up the English legend of the Jew were, in chronological order, the theological, the economic, the romantic, and the realistic. To these four, *Daniel Deronda* added a fifth layer, the heroic, and in the three quarters of a century since the appearance of the novel this layer has come ever more to the fore. . . .
>
> The third layer . . . was the legend of the angelic Jew, an exotic picturesque figure akin to the gypsy, a saintly sage about whom there was a gleam of past glory and whose daughter was beautiful, kind, and suffering. Richard Cumberland, Walter Scott, Byron, Shelley, and others idealized this museum-specimen of ancient days, but none of these writers was interested in the future of the Jews. . . . *Daniel Deronda* superimposed a fifth layer on the other four . . . the legend of Israel Reborn.[6]

As a substantive discrimination between Cumberland's kind of paragon and Eliot's, Liptzin's typology seems to me the soundest possible. At worst, it ignores the equally fundamental similarities: the tendency to idealize the characters beyond recognition, to invest them with a major grievance and little else, to turn them loose on the reading public with set speeches. There may be some prior excuse for this in the case of Mordecai, for it is, I imagine, in the nature of prophets and resurrected Isaiahs to spend themselves mostly in speechmaking. Mordecai's failure as a convincing character partly grows out of Eliot's tendency to confuse rather woolly ideals with explicit doctrine, partly out of her inability, when dealing with Mordecai, to visualize the appropriate mise-en-scène—writing, one is made to feel, in an inspired frenzy without knowing unerringly what it is she is saying. Whenever Mordecai begins to talk, Speaight notes, "it is clear that George Eliot's enthusiasm has taken leave of her critical senses and that we are in for an outflow of moral fervor."[7] As a result, conversation flags and exhortation of a vague (though burning) character takes over.

"It will be seen—it will be declared," said Mordecai triumphantly. "The world grows, and its frame is knit together by the growing soul; dim, dim at first, then clearer and more clear, the consciousness discerns remote stirrings. As thoughts move within us darkly, and shake us before they are fully discerned—so events—so beings: they are knit with us in the growth of the world. You have risen within many like a thought not fully spelled: my soul is shaken before the words are all there. The rest will come—it will come."

"Such laboured nothings in so strange a style / Amaze the unlearned." What Mordecai is really talking about is his plan for an independent Jewish state (he hardly talks about anything else when given half a chance), but it would be difficult to gather this from the above passage. It is all woolly vagueness, delivered, one feels, in a sort of dramatic limbo; one has not the sense that there is an interlocutor present to pick up Mordecai's orotund phrases; one has not even the consciousness of Mordecai's own physical presence, only of a voice lulling us to sleep with sad and necessary panaceas.[8] Listening to these endless recitals one might allow that "Madam, if we only sat down, this would be a comedy," were one not stopped by the reflection that of course Mordecai is seated all the time, hunched over his dusty and prophetic lore, dying a little ostentatiously, passing on his program to the beautiful young man who is fast becoming as eloquently mummified as the Prophet himself. This impression of being tuned in on a Sunday morning broadcast when one merely wants to tune in on a human being talking to another human being persists even in passages in which the Prophet is positively boring into the Assistant Prophet:

"You will be my life: it will be planted afresh; it will grow. You shall take the inheritance; it has been gathering for ages. The generations are crowding on my narrow life as a bridge: what has been and what is to be are meeting there; and the bridge is breaking. . . . You will take the inheritance which the base son refuses because of the tombs which the plough and harrow may not pass over or the gold-seeker disturb: you will take the sacred inheritance of the Jew."

"Deronda had become as pallid as Mordecai," Eliot comments in this place; the adjective could hardly be more apt. But Eliot, for one, wholly believes in Mordecai's beliefs, or at any rate believes that he (and she) know unmistakably what it is he believes in, with the result that her own prose sinks almost to the same deadly level as his whenever she comes near him. "Despondency, conjured up by his own words, had floated in and hovered about him with eclipsing wings."

This is not excellent English. Mordecai, as the most verbose of the lot, merely highlights a defect that all the major Jewish characters share with him. Mirah's locutions are often as exasperating as anything her prophetic brother has to offer:

"It darted into my mind that the unhappiness in my life came from my being a Jewess, and that always to the end the world would think slightly of me and that I must bear it, for I should be judged by that name; and it comforted me to believe that my suffering was part of the affliction of my people, my part in the long song of mourning that has been going on through ages and ages."

In her splendid essay on George Eliot, Virginia Woolf wrote:

The more one examines the great emotional scenes the more nervously one anticipates the brewing and gathering and thickening of the cloud which will burst upon our heads at the moment of crisis in a shower of disillusionment and verbosity. It is partly that her hold upon dialogue . . . is slack; and partly that she seems to shrink with an elderly dread of fatigue from the effort of emotional concentration. She allows her heroines to talk too much. . . . "Whom are you going to dance with?" asked Mr. Knightley, at the Westons' ball. "With you, if you will ask me," said Emma; and she has said enough. Mrs. Casaubon would have talked for an hour and we should have looked out of the window. . . .

"I have always been finding out my religion since I was a little girl," says Dorothea Casaubon. "I used to pray so much—now I hardly ever pray. I try not to have desires merely for myself. . . ." She is speaking for them all. That is their problem.[9]

In their speech-habits—their tendency to say not what is in *their* minds but what is in the author's mind—and in their idealized character and behavior, Eliot's Jewish people, then, are not at bottom significantly discriminated from their eighteenth-century prototypes. Though their speeches ring a political and prophetic note totally absent from Sheva's domestic concerns, they manage to be quite as long-winded and wooden as their precursors used to be. Their role is still to articulate a position instead of acting it out. It is not for nothing that Mordecai and Daniel are almost purely passive heroes: they are much too busy defining the parts they are meant to play in a novel which is less distinguished for its plot lines than for the multiplex viewpoints it endeavors to bring together on the Jewish question.

But it is in this sense also, it seems to me, that Eliot's Jewish group finally part company from any of the Jews we have seen. For their function is to occupy particular ethical and intellectual positions in a novel that is dialectic in intention: a variety of viewpoints are brought to bear on a particular problem—the problem of the Jew in a secularized society—and appropriate figures are invented to incorporate the respective views. It is one reason why Eliot's Jews talk so much. The point to be made here is that they are no longer justifying themselves to the Christians, but as between one Jew and another. Naturally this does not justify a wooden character to posterity.

Dialectic: The Minor Characters

Of the original Shylock myth, as I have tried to trace it through the mid-Victorians, Eliot merely retains the relationship of the repulsive and thieving father and the idealized daughter. But this relationship is no longer in any way central to the story. Lapidoth himself has dwindled into an almost supernumerary figure, of no dramatic importance in his own right, useful chiefly in so far as he casts light on his daughter—not, as used to be the custom, the other way around. It is as though Abigail, Jessica, and Rebecca had now stepped into the center of the arena while Barabas, Shylock, and Isaac had been crowded to the periphery. Lapidoth, we are to understand, is merely another one of a dozen Jewish types, more effective in his brief appearances than Eliot's pale prolocutors, but no more significant in the narrative than little Jacob Cohen. Shylock's function is no longer one of contrast with the Christians in the novel but with the other Jews. The latter, in fact, dissociate themselves from him with somewhat the same degree of inner bias with which the Christian figures in earlier works were in the habit of dissociating themselves from the Jewish characters. Mordecai and Mirah are still willing to provide sanctuary for their father, but this obligation is no longer second nature to them; it is, on the contrary, explicitly polemicised by both of them. That is, they tell Lapidoth in so many words that they are ready to take him into their household "because he happens to be their father" and because it is one's duty, as a Jew, to acknowledge one's familial ties. But neither of them makes any secret of the fact that they are ashamed of him. The filial affection of Abigail and Rebecca has given way to the affection between siblings. (Regarded in this way, Mirah and Mordecai may be thought of as Jewish descendants of Maggie and Tom Tulliver.)

Lapidoth represents the chief link with the Shylock tradition, and it is, as I have said, a tenuous link at best. Like Shylock he is basically a coward who, in emergencies, falls back on the excuse of illness, of hysteria, of "not being well."

> Lapidoth stopped short . . . not from lack of invention, but because he had reached a pathetic climax, and gave a sudden sob, like a woman's, taking out hastily an old yellow silk handkerchief. He really felt that his daughter had treated him ill—a sort of sensibility which is naturally strong in unscrupulous persons, who put down what is owing to them, without any *per contra*.

If anything, Lapidoth's conduct is even more disreputable than Shylock's, who at least had his love for Jessica to recommend him; whereas Lapidoth is base enough to try to procure for Mirah—a harsh echo of Barabas's intentions with respect to Abigail. For the rest, his main business in the novel is to keep Mirah at a certain energizing pitch of anxiety and, in his one fine and funny scene, to steal a ring from under Daniel Deronda's nose: again it may be noted that it is not Jessica nowadays who steals the father's jewelry but the father who robs property that is symbolically identified with the daughter. Eliot, who is famous for the way in which she describes the interim between the acting of a dreadful thing and its first motion, wonderfully manipulates Lapidoth's mental insurrections as he glides, slowly, toward his robbery.

> His rambling eyes quickly alighted on the ring that sparkled on the bit of dark mahogany. During his walk, his mind had been occupied with the fiction of an advantageous opening for him abroad, only requiring a sum of ready money, which, on being communicated to Deronda in private, might immediately draw from him a question as to the amount of the required sum. . . . But now, in the midst of these airy conditions preparatory to a receipt which remained indefinite, this ring, which on Deronda's finger had become familiar to Lapidoth's envy, suddenly shone detached, and within easy grasp. Its value was certainly below the smallest of the imaginary sums that his purpose fluctuated between; but then it was before him as a solid fact, and his desire at once leaped into the thought (not yet an intention) that if he were quietly to pocket that ring and walk away he would have the means of comfortable escape from present restraint, without trouble, and also without danger; . . . Lapidoth had never committed larceny; but larceny is a form of appropriation for which people are punished by law; and to take this ring from a virtual relation, who would have been willing to make a much heavier gift, would not come under the head of larceny. Still, the heavier gift was to be preferred, if Lapidoth could only make haste enough in asking for it, and the imaginary action of taking the ring, which kept repeating itself like an inward tune, sank into a rejected idea. He satisfied his urgent longing by resolving to go below . . . but—by no distinct change of resolution, rather by a dominance of desire like the thirst of the drunkard—it so happened that in passing the table his fingers fell noiselessly on the ring, and he found himself in the passage with the ring in his hand. It followed that he put on his hat and quitted the house. The possibility of again throwing himself on his children receded into the indefinite distance.[10]

With Lapidoth we have already exhausted the "bad Jews" in the book. It is convenient to consider some of the other Jewish elements Eliot introduces into the novel. In his capacity of actor and theatrical entrepreneur, Lapidoth connects up with the artistic group in the book. In *Deronda,* as in life and art more generally, the artistic genius of Judaism finds expression chiefly in music. Readers of *Trilby* will recall that as a performing artist even the noxious Svengali leaves all others in the shade; Disraeli makes a good deal of the Jewish monopoly on composers and vocalists; Baron Levy's mother made her living in the opera. "It is evident," Philipson writes in his comments on *Deronda,*

> why there could be no sculptors or painters among the Jews in ancient or medieval times, for well-nigh all the works of art treated subjects of a religious character, and the Jews, with their strict monotheism and the literal interpretation of the second commandment, could naturally pursue none of the plastic arts. Hence, music and poetry were the only channels in which the aesthetic nature among them could develop itself.[11]

Most of the Jews in *Deronda* in some manner pay their respects to the Muse Polyhymnia, often in contrast—one of the few incidental such contrasts—with the Gentiles, who are positively not musical. There is, most important, the beautiful Mirah, whose vocal talents have been anticipated in the famously silly hymn of Scott's Jewess, and whose natural musical gifts are contrasted with Gwendolen's feeble and frustrated ambitions to sing for a living. There is secondly the great Klesmer, Mirah's tutor and accompanist, allegedly modeled on Franz Liszt, "a felicitous combination of the German, the Sclave, and the Semite," whose allusive name, according to Calisch, demonstrates Eliot's thoroughgoing scholarship in Hebraic matters.[12] We have next Deronda's mother, the Princess Halm-Eberstein, who has farmed out her son to the English upper crust in order to devote herself to her operatic career. Just as Mirah's quiet talents in the *bel canto* line are juxtaposed with her father's flashy preference for backstage theatricals, the Princess's profession in the spectacular art of opera furnishes a deliberate contrast with Daniel's abhorrence of any sort of public display:

> He had often stayed in London with Sir Hugo, who to indulge the boy's ear had carried him to the opera to hear the great tenors, so that the image of the singer taking the house by storm was very vivid to him; but now, in spite of his musical gifts, he set himself bitterly against the notion of being dressed up to sing before all those fine people who did not care about him except as a wonderful toy.

In Daniel his mother's vocal genius lingers on chiefly in an extraordinarily sensitive ear and sensuous speaking-voice that is constantly compared in Gwendolen's mind with Grandcourt's bored metallic accents: "[Daniel's] voice, heard now for the first time, was to Grandcourt's toneless drawl, which had been in her ears every day, as the deep notes of a violoncello to the broken discourse of poultry and other lazy gentry in the afternoon sunshine."

Then there are Eliot's fine and engaging Dutch interiors of the Jewish bourgeois element, represented by the shopkeeper Ezra Cohen and his family, the Prophet's awed and puzzled landlords. As a clan the Cohens foreshadow the capable Jewish middle-class merchants who have since figured in a good many minor Jewish family chronicles. All the Cohens are presented as energetic and sound business people, down to young Jacob, in whose ubiquitous pen-knife we are free to detect a miniature parody on earlier and more potent knives in literature about the Jew. They are also scrupulously honest folk, if a little unpleasantly money-minded, and to that extent they serve as foils to the disgraceful commercial ethics of the Prophet's father.

In stating the contrast between Lapidoth and Ezra Cohen, we are already moving into the area of explicit religious polemic. As a Jew, Cohen, for all his instinctive adherence to material values, is a good orthodox traditionalist, who has taken in the bewildering Mordecai from a consciousness of the Jew's duties to his fellow Jews, who strictly observes the Sabbath ritual, and who wants his children educated toward a thorough understanding of Jewish worship and the Jewish way of life. At worst he lacks those consecrating spiritual qualities which Eliot so tediously admires in Daniel, Mirah, and Mordecai. Lapidoth, on the other hand, represents the worst aspects of the secularized Jew: he treats Judaism as a subject for cheap jokes. To George Eliot, who even after her Coventry apostasy believed devoutly in the need for respecting the superstitions of the faithful,[13] and who kept peopling her novels with spiritual counselors on the order of Dinah Morris and Savonarola, the spectacle of Lapidoth's Jewish anti-Semitism is repulsive; and it is the whole basis of Mirah's distrust that her father "did not follow our religion . . . and I think he wanted me not to know much about it."

On the whole, the nineteenth-century novelists liked their Jews to affirm their Jewishness. In Eliot the assimilationists do not come off well; in Disraeli they are objects of contempt.

> Mesdemoiselles Laurella were ashamed of their race [he writes in *Tancred*], and not fanatically devoted to their religion, which might be true, but certainly was not fashionable. Therese, who was of a less sanguineous temperament than her sister, affected despair and unutterable humiliation, which permitted her to say before her own people a thousand disagreeable things with an air of artless frankness. The animated Sophonisbe, on the contrary, was always combating prejudice, felt persuaded that the Jews would not be so much disliked if they were better known; that all they had to do was to imitate as closely as possible the habits and customs of the nation among whom they chanced to live; and she really did believe that eventually, such was the progressive spirit of the age, a difference in religion would cease to be regarded, and that a respectable Hebrew, particularly well dressed and well mannered, might be able to pass through society without being discovered, or at least noticed.[14]

Eliot, who did not think highly of Disraeli, tends to go along with him on this point; the difference between the two writers remains to be noted presently. "Lady Mallinger," she remarks rather wryly of one of the sillier characters in the novel, "was much interested in the poor girl [Mirah], observing that there was a society for the Conversion of the Jews, and that it was hoped Mirah would embrace Christianity; but perceiving that Sir Hugo looked at her with amusement, she concluded that she had said something foolish." Similarly, the thing that particularly saddens the Prophet is the notion of the Jew who, like his father, mocks what Mordecai calls "the breath of divine thought": "Men would smile at it and say, 'A poor Jew!'—and the chief smilers would be of my own people"; and in the crucial discovery scene Daniel confronts his mother with the creed of the faithful and dutiful: "It is no shame to have Jewish parents—the shame is to disown it."

Of the Princess, Deronda's mother, the reviewer in the *Edinburgh Review* sourly declared that she "is a mere tragedy queen, and as nearly absurd with her theatrical gestures and addresses as it is possible for George Eliot to be."[15] The Princess's dialectic position in the novel is nonetheless of the utmost importance, since it is she who most clearly articulates the position of the assimilationist. For the Princess, Judaism and, by implication, any rigid religious code, consists of a mass of outmoded and dogmatic superstitions that tend to confine the human being to an intolerably narrow role in the modern world and enslave him to a conglomeration of absurd rituals. "'I had a right to be free. I had a right to seek my freedom from a bondage that I hated.'"

"I was to be what [my father] called 'the Jewish woman' under pain of his curse. I was to feel awe for the bit of parchment in the *mezuza* over the door; to dread lest a bit of butter should touch a bit of meat; to think it beautiful that men should bind the *tephillin* on them, and women not—to adore the wisdom of such laws, however silly they might seem to me. I was to love the long prayers in the ugly synagogue, and the howling and the gabbing, and the dreadful fasts, and the tiresome feasts, and my father's endless discoursing about Our People, which was a thunder without meaning in my ears. . . . Teaching, teaching for everlasting—'this you must be,' 'that you must not be'—pressed on me like a frame that got tighter and tighter as I grew."

Daniel and Mordecai are thus thematically identified in the novel not only by their immediate aspirations toward an independent Jewish homeland, but, more fundamentally, by their desire to restore to Judaism the spiritual values from which their parents have turned away either in mockery or hate. Both—the phenomenon is a common one—are orthodox children in revolt against "reformed" parents. Both have a habit of associating the "good" side of Judaism with the very old, and the "bad" side with the contemporary. Listening to them, one often has the impression that the one thing needful for world Jewry is a return to the good Old Testament days. The opposition is found in a dozen lesser novelists, and I shall say a word about them later; the antithesis is at bottom a rhetorical one: "Isaiah, 'Hear, O heavens, and give ear, O earth,' and Levi of Holywell-street—'Old Clothes'—both of them Jews, you observe." Coleridge's antithesis keeps turning up in *Deronda* with exasperating monotony, as though the difference between Jerusalem and Holborn spelled out all moral criteria.

Deronda, not in a cheerful mood, was rashly pronouncing this Ezra Cohen to be the most unpoetic Jew he had ever met with in books or life: his phraseology was as little as possible like that of the Old Testament; and no shadow of a Suffering Race distinguished his vulgarity of soul from that of a prosperous pink-and-white huckster of the present English lineage.

> Ezra Cohen was not clad in the sublime pathos of the martyr, and his taste for money-getting seemed to be favoured with that success which has been the most exasperating difference in the greed of Jews during all the ages of their dispersion. This Jeshurun of a pawnbroker was not a symbol of the great Jewish tragedy; and yet was there not something typical in the fact that a life like Mordecai's . . . was nested in the self-congratulating ignorant prosperity of the Cohens?

The tone in these passages is sporting enough, as though Eliot herself thought Daniel a little foolish for expecting the Messiah to turn up in a pawnbroker's shop. The trouble is that she tacitly assents to Daniel's distinction and to the sense of values implied, and that, in her perfervid moments, she says substantially the same things which, in her frivolous moments, she chides Daniel for thinking. The result is a certain amount of confusion in the Prophet's program. In so far as that program crystallizes into intelligible particulars, it hinges largely on Mordecai's notion of Jewish racial separateness; and I turn here to whatever positive creed emerges from his often unintelligible diction.

Race: Sidonia and Mordecai

The problem of racism, as it bears on the treatment of the Jew in literature, had not been a conspicuous issue for the fictionists with whom I have dealt in the body of this essay. The reasons behind the stereotype were not racist but religious, and eventually the element of economic hostility came to support the religious animus. The question of biology entered the picture mostly as a means toward comic caricature: Jews had long noses and did not bathe. Whatever evils they committed, from infanticide to petty larceny, they committed in the name of their religion and their commerce. These indeed determined most of their physical characteristics. Israelites were exceedingly hirsute because their religion encouraged them to grow beards; they were, of all tribes, the most unwashed, because the ghetto to which their confession abandoned them was intolerably unsanitary; they had long and bony fingers because they stole money, as well as little children. Their physical weakness might be the effect of their crowded and malodorous living quarters or, if they were rich and emancipated, it might equally result from their passing all their time indoors, in the countinghouse, guarding their treasures. But there was no real effort to examine their vices in the light of their racial impurities. For the novelists from Edgeworth to Trollope the single most decisive factor about the Jew-villain was his professional cupidity, and the single most decisive factor about the good Jew was his professional liberality.

Between the religious and the economic impulses the sterotypes, both the good and the bad, pretty well exhausted themselves. Ancillary types and characteristics had, of course, become possible by the end of the century. Deronda is not a businessman but a civilized man of leisure. Sigismund Alvan is an eminence out of the political arena, a leading left-wing ideologist and publicist. Yet even in *Deronda* there would be no story if the hero did not experience intimately religious aspirations. And Alvan's leadership of the socialist party may be interpreted as a profession, on the level of mass politics, of the same Good Samaritanism which characters like Sheva, Montenero, Riah, and David Levi conduct in private. The fact that Alvan, like his historical prototype Ferdinand Lasalle, is a sympathetic theorist of labor movements, intent on bettering the conditions of the working classes, suggests, as I have said, that he may well be the logical culmination of a type which, in the late eighteenth century and throughout the nineteenth, found its exponents in private Jewish philanthropists and idealized Jewish bankers. The ideal remains a resolutely economic one. Liberality in financial practice and a willingness to abide by the traditional forms of religious observances are still, by the end of the century, the credentials of the good Jew, while his antipode remains a cutthroat in the market place and, more often than not, has stopped going to synagogue.

There is no racism in any of this. Jews were measured by standards other than biological ones. But it is a fact worth noting that where the issue of race did come up, as inevitably it did about the middle of the century,[16] it generally occurred in the context of the good Jew rather than in the context of the Shylock-type. In so far as the Jew was at all defined by his racial attributes, the terms of the discussion were not on the whole abusive but complimentary. Certainly there was no question as yet of the Jew's degeneracy. His blood composition was more likely to ennoble than to degrade him. When *The Tragic Comedians* appeared in 1880, it was difficult to ignore the race factor entirely, and so Meredith takes note of it. The odd thing, considering the popular race theories on the Continent, is that in English fiction the Jew's race usually stamped him as a superior beast. Meredith's hero is much too egalitarian in his sympathies to consider such theories more than a fashionable *jeu d'esprit*, but even he will, in a pinch, claim a superior status for his own race, and there is no indication that Meredith intends this to be self-inflation in him.

> We Jews have lusty blood. We are the strong of the earth. . . . We have truly excellent appetites. And why not? Heroical too! Soldiers, poets, musicians; the Gentile's masters in mental arithmetic—keenest of weapons; surpassing him in common sense and capacity for brotherhood. Ay, and in charity; or what stores of vengeance should we not have nourished! Already we have the moneybags. Soon we shall have the chief offices. And when the popular election is as unimpeded as the coursing of the blood in a healthy body, the Jew shall be foremost and topmost, for he is pre-eminently by comparison the brain of these latter day communities. But that is only my answer to the brutish contempt of the Jew. I am no champion of race. I am for the world, for man![17]

Such a claim might sound intolerably strained and aggressive, were it not for the gruff disclaimer in the final sentences and the explicit insistence on the defensiveness of Alvan's position in the sentence that precedes these. No such qualifications attend the writings of Disraeli. Disraeli is as decidedly not "for the world, for man" as he is, positively, the champion of a single race, his own. Among the novelists of the century, who either ignored the problem altogether or treated it marginally, Disraeli is exceptional. "The racial dream," Walter Allen writes, "represented what was probably the stabilizing factor in Disraeli's character."[18] Indeed, Disraeli harps on the racial supremacy of the Jews in a manner that nineteenth-century intellectuals found vapid and that twentieth-century Jews, with the experience of the Master Race behind them, find embarrassing. "The Arabian tribes rank in the first and superior class, together, among others, with the Saxon and the Greek." "The Hebrew is an unmixed race." "The Mosaic Arabs are the most ancient, if not the only, unmixed blood that dwells in the cities." "The fact is, you cannot destroy a pure race. . . . It is a physiological fact; a simple law of nature."[19] "All is race; there is no other truth." "'What is individual character but the personification of race,' said Sidonia, 'its perfection and choice exemplar?'" "'If I were an Arab in race as well as in religion,' said Tancred, 'I would not pass my life in schemes to govern some mountain tribes.'"[20]

Such notions as these are perhaps not permanently meaningful, but they do not sound well. Disraeli's racism is no doubt intended chiefly to support his more fundamental—if equally distressing—idea that the Jews are ordained on historical and religious grounds to assume the moral and intellectual leadership of the universe. Charitable interpreters, indeed, have seen their way clear to explaining away the racist basis of Disraeli's ideology by investing it with rather strained humanitarian motives.[21] The general idea is that the world's governing minority, the pure Sephardim, are impelled by a haunting sense of obligation to the less fortunate races, those stricken millions who have been barred from penetrating "the great Asian mystery." There is a kind of racial philanthropism about figures like Alroy, Sidonia, and Eva. One is made to feel that they would like to lend the Gentiles their blood composition if it could be done. There is nothing positively selfish in their racial claims; can they help it if they were hand-picked by Jehovah to rule supreme? Since they cannot very well diffuse their race among the hundred neediest, they are eager to do the next best thing: to make the benefits which their race has conferred upon them available to the lesser species in such a way that the non-Jew stands to gain the maximum profit from his contact with *homo Sidoniae*. So interpreted Alroy and his descendants begin to bear a certain family resemblance to the good Jews of the main tradition with its insistent Good Neighbor Policy—to "the worthy Hebrew," "the compassionate Israelite," whose dominant characteristic is his single-minded benevolence. But the fact remains that no amount of whitewashing can rationalize away the obtrusiveness of the race factor in Disraeli's philosophy, and modern-day readers may be forgiven for reacting nervously to a code that affirms in so many words that "Race is everything."

It was part of George Eliot's emancipated heritage to find Disraeli's theory of racial supremacy—like everything else about his novels—silly, pretentious, and insincere.

> The fellowship of race [she writes in 1848] to which D'Israeli exultingly refers the munificence of Sidonia, is so evidently an inferior impulse which must ultimately be superseded that I wonder even he, Jew as he is, dares to boast of it. My Gentile nature kicks most resolutely against any assumption of superiority in the Jews and is almost ready to echo Voltaire's vituperation. I bow to the supremacy of Hebrew poetry, but much of their early mythology and almost all their history is utterly revolting. . . . Everything *specifically* Jewish is of a low grade.[22]

One may well be tempted to convict Eliot out of her own mouth of inconsistency when it is remembered that her ultimate capitulation to the theories of Comte and Bray brought her very close to a racial determinism such as informs *The Spanish Gypsy* and *Deronda*. Both Fedalma and Deronda entertain a sort of preconscious kinship with their people long before they have the least evidence that they are *de facto* members of the race toward which they have emotionally gravitated all along. In *Deronda,* especially, the hero's elective affinity with the Jews is worked out in positivistic rather than theological terms: though Deronda dabbles in Jewish lore, haunts synagogues, and dwells upon Hebrew ritual, the point, of course, is that he should be drawn toward Judaism at all when, as far as he knows, there is nothing in a biological way to warrant the attraction. When, in the discovery scenes, the Spanish gypsy and Sir Hugo's adoptive son resolve, quite joyfully, to "wed the curse that blights our people," their resolution has long been anticipated by their extrarational commitments. The wish is father to the fact. And the wish itself betrays the enormous force of one's blood ties.

Still it would never do to confuse Disraeli's theory of the super-race with Eliot's allegiance to the prevailing scientific doctrines of her age. The two novelists represent, if anything, antithetical viewpoints. Where Disraeli publicizes the need for a racial hierarchy, with the Jews at the top and everybody else at the bottom, Eliot insists on the futility of rank classifications. She is chiefly interested in recognizing, not the superiority of any one race to another, but the sheer diversity of races. Beyond this her views are as securely egalitarian as Disraeli's are oligarchic, and as democratic as his are theocratic. If the Jews are no more "pure" than any other people, they are decidedly different from any other people, and their very separateness might well teach the rest of the world a salutary respect for the disparate minorities. "There is nothing I should care more to do," she writes to Harriet Beecher Stowe after the publication of *Deronda,* "if it were possible, than to rouse the imagination of men and women to a vision of human claims in those races of their fellow-men who most differ from them in customs and beliefs. But towards the Hebrews we western people who have been reared in Christianity, have a peculiar debt and, whether we acknowledge it or not, a peculiar thoroughness of fellowship in religious and moral sentiment."[23]

This, substantially, is the lesson Mordecai attempts to formulate in his rather protracted conversations with Deronda. The Jewish "inheritance" that he wants Daniel to assume is based on the recognition that the Jews are an inviolably separate people, neither better nor worse than others, but undeniably different; and this diversity needs to be implemented and strengthened by a return to the faith of our fathers. On the political plain it means nothing less than an independent national existence.

> Looking towards a land and a polity, our dispersed people in all the ends of the earth may share the dignity of a national life which has a voice among the peoples of the East and the West—which will plant the wisdom of our race so that it may be, as of old, a medium of transmission and understanding. Let that come to pass, and the living warmth will spread to the weak extremities of Israel; and superstition will vanish, not in the lawlessness of the renegade, but in the illumination of great facts which widen feeling and make all knowledge alive as the young offspring of beloved memories.

The difference between Disraeli's brand of Zionism and Eliot's defines itself clearly enough in the foregoing passage. Where Disraeli regards Palestine as the *fons origo* and appointed nerve center of all spiritual life, the Mecca of the Western and the Eastern worlds, Eliot regards it as a politically expedient means of gathering the Jews from the Diaspora and of conferring upon them a status comparable to that of other nations. Israel is to have "a voice among the peoples." Such a national existence is not intended to be an expression of Jewish supremacy, but a means of revitalizing the decayed foundations of

Judaism itself, by creating a kind of utopia strictly *intra muros*. While Disraeli legislates a ruling state from which to issue edicts to the pharisees, Eliot proposes what is largely meant as a defensive measure: "our race shall have an organic center, a heart and brain to watch and guide and execute; the outraged Jew shall have a defence in the court of nations as the outraged Englishman."

Duty: Daniel and Gwendolen

Once the Prophet has enunciated the Zionist doctrine and passed on his mission to Daniel, he dies; and Daniel and Mirah proceed to the Holy Land. Whether Daniel accomplished his mission is another question; Philipson, for one, doubts it.

> He has now found an ideal and an object; he is a Jew; he will assimilate Mordecai's ideas. . . . He will identify himself as far as possible with his people, and if any work can be done for them that he can give his soul and hand to, he will do it. But we feel he will not do it. He is no enthusiast; he will do nothing.[24]

Eliot's failure with her Jewish characters is perhaps most painfully manifest in Daniel, a wholly idealized person in search of his spiritual identity. Leslie Stephen has said of him:

> That young gentleman is a model from the first. He has a "seraphic face." There is "hardly a delicacy of feeling" of which he is not capable—even when he is at Eton. He is so ethereal a being that we are a little shocked when he is mentioned in connection with entrées. One can't fancy an angel at a London dinner table. That is, indeed, the impression which he makes upon his friend. A family is created expressly to pay homage to him. . . . To Gwendolen this peerless person naturally becomes an "outer conscience"; and when he exhorts her to use her past sorrow as a preparation for life, instead of letting it spoil her life, the words are to her "like the touch of a miraculous hand."[25]

Deronda's function in the novel is almost prescriptively passive. Unlike the other characters, he does not really have a positive point of view; his role is chiefly to be accessible to the opinions of others and somehow register these opinions. Within the Eliot canon he is also the conventional protagonist whose occupation it is to find an appropriate moral creed. Regarded in this way, he fulfills somewhat the same role which Eliot used to assign to her heroines; it may be one reason for his basic effeminacy. In this sense, too, Mordecai takes on the function of spiritual director previously given over to Dinah and Savonarola, Felix and Dorothea. The upshot of Mordecai's guidance, we know, is that Daniel embraces Judaism, or rather, acknowledges the birthright which his mother has endeavored to withhold from him.

By a sort of telescoping in dramatic roles, Daniel, in turn, assumes Mordecai's function of theological guide in his relation to Gwendolen Harleth, whom he plies with good advice and whom he tries to steer toward an acceptance of the positivist position which he has himself adopted on learning of his Sephardic ancestry. The positivist, to quote Leslie Stephen, "insists upon a view of duty as corresponding to the vital instincts of the 'social organism,' the identification of the individual with the body of which he is the product, and the constituent and consequent readiness to sacrifice life and happiness to the interest of the community into which he is born."[26] The doctrine had already been preached by Felix Holt to Esther, by Savonarola to Romola, and by Dorothea to Lydgate; and it found its most explicit application in *The Spanish Gypsy*.

In *Deronda* one is conscious of a certain fraudulence in Daniel's positivist attitude toward Gwendolen, though Eliot seems determined to ignore this. The difficulty with his position is that, unlike Dorothea Brooke and Felix Holt, Deronda has found his spiritual search such very easy going (while Gwendolen has found hers so very difficult) that there is absolutely no correspondence between the kind of "duty" he assumes for himself and the "duty" he expects her to shoulder. Dorothea at least suffered a catastrophic marriage and Felix languished in prison before they took it on themselves to shrive and impose vague penance on their advisees; one feels that their own martyrdom has entitled them to exercise the office of confessor. But Daniel merely drifts; eventually he drifts into Judaism; and no amount of author-analysis and buoyant rhetoric can disguise the fact that his "duties" sit very lightly on him. The *Edinburgh* reviewer described him as "a kind of Hamlet without a grievance, without anything to avenge, or indeed necessarily anything to do in this world; in whom a vague yet lofty ambition, perpetually foiled by over-thought . . . takes the place of that definite mission which the Prince of Denmark can never decide upon executing." One is thus made to feel that Judaism has been dropped into Daniel's lap, that he finds it congenial; and now he will sail to Palestine with Mirah—virtue has been rewarded, but untried virtue. Leavis has admirably stated the moral dilemma in which Eliot finds herself here:

> Since poor Gwendolen is not in a position to discover herself a Jewess, and so to find her salvation in Deronda's way, she might in time . . . come to reflect critically upon the depth and general validity of his wisdom. We . . . are obliged to be critical of the George Eliot who can so unreservedly endorse the account of the "higher, the religious life" represented by Deronda. A paragon of virtue, generosity, intelligence and disinterestedness, he has no "troubles" he needs a refuge from; what he feels he needs, and what he yearns after is an "enthusiasm"—an enthusiasm which shall be at the same time a "duty." . . . It is quite plain that the "duty" that Deronda embraces . . . combines moral enthusiasm and the feeling of emotional intensity with essential relaxation in such a way that, for any "higher life" promoted, we may fairly find an analogy in the exalting effects of alcohol. The element of self-indulgence is patent. And so are the confusions.[27]

The confusions are—once again—reflected in the character of Daniel's counsel to Gwendolen, in the rhetoric, the style; issues are being obscured; one does not precisely know what he means Gwendolen to do. " 'Keep your dread fixed on the idea of increasing that remorse which is so bitter to you. Fixed meditation may do a great deal towards defining our longing or dread. . . . Take your fear as a safeguard. It is like quickness of hearing. It may make consequences passionately present to you. Try to take hold of your sensibility, and use it as if it were a faculty, like vision.' "

On that note he departs, going off to build up Palestine. "But we feel he will not do it. . . . He will do nothing." In the meantime Eliot vaguely promises us that his advice to Gwendolen has been wholesome and that Gwendolen will profit by it. Daniel and Gwendolen have themselves one of those emotionally charged scenes which Eliot was incapable of bringing off, he wiping Gwendolen's tears and she wiping his; and then he goes to Palestine, leaving Gwendolen with her fears for a safeguard and her sensibility for vision.

"Well," said Theodora at last, "I wonder what he accomplished in the East." Pulcheria took the little dog into her lap and made him sit on the book. "Oh," she replied, "they had tea-parties at Jerusalem—exclusively of ladies—and he sat in the midst and stirred his tea and made high-toned remarks. And then Mirah sang a little, just a little, on account of her voice being so weak."[28]

But *Daniel Deronda,* translated into Hebrew, became a Zionist Bible; and in 1948 George Eliot, though she spoiled a potentially very great novel by presenting a dozen unforgivably wooden Jews, received the monumental tribute of having a street named after her in Tel-Aviv.[29]

PART THREE

Myth

Est-il rien sur la terre
Qui soit plus surprenant
Que la grande misère
Du pauvre Juif errant!
Que son sort malheureux
Parait triste et fâcheux.

DÉSIRÉ NISARD, *Histoire des livres populaires*

VIII

The Evolution of the Wandering Jew

In *Daniel Deronda* the Jewish paragon had his say as emphatically as anywhere among Victorian novelists. If he said far more than he need have said in behalf of the Jews, we know that his mellifluence was part of the game, a piece of the tradition dating back to Cumberland. For if the essential fact about Shylock was that he over-acted his role, the essential fact about Sheva was that he over-reacted to Shylock. The good Jew's whole mode thus exhausted itself in an effort to consolidate and articulate a position that was purely one of self-defense, with the unhappy literary consequences culminating in George Eliot's last novel.

With *Daniel Deronda* one stage of my inquiry has reached its terminal impasse. I have tried to trace the development of two extreme conventions, though I am by no means certain that the real issue is one of development, nor am I certain that it involves two discriminated channels of thought. At the heart of the problem is Shylock, and the Shylock myth is not a continuous fact of literature, capable of evolving new and complex configurations and relationships, but a stable one, which different generations do not so much reinterpret for themselves as they rehabilitate it. Every so often Shylock is patched up, moved up or down the economic ladder, invested with aberrant religious motives or divested of his religion, and sent into the world as Rachub, Abraham, Fagin, Nucingen, Levy. The essential Shylock has always a knife and has always the moneybags; he is always funny and always horrible.

And Sheva has, after all, only Shylock to fall back on. The impulse behind his conception, as we know, was a desire to rationalize Shylock out of the world by providing the anti-Shylock; and such a figure leads, as it were, an existence at second hand. The one type begat the other. Fagin stole; so Mordecai (or Trendelssohn or Honest Oppovich) had to insist that Jews are not in the habit of stealing. The referent is one and the same. To all intents I have been dealing here not with two myths, but with one.

The situation is unfortunate; it is unfortunate for the intelligent reading public who want *some* reflection, no matter how dim, of "life," and who are asked to settle, not for a plausible human being, but a grimace; not for a credo, but an excuse. It is doubly unfortunate for the scholar-critics who, in addition to all these things, want their fictional personnel to reveal the historic force behind the human fact; who are committed to a belief in the "history" of literature and, on the analogy from political history, rightly think of literature as an evolutionary process. A study of the Jew in English fiction, however, is fundamentally a study in the stasis of thought. If the figure of the Jew in literature is to tell us anything about the sensibilities of the age that produced him, one had better look beyond the Shylock myth and search for independent legends.

There is the myth of the Wandering Jew. The story of Cartaphilus, who struck Christ on His way to the Cross and was condemned to tarry until His second coming, has left far less of an impact on literature than the Shylock story; but it is in many respects a more useful legend. It answers the purposes of literary history more readily; it changes; it adapts itself to the demands of diverse generations and diverse beliefs. It provides a more reliable and more "readable" barometer than Shylock to the kind of civilization, ideology, and regnant literary convention in which it flourishes, for each age recreates the Wandering Jew in its own image. I should therefore like to devote the remaining pages of this study to an analysis of Cartaphilus and the sons of Cartaphilus, chiefly as they appear in the century from 1794 to 1894, from the composition of Lewis's *Monk* to the appearance of Du Maurier's *Trilby*. I hope that such a discussion will correct some of the deficiencies of the earlier chapters, deficiencies inherent, I believe, in the material covered: the defects of inflexible constancy and depressing sameness.

For the story of Cartaphilus is a story, if not of progress, at least of change, a chapter in the history of ideas. The character of the Wandering Jew, unlike Shylock and anti-Shylock, resists definition in two or three strokes, for his appearance and function take on their colors from the wider context of their epoch. A study of the Shylock story down the ages involves little more than a knowledge of the prototype, but the Wandering Jew can mean all things to all men and all ages. In an era dominated by the Church Universal he may be an object of piety or religious horror. In periods of anticlerical enlightenment, he is likely to go underground, for the conditions of his existence are always fabulous. The novel of terror translates him into a black magician, a necromancer conjuring meaningless specters, a Satan in a godless universe. If the Gothic writers paint him as Mephisto, the Romantics worship him as Faust or Prometheus, as an elemental malcontent who turns the curse of immortality against the God who pronounced it. From Faust, engaged in forbidden alchemical practices, he passes easily into the figure of the Olympian scientist-philosopher in whose image Bulwer-Lytton was fond of portraying him; and from the necromancer he passes into the hypnotist who emerges, at the end of our study, as the ogre in Du Maurier's sensation-piece.

But if the Wandering Jew thus appears to satisfy almost all sorts and conditions, he also fails singularly to satisfy the very purposes that Shylock answered above any others. He is not conspicuously comic, nor is he distinguished for his criminality. Although the foundations of the Judas legend involve a crime against the person of Christ, Cartaphilus is not turned loose as the hideous caricature, half devil and half beast, into which the medieval mind transformed the Jew-traitor. On the whole he is a serious figure, accessible to tragic interpretations. Instead of playing up to the fears and hatreds of an inimical society, he chooses to become his own scapegoat. He wanders down the centuries, a perpetual emblem of atonement, a miraculous witness and dragoman, a creature not of strife but conciliation, a figure deeply spiritualized by the penalty Christ inflicted upon him.

The real answer to Shylock the miser is not Sheva the philanthropist, for in the long run their values come to the same thing. Against the material ethics of Shylock the wolf and Sheva the good dog the Wandering Jew opposes the intelligence of his beggardom and long life. If both he and Shylock torment themselves alike with the fundamental question, "how long, oh Lord?" we know that while the one is dreaming of revenge, the other is dreaming of release. At the crux of Shylock's crime is the mutilation of the flesh, the gesture of the cannibalist. But the Immortal Jew, like a more recent longevity expert, may well console himself with the boast that "A man of my spiritual intensity does not eat corpses."

Antecedents: Cartaphilus into Ahasuerus

In the year 1228 an Armenian Archbishop visited the monastery at Saint Albans and regaled his hosts with fabulous Oriental stories.[1] For example, he claimed to have seen Noah's Ark preserved in the Armenian mountains. Most particularly did the holy brothers want to know whether the Archbishop had heard anything concerning a certain Joseph who had supposedly talked with Christ shortly before the Crucifixion, and whose name had lately come to attract a good deal of attention. The Archbishop replied that he knew the man very well. He had dined with him shortly before setting out for England.

The man's name, the Archbishop reported, had originally been Cartaphilus. A Roman by birth, he had been Pilate's doorkeeper at the time of Christ's conviction. When Jesus was being led from the hall of judgment, Cartaphilus had struck Him on the neck and driven Him from the gate with the words "Vade Jesu citius, vade, quid moraris?" "I will go," Christ answered, "but as for thee, thou shalt tarry until I return": "Ego vado, et tu expectabis me, donec redeam." Cartaphilus has been waiting ever since. Overcome by remorse, he entered the Church shortly after the Crucifixion. For twelve centuries he has been living the life of a devout Christian in Armenia and the countries around Armenia. Every hundred years he is seized by a trance and on recovering from it finds himself remitted to the age of thirty, the age at which he had insulted Christ. In all other respects, his manners are laudable. He eats little and speaks only when he is spoken to. He refuses gifts from anyone. He never laughs, but occasionally he has been seen to burst into tears. On the rare occasions when he does speak, his subject is obsessively the same: Christ's Passion and Crucifixion. He still hopes for salvation because he sinned ignorantly and is fond of applying to himself the words Christ uttered on the Cross: "Forgive them, for they know not what they do." His conduct is, to all intents, that of a holy man.[2]

This, substantially, is the account that found its way into Roger of Wendover's *Flores Historiarum* not long after the Armenian Archbishop's verbal report. Wendover was himself a friar at Saint Albans; and when Matthew Paris, his brother-in-Christ at the same monastery, expanded Wendover's chronicle into his own *Chronica Maiora,* he took over the story of Cartaphilus verbatim. Matthew Paris had occasion to record the story independently some twenty-five years later when, in 1252, the Archbishop's brother likewise stopped off at Saint Albans and confirmed the original report on his own authority. These are our first literary prefigurations of that shadowy and multifarious character who was eventually to transmogrify into the Wandering Jew. As yet he was neither Wanderer nor Jew, but a baptized Roman, stationary in the Near East, doomed to live forever from the age of thirty to the age of a hundred.[3]

Like the foundations of the Judas myth, the foundations of the legend Wendover inherited are Biblical.[4] But they are far vaguer and more elusive than the myth which begat the Jew-villain. The twelve centuries that intervened between the Biblical event and its first appearance in Anglo-Latin literature are, with respect to the legend, shrouded in darkness. Analogues, themselves vague and general, are found here and there, but these have nothing more tangible in common than the curse of an immortal existence. In Italy Cartaphilus turns up again as Johannes Buttadeus;[5] in English literature the figure of the old man in Chaucer's "Pardoner's Tale" has sometimes been cited as an avatar of the Wandering Jew.[6] None of these stories brings us any closer to the prototype; rather than refining on Wendover, they generalize away from him. To all intents the myth of Cartaphilus goes underground again as soon as it has emerged, living on only in shadowy fictions concerning mystifying old men condemned either to flee perpetually from death or to seek him out perpetually.

The legend reappears in a new light some three hundred and fifty years later in a German *Volksbuch* dated 1602. It occupies a mere four pages, of which a substantial part is taken up by its resounding title: "A Brief Description and Narrative of a Jew named Ahasuerus, who was bodily present at Christ's Crucifixion, who joined in the Clamour to crucify Him and to spare Barabas, who was barred from returning to Jerusalem ever after, who never again beheld either his wife or his children: who has remained alive ever since, came to Hamburg some years ago, and was likewise seen in Danzig Anno 1599, in the month of December."[7] The title recapitulates almost all there is to the story. The author of the *Volksbuch* claims as his authority a report transmitted to him by the Bishop of Schleswig, Paulus von Eitzen. Some fifty years earlier, while attending church at Hamburg, Eitzen's notice had been attracted by an extraordinary figure, a tall, stately individual who seemed to follow the sermon with undue intensity. The man displayed the strongest signs of emotion; he sighed; he groaned; at the mention of Christ's name he smote his breast. It was also remarked that he had long wavy black hair and that he was barefoot. Eitzen judged him to be about fifty years old.

After the service Eitzen interrogated the stranger, who gave his name as Ahasuerus, late of Jerusalem, shoemaker by calling—a profession least adapted, one would think, to one who dispensed with wearing shoes himself. He remembered the Crucifixion vividly; he remembered bringing his family to watch it with him. On the way to Calvary Christ had asked to rest and lean against him, but Ahasuerus, seized perhaps by a desire to show off to the mob, drove Him furiously away. It was then that Christ pronounced on him the curse with which we are familiar. The rest of Ahasuerus's story is indicated in the title of the chapbook: he no longer found it possible to tarry at home; he was seized by a fearful restlessness that drove him from country to country; he never again saw his family. Centuries later he returned to Jerusalem to find the city annihilated. He has been on the move ever since. His traits and his conduct agree substantially with those already prefigured in Wendover's account: he is holy, frugal, and penitent; when he speaks of God, his speech is punctuated with sighs; to hear any one take Christ's name in vain infuriates him. The author of the *Volksbuch* adds that in 1572 the same Jew allegedly turned up in Spain, with a fluent command of Spanish; and, drawing a number of pious conclusions from the foregoing, he ends his report.

The *Volksbuch* is of signal importance in the history of the myth. Though the Ahasuerus of Eitzen's story retained many characteristics of the Cartaphilus-type, the author reformed the legend in certain obvious ways. Most important, the Roman doorkeeper was translated into a Jewish cobbler; and the figure of the immortal sinner turned into that of an immortal fugitive. As to the reasons behind these changes, we are again left to speculate. Conway suggests that the restlessness thereafter associated with the Wandering Jew may reflect the dispersion of the Jews "under the remorseless police of Christendom" and their subsequent movements in the Diaspora;[8] Railo thinks that the whole context of restlessness may be traced back to the Crusades, as can also the related notion that the Orient harbored vast tracts of mysterious and unexplored territories, whose customs and histories some such figure as the Wandering Jew would be singularly qualified to describe.[9]

The *Volksbuch*, more than anything else, created a market for the Wandering Jew. By 1800 the book had gone through at least seventy editions. By getting the Jew to make a personal appearance in Germany, the author brought him very close to the public; so long as he was kept in the Orient, he remained necessarily remote. It was now possible to spot him almost anywhere. Henceforth his mobility increased impressively. The 14th of January, 1603, finds him in Lübeck. The following year he turned up at Beauvais, surrounded by children. In 1640 he appeared in Brussels. In 1642 he entered Leipzig as a beggar. He may have passed through Ulm in 1653. At Naumburg in Thuringia he could neither sit nor stand still; even during the sermon he moved about incessantly. To judge from these reports he appears to have preferred the climate of Central and Western Europe.[10]

By way of the *Volksbuch* the Wandering Jew returned to England in the seventeenth century. His first known reappearance seems to date back to a ballad of 1612, reprinted in Percy's *Reliques* under the title "The Wandering Jew, or the Shoemaker of Jerusalem. Who lived when our Lord and Saviour Jesus Christ was crucified, and by him appointed to live till his Coming again. Tune of 'The Lady's Fall.' "[11] The poem makes no effort to recapture the air of historical authenticity apparent in the *Volksbuch*; it simply tells the story. In 1634 he turns up as the subject of a street ballad, "The Wandering Jew's Chronicle," by Thomas Lambert. Though Lambert's performance involves the shoddiest kind of doggerel, it possesses a certain adventitious interest in suggesting the extreme and peripheral uses to which the Wandering Jew already lent himself. By virtue of his extraordinary old age, he could be made over into an ideal witness to ancient historical events; or he might simply furnish the framework for an historical narrative. It is in this latter capacity that Lambert employs him. The ballad parades onstage a number of English rulers, and the business of the Wandering Jew begins and ends with his having been alive long enough to have seen them all. His presence furnishes an elementary thread of continuity; for the rest, he provides an excuse for the author to talk about something else. The tone of the poem (to the melody of "Our Prince Is Welcome out of Spain") may do very well for a street ballad but ill accords with the pathetic object of Christ's vengeance:

When William Duke of Normandy,
With all his Normans gallantly
This Kingdom did subdue,
Full fifteen years of age I was,
And whate'er since hath come to pass,
I can repeat as true.[12]

The automatic question, how the Wandering Jew could have been fifteen years old in 1066, merely points up the odd degree to which the original had been distorted to suit the author's purpose. "The indifference toward the legend," Zirus well adds, "could not be expressed more crassly."[13]

A similar indifference characterizes a prose work of 1640 entitled "The Wandering Jew telling Fortunes to Englishmen. A Jew's Lottery."[14] That a purely nominal significance is attached to the legendary figure is apparent from the title of an almost indistinguishable early version of 1609 which has, not the Wandering Jew, but "The Man in the Moon telling Strange Fortunes." The status of the Jew is only a trifle more specifically defined than it is in Lambert's ballad. The author, apparently a Puritan, relates how, straying one day into a deserted neighborhood, he came upon a strange and lonely dwelling. The inhabitant invited him in and in the course of conversation revealed himself to be a dignified and cosmopolitan human being, who had retired from the world in the recognition of his own paltriness. The name to which he answers suggests him to be not so much a man as a whole genealogy of men: Gad Ben Arod Ben Balaam Ben Alimoth Ben Baal Ben Gog Ben Magog. His profession is that of soothsayer. The prefatory credentials out of the way, Gad Ben Arod etc. dwindles into the same frame-figure already observed in the Wandering Jew of Lambert's poem, whose function it is to play master of ceremonies to a series of sinners in search of their future. These are then presented almost in the manner of Overburian characters: there is the drunkard, the prodigal, the lewd woman, the usurer, the glutton, as well as the lover and the tobacconist. Prodigal, tobacconist, and lover all receive a noisy verbal lashing from the prophet, who paints their future in such dismal colors that they wend their way home in a profoundly pensive cast of mind. "Fuga opportunitatem!" says the prophet by way of terminating the interview, and he retires into his inner chambers, scheduling new appointments for those sinners who are still, as it were, left in the waiting room.

What have these tangential figures, these Sunday recitalists and sunshine prophets, to do with the pitiful and self-lacerating worshipper whom Bishop von Eitzen discovered in the church of Hamburg? Substantially, next to nothing—no more than the Man in the Moon has. Perhaps the very fact that the designation Wandering Jew could be attached to all sorts of vaguely symbolic or allegorical *personae*—who had nothing but their genius for longevity to relate them to the legend—itself indicates how deeply the image of Ahasuerus had already penetrated the popular consciousness. Two very useful services he did continue to perform, one by reason of his immortality, the other by reason of his restlessness. He cut across all limitations of time, and all limitations of space. As a result, he could be used as an authority on almost every topic under the sun—history, geography, and the study of exotic *mœurs* being his particular provinces. If the author wanted to give an illusory authenticity to a narrative about, let us say, the sacking of Rome, he could always get the Wandering Jew to deliver a first-hand account. If the author decided to delve into remote Afro-Asian corners and talk about the behavior of the Persians, he needed only to pack the Wandering Jew off to Persia. As a plausible source of implausible information Ahasuerus was inexhaustible and indispensable. And if the author wished also to preserve the religious nexus, what figure better adapted to point a moral than one who was himself a walking Moral, a perpetual embodiment of Sin in process of being punished?

Moreover, any writer who wished to explore the specifically ethical implications of the subject, had ready to hand a character so situated that he could be examined from almost any point on the moral spectrum. Someone like Ahasuerus quite singularly incorporated the greatest possibilities at once for depravity and for sanctity. A figure who perpetrated a crime so foul that he heard his doom pronounced by the lips of Jesus himself and who, at the same time, lives the blameless life of an ascetic, dedicating his immortality to acts and gestures of penitence, invites every kind of interpretation. He is something of Christ and Anti-Christ both; his existence finally points at an insoluble paradox. Some such ambiguity is apparent in a quite mechanical way, even in so frivolous a work as "The Jew telling Fortunes," in which the title figure on the one hand bears all the idolatrous names from Baal to Gog and Magog and, on the other, behaves like a righteous Presbyter, phophesying doom and disaster to a congregation of scoundrels.[15]

From the point of view of an evolutionary study, such generalizing tendencies may have their disadvantages, for there is always the chance that at the end of the line the Wandering Jew no longer bears the remotest resemblance to the ancestral portrait. A character so indefinitely comprehensive and so infinitely fissile that he can be made to look like Prometheus, Judas Maccabaeus, Tithonus, Satan, Svengali, an anchorite, and a Rosicrucian invites the suspicion that his paternity has never been properly legitimated. But every age, as has been said, has a way of translating its myths to suit itself, and so extreme distortions are perhaps inevitable. Shelley decreed that his Ahasuerus should shake his fists against God; and Eugène Sue decreed that his Ahasuerus should be married to a woman clamoring for the emancipation of women. We have already noted that the Wandering Jew did not need to be a Jew at all; the one burden definitely laid upon him was his inability to die. By the time the Romantics got through with him, even that dispensation could be repudiated; and by the time Du Maurier got through with him, he was eligible to die, not with a whimper of atonement but a theatrical bang. Meanwhile, however, other attractive features gave him a new lease on life and immortality.

The Romantic Agony

In the nineteenth century Ahasuerus turned, predictably enough, from a sinner into an accuser, from a figure of expiation into a figure of revolt. Among the romantic poets he still suffers all the age-old agonies of the immortal wanderer, but he no longer atones for his crime; instead he rebels against a punishment administered unjustly by a tyrannical deity. His sufferings no longer derive from the consciousness of having sinned, but rather from an overwhelming world-weariness, an urge to be released from the fetters of immortality. The motif of rebellion is thus often attended by the ancillary symptoms of *Weltschmerz*. In this double aspect, Ahasuerus appears prominently in the work of the Swabian poet Christian Daniel Schubart, who is generally credited with having made Ahasuerus available to the English romantics. Schubart composed his "lyrical rhapsody" *Ahasver* in 1783 and published it three years later. "With his poem," Railo notes, "Schubart lifts with unerring hand the Ahasuerus-theme from the region of folklore into that of artistic literature."[16]

Schubart is an interesting minor figure in the history of Storm-and-Stress, and the *Ahasver* poem is a fair sample of his talents and defects. Hermann Hesse characterizes him as "wild, noisy, braggart, and sentimental";[17] and Schubart's own autobiographical fragment reveals moreover an extraordinary capacity for lachrymose self-indulgence and a kind of Thrasonic pietism.[18] The stabilizing factor in his emotionalism seems to have been a strong prejudice in favor of cemeteries, which is reflected in the titles of half his poems. Schubart thus straddles the conventions both of the graveyard school and of the romantic rebel; and it is in this dual function that his treatment of the Ahasuerus legend represents an important advance in the development of the myth.

What interested Schubart were none of the specifically religious associations that the Wandering Jew had traditionally carried with him. The attractions were of a more generally cultural kind and have been ably summed up by Zirus:

> The "gigantic idea" of a superhuman being, "lifted above space and time," was [Schubart's] favorite conception. . . . His thousand-year-old Jew had witnessed the heights and depths of mankind, had seen Rome and the Papacy, Columbus and the Reformation; now, from the vantage point of his rock, he was to view in retrospect this "furrowed ocean of time." Exalted above books and above human forces, he was for all that to bear "the full stamp of humanity." What actually remains of this grandiose vision is a singular mixture of genuine plastic power and verbose bardic posturing.[19]

Schubart's poem, so far from following the prescribed theology, tends to be anti-Christian in character; and his Ahasver, instead of submitting to the will of God, feels himself under the pressure of a penalty which is in no way commensurate with his crime. Though Ahasver is still nominally under the influence of the divine curse, what really urges him on is a "demon fled from hell": his restlessness has become part and parcel of a personality that admits a large admixture of satanism. Hitherto the Jew's restlessness had been shown as the consequence of a single damnable action, as something imposed from without and at bottom extraneous to his character. In the original versions of the myth, the relation of the punishment to the offense, and of the offense to the character of the offender, had rested, I should say, in nothing more substantial than a *bon mot* on the part of Jesus: "Thou shalt go," said Cartaphilus; "and thou," said Jesus, "shalt stay." Schubart internalized the Jew's restiveness and made it a facet of his character. For Ahasver's urge to be on the move is inextricably bound up with his fundamental death-wish, the desire to cease from all movement and make his peace with the God Whom he denies.

His efforts at self-annihilation are indeed ingenious and wonder-

The Wandering Jew in Town

The Wandering Jew in the Wilderness

ful. The general impression in the poem is one of rocks and inclement weather. The rhapsody begins by depicting Ahasver as he creeps forth from his cavern on Mount Carmel, hurling the skulls of his parents, his siblings, and his descendants into the cavern below. "That is my father!" he laughs frantically, throwing skull No. 1; "Those are my wives!" (seven more skulls are accounted for); "These my children! They could die, but I—outcast—cannot die!"[20] It is not for want of enthusiasm that he cannot. He has sought death in battle and among vipers. He has hurled himself into the flames of burning Jerusalem and into the mouth of Etna. "Under my feet the mine exploded and threw me high into the air; senseless I fell down, and found myself roasted amongst blood, brains, and bones."[21] He begs God to make an end of him by compounding the dangers of jactation and electricity: to cast him from a lofty precipice in the midst of a howling tempest. And at last he does find rest: in a conventionally pietistic sort of postscript that bears no organic relation whatever to the titanic businesses which have preceded and that ill accords with dragons and large snakes, Ahasver falls into a small slumber; an angel bears him into some shrubbery and, in a quiet dream-vision, Ahasver receives the assurance that Christ will come and redeem him—that, as it were, he will wake up to find himself dead.

Schubart's use (or abuse) of the myth set the pace for the Wandering Jew when the English romantic poets picked him up in the opening decades of the nineteenth century. His primary innovations, as I have tried to indicate, alighted on two traits which one would like to dismiss as mutually exclusive if one did not constantly find them to coexist in life, art, and certain proto-Romantic political movements. One is the impulse to self-annihilation, the exhaustion of all vital energies; the other is the impulse to rebellion, and the—frequently misdirected—concentration of all vital energies.

It was this second aspect of Schubart's Ahasver that attracted poets like Southey and Shelley. In Southey's *Curse of Kehama,* the Hindu sorcerer of the title condemns the romantic hero of the poem, Ladurlad, to everlasting life. In spite of its Oriental setting[22] the story of Ladurlad falls more or less strictly within the framework of the Ahasver myth. Kehama's curse, with its provision that Ladurlad remain indestructibly immune to natural phenomena, is a source of bitter anguish to the hero:

Oh! he hath laid a Curse upon my life,
A clinging curse, quoth he;
Hath sent a fire into my heart and brain,
A burning fire, for ever there to be!
The Winds of Heaven must never breathe on me;
The Rains and Dews must never fall on me;
Water must mock my thirst and shrink from me;
The common Earth must yield no fruit to me;
Sleep, blessed Sleep! must never light on me;
And Death, who comes to all, must fly from me,
And never, never set Ladurlad free.[23]

Ladurlad's adventures roughly parallel those of Schubart's Ahasver, although Southey permits his hero to travel in the company of a daughter, whom he is fond of rescuing from fires. For the rest, Ladurlad encounters the customary death-traps and side-steps them all. Poisoned arrows bounce off his body; the waves retreat before his person; he is immune to fire as well as to marine monsters. But unlike Ahasver Ladurlad eventually begins to plume himself on his superhuman prowesses and to make a virtue of necessity by translating the curse itself into a threat against the tyrant who pronounced it. Instead of dissolving in *Weltschmerz* or capitulating to the Tyrant Omnipotent, he rouses himself to positive energetic deeds.[24] In Southey's handling of the legend, as one might expect, protagonist and antagonist have changed roles: the cursed is ethically in the right whereas the articulator of the curse takes on the role of villain. Southey's motto to the poem gives as much away: "Curses Are like Young Chickens, They Always Come Home to Roost." Ladurlad's allusions to Kehama—"The Tyrant of the Earth, / The Enemy of Heaven!"—foreshadow Shelley's Prometheus figures, and the hero's confrontation of his maligner bears the same traces of heroic obstinacy:

her Father's eye
Was fix'd upon Kehama haughtily;
It spake defiance to him, high disdain,
Stern patience unsubduable by pain,
And pride triumphant over agony.[25]

The Curse of Kehama appeared in 1810, and in the same year Shelley added no fewer than four versions of his own to the legend of the Wandering Jew. Of these "The Wandering Jew's Soliloquy" is most directly in the Schubart-Southey tradition: the poem turns the myth into an accusation against the tyrannical god.[26] The Ahasuerus of the piece has discarded all the trappings of the sinner in exchange for those of the martyr who refuses to acquiesce in his martyrdom. The thirty-line monologue bristles with invectives against the "Eternal Triune," the "Tyrant on Earth," "pale misery's jackal," and, proceeding by a series of rhetorical accusations against God's abuse of His omnipotence, culminates in the speaker's affirmation of his undying enmity.

Yes! I would court a ruin such as this,
Almighty Tyrant! and give thanks to Thee—
Drink deeply—drain the cup of hate—remit this
    I may die.[27]

Plainly the Wandering Jew of the poem is already conceived in the lineaments of a Prometheus Adrift. More famous and equally emphatic in his indictment against the deity is the Ahasuerus who is conjured up in Canto VII of *Queen Mab,* composed the year following. He appears in one of the guises that he had already assumed in the seventeenth century and was to assume again throughout the nineteenth: as witness to the destiny of mankind, past, present, and future. Given the panoramic structure of the poem, it is perhaps natural that Queen Mab should summon the Wandering Jew, conqueror of time and space, and place him in the witness box to support her prosecution of God.[28] In his physical make-up, Ahasuerus combines some of the age-old dignity of his prototype with the youthful energy emblematic of muscular atheism.

    A strange and woe-worn wight
Arose beside the battlement,
    And stood unmoving there.
His inessential figure cast no shade
    Upon the golden floor;
His port and mien bore mark of many years,
And chronicles of untold ancientness
Were legible within his beamless eye:
    Yet his cheek bore the mark of youth;

Freshness and vigour knit his manly frame;
The wisdom of old age was mingled there
With youth's primeval dauntlessness;
And inexpressible woe,
Chastened by fearless resignation, gave
An awful grace to his all-speaking brow.[29]

To the Spirit's rhetorical question, "Is there a God?" Ahasuerus replies that indeed there is "an almighty God, / And vengeful as almighty!" and in a philippic of some two hundred lines he proceeds to unfold a catalogue of Jehovah's crimes. God is presented as a monster of gratuitous malice, "the omnipotent fiend" whose "costly altars smoked / With human blood." Moses emerges as some Old Testament Castlereagh, "A murderer . . . Accomplice of omnipotence in crime"; while God is made to sound like a combination of Tamburlaine and Machiavelli, cynically boasting that he created man on purpose "to turn / Even like a heartless conqueror of the earth / All misery to my fame." By his own admission, Jehovah conceived of Christ's birth and death as a crafty stratagem to tempt human beings into sin and everlasting torment—a proposal so sanguinary in the unfolding that "Even the murderer's [Moses's] cheek / Was blanched with horror." Between God the Father and Christ His Son there is not much to choose; Jesus is variously described as "veiling his horrible Godhead in the shape of man," "a parish demagogue" satiating his "malignant soul" with "the blood of truth and freedom."[30] When Ahasuerus comes at length to narrate the central and permanent episode of the myth, the offense against Jesus before the high priest, the extent of Shelley's iconoclasm becomes rather oppressively glaring: Christ's anguish on the Cross, if we are to believe Ahasuerus, was so much play-acting; Christ merely pretended to suffer in order to impress the rabble and give posterity something to atone for.

At length his mortal frame was led to death.
I stood beside him: on the torturing cross
No pain assailed his unterrestrial sense;
And yet he groaned. Indignantly I summed
The massacres and misery which his name
Had sanctioned in my country, and I cried,
Go! go! in mockery.

A smile of godlike malice reillumined
His fading lineaments.—I go, he cried,
But thou shalt wander o'er the unquiet earth
Eternally.—The dampness of the grave
Bathed my imperishable front. I fell,
And long lay tranced upon the charmed soil.
When I awoke hell burned within my brain,
Which staggered on its seat; for all around
The mouldering relics of my kindred lay,
Even as the Almighty's ire arrested them,
And in their various attitudes of death
My murdered children's mute and eyeless skulls
Glared ghastily upon me.[31]

Since Shelley was a distinguished poet, it is only to be expected that his treatment of the legend should explain at least as much about Shelley as it does about the legend. This is yet more markedly true of the Ahasuerus who appears in Shelley's *opus posthumus.* In *Hellas* the visionary looms much larger than either the rebel or the dreamer. As in *Queen Mab,* the antagonist is still the political tyrant, but since the poem owes its existence more or less directly to the Greek struggle for independence, the symbol of despotism is vested this time in a more concrete figure than Zeus or Jehovah, the Islamic tyrant Mahmud.[32] Mahmud, who has been plagued by the nightmares to which tyrants are traditionally said to be prey, learns of a mysterious Jew who is rumored to have "outlived the world's decay." He dwells in a lonely cave on the Island of Demonesi, surrounded by friendly spirits. Like his namesake in *Queen Mab* he manages to be both bodily decrepit and mentally alert.

The Jew of whom I spake is old, so old
He seems to have outlived the world's decay;
The hoary mountains and the wrinkled ocean
Seem younger still than he; his hair and beard
Are whiter than the tempest-sifted snow;
His cold pale limbs and pulseless arteries
Are like the fibres of a cloud instinct
With light, and to the soul that quickens them
Are as the atoms of the mountain-drift
To the winter wind; but from his eye looks forth
A life of unconsumed thought which pierces
The present, and the past, and the to-come.[33]

In answer to Mahmud's summons, Ahasuerus leaves his insular refuge to expound his doctrines to the tyrant. It is evident that Shelley uses the Wandering Jew's immortality mostly as an excuse to launch into a quasi-Platonic discourse on the nature of reality and the eternal substances. The world, Ahasuerus explains, is coextensive and coeval with thought; "Thought Alone and its quick elements, will, passion, reason, imagination cannot die." The material activities of past, present, and future remain without essential consequence:

—this Whole
Of suns, and worlds, and men, and beasts, and flowers
With all the silent or tempestuous workings
By which they have been, are, or cease to be,
Is but a vision; all that it inherits
Are motes of a sick eye, bubbles, and dreams;
Thought is its cradle and its grave, no less
The future and the past are idle shadows
Of thought's eternal flight—they have no being;
Nought is but that which feels itself to be.[34]

To inculcate his lesson that Mahmud's power is as transitory as all earthly activity, Ahasuerus conjures up the ancestral Ghost of Mohammed II, who had figured earlier as one of Mahmud's dream-phantoms, and who now prophesies that Mahmud's dominions, and with them the whole of Islam, will be overthrown in his own lifetime.

The metaphysical aspects of the poem need not detain us here. But in so far as the Ahasuerus section of *Hellas* represents an attack on the senselessness of material values and a hymn to the eternality of the spirit, it foreshadows in a curious way some of the later handlings of the Wandering Jew legend. Bulwer's Mejnour, for example, embodies the immutability of Thought somewhat as does Ahasuerus. Both Ahasuerus in his grotto and Mejnour in his Alpine retreat have attained to a kind of nirvana; old age has brought them not suffering but serenity. For in Shelley's final treatment of the myth of the Wandering Jew, immortality is once again viewed not as a penalty but as a positive good, capable of conferring a relaxed wisdom, an ability to see life steadily and see it whole. After two thousand years, the Wandering Jew has returned to his prelegendary origins, to the dark regions that were built before Pilate's servitor struck Christ.

More specifically, the visionary powers of Shelley's last Ahasuerus relate him to the whole tribe of Wandering Jews who have infinite knowledge at their fingertips, who know the past empirically and are able to construe the future on the general principle that "what has been, shall be." If they are also gifted with extraordinary prophetic insights, they frequently owe their gift to their talents for reading the right books, studying the right philosophers, and rolling all the world's wisdom into a crystal ball.

Even so, the Ahasuerus of *Hellas* is perhaps too emblematic of Shelley's particular brand of Platonism to fit very comfortably into the framework of the myth. For the academic purposes of tracing the legend through its meanderings down the nineteenth century, *Hellas* is probably less useful than two earlier productions of Shelley's, *St. Irvyne* and "The Victim of the Eternal Avenger." The transcendental and allegorical function of the Ahasuerus in *Hellas* brought to a terminal point one aspect of the Romantic agony. The immortal had now been translated into the eternal sinner, the eternal sinner into the eternal wanderer, the wanderer-malgré-soi into the eternal martyr, the martyr into the rebel. In *Hellas* he came home to roost, having employed his pilgrimage to learn what there was to learn. If the legend was to continue beyond this point, it would probably have to develop along different and more popularly available lines than those indicated in Shelley's visionary poetry.

Such lines had already been provided by the Gothic novelists whom the youthful Shelley imitated; and by the time Shelley died the legend of the Wandering Jew had been irretrievably claimed by a host of writers who decided that their man could be made to swallow elixirs and look like Faustus. I turn, in the following chapter, from the poets to the fictionists, and from Ahasuerus the rebel to Ahasuerus the sorcerer.

> Need I remind the reader that while that was the day for polished skepticism and affected wisdom, it was the day also for the most egregious credulity and the most mystical superstitions,—the day in which magnetism and magic found converts amongst the disciples of Diderot,—when prophecies were current in every mouth,—when the *salon* of a philosophical deist was converted into a Heraclea, in which necromancy professed to conjure up the shadows of the dead,—when the Crosier and the Book were ridiculed, and Mesmer and Cagliostro were believed? In that Heliacal Rising, heralding the new sun before which all vapours were to vanish, stalked from their graves in the feudal ages all the phantoms that had flitted before the eye of Paracelsus and Agrippa.
>
> EDWARD BULWER-LYTTON, *Zanoni* (1842)

IX

The Jew as Sorcerer: Monk Lewis and Godwin

When the legend of the Wandering Jew was joined by the legend of Faust, Ahasuerus was invested with certain specific supernatural gifts which did not necessarily grow out of his longevity and which half the time were induced by sources other than Christ's wrath. The history of Ahasuerus in the period between the appearance of Lewis's *The Monk* in 1796 and the publication of *Trilby* in 1894 is largely the story of his translation from a religious figure of whom Christ made an example for the edification of other sinners, to a black magician whose sorcery was interesting on secular grounds. Although novelists like Lewis, Godwin, and Bulwer found it convenient to retain the Jew's immortality and even continued to regard it as a source of his unhappiness, they no longer made the conventional associations that had given rise to the myth in the first place. In *The Monk,* for example, Ahasuerus is already divested of all his Scriptural trappings. Lewis conjures him up as a stock-figure in a horror story, and the Jew's longevity is used both to intensify the horror and "authenticate" his credentials as a sorcerer. But it is the sorcery, not the longevity, that counts.

Godwin also stresses the Jew's magical prowesses and neglects whatever sinfulness, in the Christian meaning of the word, inheres in his character. Unlike Lewis, however, Godwin attaches his own brand of didacticism to the Wandering Jew. What plainly attracts Godwin to this figure is the degree of isolation from the social community to which his fate must needs condemn him, and the opportunity thus afforded of preaching a good text on the virtues of human fraternalism. And so his Zampieri becomes a minor exemplar in a kind of secular morality play. It is probably of some significance that Godwin allows his man to die after he has made his point and to transmit his wizardry to the hero of the novel, in whom the curse of isolation shows up more potently than it does in a peripheral figure like Zampieri.

It may be noted, however, that both Lewis and Godwin continue to treat the Wandering Jew's magical legacy as a curse: Lewis, because such a doom surrounds his figure with an air of heavy, unassimilated, and fraudulent emotionality; Godwin, because he is trying to say something about the need for ordinary human ties. In Bulwer, even this nexus with the legend is dispensed with. Bulwer, who owes a good deal to Godwin, acknowledges his debt by assuming, like Godwin, that one's living forever is not the most promising condition for making friends easily and that isolation promotes unhappiness. But there is no longer, as there is in Godwin, the slightest implication that the magical practices which ensure immortality are on that account evil. A character like Zanoni is admirable in his theosophic scientism. If his detachment makes for romantic grief, it is to be remembered that his tears are the tears of the lonely superior man: the tears of Werther and Torquato Tasso. *Zanoni* appeared in 1842, and the Wandering Jew, who has ceased to be either a Wanderer or a Jew, is also no longer a sinner. Bulwer celebrates the Heroic Cartaphilus.

The Wandering Jew did not, of course, turn into a black magician overnight toward the end of the eighteenth century. Probably his wizardry evolved as slowly as his other traits. A man who is capable of living forever is very likely capable of ancillary talents. Nor must it be thought that the element of the miraculous is quite so sharply separated from the other romantic elements of the legend as my chapter division might suggest. Miracles, in one form or another, are present in most versions of the myth after the seventeenth century. But in poets like Schubart, Southey, and Shelley, they were consistently subordinated to considerations of a somewhat more intelligent kind: considerations of characterization, ethos, and the like. Ladurlad's immunity to fire and monsters is not nearly so important, or even so remarkable, as his moral fibre under stress; and the immunity of Schubart's Ahasver to volcanoes and the laws of gravity is not so important as his consuming wish to die. The supernatural investiture in these poems is almost gratuitous: even without it Ladurlad and the half-dozen Ahasueri we have encountered possess whatever stature the poet confers upon them, and articulate whatever moral the poet wishes them to articulate. In the novelists to be considered hereafter, on the other hand, the supernatural machinery, with all the paraphernalia used to create horror and suspense, cannot be thought away.

By the end of the eighteenth century—by the time Goethe, Monk Lewis, and Godwin promoted their Easter elixirs and publicized their blood pacts—it had become standard practice to invest the Wandering Jew not only with miraculous bodily strength but with all the external paraphernalia of the miraculous: with fabulous bottleware and invisibility uniforms, with deep, bloody gashes for stigmata, and with a speaking knowledge of cabalistic incantations. The age demanded marvels; the religious bodies patronized and looked favorably upon them, if only to oppose the rising tendency toward enlightenment, skepticism, atheism. We are so apt to think of the late eighteenth century in the idolatrous images of Voltaire and the Encyclopaedists that we forget it was also the age of hypnotism, of occultism, of secret fraternities—some of which (like the Freemasons) oddly cut across the boundaries of enlightenment and mysticism both. It is probably no coincidence that Mozart's High Priest of Freemasonry in *The Magic Flute* looks and sounds like a Middle Eastern sorcerer. It was, as Dickens crudely put it in the first chapter of *A Tale of Two Cities,* the epoch of belief; it was the epoch of incredulity. For each d'Alembert there were three Cagliostros and three more Count Saint-Germains, unriddling the philosopher's stone. The story of Christian Rosenkreuz, eponymous father of Rosicrucianism, who had been initiated by the Arabians into the darkest secrets of nature about the year 1378, gained new converts all over Europe.

And the Wandering Jew, satisfying all sorts and conditions, lent himself also to the marvelous usages which that odd Spirit of the Times exacted. One aspect of the legend, in particular, could scarcely have been overlooked by people like Monk Lewis and Charles Maturin. As far back as Wendover the curse upon Cartaphilus had involved a centennial rejuvenation. It would have been odd if the Gothic writers had not seized on this detail by mobilizing all the machinery which had accumulated in their cellarage: vital elixirs, diabolical covenants, ancestral portraits stepping from their frames. The insatiable curiosity of the Wandering Jew's blood relation, Faust, could be put into requisition, too. Given world enough and time, Godwin's St. Leon and Bulwer's Glyndon and Mejnour will employ their powers in more active services than in the service of atonement. As a result, the whole immortality issue shifts correspondingly. Did the Wandering Jew, transformed into a sorcerer, use his powers for good or ill? In his earlier manifestations, once Christ's curse had begun to operate, the Wandering Jew, for all the horror he may have inspired in his auditors, cut anything but an evil figure, nor was he a force for evil. He could not very well undo his original offense, but whatever restitution he could humanly make, he offered up in fasting and prayer.

It is quite another matter, however, when the Wandering Jew owes his immortality not to Christ's private directive, but to unholy alliances of his own choosing, forbidden alchemical practices, Faustian ambitions to be like God. Sorcery might or might not be forgivable, depending on the ends to which it was employed, but even when it led to heinous consequences, the anathema pronounced upon it no longer had anything but factitious theological origins. Lewis, for example, chose to forgive his Wandering Jew for his conjuring tricks, since he used them to stop the Bleeding Nun's ghostly agonies and thus eased her perturbed spirit; but he could not forgive Ambrosio or Matilda who were plainly in league with some kind of secularized devil and conspired between the two of them to kidnap, ravish, and murder some blameless females. As a rule, the magic practice called for punishment, but never with a real sense of the sin involved. A vague and ghastly aura of religiosity might be retained, but it was a religiosity without religious content. The Wandering Jew who figures briefly in *The Monk,* for example, engages in all the regulation maneuvers preparatory to exorcising the ghost of the unhappy Beatrice; but the object is not to remind the reader of some awful power conferred by Christ on a great sinner; it is to create a spectacular effect. The moral has been sacrificed to the tableau, theology to decor.

The Monk

The first thing which [the Wandering Jew] produced was a small wooden crucifix; he sank upon his knees, gazed upon it mournfully, and cast his eyes towards heaven. He seemed to be praying devoutly. At length he bowed his head respectfully, kissed the crucifix thrice, and quitted his kneeling posture. He next drew from the chest a covered goblet; with the liquor which it contained, and which appeared to be blood, he sprinkled the floor; and then, dipping in it one end of the crucifix, he described a circle in the middle of the room. Round about this he placed various reliques, sculls, thighbones, etc. I observed then that he disposed them all in the forms of crosses. Lastly, he took out a large Bible, and beckoned me to follow him into the circle. I obeyed.[1]

This was written in 1794; but readers of *Dracula* will recall that a hundred years later blood-sucking vampires could still be kept at bay by holy wafers, crucifixes held at certain angles, and magic circles illumined by the emblems of Christianity. Since the Wandering Jew of Lewis's horror story is widely regarded as the forerunner of the types to be found in the novels of Godwin, Shelley, Maturin, and Bulwer, it may be worthwhile to fix the episode in which he figures within the framework of the whole novel. The book, it will be remembered, deals chiefly with the prurient activities of Ambrosio, a popular and appealing Spanish monk, who exercises a certain sexual fascination not only over his congregation but over the nuns under his supervision. The mother superior, in particular, has conceived a passion for him—necessarily frustrated—which she sublimates by enforcing, with needless brutality, Ambrosio's fanatic religious imperatives. For example, she cruelly maltreats one of her better-looking novices who has gotten herself pregnant in the course of the novitiate and who still receives occasional billets-doux from her lover during religious processionals. I have now to call these people by their names. The enceinte novice is Agnes de Medina. The lover is the Marquis Raymond de las Cisternas. The brother of Agnes is Lorenzo de Medina, an acquaintance of Raymond's, and he is in love with Raymond's niece Antonia.

Don Raymond and Agnes are rather on the periphery of the novel; our attention is chiefly engaged by the sexual activities of Ambrosio, whom Lewis after about page 100 is fond of calling "the lustful monk."[2] These are soon complicated by more serious matters, for to gain the blameless Antonia Ambrosio accepts the devil's asssistance, offered him by his erstwhile seducer, Matilda. With Satan on his side, he succeeds in gratifying his lust for Antonia. But just barely; Lorenzo and some members of the Inquisition soon arrive upon the scene, though not in time to save Antonia's life. The rest of the story may be quoted in Montague Summers's paraphrase.

> Torture is applied, a full confession being extorted from the fears of his accomplice, when both are condemned to the stake. Matilda obtains freedom by devoting herself to the demon, and at the last moment Ambrosio also vows himself to the fiend on the condition of instant release. He is borne to the wilds of the Sierra Morena where the mocking spirit informs him that Elvira, whom he slew, was his mother, Antonia, whom he raped and killed, was his sister. The condition of release has been fulfilled, no more will be granted. The wretched monk is then hurled into the abyss.[3]

For the better part of the narrative Agnes is confined in a damp vault of the nunnery and Don Raymond, believing her dead, is reduced to a condition of despair and delirium. To force the Raymond-Agnes relationship into the novel proper, Lewis resorts to an elaborate flashback of some hundred pages, cast in the form of a narrative by Raymond, in which the narrator reconstructs his adventures before Agnes entered the fatal nunnery. It is Raymond's narrative which provides most of the strictly gratuitous supernatural horror and which produces the Wandering Jew. The antecedents are quite ghastly and entertaining, and without them the Wandering Jew would be even more inexcusable than he is.

Don Raymond, having fallen in love with Donna Agnes, follows his betrothed to the Castle of Lindenberg, the estate of her German relatives. The Lindenberg branch violently opposes Agnes's marriage; her aunt, in particular, a superstitious woman given to pietistic seizures, desires to put Agnes away in the nunnery where, as we know, she finally does find a haven and maternity ward. One of the aunt's Catholic superstitions, as the sequel discloses, has some foundation in the Gothic reality; for she is under the impression that Lindenberg Castle is haunted by the ghost of an ancestral Lindenberg, the Bleeding Nun.[4] A portrait of this alarming creature is on view in the gallery. The Bleeding Nun allegedly returns to haunt the castle every five years, on the fifth of May, the anniversary of whatever crime propelled her into the ghostly state. As a courtesy to her the gates of the Castle are left open on the eve of the anniversary; and the lovers now resolve to profit by this circumstance to elope, deciding upon an expedient which is not without its inventive touches. Agnes is to be dressed up in the garments of the Bleeding Nun (whose Sabbatical visits the girl thinks nonsense) and, sprinkled with red fluid, she is to walk out of the Castle in which she has been a virtual prisoner of the aunt's. Raymond is to wait for her in the garden. "The fifth of May arrived," says Raymond, "A period by me never to be forgotten!"

While I sat upon a broken ridge of the hill, the stillness of the scene inspired me with melancholy ideas not altogether unpleasing. The castle, which stood full in my sight, formed an object equally awful and picturesque. Its ponderous walls, tinged by the moon with solemn brightness; its old and partly ruined towers . . . made me sensible of a sad and reverential horror. . . . A few rays of light still glimmered in the chamber of Agnes. I observed them with joy. I was still gazing upon them when I perceived a figure draw near the window, and the curtain was carefully closed to conceal the lamp which burned there.

The figure, whom Raymond supposes to be Agnes, enters the carriage, and they drive off. Actually, of course, she is the real thing, the Bleeding Nun herself. The reader is aware of this, and Lewis, who knows unerringly what to do in a situation of this sort, beautifully plays on our nerves while we are waiting for Raymond to discover the Nun's identity. In the course of the escape, their carriage is dashed to bits; Raymond suffers a brain concussion and, on coming out of it, he finds not only that Agnes is not with him but that, according to all witnesses, he had been traveling alone at the time the accident occurred. In this tenebrous and gloomy atmosphere the unhappy and bewildered man seeks repose on his bed, and then:

> Suddenly I heard slow and heavy steps ascending the staircase. By an involuntary movement I started up in my bed, and drew back the curtain. A single rush-light, which glimmered upon the hearth, shed a faint gleam through the apartment, which was hung with tapestry. The door was thrown open with violence. A figure entered, and drew near my bed with solemn measured steps. With trembling apprehension I examined this midnight visitor. God Almighty!—It was the Bleeding Nun! it was my lost companion! Her face was still veiled, but she no longer held her lamp and dagger. She lifted up her veil slowly. . . .
>
> I gazed upon the spectre with horror too great to be described. My blood was frozen in my veins. I would have called for aid, but the sound expired ere it could pass my lips. My nerves were bound up in impotence, and I remained in the same attitude inanimate as a statue. . . .
>
> In this attitude she remained for a whole long hour, without speaking or moving; nor was I able to do either. At length the clock struck two. The apparition rose from her seat and approached the side of the bed. She grasped with her icy fingers my hand, which hung lifeless upon the coverture, and, pressing her cold lips to mine . . . repeated:
>
> Raymond! Raymond! Thou art mine!
> Raymond! Raymond! I am thine![5]

The Bleeding Nun now haunts Raymond every night; Raymond wastes away under these continual shocks and gives every promise of dying of them; and at this point the Wandering Jew enters and takes control of the situation.

As a matter of fact, he has already entered briefly on a former occasion. Raymond's servant had run into him while he and his master were passing through Munich. The mysterious stranger was then residing at a hotel named "The King of the Romans," a touch obviously meant to suggest the relation with the legend. According to the landlord, the stranger "seemed to have no acquaintance in the town, spoke very seldom, and never was seen to smile." The borrowings here are transparent. "He had neither servants nor baggage, but his purse seemed well furnished, and he did much good in the town. Some supposed him to be an Arabian astrologer, others to be a travelling mountebank, and many declared that he was Doctor Faustus, whom the devil had sent back to Germany." Passing Raymond's valet on the stairs, the stranger had stopped him to impart the baffling information that "his hand alone could dry up blood" and that Raymond was to "wish for him when the clock strikes 'one.'" Since this is the hour when the Bleeding Nun begins her nightly sittings, Raymond now recognizes in the stranger some secret emissary from the spirit world and sends for him.

> He was a man of majestic presence; his countenance was strongly marked, and his eyes were large, black, and sparkling; yet there was something in his look which, the moment that I saw him, inspired me with a secret awe, not to say horror. He was dressed plainly, his hair hung wildly upon his brow, and a band of black velvet which encircled his forehead spread over his features an additional gloom. His countenance wore the marks of profound melancholy, his step was slow, and his manner grave, stately and solemn.

The detail by which the stranger is endowed with a pointedly striking glance has considerable bearing on the discussion, less for the sake of its occurrence in *The Monk* than for its effect on later treatments of the Wandering Jew legend. In *St. Irvyne,*[6] *Zanoni,* and *Trilby,* the Jew's penetrating glance is not only an intimately rendered physiognomic trait but an essential datum in the plot. From here on it is possible to follow with increasing clarity the gradual transformation of the Wandering Jew into a hypnotist—the transformation which was to be completed in Du Maurier's novel. Railo suggests that only beginning with *The Monk* did the Jew's glance become an important feature of the legend. "As Lewis's own contribution," he writes, "I am inclined to regard the Jew's large, black, flashing eyes, whose glance awakened horror, his melancholy, and his noble majesty." As we have had occasion to notice, Lewis certainly did not invent the Wandering Jew's melancholy and his noble majesty, but there may have been good historical reasons for his inaugurating that aspect of the myth which culminated a century later in Svengali.

The glance of the Wandering Jew, whose sinister power Lewis had so well expressed, is a special characteristic of romantic, saturnine persons, from Eblis (the Oriental Lucifer of *Vathek*) onward, increasing in significance as a source of mysterious influences as attention is drawn to the general possibilities of power in the human eye. The latter half of the eighteenth century was the heyday of Mesmerism, a time when "animal magnetism" and quackery based on that idea were extremely fashionable; the species of "magnetism" which flowed, according to Mesmer, from the human eye, in other words the hypnotic power of the eye, was adopted by the romanticists to serve their own purposes, its source, the eye, being endowed by these writers with a dark mystical colouring harmonizing with their own special conception of beauty.[7]

If the Jew's hypnotic eyes are new to the legend, his other features recall the prototypes quite forcibly. Lewis's debt to his sources is, in fact, easily as conspicuous as anything original he had to offer. There is, to begin with, the Jew's *vita,* which agrees in all essentials with what we already know of him as a type:

He named people who had ceased to exist for many centuries and yet with whom he appeared to have been personally acquainted. I could not mention a country, however distant, which he had not visited, nor could I sufficiently admire the extent and variety of his information. I remarked to him that having travelled, seen, and known so much must have given him infinite pleasure. He shook his head mournfully.

"No one," he replied, "is adequate to comprehending the misery of my lot; Fate obliges me to be constantly in movement; I am not permitted to pass more than a fortnight in the same place. I have no friend in the world, and, from the restlessness of my destiny, I never can acquire one. Fain would I lay down my miserable life, for I envy those who enjoy the quiet of the grave; but death eludes me, and flies from my embrace. In vain do I throw myself in the way of danger. I plunge into the ocean; the waves throw me back with abhorrence upon the shore: I rush into the fire; the flames recoil at my approach: I oppose myself to the fury of the banditti; their swords become blunted and break against my breast. The hungry tiger shudders at my approach, and the alligator flies from a monster more horrible than itself. God has set his seal upon me, and all his creatures respect this fatal mark."

It will be noted that the above passage pretty well combines the traditional materials with those popularized by the Romantics. The suicide attempts, of course, recall Schubart and point ahead to Southey and Shelley, down to the exact methods employed. For the "blunted swords" breaking against the Wandering Jew's breast, read Schubart's "An mir sprang der Stahlkolben des Riesen"; similarly, Schubart's "Des Tigers Zahn stumpfte an mir" becomes in Lewis "the hungry tiger shudders at my approach": for Lewis's "the waves throw me back with abhorrence upon the shore" substitute Southey's "the coming Wave / Which knew Kehama's curse, before [Ladurlad's] way / Started, and on he went as on dry land"; and the retreating alligator in Lewis recalls the various dragons, sharks, and maritime serpents to be met with in Schubart and Southey alike. The Jew's immunity to fire appears to be a particular favorite: Ladurlad rescues his daughter from the flames; Schubart's Eternal Jew dangerously skirts the slopes of fire-breathing Etna; Croly's Salathiel seems to walk in and out of municipal Roman conflagrations as though walking through fire were the natural condition of man; and one of Bulwer's spectacular scenes takes Zanoni and Glyndon on a near-fatal excursion to Mount Vesuvius.

The dominant note in Lewis's Wandering Jew, however, is neither one of religious submission, as it is in the writers before 1780, nor one of anticlerical rebelliousness, as it is in Schubart, Shelley, and Southey. It is, rather, a note of meaningless horror. The Jew himself consciously emphasizes his gift for scaring people.

> He put his hand to the velvet which was bound round his forehead. There was in his eyes an expression of fury, despair, and malevolence that struck horror to my very soul. An involuntary convulsion made me shudder. The stranger perceived it.
>
> "Such is the curse imposed on me," he continued; "I am doomed to inspire all who look on me with terror and detestation. You already feel the influence of the charm, and with every succeeding moment you will feel it more. . . . Farewell till Saturday! As soon as the clock strikes twelve expect me at your chamber-door."

His capacity for inspiring horror becomes increasingly plain when, as promised, he returns to Don Raymond's chambers on the following Saturday to proceed with the business of disembarrassing his client of the insufferable Nun. We have already described his mechanical aids. Skulls, thighbones, and covered goblets are all laid out. Crucifix and Bible are in their appointed places. All eventualities have been foreseen, all contingencies anticipated. The Jew thrice invokes the name of Beatrice, and the apparition of the Nun appears. The Jew puts her through a short preliminary catechism. His voice is "distinct and solemn." Hers, "hollow and faltering." The rest must be quoted; the scene is justly famous as *locus classicus* of the terror novel:

He spoke in a commanding tone, and drew the sable band from his forehead. In spite of his injunctions to the contrary, curiosity would not suffer me to keep my eyes off his face; I raised them, and beheld a burning cross impressed upon his brow. For the horror with which this object inspired me I cannot account, but I never felt its equal. My senses left me for some moments; a mysterious dread overcame my courage; and, had not the exorciser caught my hand, I should have fallen out of the circle.

When I recovered myself, I perceived that the burning cross had produced an effect no less violent upon the spectre. Her countenance expressed reverence and horror, and her visionary limbs were shaken by fear.

"Yes!" she said at length; "I tremble at that mark! I respect it! I obey you! Know then, that my bones lie still unburied; they rot in the obscurity of Lindenberg Hole. None but this youth has the right of consigning them to the grave. His own lips have made over to me his body and his soul; never will I give back his promise, never shall he know a night devoid of terror, unless he engages to collect my mouldering bones, and deposit them in the family vault of his Andalusian castle. Then let thirty masses be said for the repose of my spirit; and I trouble this world no more. Now let me depart. Those flames are scorching!"

The Wandering Jew then goes through the regulation maneuvers with his Crucifix, and the Bleeding Nun melts into air. Her power over Raymond is about to come to an end. The Wandering Jew also takes his leave of the bedeviled Marquis, treating him to a few words of advice as he bows himself out:

"Don Raymond, you have heard the conditions on which repose is promised you: be it your business to fulfill them to the letter. For me nothing more remains than to clear up the darkness still spread over the spectre's history, and inform you that, when living, Beatrice bore the name of las Cisternas. She was the great aunt of your grandfather. In quality of your relation, her ashes demand respect from you, though the enormity of her crime must excite your abhorrence."

What these crimes are the Wandering Jew briefly describes in his ensuing narrative about Beatrice de las Cisternas who "not satisfied with displaying the incontinence of a prostitute . . . professed herself an atheist." The recital done, the wandering Jew leaves. Raymond tries to get him to tell *his* autobiography in turn, and the Jew feebly promises to satisfy Raymond's curiosity on a return visit the next day. But the following morning he has disappeared into the dark places out of which he came. His destination, like his origin, is shrouded in unknowables.

The above account of *The Monk* has somewhat slighted such religious and antireligious opinions as the book has to offer, though I have tried to indicate these parenthetically. They are relevant only in that any discussion of the Wandering Jew has finally to establish how closely the author has stuck to the—exclusively religious—prototype. Lewis's position is a good deal less viable, certainly, than Shelley's, whose dogmas on the necessity of atheism and whose transfigurations of Ahasuerus into the image of the arch rebel at least affirm a thoroughly explicit theology. Compared with Shelley's efforts in the satanic line, Lewis's are tinsel. There is a certain fashionable as well as juvenile anticlericalism in *The Monk* (Lewis wrote the book at nineteen), borrowed, according to Tompkins, from the popular German *Schauerroman*.[8] Organized piety does not come off well in Lewis's book; but one may well deny his attacks on the clergy much seriousness when its two chief pillars in the novel, Ambrosio and the mother superior, are positive ogres. As religious fanatics they are naturally grist to Lewis's mill, on the general hypothesis that fanaticism easily brings on the desirable bloodshed. The fact that Agnes violates her monastic vows, entertains a lover, and bears her child in the nunnery, seems not to bother Lewis overmuch; by the end of the novel it is Agnes, rather than the blameless Antonia, who is happily installed with her husband. But it must not be thought that there is any particular method in any of this; Beatrice's elopement from the nunnery, for example, is alleged as one of the counts against her when Lewis wants to translate her into the Spectral Bleeder. Ambrosio and Matilda have naturally got to be damned; but again their damnation must not be viewed with any kind of theological finesse; it is simply that Lewis, having wound himself up to such an intolerable pitch of horror, cannot now leave the reader with the vapid impression that these ghastly dummies will perish through the ordinary channels. As their crimes have been unspeakable, so must their agonies be incomparable.

To the Wandering Jew, as I have indicated, no such doom is vouchsafed. Though he is indeed a sorcerer, Lewis does not imply that he is therefore in league with the nether phenomena. Instead he stresses his sorrow, his dignity, his willingness to lend himself to samaritan performances. He is still, in a way, the great penitent, though with a hitherto impertinent knack for manipulating skulls, thighbones, and mystical silverware. It is not until four years later, in William Godwin's *St. Leon,* that the Jew's sorcery is joined to his unrest and that the legend of Ahasuerus is assimilated to the Faust story.

St. Leon

The best way of approaching Godwin and (via Godwin) Shelley and Bulwer-Lytton is by reverting for a moment to a passage in *The Monk*. It occurs in the main plot involving Ambrosio and Matilda. Matilda is in process of explaining to the monk the sources of her unearthly powers, as these have been instilled into her mentor and thus devolved on her:

> I formerly mentioned that my guardian was a man of uncommon knowledge. He took pains to instil that knowledge into my infant mind. Among the various sciences which curiosity had induced him to explore, he neglected not that which by most is esteemed most impious, and by many chimerical: I speak of those arts which relate to the world of spirits. His deep researches into causes and effects, his unwearied application to the study of natural philosophy, his profound and unlimited knowledge of the properties and virtues of every gem which enriches the deep, of every herb which the earth produces, at length procured him the distinction which he had sought so long, so earnestly. His curiosity was fully slaked, his ambition amply gratified. He gave laws to the elements: he could reverse the order of Nature: his eye read the mandates of futurity; and the infernal spirits were submissive to his commands.

In *St. Leon, St. Irvyne,* and *Zanoni,* "deep researches," "unwearied application to the study of natural philosophy," and "profound and unlimited knowledge" are far more essentially bound up with the very themes of these novels than they are in *The Monk,* in which so many Gothic elements are mobilized that any one motif is immediately overshadowed by a dozen others. The magical practices, which operated incidentally in Lewis's novel, determine the very shape of Godwin's. "It is well known," Godwin notes in the Preface to *St. Leon,* "that the philosopher's stone, the art of transmuting metals into gold; and the elixir vitae, which was to restore youth, and make him that possessed it immortal; formed a principal object of the studies of the curious for centuries."[9] The same dominant chord is struck by the hero-narrator in the opening sentences of the novel proper: "In my own times, and for upwards of a century before them, the subject which has chiefly occupied men of intrepid and persevering study, has been the great secret of nature, the *opus magnum,* in its two grand and inseparable branches, the art of multiplying gold, and of defying the inroads of infirmity and death." In Godwin's novel and in his son-in-law's heavily Godwinian fragment, the hunger for forbidden knowledge leads to certain disastrous consequences that Lewis at best anticipated and that enable a novelist like Godwin to preach an interesting doctrine under the cover of a horror story.

St. Leon appeared four years after *The Monk*. Whatever else may be said about it, it is not a felicitous production.[10] Its first dialogue occurs on page 152, which is not an encouraging sign in a novel. Thereafter much is said by every one in the book, and one immediately wishes oneself translated back into the condition of silence that prevailed before page 152; for once a Godwinian character begins to speak, it takes all of Godwin's will power to make him stop again. St. Leon's goodwife Marguerite, for example, has the greatest difficulty in saying anything in less than seven pages, of which six have nothing to do with the story. "St. Leon," she will address her husband on page 134 of Book Two, "listen kindly to what I am going to say to you, and assure yourself that I am actuated by no spleen, resentment, or ill humour, but by the truest affection," etc., etc., and in this admirable frame of mind she will go on talking to the bottom of page 141. The fact is that Godwin's characters do not, of course, engage in dialogue at all, in the proper sense of the word, but merely recite written Godwin.[11] *St. Leon* is largely a novel of ideas, and the characters in *St. Leon* are the exponents of these.

What ideas? Godwin himself provides part of the answer in the Preface, in which he notes that the novel was intended as a corrective to some of the skeptical notions concerning familial ties which he had propagated four years earlier in his treatise on *Political Justice*.[12]

Some readers of my graver productions will perhaps, in perusing these little volumes, accuse me of inconsistency, the affections and charities of private life being every where in this publication a topic of the warmest eulogium, while in the Enquiry concerning Political Justice they seem to be treated with no great degree of indulgence and favour. In answer to this objection all I think it necessary to say on the present occasion, is that for more than four years, I have been anxious for opportunity and leisure to modify some of the earlier chapters of that work in conformity to the sentiments inculcated in this. . . . I apprehend domestic and private affections inseparable from the nature of man, and from what may be styled the culture of the heart, and am fully persuaded that they are not incompatible with a profound and active sense of justice in the mind of him that cherishes them.

This is, I believe, a fair statement of Godwin's chief purpose, and it is borne out by the events of the novel. Certainly everything in the book is calculated to illustrate the benefits of domestic attachments and the miseries attendant upon the unsocial and the unsociable. St. Leon himself insists upon the miseries of his self-inflicted solitude with unflagging redundancy. " 'Must I,' he lamented, 'for ever live without a companion, a friend, any one with whom I can associate upon equal terms, with whom I can have a community of sensations, and feelings, and hopes and desires, and fears?' " " 'Man was not born to live alone. He is linked to his brethren by a thousand ties; and, when those ties are broken, he ceases from all genuine existence.' " " 'I can no longer cheat my fancy; I know that I am alone. The creature does not exist with whom I have any common language, or any genuine sympathy. Society is a bitter and galling mockery to my heart; it only shows in more glaring colours my desolate condition.' " And, for a paragraph at a time:

> It is indeed absurd, it may be termed profanation, to talk of solitary pleasure. No sensation ordinarily distinguished by that epithet, can endure the test of a moment's inspection, when compared with social enjoyment. It is then only that a man is truly pleased, when pulse replies to pulse, when the eyes discourse eloquently to each other, when in responsible tones and words the soul is communicated. Altogether, we are conscious of a sober, a chaste, and dignified intoxication, an elevation of spirit, that does not bereave the mind of itself, and that endures long enough for us to analyse and savour the causes of our joy.[13]

The theme of isolation is, of course, a recurrent one in Godwin's fiction; indeed it may be said to supply his novels with their stable element. It has often been noted that each one of his heroes suffers in one way or another all the anguish of the solitary. Caleb Williams is cut off from the social body by the persecutions of Falkland; Fleetwood by a combination of Wertherian sensibility and Byronic cynicism which makes him incapable of enduring friendship; Mandeville by his wealth and his plutocratic prejudices; St. Leon by inheriting the cursed legacy of the Wandering Jew.[14] In enforcing his thesis in the body of *St. Leon,* Godwin is something less fortunate than in enunciating it in the Preface. By his own profession, his story called for a judicious mixture of "human passions and feelings with incredible situations," or, in plain language, for melodrama encumbered with sentimentality. Why incredible situations should be profitably mobilized in order to preach the doctrine of domestic affability is not clear, and one rather sympathizes with the impatient query of the critic in *The Monthly Review,* "Of what use are such idle fictions to man in the actual state of existence?"[15]

The purely sentimental aspects of the book obtrude themselves most disagreeably in the opening volume, while St. Leon is still enjoying the advantages of hearth and home. It is at the beginning of Book Two that the Wandering Jew appears to deprive him of his domestic blessings, so that the "extraordinary situations" take over increasingly once St. Leon has stepped outside the charmed circle of his family and gone off, with his elixirs and heaps of gold, to forge the chains of his solitary desolation. Book One finds the St. Leons rusticating in the Alpine territories and on the shores of Lake Constance, and it is only to be expected that these scenes should be surcharged with the ideas and memories of Rousseau. "[Godwin] is in sympathy with the great body of sentimental literature that depicts the delights of a thatched cottage and humble repast of curds and cream," Allen writes;[16] and we must bear with the St. Leons as they each one of them, down to the six-year-old Little Marguerite, trot out their several versions of pastoral.

[Little Marguerite] came towards me, and, with much anxiety in her enquiring face, asked why we must go away from the cottage? If I had got some money, I might go to the town, and buy sweetmeats, and ribbands, and new clothes, and a hundred more pretty things, and bring them home. For her part, she should be better pleased to put on her finery and make her feast in the pretty old summer-house . . . than in a palace all stuck over with emeralds and rubies. Her mother wiped away a tear at the innocent speech of her darling, kissed her, and bid her go and feed the hen and her chickens.[17]

St. Leon himself feels it to be a double blessing to reside at once in the bosom of nature and in the bosom of his family; indeed the two are vaguely felt to be the same thing.

I lived in the bosom of nature, surrounded with the luxuriance of its gifts, and the sublimity of its features, which the romantic elevation of my soul particularly fitted me to relish. In my domestic scene I beheld the golden age renewed, the simplicity of pastoral life without its grossness, a situation remote from cities and courts, from traffic and hypocrisy, yet not unadorned with taste, imagination, and knowledge.

Before the Wandering Jew enters to cut off her elevated torrents, we had better give ear once more to St. Leon's wife. On the subject of curd and cream she is able to speak volumes, and to speak them very well.

Let us at length dismiss artificial tastes and idle and visionary pursuits, that do not flow in a direct line from any of the genuine principles of our nature! Here we are surrounded with the sources of happiness. . . . What is chivalry, what are military prowess and glory? Believe me, they are the passions of a mind depraved, that with ambitious refinement seeks to be wise beyond the dictates of sentiment or reason! There is no happiness so solid, or so perfect, as that which disdains these refinements. You, like me, are fond of the luxuriant and romantic scenes of nature. Here we are placed in the midst of them. . . . Alas, Reginald! It is I fear too true, that the splendour in which we lately lived, has its basis in oppression. . . . Here we see a peasantry more peaceful and less oppressed, than perhaps any other tract of the earth can exhibit. They are erect and independent, at once friendly and fearless. Is not this a refreshing spectacle? . . . How cumbrous is magnificence!

We may be forgiven for skipping three pages:

There is no character [Marguerite is still talking] more admirable than the patriot yeoman, who unites with the utmost simplicity of garb and manners, an understanding fraught with information and sentiment, and a heart burning with the love of mankind. Such were Fabricius and Regulus among the ancients, and such was Tell, the founder of the Helvetic liberty. For my part, I am inclined to be thankful, that this unexpected reverse in our circumstances, has made me acquaintanced with new pleasures, and opened to my mind an invaluable lesson.

I have lingered over Godwin's thesis not merely because to do so gives an idea of his doctrinaire qualities, but because the very vehemence with which he preaches his doctrine of the social virtues helps to place his Wandering Jew in the context of Godwin's ethic and to explain the importance that Godwin attached to the legendary figure. To palm him off simply as a continuator of the Gothic tradition, standing midway between Horace Walpole and Charles Maturin, would be to overlook sententious qualities in *St. Leon* which are almost entirely absent from, say, *The Monk,* and only incidentally felt in *St. Irvyne;* and to palm off Zampieri as merely another wicked sorcerer, unhappy in his wickedness, would be, I think, to miss some of the attractions which he had for Godwin. In a novel whose chief lessons are the need for domestic solidarity and the vicious influence of unproductive wealth, the Wandering Jew serves an ideal function. Given his anterior status of magician, he brings to the hero the two gifts best suited to drive home Godwin's moral: the curse of human isolation, and the curse of illimitable riches.

Godwin's novel, like Lewis's, spins itself out during the dying decades of the Renaissance, possibly because Godwin, like Lewis, wants to take advantage of such fictional interest as the Inquisition has to offer.[18] The events of Book I, which lead up to Zampieri's brief sojourn, can be summed up in a page. The opening chapters find young Reginald de St. Leon setting out on what promises to be a glorious military career as officer under Francis I. Like most of Godwin's heroes he is also an irresistibly deluded man, who loosely equates the ideal of honor with the actuality of wealth and who, in pursuit of his ideal, ruins himself at the gambling table. There comes to his rescue a young lady, who by any other name is Mary Wollstonecraft and of whom little needs to be premised except that she "seemed to shed ambrosial odours around her; her touch was thrilling; her lips were nectar; her figure was that of a descended deity!" After much promotional oratory by his prospective father-in-law, Reginald marries this lady who, though she bears him several prodigious children, is powerless to subdue her husband's gambling instincts. In view of Reginald's own resolute imperatives on the need for domestic ties, it must be confessed that he tests their strength to the utmost, by plunging his family at once into the very abyss of indigence and distress.

The St. Leons emigrate into the Alps. To the devotees of Rousseau Switzerland offers many advantages, but clement weather is not one of them. If there are patriot-yeomen, uniting with the utmost simplicity of garb and manners an understanding fraught with information and sentiment, there are also glaciers; there are avalanches too, and one such buries the St. Leons' cottage and lays waste their chicken farm. To the cruelty of nature in the broad sense must be added the brutality of human nature in the finite: the landlord of the St. Leons unmasks himself as an extortionist, a criminal, not the type of person Marguerite expected to find among the descendants of Fabricius and Tell. In the meantime, neither the experience of poverty nor the wind of fashionable doctrine has managed to reconcile Reginald to the importance of his familial responsibilities; he rather pouts his way through his Alpine phase, spends much time aimlessly on horseback, and seems on the whole to be in want of employment. After the business of the avalanche and the landlord, the family moves to safer grounds on the shore of the Bodensee, and they are in a fair way of acclimating themselves to the refreshing spectacles and invaluable lessons provided by cow and ewe when the Wandering Jew appears on the scene, and with him trouble.

> It was in the evening of a summer's day [begins Book Two] in the latter end of the year fifteen hundred and forty-four, that a stranger arrived at my habitation. He was feeble, emaciated, and pale, his forehead full of wrinkles, and his hair and beard as white as snow. Care was written in his face; it was easy to perceive that he had suffered much from distress of mind; yet his eye was still quick and lively, with a strong expression of suspiciousness and anxiety. His garb, which externally consisted of nothing more than a robe of russet brown, with a girdle of the same, was coarse, threadbare, and ragged. . . . Ruined and squalid as he appeared, I thought I could perceive traces on his countenance of what had formerly been daring enterprise, profound meditation, and generous humanity.

This phenomenon now asks St. Leon for sanctuary, stipulating with much ill-grace that his presence remain concealed from the lesser St. Leons. Reginald accedes to all his wishes and puts him up in that same summerhouse which Little Marguerite has been heard to place above a palace all stuck over with emeralds and rubies, little suspecting that her sudden supercessor in the cottage quite shares her contempt for rubies and emeralds, though for reasons rather less sentimental than hers. But when St. Leon begins to ask his guest the questions one customarily puts to a new acquaintance, the mysterious gaffer becomes as evasive as the Wandering Jew in *The Monk*. "My name," he replies with needless churlishness, "shall be buried with me in the grave; nor shall any one who has hitherto known me, know how, at what time, or on what spot of earth I shall terminate my existence. The cloud of oblivion shall shelter me from all human curiosity." Eventually he relents just far enough to disclose his name, which is Zampieri, and St. Leon discovers further that the man is being sought, either by the local constabulary or by agents of the Inquisition, on some as yet unspecified charge.

It is evident from Zampieri's dossier, meager though it is, that he already anticipates the species of Wandering Jew whose immortality is not absolute but may be abrogated under special conditions. St. Leon, in turn, gradually reveals a degree of fascination for his guest which, we are given to understand, is not healthy. As Zampieri extends his sojourn he becomes a little more talkative and engages his host in a series of increasingly tantalizing conversations, always behind closed doors. In the weeks to follow he is given a chance to manifest those traditional traits with which we are already familiar: the astonishing first-hand acquaintance with the past, the intensity of his suffering, and the general dignity with which he endeavors to bear up under his lot.

When we discoursed of events that had passed, and persons that had died, more than a century before, the stranger often spoke of them in a manner as if he had been an eye-witness and directly acquainted with the objects of our discourse. This I ascribed to the vividness of his conceptions, and the animation of his language. He however often checked himself in this peculiarity, and always carefully avoided what might lead to any thing personal to himself. I described to him the scenes of my youth, and related my subsequent history; he on his part was invincibly silent on every circumstance of his country, his family, and his adventures.

"The greatness of his powers, the dignity of his carriage, the irresistible appearance of sincerity that sparkled in his eye, and modulated his voice" are also old hat for the myth-monger, as is the general tenor of his lamentation: "Why should my distresses and disgraces be published to any one? Is it not enough, that they have lacerated my bosom, that they have deprived me of friends, that they have visited me with every adversity and every anguish," etc., etc. But among the reasons he alleges for his secrecy there is one which deserves some attention here because it comes up again in a significant way in Bulwer's novel. His occult powers, he tells St. Leon (at a point when we all take it for granted that he is in possession of occult powers) might fall into the hands of some creature who will misuse them to the detriment of all mankind.

The talent he possessed was one, upon which the fate of nations and of the human species might be made to depend. God had given it for the best and highest purposes; and the vessel, in which it was deposited, must be purified from the alloy of human frailty. It might be abused, and applied to the most atrocious designs. It might blind the understanding of the wisest, and corrupt the integrity of the noblest. It might overturn kingdoms, and change the whole order of human society into anarchy and barbarism. It might render its possessor the universal plague or the universal tyrant of mankind.

This is substantially the burden of Mejnour's answer in Bulwer's *Zanoni* when Glyndon, in process of being initiated, wants to know why his mentor is being "so churlish in withholding the diffusion" of his secrets. "Suppose," Mejnour argues,

"we were to impart all our knowledge to all mankind, indiscriminately, alike to the vicious and the virtuous — should we be benefactors or scourges? Imagine the tyrant, the sensualist, the evil and corrupted being possessed by these tremendous powers; would he not be a demon let loose on earth? . . . It is for these reasons . . . that we place our ordeal in tests that purify the passions and elevate the desires."[19]

If the substance of the two speeches sounds alike, Mejnour's concluding sentence sharply marks the difference between his own motive and Zampieri's. For Zampieri the possession of the *elixir vitae* and of the philosopher's stone tends to results quite other than any which might "purify the passions and elevate the desires"; and he is willing in the long run to initiate St. Leon into his secrets not because St. Leon has been singled out for some supernal favor, but because Zampieri needs to captivate some soul into taking from him a burden which he experiences as an unending nightmare. Zampieri, in brief, has been wandering up and down the earth in an effort to hunt up a creature who is ready to play the Wandering Jew *in loco parentis*, to whom he may render up his secret and who is thus to free him from his endless existence. St. Leon is to be lured into what is in effect a devil's compact. Zampieri's merchandise is extremely attractive: eternal youth, infinite riches. St. Leon listens, marvels—and falls. Zampieri, free from the onus of immortality, sensibly wastes away; the constabulary appear one day to search for some mysterious alien who is under suspicion of black magic by the Inquisition; Zampieri has just strength enough to crawl to a hiding place a few yards away; and there he dies the following morning.

St. Leon is beside himself with triumph. "Time," he exults,

> "shall generate in me no decay, shall not add a wrinkle to my brow, or convert a hair of my head to grey! This body was formed to die! this edifice to crumble into dust; the principles of corruption and mortality are mixed up in every atom of my frame. But for me the laws of nature are suspended; the eternal wheels of the universe roll backward; I am destined to be triumphant over fate and time!"

But of course he is not; and the remaining two volumes and a half are intended to demonstrate the depth of his folly and his self-deception.

It can be seen from the foregoing that in his own right Zampieri is of no great importance to Godwin, who keeps him on scene scarcely longer than Lewis keeps his Ahasuerus on scene. Still, the two figures play manifestly different roles, and Zampieri's is much the more far-reaching. Lewis's man is brought into the book, performs his magic tricks, is ushered out again; and that is that. His performance is merely a set piece in a disjointed narrative; it sets up no reverberations; it points nowhere; one cannot generalize away from it. The incident of the Bleeding Nun is itself a gratuitous episode, productive of momentary horror; its effects are situational and stationary. But the importance of Zampieri's brief presence is defined wholly by its consequences. His appearance, in fact, marks the turning point of the novel. For having depicted his hero in the ideal circumstances conferred upon him by pastoralism-cum-Wollstonecraft, Godwin now plunges him into those "extraordinary situations" by which the moralist means to point up the fatality attached to St. Leon's inheritance.

What we get from here on in is a sequence of calamities by which Godwin increasingly isolates his character, depressing him step by step almost in the manner of Balzac's famous *coupes*. To begin with, his son Charles creates an unpleasant scene when he finds that St. Leon is unable to account for his sudden wealth before some strangers who cast aspersions on his honor; and, after reading his father an extended homily, he deserts him. Next St. Leon is incarcerated for his failure to satisfy the local police in the matter of Zampieri's mysterious disappearance. He breaks jail and escapes to Italy where his house is burnt down. Wherever he goes his wealth excites suspicion and creates animosity. Next his wife dies—of loneliness, of neglect, of life. In Italy St. Leon is jailed a second time, his imprisonment lasting twelve years and taking up the better part of Book Three. He escapes again. Disguised as a Spanish grandee he visits his impoverished orphan daughters, gives himself out to be their father's testamental executor, and restores them to riches.

He proceeds to Hungary. While there he saves the country single-handed from the ravages of war by means of his portable bank-account and befriends the patriotic Bethlem Gabor, finding "an inexhaustible and indescribable pleasure in examining the sublime desolation of a mighty soul," "a soul that soared to a sightless distance above the sphere of pity." (It is one of the incidental defects of Godwin's prose that one does not quite know whether a phrase like "a soul that soared to a sightless distance above the sphere of pity" is intended as a compliment or a criticism.) The soul presently exercises its privilege of soaring above the sphere of pity by casting the savior of Hungary into yet another dungeon, as though to punish him for his wealth;[20] and there St. Leon is still languishing when the fortress is besieged by the anti-Bethlemites, led by a certain De Damville, who turns out to be St. Leon's renegade son Charles and who seizes the occasion thus unexpectedly thrown in his path to repudiate his father a second time. At long last, having had ample means of reflecting on the futility of his devil's pact, the uselessness of his wealth, and the degradation of the outcast, St. Leon is able to watch from afar and in disguise as his children grow into happy and useful human beings. In the closing sentence of the book, St. Leon murmurs his acquiescence in "the actual state of existence," and, in a final gesture which is grossly out of character with the crescendi that went before, he urges the pious conclusion that "this busy and anxious world of ours yet contains something in its stores that is worth living for."

What is Godwin's contribution to the legend? His Wandering Jew dies in the early part of the book; but Zampieri's death, taken by itself, is nothing new. Schubart's Ahasver did not live interminably: angels descended to herald his reprieve. What is new is Godwin's ability to intertwine the stories of the Wandering Jew and the devil's compact in such a way that the fusion of the wanderer and the black magician became accessible to later novelists. Lewis had used both stories separately in *The Monk*; but it seems not to have occurred to him to do anything with them, and so he assigned the satanic pact to Ambrosio and Matilda, and the Ahasuerus legend to a totally disparate narrative. In making his Wanderer a party to the pact and in introducing, as central figure, the legatee of the curse, Godwin gave the myth a new lease on life, at least for a few decades. Shelley, as I noted, took over Godwin's plot innovation along with his morality in *St. Irvyne*; but the theme of the Eternal Wanderer who discovers the horror of his compact and devotes his life to the search for a proxy reaches its full climax only with the story of Melmoth. Maturin's chief interpreter assigns to Melmoth a fundamentally religious theme: that no human being, even in the deadliest crisis, likes to surrender his soul for worldly advantages.[21] St. Leon, in fact, makes the same discovery; and Maturin's theme is, I think, no less strongly anticipated in Godwin for his treating it in a basically secular spirit.

After the Gothic novelists were done with him, the Wandering Jew appeared sporadically. Bulwer picked him up again in 1842, but by then he had become scarcely recognizable. He shared the *mal' occhio* with his immediate forebears; and like his earlier prototypes lived to be upwards of 5,000 years old; but we shall be concerned not

Ahasuerus

Fagin at the Three Cripples

"'Et maintenant dors, ma mignonne!'"

with the similarities but with the fundamental divagation from the myth.

Bulwer thought *Zanoni* his best book, and Carlyle spoke of it courteously. In his preface in the 1853 edition, Bulwer notes with his customary complacency that "as a work of imagination Zanoni ranks, perhaps, among the highest of my prose fictions"; and in his dedicatory epistle to the sculptor John Gibson he proclaims: "I, Artist in words, dedicate, then, to you, Artist, whose ideas speak in marble, this well-loved work of my matured manhood. I love it not the less because it has been little understood and superficially judged by the common herd. It was not meant for them." The theosophists, for whom it was meant, have taken it very seriously, however; thus, a monograph on Bulwer printed under the aegis of the Theosophical Publishing House records that "If one were asked to name the book which more than any other provides a matrix for the building-up of modern theosophical philosophy in the English language, *Zanoni* seems an inevitable choice.[22]

Zanoni is a rather queer book; and the reader who comes upon it without the theosophist's professional equipment may find it difficult to escape a certain sense of oppressiveness as he struggles through pages of pseudo-scientific phraseology. In trying to place the novel within the framework of the myth, one is likely to be struck by Bulwer's departures from earlier works rather than by his debts. The most important of these departures I have already anticipated. To begin with, Bulwer drops all pretenses that his figure is a Jew. Lewis and Godwin treated their Wandering Jews so vaguely and diffidently that the question of religious affiliation is left in the air; it did not matter whether Zampieri and Lewis's man were Jews or not. Bulwer's Zanoni is definitely and specifically not a Jew but a Chaldean, in love with an Italian Catholic.

The more important difference is that the moral definition of the magician figure has shifted noticeably. In Godwin's novel, as we saw, the hunger for forbidden knowledge leads to disastrous consequences; similarly in Shelley's and Maturin's. In Bulwer's novel, on the contrary, the phrase "forbidden knowledge" already implies a paradox: all knowledge is open to all comers who are qualified to cope with Rosicrucian secrets. In *St. Leon* and *St. Irvyne* the Faustian offense is directed against a somewhat sentimentally conceived overlord; in *Zanoni* the unriddling of arcane formulae is not so much a punishable heresy as it is (at worst) a threat to mankind. Hence, whereas Godwin treats sorcery as a positive evil, Bulwer treats it as a contingent good. The possession of the philosopher's stone does not so much argue presumptuousness in Mejnour and Zanoni as it argues infinite patience and travail. For Godwin Zampieri's sorcery automatically confers on Zampieri the mark of ineradicable woe; for Bulwer the same thing confers upon Mejnour the patent of supreme virtue.

Moreover, the isolation that Zampieri and St. Leon experience as a result of their superhuman powers constitutes in itself something of a life-sentence in the eyes of a sentimental moralist like Godwin. In Bulwer's novel, such insulation from ordinary distractions is essential and profitable to people of Mejnour's stamp: it keeps them at their desks and in their laboratories. From his Olympian elevation, Mejnour surveys men and affairs with an impartial and a frigid eye. He wants nothing to do with them. At worst what may happen is what happens as a recurrent commonplace in Goethe's dramas: the man of icy or of hypersensitive intelligence experiences his separateness as an insufferable strain and longs for decent, normal, ordinary contacts. He wants his Charlotte, cutting bread and butter, or Gretchen, humming at the spinning wheel. Zanoni (like Svengali after him) will settle for the world's great soprano as the next best thing. His yearning for human commitments, which places him a notch below the totally detached Mejnour, eventually leads to his death, though Bulwer does not positively think worse of him for desiring the company of a mortal. The point is that by the time Bulwer adds his bit to the legend, immortality no longer presumes an act of evil and therefore can no longer be treated as a sinner's just punishment. So far from having sinned, Mejnour and Zanoni have been in some sense divinely elected. Their isolation from worldly affairs does not mean that they are bogies but that they are men of scientific genius.

Finally, Bulwer introduces a certain arbitrary element into the whole story of the Wandering Jew by having not one, but two potential immortals, of whom one is relatively more immortal than the other. The difference between Mejnour and Zanoni is marked by the degree to which they succumb to the temptations of the bread-and-butter world. Mejnour remains immune to all human claims and is rewarded by living forever in a Lotus Land of scientific detachment. The theosophist in Bulwer admires Mejnour's imperturbable devotion to his business; the romancer in him thinks only indifferently of it; and one is not certain, finally, what to make of Mejnour. Zanoni is both the weaker vessel and the more charming: he falls in love with a gifted singer whose voice control he regulates on occasion; having found his mate on earth, he proceeds to hand on his immortality to an eager Anglo-Saxon who does not quite know what to do with it; finally, he pays the price of his weakness by being guillotined during the Reign of Terror. But as a romantic hero he cuts an attractive figure.

After Bulwer, Ahasuerus enjoyed a major rest. When he reappeared as Svengali fifty-three years afterward, he bore more resemblance to Shylock than to the Wandering Jew. Very late in the day, on the threshold of the twentieth century, the myths of Judas and of Cartaphilus meet in the figure of a Victorian bogey-hypnotist; and with our discussion of *Trilby* we must rest our case.

> We are approaching a frontier, and the voices that come to us from the other side, *Modern Love* and *Ecce Homo,* Swinburne's first poems and Pater's first essays, are the voices of a new world, of which the satirist is not Cruikshank but Du Maurier, the laureate not Tennyson but Browning, the schoolmaster not Arnold but his son.
>
> G. M. YOUNG, "Portrait of an Age" (1934)

X

The Jew as Degenerate and Artist: Du Maurier

A good way of placing Svengali in the main tradition of the Jewish stereotype is to take G. M. Young's above hint. One may conveniently compare Cruikshank's drawing of Fagin in his condemned cell, or the illustration to Chapter XLII of *Oliver Twist,* picturing Fagin at the "Three Cripples," with Du Maurier's drawing of Svengali in the act of hypnotizing Trilby. Detail for detail the two Jews run equally true to type: the same unkempt hair, the same bushy eyebrows and penetrating stare, the same protruding Hapsburg lip. The noses are beaked in the same way, not so much jutting outward as resting flat against the mustaches, so that the characters may be imagined sniffling into their beards as they converse; the beards, too, are of identical cut, straggling Vandykes. The fingers which Fagin strikes cunningly against the side of his nose and those with which Svengali beckons toward Trilby are the same long, bony, by no means unbeautiful fingers. The shabby clothes, too, are shabby in the same way. The only difference is that Fagin still wears the broad-brimmed hat and the long black kaftan perpetuated by orthodox Jews, whereas Svengali is done up indifferently in the garb of the Parisian bohemian. And their sleeves are a world too wide for their shrunken wrists.

Still, it would be quite impossible to transpose the two figures. On second glance all similarities disappear. No such creature as Fagin ever trod the boards of the Adelphi. The shaft of light that breaks into the condemned cell strikes the prison wall and illuminates a patch on the floor; but Fagin remains twice imprisoned in an island of darkness. Compared with this picture of human evil left to reflect upon itself, Svengali looks like a *papier-mâché* Mephistopheles. The features are, in an elementary way, those of the devil all right, but of the devil who is about to get up and sing *Le veau d'or*. The light that radiates round Trilby's head, while on one side of her Svengali puts her to sleep and on the other the old Jewess places a diadem on her head, is the merest embellishment; or perhaps there may be some wax candles about. The diadem itself is decorative claptrap; there is nothing about a diadem in the score. There one has the whole conventional tableau: the drawing-room heroine all in white *crêpe-de-chine,* the aging villain, the old crony of a confidante. "Et maintenant," says Svengali, "dors, ma mignonne." It is the devil out of *Punch* whispering. Presently he will put on evening clothes and drive Trilby to the opera. The end of the nineteenth century finds the Wandering Jew driving about London in a gilded landau, with a nice Gibson girl in tow.

Du Maurier as Novelist

Du Maurier's fame rests chiefly on his work as an illustrator; hence the foregoing demonstration. As a novelist he is something of a dead letter. Such as they are, his literary accomplishments have received next to no critical attention, nor is it likely that his fiction will ever be treated very seriously. (Of the dozen articles he has provoked in the past twenty years, half are concerned with his work as a graphic artist.)[1] His three novels were written within a period of seven years after Du Maurier had already served a glorious career as the most eminent of late Victorian draftsmen.[2] Of the three novels *Peter Ibbetson* led the way in 1891; *Trilby* followed in 1894; *The Martian* was published posthumously in 1897. All three were issued with copious illustrations by the author, in *Punch* style. If I were to commit myself to a spontaneous critical estimate of the books, I should say at once that the illustrations are the best things in them. As literature the novels are fairly abominable; criticism is right in dissociating itself from these immortal potboilers. The publication histories of *Ibbetson* and *Trilby* are in their way exciting stuff, but their proper repository is a study of popular culture.[3] Just what finally distinguishes a genuine artist from a popularizer with the kind of lasting appeal Du Maurier seems to have secured is perhaps a moot point; but one of the distinctions, I imagine, is that the popularizer has a flair for summarizing and rushing indiscriminately over the events of the narrative, sacrificing detail, intensiveness, and a willingness to pause and look, to a hurried and superficial coverage. Years are as minutes; vast spaces are traversed in no time at all; the rush of incidents—themselves never genuinely apprehended but merely sighted in transit—this is what matters. It is what matters to Du Maurier, certainly, who never pauses. His glorious achievements in fiction are his transitions. One reads his books and one says: what an imperturbable mind.[4]

Du Maurier's positive faults are embarrassingly obvious in his style, which reflects the general breathlessness; it is gushy and exclamatory—literally so in that every other sentence ends in an exclamation point, or two exclamation points or occasionally three ("Paris! Paris!! Paris!!!")—revealing an inexhaustible and fatiguing capacity for unsophisticated astonishment.

> *It was Trilby!*
> Trilby the tone-deaf, who couldn't sing one single note in tune! Trilby, who couldn't tell a C from an F!!
> What was going to happen?![5]

Elsewhere his prose degenerates into cloyingly sophomoric asides: "Hélas! ahime! ach weh! ay de mi! eheu!—in point of fact, alas! That is the very exclamation I wanted." As a rule, Du Maurier deploys his linguistic equipment a trifle more tactfully than this; but even so his books remain without a doubt the most fantastically bilingual novels on the market. His pages teem with French conversational matter, interjections, parenthetical confidences, which the narrator sometimes translates and sometimes not, but which in any case augment the hectic schoolgirlish chit-chattiness behind the material revealed. "It gave him unspeakable excitement and a strange tender wistful melancholy for which there is no name. *Je connais ça.*" "Little Billee handed sixty francs to the massier for his bienvenue."

Du Maurier, of course, was Anglo-French, as was his material. Each one of his novels is, in a geographical way, a tale of two cities. Peter Ibbetson is reared in the Parisian suburbs, is brought to England after the death of his parents; he returns to France in his dream existence, which occupies the final third of the book, while living out his corporeal existence in a London prison for lunatics. Trilby (the narrative as well as the character) shuttles back and forth between London and Paris with such awe-inspiring breeziness that one is never sure whether one is in the one place or the other; the chances are, however, that in either country the *mise-en-scène* will be an *atelier* or a *restaurant,* or the passage between; for Du Maurier's characters eat immensely. *The Martian* is still more cosmopolitan, even interstellar, in its setting: the hero, Barty Josselin, Anglo-French like his author, with ties to the Scottish peerage, attends boarding school in France, travels in Belgium in the company of some Italians; in Germany he proposes to an English Jewess, despite the warnings against the marriage which he receives in his sleep from a woman on the planet Mars.

It is perhaps a pity that Du Maurier did not deal with his dual nationality more problematically. He merely uses it in a rather obvious way, to provide a colorful backdrop and a maximum of linguistic gobbledygook. Even so, the subject with which he did choose to concern himself might have been treated quite seriously by a better writer. Du Maurier's recurrent theme has to do with the influence of some occult force on the gifted bohemian.[6] All his important characters are artists of one description or another. The ways in which Du Maurier exposes them to the psychic machinery admit of occasional variations: for example, in *Trilby* Svengali, who is a performing artist of genius, incorporates the occult possibilities himself, while in the same novel Billee becomes a painter of considerable stature through the ordinary channels: *odium vitae* and hard work. But in general the idea is to let the occult loose on the potential artist at a critical juncture in his life, when some emotionally harrowing experience has anyhow, so to speak, sensitized his antennae. Trilby, after an unhappy love affair, falls under the evil spell of the Jew. Ibbetson, after killing his uncle, learns "the secret of dreaming true," which consists not merely of willing one's own dreams, but of having the assurance that the beloved dream-object shall, reciprocally, dream right along. If, for example, Peter Ibbetson (in *his* dream) asks Mimsey Seraskier to leave a note for him next morning, appointing a trysting place for tomorrow night's dream, and if Mimsey (in *her* dream) so promises, Peter will, on waking up, find a real note from her in his real cell for the criminally insane. The idea is somewhat that of two people talking to each other in their sleep and resuming the conversation at breakfast. In *The Martian,* finally, Barty Josselin, on the point of going blind and killing himself, receives in his sleep an admonitory letter written in his own handwriting and bearing the signature of a vital female essence named Martia after the planet of issuance.[7] Under Martia's recondite influence Barty grows to be the world's most daring novelist, author of the immortal *Sardonyx.* Just what these novels are about, Du Maurier leaves unsaid, but from the respectfully shocked tone which his narrator adopts toward them one gathers that they manage to be both messianic and unspeakable—the sort of novels Wilde might have written, or Mark Ambient, the author of *Beltraffio. The Martian* concludes on a garbled Bergsonian note: Martia, charmed with the notion of evolving a biologically and cerebrally perfect species, resolves to quit Mars and to be born as daughter to Barty and his Jewish wife.

Of such stuff science fiction is made.[8] Du Maurier, however, subjoins a message of sorts: there are, in effect, says Du Maurier, two norms of existence, the actual and the illusory. But the conventional meanings of these two norms ought really to be turned upside down. Reality, as the world goes, is as nothingness compared with the sublime reality imparted by that otherworldly impulse which, in the absence of a more specific terminology, I have called the occult, but which may, in fact, involve a variety of agencies: mesmerism, dreaming, telepathy, and an interplanetary Western Union service.[9] The point is that whatever greatness, genius, bliss, is granted to mortals is granted by virtue of this occult insemination. Once the Duchess of Towers has insinuated herself into Peter's dream life, his existence is translated into one of the sheerest incandescence: "She has filled my long life of bondage with such felicity as no monarch has ever dreamed, and has found her own felicity in doing so. . . . The most sympathetic reader is apt . . . to be skeptical of the beauties and virtues and mortal gifts of one he has never seen." "[The Duchess] did not stay long, and when she departed all turned dull and commonplace that had seemed so bright before she came." The most sympathetic reader will take the beauties and virtues on faith and is apt to be most skeptical of Mimi's talents when they attain their apotheosis in a mere riot of punctuation:

"And there is no end, and never can be—no end to Time and all the things that are done in it—no end to Space and all the things that fill it, or all would come together in a heap and smash up in the middle—and there *is* no middle! no end, no beginning, no middle! *no middle,* Gogo! think of *that*! it is the most inconceivable thing of all!!!"[10]

Part of Du Maurier's difficulty in passages such as this is his positive genius for adopting the most unsuitable focus of perception from which to broadcast his occult disclosures. There is every indication that he intended his psychic messages to be taken seriously; but the narrators whom he appoints are so gabby that the mysterious is deprived of all its latent mystery and reduced to the level of sentimental kitchen gossip. The result is a ludicrous disharmony between narration and narrative. Svengali sends messages "out of the mysterious East," but the mysterious East, and the whole dreadful *mystique* of the Perpetual Wanderer, take on a kind of warmed-over domestic property when the hypnotic Easterner is breezily said to be "as bad as they make 'em" and endowed by the narrator with a German-Jewish brogue which smacks a little less of Rasputin and a little more of vaudeville.

Against this setting, then, of bohemian ebullience, always ready to be darkened by the shadow of the occult directive, we have to imagine the figure of Svengali, the Wandering Jew as he looked to the late Victorians.

Svengali: Black Magician

By the time Du Maurier added his contribution to the myth of the Wandering Jew, the type had already been fused with that of the Black Magician. As we know, the Scriptural significance of the prototype had long been distorted to the point where it seemed no longer to matter whether Ahasuerus had ever so much as heard of Christ.

By 1890 the Wandering Jew could assume almost any mask. He could be a bogey; a harmless ascetic; a member of a secret masonic order; a dromomaniac in romantic places; a sorcerer; a satanic malcontent; a megalomaniac; a necrophiliac; a visionary; a proletarian social reformer. As Railo notes, he might stand as an eternal warning against unbelief; as a vehicle for ideas concerning the past and future of mankind; as the symbol of the Christian's desire to cast off the fetters of mortality.[11] All these possibilities were open to Du Maurier. Given his dual interest in the occult and the problem of evolution, which he had already demonstrated in *Peter Ibbetson,* it would have been natural for him to focus on the aspect of the legend that emphasized the notion of an organic eternalism. As a matter of fact, Du Maurier retained the Wandering Jew's gypsy-like attributes, but he did not stress them. Instead he played up the other chief aspect of the myth, the magical. The occult can move in many ways; it can, for example, be handled in terms of the mysterious influence of mind upon mind.[12] In *Ibbetson* these influences had been explored on the level of the wholly unconscious; the two minds that react on each other are legislating their mutual destinies in their sleep. In *Trilby* the occult influence was to operate through the more familiar agency of mesmerism. In making Svengali over into a hypnotist, Du Maurier was following out implications long anticipated by Monk Lewis, developed in *St. Irvyne,* and almost decisive in *Zanoni*: for precisely a century the *mal' occhio* had been the Wandering Jew's most conspicuous fixture.

*Trilby** introduces us to the studio of three English expatriates

* On the title *Trilby,* see *Notes and Queries,* September 26, 1942, p. 207. On the genesis of the novel, see Deems Taylor, "Introduction," *Peter Ibbetson,* p. ix, and Wood, *George Du Maurier,* p. 92. It is amusing to think that Du Maurier originally offered the plot of *Trilby* to Henry James during an evening stroll, in the course of which he spun out his "idea for a novel" in some detail. Perhaps James would like to make it into a book? However, *Trilby* was, of course, the last thing Henry James wanted to make into a novel just then. He told Du Maurier in all seriousness that the story idea was "too valuable" a gift to be accepted by him and invited Du Maurier "to speak for himself." This ill-considered advice seems to have launched Du Maurier on his literary career, for he commenced to perpetrate his first novel, *Peter Ibbetson,* that same evening. It sold so well that Harper's offered him twice the sum for a second novel. *Trilby,* a phenomenon in the publishing business, has been called the first modern best-seller.

in the Parisian Latin Quarter. Had anyone else written the novel, one might justifiably read into it an allegory on art; as it is, Du Maurier cuts across an impressive number of artistic types. At the lowest level of achievement there is Trilby herself who is, as one of the characters later expresses it, "just a singing machine," "an echo," "the unconscious voice that Svengali sang with." Trilby is a purely receptive being, performing without effort, without consciousness, at the bidding of some magician whose power she can neither resist nor understand. Next there are Billee's two bohemian friends, Taffy the Yorkshireman and the Laird.[13] Both are British to the bone, and in a minute Du Maurier is going to juxtapose them with the horrible Jew Svengali. As painters, however, they leave much to be desired. The Laird is always drawing "little" things: little landscapes, little floral affairs: not much. Taffy grows to be very fat, very rich, on the academic style. In their spare time the two fall in and out of love with Trilby and minister to the romantic griefs of Little Billee, the hero of the book. Billee himself, finally, younger and more sensitive than his friends, destined to die in early manhood, turns into a painter of talent under the impact of losing Trilby to Svengali.

Good as Billee is, he is not so fine as Svengali, the figure at the apex of Du Maurier's artistic hierarchy and his big-time villain. Like Disraeli's and George Eliot's Jewish artists, Svengali is a musician: the type recalls Klesmer, the Princess Alcharisi, Mirah, and Disraeli's implausible Baroni family in *Tancred*. As if to underline the major contrast between the merely talented painter and the genial performing artist, Du Maurier places them side by side on Svengali's first appearance. Svengali is ushered into the novel in a few thoroughly unflattering paragraphs; he cuts a wicked appearance and speaks a ludicrous mishmash of dialects; he picks up a flageolet, a mere whistle of a thing, not the instrument best suited to the display of one's musical genius:

> And it would be impossible to render in any words the deftness, the distinction, the grace, power, pathos, and passion with which this truly phenomenal artist executed the poor old two-penny tune on his elastic penny whistle—for it was little more—such thrilling, vibrating, piercing tenderness, now loud and full, a shrill scream of anguish, now soft as a whisper, a mere melodic breath, more human almost than the human voice itself. . . .

> [Billee] had never heard such music as this, never dreamed such music was possible. He was conscious, while it lasted, that he saw deeper into the beauty, the sadness of things, the very heart of them, and their pathetic evanescence, as with a new, inner eye . . . a vague cosmic vision that faded when the music was over, but left an unfading reminiscence of its having been, and a passionate desire to express the like some day through the plastic medium of his own beautiful art.

Just who is Svengali? What features relate him to the myth we are attempting to trace?

He is still the Immortal Wanderer, the Eternal Jew, though little more than a faint replica of the prototype. The most explicit allusion to his *wanderlust* occurs early in the novel, in the remark, "Svengali walking up and down the earth seeking whom he might cheat, betray, exploit, borrow money from, make brutal fun of, bully if he dared, cringe to if he must—man, woman, child, or dog—was about as bad as they make 'em." His origins, too, remain for a while shrouded in mystery. His first appearance in the novel is at least moderately unsettling; one might wish that Du Maurier had kept him at this level of perception:

> First [entered] a tall bony individual of any age between thirty and forty-five, of Jewish aspect, well-featured, but sinister. He was very shabby and dirty, and wore a red beret and a large velveteen cloak, with a big metal clasp at the collar. His thin, heavy, languid, lustreless black hair fell down behind his ears on to his shoulders, in that musician-like way that is so offensive to the normal Englishman. He had bold, brilliant black eyes, with long heavy lids, a thin, sallow face, and a beard of burnt-up black which grew almost from under his eyelids; and over it his mustache, a shade lighter, fell in two long spiral twists.

The passage promises a respectably Ahasver-like version of the type. For the next hundred pages or so, Svengali's entrances and exits remain satisfactorily inexplicable, but then so are the entrances and exits of all Du Maurier's characters, so that Svengali's mysterious movements explain perhaps less about Svengali than about Du Maurier's nonchalant way of putting a novel together. Moreover, life in the Latin Quarter dictates a certain informality of movement anyhow, and Svengali's unscheduled visits must be tolerated under the bohemian laws of hospitality.

As the opening description informs us, Svengali is also very wicked, capable of diabolic businesses. It is fairly evident from the outset that Du Maurier has endeavored to restore to his character some of the ghastly attributes which had been toned down by his predecessors early in the century, and, while steering clear of all religious implications, to use Svengali's hypnotic powers in order to show up his malevolence. "When he cringed, it was with a mock humility, full of sardonic threats; when he was playful, it was with a terrible playfulness, like that of a cat with a mouse—a weird ungainly cat, and most unclean; a sticky, haunting, long, lean, uncanny, black spider-cat, if there is such an animal outside a bad dream." "In her gratitude [Trilby] kissed Svengali's hand; and he leered, and showed his big brown teeth and the yellow whites at the top of his big black eyes, and drew his breath with a hiss."

Bit by bit, however, Svengali's identity is pieced together; and as the book progresses, his claims to be the Wandering Jew from the longevity point of view recede as his wizardry is given increasing prominence. Though he may be "walking up and down the earth," it must not be thought that he has been at it since the Crucifixion, suffering the centennial rejuvenation stipulated in the early legends. He *could* go home. He has "people in Austria." It is a little unsettling to discover that the Wandering Jew is sufficiently domesticated by 1894 to get cash from his family, which consists of "his old father and mother, his sisters, his cousins, and his aunts." He turns out, in fact, to be rather unpleasantly bourgeois for a sorcerer. For example, he keeps a thoroughly commonplace mistress, Mimi Cahen alias Honorine la Saloppe, to whom he administers beatings and voice lessons. His real name is nothing more exciting than Adler. He may send Trilby messages "out of the mysterious East"; but his musical studies were completed at the perfectly solid and verifiable Leipzig conservatory.

Moreover, if his origins and movements remain always a trifle vague, there is nothing vague about his final destination: he dies, in his fifties, of a heart attack. It had been a long time since the Wandering Jew needed to be kept alive indefinitely; but heretofore his death had been handled with a certain degree of discretion. In Godwin's novel, Zampieri does not expire very circumstantially, though the consequences of his death are, in the nature of the case, very important indeed. In Croly's romance, Salathiel the Immortal's hour of mortality is merely noted by the author as a redeeming afterthought; Salathiel is, in a general way, going out with the tide. What finally becomes of the ancient Melmoth no man knows. To judge from the scarf that is found on a crag near the ocean, he may literally have gone out with the tide. It hardly matters.

Svengali's death, by contrast, is spectacular, one of the major set scenes in the novel. It is also the decisive event in the plot, for it marks Trilby's return to a normality of sorts. Svengali, as we know, has been conducting his wife's vocal genius by virtue of the *mal' occhio.* On the present occasion he stations himself in a loge opposite her, so that the *mal' occhio* may continue to operate from that remote post. Trilby comes onstage, faces Svengali, and in a scene abounding in bilingual melodrama begins to sing in her ordinary extra-hypnotic voice, which is a barmaid's falsetto, idiotically out of tune. The house is up in arms. What has happened? Svengali, of course, has already died up there in his box, though he continues to leer down at his distraught Galathea. His powers are ended. Du Maurier marks the fact with a suitable number of italics and exclamation points, and Madame Svengali alias Trilby O'Farrell, very tired after a life compounded of gratuitous human hardships and extraordinary inhuman shocks, fades away in an aura of decorative floral arrangements. She recaptures her voice once more; just in time for her swan-song arrives Svengali's portrait, God knows how, and under the impact of those irresistible incantatory eyes Trilby transports herself into her stall of night.[14]

It can be seen that Du Maurier, like his predecessors since the days of Monk Lewis, is a great deal more interested in the Jew's hypnotic performances than in his walking feats. The question of longevity interests Du Maurier only in so far as it impinges on the related problem concerning the reaches of the human mind when it operates in a condition of unconsciousness. The *mystique* of the Wanderer is retained in a few parenthetical, largely externalized strokes: in Svengali's unaccountable maneuvers generally, and in the criminal and ghoulish features which set him apart from lesser men. His ability to excite wonder as well as hatred marks him out as being just exotic enough to qualify within the myth.

Du Maurier's refusal to do more with Svengali either as Immortal or as Wanderer need not, then, surprise us in view of the almost unrecognizably generalized quality at which the legend had arrived by the end of the century. His contributions to the myth of the Wandering Jew lie elsewhere. For one thing, he deprived him, as has been suggested, of the sympathy to which the Wandering Jew, in contra-distinction to the Jew-villain of the main tradition, had been persistently entitled. For another he presented Svengali as a largely comic figure. With the evil eye of the Cartaphilus tradition Du Maurier combined the far-reaching nose of the Judas tradition. This was atypical, certainly. Hitherto, in whatever guise the Wandering Jew appeared throughout his long evolutionary course, and in whatever doctrine he was commissioned to espouse, he had been treated as an unfailingly serious type. For the writers from Wendover down to the poets and novelists of the nineteenth century he had been too intimately involved in the Crucifixion to be a source of laughter. Among the Gothic novelists his alliance with the superhuman powers ensured him the distant respect which nature traditionally pays to supernature. For romantic poets like Shelley and Southey he functioned so frequently as an extension of their own egos that to have laughed at him would have involved half the time a measure of self-denigration. Godwin and Bulwer enlisted him for the purpose of making an occasional speech. The doctrines of Moral Virtue and the mysteries of Christian Rosenkreuz are grave matters and they demand grave emblems. Whether by an historic accident or because of something resolutely and intractably serious in the prototype, there is in none of the major English analogues a single strand of humor.

The legend was occasionally parodied, of course, and it might even be susceptible to tendentious satirical treatment; most legends are.[15] The Wandering Jew could also be used allusively or metaphorically in a comedic context;[16] but such usage in itself is meaningless; it merely suggests that the myth was sufficiently familiar to pass into a figure of speech. The leading character of the legend, however, and the story in which he appeared, remained unalterably humorless.

Du Maurier changed all that. What he did was to combine certain elements of the traditional Ahasuerus-magician type with elements of the stereotype of the Shylock tradition, and to make Svengali over into a grotesque.

To begin with, he endowed him with a ludicrous brogue, which consists mainly in Svengali's inverting soft and hard consonants. His dialect is essentially that of the comic stage-Jew. "Ponchour, mes enfants," says Svengali on his first appearance. Also he says: "Che vous amène mon ami Checko, qui choue du violon gomme un anche! . . . Ch'espère qu'il est pon, et pien t'accord!" In his amatory moods, he salutes Mimi la Saloppe as his "bearl of Pabylon" and his "cazelle-eyed liddle Cherussalem skylark." I do not know that anything is to be gained by these phonetic disturbances, but Du Maurier seems determined to have fun with them. The friend Gecko whom Svengali brings along is another figure out of the main tradition: the comic underling. The Wandering Jew had not heretofore been in the habit of traveling in company. Sorcerers, of course, may keep apprentices; and in somewhat this relation we may picture Svengali and the friend Gecko, who plays the violin like an angel. When in the company of Trilby, Svengali is sufficiently overcome to drop his *patois* at short notice and conduct his suit in English. Diabolically strange, however, is the manner of his suing. His love-making consists very largely of submitting Trilby to prolonged dental inspections, a procedure in which the reader is free to detect obscure hints of voyeurism.

> "Himmel! [says Svengali]. The roof of your mouth is like the dome of the Pantheon; there is room in it for 'toutes les gloires de la France,' and a little to spare! The entrance to your throat is like the middle porch of Saint Sulpice when the doors are open for the faithful on All-Saints' Day; and not one tooth missing—thirty-two British teeth as white as milk and as big as knuckle-bones! And your little tongue is scooped out like the leaf of a pink peony, and the bridge of your nose is like the belly of a Stradivarius."

Was ever woman in this humor woo'd? As a rule, Svengali's comic diablerie takes on rather more grisly colors. One may ignore his brown teeth, so different from Trilby's ivory constructions; and as for his overdeveloped optic apparatus, one is almost made to feel that the matter is beyond his private jurisdiction. But that leer! "He leered all round with a leer that was not engaging"; he will "shake his dirty mane and shrug his shoulders and smile and leer at the audience" in a way that is not to be borne; "he leered and showed his big brown teeth and the yellow whites at the top of his big black eyes"; "his teeth were bared in a spasmodic grin of hate"; our last view of him is of his "ghastly, sardonic smile." On the other hand, one is never quite certain how funny Du Maurier intends him to be or how funny he looks, because Du Maurier pulls all the stops. Every so often Du Maurier endeavors to define his perspective by noting that Svengali "was almost droll in the intensity of his terrible realism"; one suspects that he may be a good deal more droll than Du Maurier meant him to be.[17]

All the same, as a hypnotist Svengali must be viewed in earnest; Du Maurier does not take matters lightly when the occult is at stake; and, after all, Trilby does grow into a vocalist of immense stature under Svengali's tutelage, "a combination," as Edmund Wilson notes, "of Adelina Patti and Yvette Guilbert."[18] Once more the central Du Maurier dualism comes into play, the world of the occult genius impinging on Trilby's ordinary world, translating her vocal ineptitude into something rich and strange. The interesting thing is that Du Maurier has rather twisted around the moral implications of Svengali's agency, as compared with the function of the supernatural in his other books. In *Ibbetson,* Peter's inspired dream life is meant to be taken for a sort of ultimate good—good in a moral sense inasmuch as the ending of the novel rings a note of universal harmony and fraternalism, to be brought about, a little vaguely, by everybody's learning "the secret of dreaming true." Again, in Du Maurier's last novel, the Martian influence is shown to have morally desirable results on the hero's slumbering genius. Trilby's accomplishments, by contrast, though they identically implicate the powers of the unconscious, are on that very account dismissed as hollow, artificial, and meaningless.

"I will tell you a secret [says Gecko]. *There were two Trilbys.* There was the Trilby you know, who could not sing one single note in tune.

She was an angel of paradise. She is now! But she had no more idea of singing than I have of winning a steeple-chase. . . . Well, that was our Trilby . . . a gentle martyr on earth, a blessed saint in heaven! . . .

"But all at once—Svengali could turn her into the other Trilby, *his* Trilby—and make her do whatever he liked. . . . It was not worth having!

"That Trilby was just a singing machine—an organ to play upon—just the unconscious voice that Svengali sang with. . . . When Svengali's Trilby was singing—or seemed to *you* as if she were singing—our *Trilby* was fast asleep . . . in fact, *our* Trilby was dead."

It is as though Du Maurier could not, after all, bring himself to credit the vile Svengali with anything like the same morally uplifting qualities that he grants to the comparable forces in his other books. The genius in Svengali is constantly checked by the squalid Jew, with the result that there are really, as Bernard Shaw and Edmund Wilson have pointed out, two Svengalis just as there are two Trilbys: the supernaturally endowed hypnotist, who traces his ancestry back to Cartaphilus—Svengali in his academic relations with Trilby—and the comically vulgar coward who functions within the stereotype—Svengali in his sexual relations with Trilby. Shaw, in some good pages of dramatic criticism, draws the line here between the Svengali of Du Maurier's novel and the Svengali of Beerbohm Tree's theatrical interpretation; and though we are concerned only with the first named, most of the humbug which Shaw imputes to Beerbohm Tree is fully provided for in the book, so that there is something a trifle capricious in Shaw's drawing the line just where he does. For Shaw there is "the original Svengali, the luckless artist-cad," of whom Shaw approves, "understanding neither good manners nor cleanliness, always presuming, and generally getting snubbed and nose-pulled and bullied"; and there is secondly the playhouse Svengali, whom Shaw dismisses as "vulgar nonsense," who "absurdly declines into the stagey, the malignant, the diabolic, the Wandering Jewish" and who "vainly endeavours to make our flesh creep . . . Svengali defying Heaven, declaring that henceforth he is his own God, and then tumbling down in a paroxysm of heart disease . . . and having to be revived by draughts of brandy."[19] In the same passage Shaw remarks that he likes "an imagination without gall, to which poor

Svengali is *not* a villain, but only a poor egotistical wretch who provokes people to pull his nose, although he has better grounds for egotism than any one else in the book except Little Billee and Trilby." The sordid Svengali, you see, looks the genuine article, and so all praise to him; the "malignant, the diabolic, the Wandering Jewish" is a hopeless operatic fraud, a concession to the stage of the 'nineties. Behind Shaw's attempt to absolve Svengali from the label "villain" (and Du Maurier from the job of pinning it on him) you sense Shaw's exasperation with people who cannot see, as he is all the time trying to show you, that "villains," taken at Beerbohm Tree's evaluation, are at least obsolescent if not fictive creatures, who have no place in the contemporary theater. Still, Shaw's crusade ought not to obscure the certainty that both these elements—the ill-mannered Jew and the heaven-defying Jew—are present in the nondramatic original, and one has got to discount somewhat Shaw's aesthetic prejudices to get at a just estimate of this double facet in Svengali's personality.

Next we have Edmund Wilson, whose brief comments on Du Maurier's peculiar brand of respectful anti-Semitism remain the very best and most illuminating things yet written on the subject. Wilson, who quotes Shaw's remarks with approval, undertakes an interpretation of Svengali along interesting sociological lines, to which the terms of Shaw's distinction are not without relevance. Wilson's remarks occur in the context of an essay in which he examines very amusingly the tendency among some nineteenth-century American writers (he singles out Lowell and John Jay Chapman) to credit the Jews with supernatural powers, presumably for evil—quite as though these writers, up-to-date as they were in some other matters, found themselves transported back to the Dark Ages on the bugaboo subject of the Jews.[20] Lowell, who apparently personified this state of mind in its extreme form, seems to have gone through a period of violently anti-Semitic crankiness, of the kind that sees a Jew behind every bush and is obsessed with the idea of world-wide Jewish conspiracies to overthrow all civilized forms of life. The belief in such a threat can only be upheld, of course, if you see the Jews at once as wicked enough to desire another Armageddon, and powerful enough to bring it off. The whole notion sounds like a medieval commonplace: the Jews' wickedness being taken for granted, the power threat operated as a constant stimulus to vigilance and an excuse for massacre. The interesting thing is that for such writers as Lowell the danger of Jewish political supremacy was uncomfortably associated with the Jew's Old Testamental status of divine prolocutor, whose prophetic gifts could hardly be attributed to the devil when, presumably, they emanated from the opposite source. It can be seen that such a view promotes a peculiar ambivalence in one's attitude toward the Jews: the idea of the Jew's supernatural competence, with its appalling consequences, is enough to make Lowell's flesh creep; at the same time, and considering its original sanction and prehistory, the Jew's supernature (call it his prophetic voice or his evil eye or what you will) compels a certain degree of quaking and gibbering veneration. If the Jews have been turned into Judases and Shylocks, they have not quite given over being a lot of inelegant Jeremiahs; and this genealogical confusion makes these American writers uncomfortable.

Wilson picks up Du Maurier as "an odd non-American example of this tendency to credit the Jews with supernatural powers," and he cites Svengali as embodying the classic dilemma, already noted in this study, between the popular conception of the Jew in his sordid role and the attempt to reconcile this with the Jew's pre-Christian function as the mouthpiece of God.

There is always in these novels of Du Maurier—binational, bilingual as he was—a certain light playing off of French civilization against English; but the picture is further complicated—it is one of the things that makes them interesting—by this dual role of the Jew, who appears—in Colonel Ibbetson, Svengali in his ordinary relations—now as a malignant devil, whose malignancy is hardly accounted for; now—in Leah, Little Billee and the Svengali who animates Trilby—as a spirit from an alien world who carries with it an uncanny prestige, who may speak in a divine tongue.[21]

In the passage directly preceding, Wilson elaborates this dualism as it applies to Svengali,

the fabulous musician who cannot sing but who, by hypnotizing the tone-deaf Trilby and exploiting her wonderful voice, makes of her a great artist. Svengali, in other connections, is always represented as everything that these gentlemanly Britishers most abhor: he is dirty, insulting, boastful, mendacious, malicious, quarrelsome; they have constantly to put him in his place. Yet Trilby, in spite of her voice, has not only no ear whatever for music, no range of emotion or expression which would be adequate, even if she had one, to achieve the outstanding effects which Svengali is able to teach her by turning her into a simple automaton. . . . The whole thing is an emanation of Svengali's musical soul; and if this is true, the horrid Svengali must have, after all, as Bernard Shaw says, "better grounds for [his] egotism than anybody else in the book except Little Billee and Trilby." . . . What is really behind Svengali is the notion, again, that the Jew, even in his squalidest form, is a mouthpiece of our Judaico-Christian God, whose voice he has, in this case, transferred, ventriloquially, to the throat of Trilby.

If we try to put some of these ideas together, we get in Du Maurier a fairly clear double-intention, a case of wanting one's cake and eating it. There is the Du Maurier who finds in the Jew a peculiarly congenial (because historically acceptable) type of supernaturalist, whose supernaturalism he has got to respect. Remembering, moreover, the close affinity between prophecy and song, we can see that Svengali's combination of gifts is practically made to order for Du Maurier's brand of occultism. But it also seems to have suited Du Maurier to keep his man moving within the conventional framework, in which the Jew is both a very sordid and nasty creature; and since Svengali's sordidness is really, as Shaw says, a good deal more impressive in the long run than Svengali's genius, one is apt to remember the smuttiness after one has forgotten the power and the glory.[22]

As a matter of fact, in at least one respect, Du Maurier goes the Shylock convention one better. The year is 1894. If, in 1594, it was a truth universally acknowledged that Jews had killed the Saviour and ruined their debtors, it was equally clear three centuries later that such corruption of the soul argued a pollution of the body, a failure of the nerves, a poisoning of the blood stream. Shylock may be evil, but Svengali is sick. Shakespeare's Venice is infested with bloodsucking parasites; but the "spider-cat" who makes passes at young Trilby is a degenerate: the Jew as contaminator of the race. Taken by himself, Svengali remains, as Wilson says, "everything that these gentlemanly Britishers most abhor"; and it is his collision with these that we must briefly glance at.

Blood Types: Svengali and Leah Gibson

Peter Ibbetson is meditating:

To pray for any personal boon or remission of evil—to bend the knee, or lift one's voice in praise or thanksgiving for any earthly good that had befallen one, either through inheritance, or chance, or one's own successful endeavour—was in my eyes simply futile; by putting its futility aside, it was an act of servile presumption, of wheedling impertinence, not without suspicion of a lively sense of favours to come.

It seemed to me as though the Jews—a superstitious and businesslike people, who know what they want and do not care how they get it—must have taught us to pray like that.

It was not the sweet, simple child innocently beseeching that tomorrow might be fine for its holiday, or that Santa Claus would be generous; it was the cunning trader, fawning, flattering, propitiating, bribing with fulsome, sycophantic praise (an insult in itself), as well as burnt offerings, working for his own success here and hereafter, and his enemy's confounding.

It was the grovelling of the dog, without the dog's single-hearted love, stronger than even its fear or its sense of self interest.

What an attitude for one whom God had made after His own image—even toward his Maker!

Well: That certainly has all been heard before—Du Maurier is describing a thoroughly familiar type, with all the standard features of Shylock brought together on a single page. They are all there, down to the canine metaphor: the implied charge of religious obscurantism, Shylock as cut-throat, Shylock as sycophant. "Superstitious and businesslike"—the dual indictment rings down the centuries. And yet, I think, a new and unpleasantly hysterical note has come to intrude three hundred years after Shylock. It used not to be the custom to lump Jews together so freely. Hitherto the creators of the Jewish criminal had not so pointedly phrased the major premise to read, "all Jews are bad." Writers like Dickens and Trollope might have conceded on general principles that the wickedness of their characters was inseparable from their Jewishness; they might have gone so far as to grant that Fagin and Melmotte were intended to be representative of vices associated peculiarly with Jews. Indeed Dickens said so in so many words; and Trollope puts rather the same construction in the mouth of Roger Carbury. But neither

Dickens nor Trollope really bothered to generalize Fagin and Melmotte in such a way as to warrant the assumption that they were indicting the whole tribe of Jews. Even within their own race the century's two greatest Jewish scoundrels, the little and the big swindlers, looked like marginal figures, Fagin largely because Dickens's sensational vision removed his Jew from the sphere of a socially valid type, Melmotte because the sheer supremacy of his position in the world of finance underlined his singular and extraordinary qualities. Eclipse, says Macaulay, is first, and the rest nowhere; and once a character is presented, like Melmotte, by a string of superlatives, all comparisons cease to make sense. Fagin and Melmotte are as certainly Jews as they are, within the stereotype, *sui generis*. As for the minor Jewish villains who flit in and out of half a hundred Victorian novels—that multitude of pawnbrokers, receivers of stolen goods, small tradesmen, acting assistant murderers, and the like—they were either treated so patently as caricatures or social deviants or both as to discourage intelligent readers from jumping to damaging conclusions. Since anyhow the Jew-villain was generally the product of the sensation-novel, while the good Jew was appropriated by the domestic realists, the chances after about the middle of the century were that one's Jewish neighbors resembled the honest Oppovich rather than the sanguinary Abraham. As I have indicated in the early pages of this study, it had traditionally been the privilege of the Jewish paragon to pose as a delegate of his tribe as a whole. If Fagin does not even remotely imply that all Jews are hideous, Riah comes very close to saying "all Jews are fine." Since he cannot very well put it quite that way, he inverts the proposition by allowing that most Jews are misunderstood by most people most of the time—which comes to the same thing.

In Du Maurier the whole group is judged and convicted. In the passage I cited from *Ibbetson,* the terms of the indictment are the traditional counts, religious and economic. But significantly Du Maurier's two chief villains, Colonel Ibbetson and Svengali, are remarkable not for their dishonesty but for the degenerate blood that flows in their veins. Neither of them, of course, is "in business"; Peter's uncle is a brutal retired military man; Svengali is a performing artist. The description of Colonel Ibbetson fairly puts Du Maurier's case against the impure:

. . . his mother (the Archdeacon's second wife) had been the only child and heiress of an immensely rich pawnbroker, by name Mendoza; a Portuguese Jew, with a dash of colored blood in his veins besides, it was said; and, indeed, this remote African strain still showed itself in Uncle Ibbetson's thick lips, wide-open nostrils, and big black eyes with yellow whites, and especially in his long, splay, lark-heeled feet, which gave both himself and the best bootmaker in London a great deal of trouble.

Otherwise, and in spite of his ugly face, he was not without a certain soldier-like air of distinction, being very tall and powerfully built. He wore stays and an excellent wig, for he was prematurely bald; and he carried his hat on one side, which (in my untutored eyes) made him look very much like a "swell," but not quite like a *gentleman.*

To wear your hat jauntily cocked over one eye, and yet "look like a gentleman!"

It can be done, I am told; and has been, and is even still! It is not, perhaps, a very lofty achievement—but such as it is, it requires a somewhat rare combination of social and physical gifts in the wearer; and the possession of either Semitic or African blood does not seem to be one of these.

A somewhat more tentative and qualified racial diagnosis is put forward in the opening pages of *Trilby,* in the passage which introduces Little Billee to the reader.

And in his winning and handsome face there was just a faint suggestion of some possibly very remote Jewish ancestor—just a tinge of that strong, sturdy, irrepressible, indomitable, indelible blood which is of such priceless value in diluted homeopathic doses, like the dry white Spanish wine called montijo, which is not meant to be taken pure. . . . Fortunately for the world, and especially for ourselves, most of us have in our veins at least a minim of that precious fluid, whether we know it or show it or not. *Tant pis pour les autres!*

The fulsome adjectives, descriptive of those Kiplingesque qualities Du Maurier admires above any others, almost make it appear as though Du Maurier had suffered a comprehensive change of heart between the composition of *Ibbetson* and of *Trilby*—unless, putting the two passages together, one were to deduce from his racial arithmetic that Colonel Ibbetson's African substances made the decisive difference whereas the Semitic chemicalia are relatively good things. However, of course, there remains Svengali, Du Maurier's demonstration piece of what happens when the montijo is swallowed pure.

There are in *Trilby* two rather revolting scenes which, I think, help to point up Du Maurier's least defensible and most nearly hysterical attitude. Both scenes show up Svengali in the presence of his racial antagonists. The first involves Trilby; the second, Taffy. Of the two the first is less obviously but more basically offensive, owing in part to the sort of ungainly humor Du Maurier flashes on. The scene describes a kind of Svengali Furioso, the Jew foaming at the mouth because the Aryan girl whom he covets refuses to be seduced. The passage has already been anticipated by the scene, similar in drift, in which Svengali peers into Trilby's oral cavity and luxuriates in her labial, uvulary, and pharyngial parts. He has not, since then, made any headway, and there follows this unlikely malediction:

"... ach! what a beautiful skeleton you will make! ... Svengali shall come in his new fur-lined coat, smoking his big cigar of the Havana, and push the dirty carabins out of the way, and look through the holes of your eyes into your stupid empty skull, and up the nostrils of your high, bony sounding-board of a nose without either a tip or a lip to it, and into the roof of your big mouth, with your thirty-two big English teeth, and between your big ribs into your big chest, where the big leather lungs used to be, and say, 'Ach! what a pity she had no more music in her than a big tomcat!' "

The passage moves Du Maurier to comment:

And here let me say that these vicious imaginations of Svengali's ... sounded much more ghastly in French pronounced with a Hebrew-German accent, and uttered in his hoarse, rasping, nasal throaty rook's caw, his big yellow teeth baring themselves in a mongrel canine snarl, his heavy upper eyelids drooping over his insolent black eyes. ... He [took stock] of the different bones in her skeleton with greedy but discriminating approval.

Svengali's pursuit of Trilby is almost consistently presented by Du Maurier as something physically obscene and shameful. The horror Trilby entertains for the Jew does not so much involve a fear of his hypnotic powers as it lays bare a revulsion of the flesh. One is made to feel that Trilby is much less afraid of being bewitched than of being bodily soiled. "So he would playfully try to mesmerize her with his glance, and sidle up nearer and nearer to her, making passes and counter-passes . . . till she would shake and shiver and almost sicken." Svengali's threats of poverty which Trilby has to face if she repulses him lose themselves in sexual fantasies:

"There is a little ugly gray building there, and inside are eight slanting slabs of brass . . . and one fine day you shall lie asleep on one of those slabs. . . . And over the middle of you will be a little leather apron, and over your head a little brass tap, and all day long and all night the cold water shall trickle, trickle all the way down your beautiful white body to your beautiful white feet till they turn green, and your poor, damp, draggled, muddy rags will hang above you from the ceiling for your friends to know you by; drip, drip, drip!"

Hence when Svengali finally gains ascendancy over her, the reader is left with the impression that the crime at the heart of the novel is not really one of occult sorcery but the specifically "Jewish" crime to which the Germans have since given the name *Rassenschande,* the (legally punishable) mating of the inferior racial type with the higher. It seems to me important to recognize that in Svengali Du Maurier recovers not only the medieval conception of the Jew as Devil, but that the other potent medieval metaphor, that of the dog, is constantly being applied to Svengali, though with a peculiarly modern emphasis. If the dog retains some of his lupine qualities, "his big yellow teeth baring themselves in a mongrel canine snarl" at those fawning publicans Taffy, the Laird, and Billee, he is still more clearly the dog whose chief offense is simply his bestiality, whose threat to the bipeds lies not in his aggressiveness but in his noxious and contaminating presence—a creature less to be feared for its calculated malevolence than for its innate foulness.

Like all cowards, Svengali bullies the weak: "Next morning he saw [Billee] again in the hotel post-office, looking small and flurried, and apparently alone; and being an Oriental Israelite Hebrew Jew, he had not been able to resist the temptation of spitting in his face, since he must not throttle him to death." But the bully, as we know, is bound to end up as *eiron*: the publicans will have their revenge. Eventually "race shame" must be brought to trial. In view of Du Maurier's respect for size, it is natural that the trial should be a trial-of-arms and that the issue should be a foregone conclusion. The passage in which Taffy beats up the Jew recalls Tarzan atop the dead monkey, yelling his barbarian victory shout, while Du Maurier approvingly pins the V.C. on his chest.

Svengali . . . recognized [Taffy] at once, and turned white.

Taffy, who had dog-skin gloves on, put out his right hand and deftly seized Svengali's nose between his fore and middle fingers and nearly pulled it off and swung his head two or three times backward and forward by it, and then from side to side, Svengali holding on to his wrist, and then, letting him go, gave him a sounding open-handed smack on his right cheek. . . .

. . . . he had, for hours, the feel of that long, thick, shapely Hebrew nose being kneaded between his gloved knuckles, and a pleasing sense of the effectiveness of the tweak he had given him. So he went about chewing the cud of that heavenly remembrance.

Shortly afterwards Svengali relives the incident in his mind, drawing all the racial inferences which Du Maurier wants him to draw:

. . . and then, suddenly and quite unexpectedly, had come upon the scene that apparition so loathed and dreaded of old—the pig-headed Yorkshireman—the huge British philistine, the irresponsible bull, the junker, the ex-Crimean Front-de-Boeuf, who had always reminded him of the brutal and contemptuous sword-clanking, spur-jingling aristocrats of his own country—ruffians that treated Jews like dogs. Callous as he was to the woes of others, the self-indulgent and highly-strung musician was extra-sensitive about himself—a very bundle of nerves—and especially sensitive to pain and rough usage, and by no means physically brave. The stern, choleric, invincible blue eyes of the hated Northern gentile had cowed him at once. And that violent tweaking of his nose, that heavy open-handed blow on his face, had so shaken and demoralized him that he had never recovered from it.*

And indeed his shame survives him. A few pages later on Svengali makes his exit from the stage of his spectacular triumphs over the Aryan race and his spectacular defeats at their hands; and the two

* Against the objection that Svengali's consciousness of being "treated like a dog" constitutes an admission that he is *not* a dog but a sympathetic human being, it is worth reflecting that Shylock refers the same analogy to himself, without being a whit less of a dog for reminding the audience that he is treated like one: "they curse me for a dog," "he calls me dog," etc.

Christians whom he has injured most, the lovers Billee and Trilby, are not very long in following him. Allegedly Svengali succumbs to a heart attack, but there is an element of humbug in this. If Du Maurier does not positively say that he died of cowardice or hate, at least he does not exclude the possibility. The general impression is that the heart attack was brought on by the sudden appearance of the three Nordic Musketeers. I remember that when I first read the novel as a child the impression was very strong on me that Svengali died simply of a fright. "And Svengali for a moment glanced at them. And the expression of his face was so terrible with wonder, rage, and fear that they were quite appalled—and then he sat down, still glaring at Taffy, the whites of his eyes showing at the top, and his teeth bared in a spasmodic grin of hate."[23] And in this posture he dies: of shock, of fear, of some hereditary taint or other, a defect in his blood stream, a failure of the nerves.

The answer to the sneaky and ill-favored non-Aryan, then, is someone like Barty Josselin who, for all his mixed ancestry, is a securely Nordic type, and whom Martia chooses to be her begetter because he represents the finest biological and physical specimen to be found between the Milky Way and Waterloo Station. Or he is someone like Taffy the Yorkshireman of whose attack on Svengali Du Maurier all but tells you, "This was his finest hour." Du Maurier, as I have implied, seems anyhow to have been infatuated with sheer physical height. Not the least important and surely the most singular of Barty Josselin's inexhaustible accomplishments is his success in contributing to the elongation of the human race.[24]

A recurrent type in Du Maurier's novels is the towering purebred female: his first dream woman actually bears the name of Towers. "The Duchess of Towers in the Ibbetson illustrations," Taylor notes, "is ten heads high; Peter averages about eleven. If [these women] were not to be found in the living world, at least they made a magnificent national ideal, a sort of 'look on this and do your best' for British womanhood."[25] Du Maurier's catalogue of Nordic Amazons is indeed long and monotonous, relatively more monotonous than Scott's in that *all* of Du Maurier's eligible women are oversized—and their mothers as well.[26]

Of the Duchess he writes:

She was so tall that her eyes seemed almost on a level with mine, but she moved with the alert lightness and grace of a small person. Her thick, heavy hair was of a dark coppery brown, her complexion clear and pale, her eyebrows and eyelashes black, her eyes a light bluish gray. Her nose was short and sharp, and rather tilted at the tip, and her red mouth was large and very mobile.

Of "la divine Madame Seraskier": "She topped my tall mother by more than half a head."

Of Trilby: "It was the figure of a very tall and fully developed young female. . . . She bore herself with easy, unembarrassed grace, like a person whose nerves and muscles are well in tune."

Of the same: ". . . she was thought much too tall for her sex, and her day, and her station in life, and especially for the country she lived in. She hardly looked up to a bold gendarme! and a bold gendarme was nearly as tall as a 'dragon de la garde,' who was nearly as tall as an average English policeman."

Du Maurier's type-casting in both *Ibbetson* and *Trilby* calls for the juxtaposition of these two racial groups, the Afro-Semitic, which provides the villainous element, and the Nordic, which furnishes the heroes and heroines. Colonel Ibbetson, whose grandfather, if you pricked him, shed the blood of the Mendozas and the Moors, is pitted against the "lusty, love-famished, warm-blooded pagan" his nephew; Svengali, the Oriental Israelite Hebrew, plays Mephisto to Trilby's Gretchen and has his nose wrenched by Taffy, the "Man of Blood," "the very big young man" with the straight features and the "kind but choleric blue eyes" who, but for a sprained ankle, would have charged and died at Balaclava and, *faute de mieux,* survives to twirl Indian clubs around his head. (The villains, in turn, by a sort of telescoping of values, may be relatively elevated when invested with lesser comic auxiliaries of their own. Thus Colonel Ibbetson is allowed to lord it over the absurd Lintot, and Svengali is made to look comparatively dignified beside that friendlier dog Gecko, with his "large, soft, affectionate brown eyes, like a King Charles spaniel." But the primary antithesis is provided by the enmity of the blood.)

What, then, are we to make of Leah Gibson, the heroine of *The Martian,* the last of our Beautiful Jewesses? If one of the traditional

Leah, who is all wax, marks the fitting culmination of her type. The word with which Du Maurier ushers her into the book is "paragon," and once he has described her as a paragon there is nothing left to say. Supremely beautiful and fit Leah must indeed be, or the choosy Martia would never consent to adopt her to be her mother. Surely the fact that this patron goddess of physical culture leaves her native planet to spend the customary period in Leah Gibson's womb represents the highest tribute she could pay to Leah's genetic fitness.

What has happened to Du Maurier's Aryan noises? Has he moved his shrine from beneath the Tree Igdrasil to the cedar groves of Lebanon?

Well, no. The figure of Leah, as I mentioned earlier, has been interpreted as Du Maurier's official symbol of apology for the presentation of Svengali—the final instance of that odd gesture, a kind of conditioned reflex, which is based on the naïve assumption that one literary emblem has the power to cancel out, as it were, an emblem committed elsewhere. It is very likely that some such ulterior motive impelled Du Maurier to make Leah over into a Jewess. On the other hand, I wonder whether her Jewishness can be taken to constitute anything like a disavowal of Du Maurier's cherished profession and prejudices, or whether it does not look rather like a confirmation of them. If Du Maurier did indeed intend to "effect an amnesty," as I suppose he did, he had already provided the means for doing so with a minimum of jeopardy to his racial principles. He merely turned Leah into another one of his Amazons and, by the analogy to Scott, called her a Jewess. Half the time, indeed, he calls her "a Rebecca" in so many words, as though to remind us that her foundations are romantic; and, for the rest, no racial inferences are drawn.

> [Hers] is a type that sometimes, just now and again, can be so pathetically noble and beautiful in a woman, so suggestive of chastity and the most passionate love combined . . . love that implies all the big practical obligations and responsibilities of human life, that the mere term "Jewess" (and especially its French equivalent) brings to my mind some vague, mysterious, exotically poetic image of all I love best in woman. I find myself dreaming of Rebecca of York, as I used to dream of her in the English class at Brossard's, where I so pitied poor Ivanhoe for his misplaced constancy. . . .

He could see that Leah and Julia often looked at each other. . . . Probably most votes would have been for Julia, the fair-haired one, the prima donna assoluta, the soprano, the Rowena, who might always get the biggest salary and most of the applause. . . . The brunette, the contralto, the Rebecca dazzles less but touches the heart all the more deeply, perhaps; anyhow Barty had no doubt as to which of the two voices was the voice for him. His passion was as that of Brian-de-Bois-Guilbert for mere strength, except that he was bound by no vows of celibacy.

On the whole, Leah's Jewishness is a gratuitous compliment to the race in that it functions extraneously to anything she does, says, thinks, wills, or emotes. Had Du Maurier not explicitly affixed the label "Jewess" (or its French equivalent), she would remain indistinguishable from the rest of his lovely giantesses. If Mimsey is described as having black hair and "a beautiful white skin" and the Duchess of Towers "thick, heavy hair, of a dark coppery brown," "her complexion clear and pale," "her red mouth very large and mobile," Leah Gibson presents "a delicate narrow face, a clear pale complexion," "very red lips." Trilby has her thirty-two faultless English teeth and Leah her "very beautiful white pearly teeth." For the rest she has nothing to do except to dazzle heroically; and none of Du Maurier's strained rhetoric is able to conceal the fact that Leah Gibson is after all little more than—Gibson-girl stuff, *Punch* material. The case presents no adjunct to the Muse's diadem.

But Svengali survives: Svengali leering, Svengali screaming anathemas, Svengali rumbling "dors, ma mignonne," Svengali having his face bashed in, Svengali baring his yellow fangs in a rictus of hate—the smutty genius, the sticky spider-cat, the Devil bedeviled, the Errant Jew solemnizing his glory and his death behind the taffeta curtain of a London music hall.

George Du Maurier died October 8, 1896. His last comment to his son Gerald were the words, "Si c'est la mort, ce n'est pas gai"—it almost seemed as though he wished to repudiate to the last the historic refrain, the cry for quiescence and release, which has rung emblematically down the centuries since Christ uttered his Tarry Thou.[27]

But that is where art parts from reality.

XI

What News on the Rialto?

With my remarks on Du Maurier, I must bring this demonstration to a close. *Trilby* appeared six years before the end of the century—three hundred years after the emergence of Shylock and the ogres of Nashe, a hundred years after the coming of Sheva and the Wandering Jew's first important appearance in the English novel. There is a consoling calendrical rightness about these things: *The Merchant of Venice* and *The Unfortunate Traveller* in 1594–95; Cumberland's *Jew* and Lewis's *Monk* in 1794–96; *Trilby* in 1894. The year 1894 must therefore do as a terminal point for this study.

In looking back on the portrayal of the Jew in the nineteenth-century novel, one is likely to be struck first by the novelist's dependence on traditional types, and by his failure to do something with the Jew in literature that had not already been done in the sixteenth and again in the eighteenth century. The major novelists with whom this essay has dealt took over their opposing types almost ready made: one, a monster of cupidity, fundamentally anti-realistic in conception, functioning as a caricature in comedy, satire, and melodrama; the other, a paragon of economic probity, equally (but dissimilarly) unrealistic, treated as an idealized figure in didactic literature and commissioned explicitly to argue his antipode out of existence. For the novelists from Edgeworth to Trollope, the basic facts about the wicked Jew were his commercial rascality and a bottomless egoism which led him to trample over human lives and thus placed him beyond the social and moral pale; and the basic facts about the good Jew after Smollett and Cumberland were his commercial probity and his insistence, in the name of humanitarianism, that he had been placed beyond the social pale unfairly, that he suffered guiltlessly and deserved better treatment.

Good Jew or bad, rich Jew or poor, tyrant or slave, money was almost bound to be at the root of his problem. The referent being one and the same, the character of the good Jew in one novel by Author X usually turned out to be as nearly as possible the strict antithesis of the bad Jew in X's previous (or next) novel. Since the Jews in Maria Edgeworth's early stories are commercial scoundrels, Montenero in *Harrington* has got to be a model of generosity. Scott's Isaac is a frightened tightwad; old Moncada a baronial coin-flinger. Dickens's Fagin is an agent of economic exploitation, and so Dickens's Riah must be a victim of economic pressures. Trollope's Melmotte commits fraud on a grand scale; hence Trendelssohn in *Nina Balatka* must stand up for the principle, afterward propounded in one of Bernard Shaw's paradoxes, that in money matters irresponsibility is more often to be found among Christians than among Jews.[1] Brehgert is a greasily honest and plain-speaking Jew; Father Joseph Emilius, the Mayfair convert of *The Eustace Diamonds,* is an unctuous hypocrite. Whether Smollett calls his Jew a "compassionating Israelite" in *Ferdinand Count Fathom,* or a "cent per cent. fornicator" in *Roderick Random,* the yardstick remains strictly one of economic decorum. A compassionate Israelite differs principally from his antipode in that he dispenses with the interest: compassion in the Jew is embarrassingly apt to exhaust itself in financial aid—although it is also likely to be attended by gestures of philanthropy in a wider sense. Even a figure like Riah the synagogue-mouse, who is exempted by his poverty from "doing good by stealth" in the Sheva meaning of the term, is so transparently contrasted with the greed of his overseer that his goodness is all the more plainly brought into direct relation with the cash nexus. Had Riah money to spend, so runs the implication, he would spend it all—on the Jenny Wrens of the world and the Lizzie Hexams—and on the odious Fledgebys, too, who have kept him in bondage.

If Author X could not make up his mind whether to present his Jew as exploiter or exploited, the logical compromise was to present him as both. This is what happens, for example, in Charles Reade's "matter-of-fact romance" *It Is Never Too Late to Mend.* Reade's solution is simply to split his Jew down the middle, let him have the best of two worlds, and make the public a present of two clichés instead of one. Reade's Jew, Isaac Levi, is ushered into the novel as a gentle and pathetic old soul, "an aged and lonely man," who has buried two children and his wife Leah, who supports himself in his

Berkshire cottage by lending money at a perfectly respectable rate; he has been a model resident among the native farmers as well as a devoutly religious Hebrew, with some traits of the Wandering Jew in his make-up, having "sojourned in Madras and Benares, in Bagdad, Ispahan, Mecca, and Bassora, and found no rest." In the opening chapters of the novel, Levi's cutthroat landlord, the villain of the book, expels him, without notice and without explanation, from the cottage in which Levi has passed his declining years, and, with a few savage comments on usurious Jews in general, sets him adrift on the world. Levi naturally trots out all the Sheva-clichés in an effort to placate his enemy, reels them off as though he had been wound up directly before he came onstage, reminds the landlord of his widowerhood, his piety, his industry, his trustworthiness, points to his grey hairs as numerical indices to his sorrows, and makes the speech about the oppressed people: to no avail. And then the Sheva-half of him is dropped and the Shylock-half mobilized. With the ominous constatation that "a Jew knows how to revenge himself," Levi follows the landlord to Australia, "resolving Oriental vengeance" and "feeding fat the ancient grudge." Positively rejuvenated by the landlord's call to action, he makes his fortune in gold-prospecting, spends the rest of the novel in grandiose exploitation schemes with the object of gaining a stranglehold on the landlord and sending him to jail, and even cheats his partners a little. He hatches plots "worthy of Machiavel," "patient as a cat, keen as a lynx," "an Oriental spider . . . the threads of which were so subtle as to be altogether invisible." When his patience forsakes him, he experiences diabolic twitches. "'A tooth for a tooth!' And the old man ground his teeth, which were white as ivory, and his fist clenched itself, while his eye glittered, and he swelled from the chair, and literally bristled with hate—'A tooth for a tooth!'"[2]

Reade manages the difficult transition from Philip Sober to Philip Drunk by pretending that none is needed, and that behind every Sheva lurks a Shylock; and in this, at least, he has literary history to back him up. But if you turn your character upside down in the first place, you virtually owe it to him to stand him right side up again in the sequel. Accordingly, on page 582, with little to prepare us except the title of the novel, we are told that Isaac has "softened." Back in the Berkshires, the title deeds to his home restored to him, he writes out a cheque to the bankrupt landlord, urges him "to repent and prosper," and assures him that "Isaac Levi wishes you no ill from this day, but rather good." Evidently, it is never too late to mend. In the novel of the nineteenth century, Reade's Jew remains a kind of final exemplar, a product of Reade's arid persuasion that there are only two sides to the Jewish question, and that gold is at the bottom of both. "What news on the Rialto?" Shylock kept asking, after turning down Bassanio's dinner invitation; his question is still, among his Victorian relations, the basic one.

Would Riah have embraced Fagin in his sympathies, too, in the great sentimental, private welfare state established by the dynasty of Nathan the Wise? Yes, definitely, and—though Fagin would have rejected the offer—with the greatest pleasure. First, because there were no limits to Riah's mercy (a quality, it will be remembered, whose properties were originally defined for Shylock's personal benefit), and second, because the Jew in literature is never really at ease except in Zion. "True friendship between Jew and Christian is impossible," remarks one of the Jewish characters in Walter Besant's novel *The Rebel Queen* as late as 1893. Whether the Jew placed himself beyond the social limits by his baroque criminality, or whether he was crowded out by the hostile mass of men, he continued to be treated as an alien, a thing apart, an object of awe or hatred or contempt, to be vilified as a monster or patronized as an oddity. In either case, he existed apart from the body politic, to which he stood in the relation of parasite or benefactor. Whether he was Shylock or Sheva, Isaac or Trendelssohn, Montenero or Melmotte, the Jew enjoyed prominent standing in a separatist community, acting as spokesman for its moral code, the key inside-figure in an outside group, the center of a dim little planet on the periphery of the universe. His separatism defined him; it explained (at worst) his unnatural will to evil and (at best) his outward eccentricities, his antique garb, his queer habits—his rationalized will to good.

His desire for social acceptance by the Gentiles did not necessarily imply a desire to share their religion. In Shakespeare's day, the gesture of apostasy from the tribe might have been the means of his salvation, but he did not care to be saved, a job his daughter performed much better; in George Eliot's day, apostasy no longer meant salvation but disloyalty, desertion, flight; and so he knew better than to cast off his faith. His refusal to convert thus cuts across moral stratifications: it was held against him when the Jew was by definition odious, one of the "phrentic and lunatic" people in the Tudor medical texts, the denizen of Satan's heart, the "foreskin-clipper" in Nashe's surreal atmosphere; it was held in his favor when it no longer mattered so much what you were as long as you knew what you were and lived up to your racial and religious identity. This is merely another way of saying that what defines the Jew in literature is his exclusive Jewishness, which may be a good or a bad thing, but in any case freezes him in the role of outsider. The pious Riah, padding down the London alleys in his Oriental costume, is as much "out of it" as the blaspheming Shylock, dragged to the baptismal font. The Jew in literature remains on the whole obstinately Jewish. At once rejecting the majority and rejected by them, he elects to display the proverbial badge of all his tribe with tenacity and a certain ostentatiousness. Even when Meredith's socialist-hero boasts, "I am for the world, for man!" one detects behind the boast not only the conventionally philanthropic motive but the gesture of the self-conscious Jew who *feels* himself playing the role assigned to him by tradition, the part of the Tragic Comedian who, while he is himself in fetters, dreams of setting his jailers free.

But there are also those few, the professional murderers, the hallucinations we thought we left in the backroom, the sensation-Jews of Dickens and Ainsworth, who are irretrievable even to their own tribe, the final infidels who elude all social meaning, for whom the profit motive is a cover-up to mask their madness, for whom gold is the least thing that glitters. "You cannot take from me," reads Fagin's exit line, "anything I will not willingly part withal—except my knife, except my knife, except my knife."

Business: Nathanheimer versus Oppovich

Other times, same manners? Not quite. The market analyst on the Rialto reveals some new alignments.

Until the nineteenth century, and well into it, the conflict in the novels we have discussed was provided by a clear-cut economic antagonism between the Christian and the Jew: the one exploited the other. Through the latter part of the eighteenth century, all the thievery was axiomatically charged to the Jews; thereafter, Gentile and Jew enjoyed a roughly equal chance of cheating the other. The importance lies in the division itself, which was either taken for granted or unmistakably spelled out down to about 1850. The good Jew, naturally, held out his hand to the Christians, but chiefly from a sense of having himself been exploited by them. This entitled him to deliver a good-natured and mildly self-righteous homily on the exploitation of the Jews, which always came round to the prayer that Heaven preserve the Jews from doing unto the Christians as the Christians have done unto the Jews, and which merely underlined the fundamental enmity between the races. One is struck by the moral strategy behind all this: in subsidizing his Christian exploiters, the Jew is so obviously intended to be moved by a policy of turning the other cheek, of engaging in what Nietzsche, in his sour and succinct way, calls the "inhuman" gesture of blessing those by whom one is being cursed, that the Jewish paragon—no matter how fiercely loyal he may remain to his tribe—is in effect made to assimilate a morality which the novelist regarded as peculiarly and definitively Christian. For the student of ethics, the implications of this sort of moral kidnaping present a rather mordant irony of their own. They suggest that the nineteenth-century novelist still has to "disinfect" his Jews with the baptismal sprinkler before the public can be brought to keep company with them. Were one to look for a slogan, it would read: Make the Jews Safe for Christianity. The decent Jew, in other words, is decent in so far as he acts out and (to keep misunderstandings at a minimum) in so far as he pays lip-service to all the specifically New Testament virtues.

Occasionally, the novelist makes a special point of stressing the incongruity which this kind of transference is apt to involve on a purely lexical level. In Reade's book, for example, one of the Gentile prospectors, who has been selling his gold dust to the Jew Isaac, worries about finding a market for his produce once Isaac has left the campsite. On being reassured by the Jew that "the Christian merchants" will continue to patronize his gold dust, the Christian automatically bursts out that "they are such—Jews." Similar verbal ambiguities are found in novels in which the morally sound Jew at the center of the story is surrounded by lesser Jewish lickspittles and parasites. In Hall Caine's *The Scapegoat,* for example, a product of the 1890's, the self-righteous Jewish hero instinctively falls into the stance of the Gentile antagonist by calling his fellow Jews Shylocks and Bildads to their faces. There is not a trace of cynicism in his outburst, and certainly no assimilationism; the man is convinced of his Judaic mission and is full of passionate intensity in carrying it through. But he has projected his own situation to the point at which he can look at "the Jew" from the outside and regard the whole notion of the Jew in the popular—that is, hostile—meaning of the term; he momentarily assumes Antonio's view of Shylock, the view of the "inauthentic" Jew. The tension so far is interracial all the way. It is Jew against Christian, or Jew against Gentile.[3]

To keep this conflict sharply in focus, the novelists, down to about the middle of the century, did not bother to distinguish among kinds and varieties of Jews, beyond observing the conventional clash between the heavy father and the romantic daughter, or between the greedy Jewish master and the starved comic underling. To do more than this would have blurred the issue. The major Jewish figures came equipped with one or two Jewish cronies—their Tubals and Kirjaths and Cohenlupes—who were not, however, notably discriminated from the principals. They merely enjoyed a little less status, less wealth, less influence. In their bearing toward the chief they generally imitated the chief's own bearing toward the Gentile: the picture is that of the spaniel fawning on the big cur who elects to fawn on *homo sapiens.* With Edgeworth's *Harrington* the novelist begins to recognize the possibilities for stratifying the Jews more distinctly along economic lines, from the peddler to the millionaire, and to individualize them accordingly. Still, Edgeworth's Jews are all—necessarily and *a priori*—cut from the same moral pattern; since they all alike spend themselves in hortatory paragraphs, delivered in flawless English, they appear to be intellectual equals as well, so that one is left with the impression of a merely fortuitous distinction among them, a sense that the indigent Jacob needed only to be treated to some of Montenero's unique opportunities on the Rialto to become indistinguishable from him.

By the middle of the century, the novelist had begun to take an interest in the dramatic conflicts among the Jews themselves. As his samples from among English and continental Jewry accumulated, it became possible to deal with intramural rivalries and competitions, sometimes (though infrequently) without emphatic reference to the Gentiles beyond the wall. As a result, what we often find among the late Victorians is the novelist's concern with the exploitation of the Jew by the Jew. The theme emerges, directly or obliquely, in novels like *The Newcomes, Hypatia, Daniel Deronda, The Rebel Queen,* and *That Boy of Norcott's*; and it is formulated with a certain Machiavellian backhandedness both in Reade's novel and in Dickens's *Our Mutual Friend,* in which the Veneerings, the Lammles, and their sort, who have adopted all the sordid upstart traits associated with "Jewish capitalism" and who are probably themselves thinly veiled portraits of Jews, personify the very vices that elsewhere in the same novel the cloddish Riah is explicitly made to repudiate. Since Dickens's parvenus are far more cunningly drawn than Riah, one not only takes more interest in them but is apt to believe in the Veneering-reality long after the Riah-artifice has become drearily transparent. By and large, it is the small-time Jew who is unfavorably contrasted with his more amply endowed coreligionists, the men of culture, wealth, and knowledge, whom he tries, in a greasy way, to hoodwink: Lapidoth robbing Deronda, Besant's Mr. Angelo scheming to attach the Elveda fortune, the transparently named Abraham Pigman in Hall Caine's novel conspiring against the heroic Israel-ben-Oliel, the mercenary procuress Miriam in Kingsley's book acting as a foil to her unacknowledged son Raphael-Aben-Ezra, the gifted and civilized man. But the exploitation could also work the other way. If the novelist liked on the whole to depict the Jewish man of property in the image of the racially unexceptionable Sephardim on whom the poor Jew sponges, he could also typecast him in the role of the robber-baron of the Melmotte variety who no longer cares whether he pauperizes Gentile or fellow Jew.

To observe how the novelist deals with the exploitation of the Jewish merchant class by the international Jewish financier, one can go to Charles Lever's interesting story *That Boy of Norcott's,* the minor production of a minor novelist whom Bernard Shaw, in his quixotic way, cited (at Ibsen's expense) as one of his countless forgotten literary divinities.[4] Like most of his stories, Lever's novel (novella really) is made up of some loosely connected episodes in the life of its Irish narrator, a romantically disinherited and as it were misfiled young nobleman whose adventures bring him to Austria-Hungary and a secretarial job with the export house of Hodnig & Oppovich, late of Fiume, specialists in "grain trade from Russia, rags from Transylvania, staves from Hungary, fruit from the Levant, cotton from Egypt, minerals from Lower Austria, and woollen fabrics from Bohemia . . . besides a fair share in oak bark and hemp." Hodnig, the senior partner, is out of the picture, having some time ago "overspeculated and died of a broken heart," with the result that he has ruined the firm and left it to the surviving partner, the patriarchal Ignaz Oppovich, "after years of patient toil and thrift" to restore the credit of the house.

Oppovich is up to a point depicted as the conventionally good Jew and treated to the understandably tired phrases: "a Jew that could teach many a Christian the virtues of his own faith," "a Jew that never refused an alms to the poor, no matter of what belief, and that never spoke ill of his neighbour," a Jew who inspires in his townsmen the rhetorical surmise "what would become of the hospital, or the poorhouse, or the asylum for the orphans here, but for him?"—in other words, the Jew as samaritan, the Jew as John the Baptist, the Jew as Florence Nightingale. But Lever, who is something of a romantic realist, a lesser English Daudet or Berthold Auerbach, is by no means unqualified in his approval of the Oppoviches: if it may be said of them that they bring "to the battle of trade resolution and boldness and persistence and daring not a whit inferior to what their ancestors had carried into personal conflict," it must also be admitted that they have left the social graces behind with the Maccabees. Lever's young hero, who is in love with the Jewish daughter and is therefore motivated to look only on the bright side, cannot help noticing the "coarseness," "unculture and roughness" he finds in both the Oppovich home and the Oppovich countinghouse: indeed, the thing that keeps appalling him is the failure to distinguish between the two, and the monomania for trade which makes Profit and Loss a subject for discussion at high table. "So unlike was all this to the tone of dinner conversation I was used to, that I listened in wonderment how they could devote the hour of social enjoyment and relaxation to details so perplexing and vulgar." For all that, Lever leaves no doubt that he wants you to admire the Oppoviches, who, in a way, constitute the commercial "yeomanry" of their age, besides being the chief benefactors to their community; they are a strong-willed as well as soft-hearted clan, traits which commend them to Lever's Irish bias.

But as the novel bounces along toward its premature ending (Lever's bookseller wanted the novel for the Christmas trade, possibly because it contains a seasonable sleighride), it becomes clear that the Oppovich economy, through no real fault of Oppovich's own, is rotten at the center, that the firm has been conducted in continual fear of being wiped out, and that if the Oppoviches talk so obsessively about money, they do so with the partly realistic obsessiveness of people who stand to lose all their financial safeguards at any moment. The maintenance of Hodnig & Oppovich has been for years at the mercy of a massive Jewish combine which controls the smaller Jewish businesses, of "the great Jew House of 'Nathanheimer' of Paris"—and Nathanheimer of Paris, by any other name, is Rothschild, with or without Lever's pointed quotation marks. "It's all Nathanheimer! If a man prospers and shows that he has skill in business, they'll stand by him, even to millions. If he blunders, they sweep him away." One of Oppovich's salesmen enlarges on the Nathanheimer policy and machinery for conquest, enslavement, and elimination; the policy is absolutist and dynastic, though Lever (and this is where he parts company from his friend Trollope) allows his tycoons a certain element of "sportsmanship," and never leaves one with the sense of purely inflating the Melmotte issue. The employee describes

> how these great potentates of finance and trade had agencies in every great centre of Europe, who reported to them everything that went on, who flourished, and who foundered; how, when enterprises that promised well, presented themselves, Nathanheimer would advance any sum, no matter how great, that was wanted. If a country needed a railroad, if a city required a boulevard, if a seaport wanted a dock, they were ready to furnish each and all of them. The conditions, too, were never unfair, never ungenerous, but still they bargained always for something besides money. They desired that this man would aid such projects here, or oppose that

other there. Their interests were so various and widespread that they needed political power everywhere, and they had it.

One offence they never pardoned, never condoned, which was any, the slightest, insubordination amongst those they supported and maintained. Marsac [the speaker] ran over a catalogue of those they had ruined in London, Amsterdam, Paris, Frankfort, and Vienna, simply because they had attempted to emancipate themselves from the serfdom imposed upon them. Let one of the subordinate firms branch out into an enterprise unauthorised by the great house, and straightway their acceptances become dishonored, and their credit assailed. In one word, he made it appear that from one end of Europe to the other the whole financial system was in the hands of a few crafty men of immense wealth, who unthroned dynasties, and controlled the fate of nations, with a word.

He went on to show that Oppovich had somehow fallen into disgrace with these mighty patrons.

By the end of the book the Nathanheimers have taken their business away from Oppovich and so ruined him. Just why and how he has incurred their displeasure is not clear. There is a suggestion that he may have become too independent in his methods to suit his principals and begun to speculate without their consent; more likely, he became too soft and feeble with age to keep up with the Nathanheimer tempo. Having outlasted his usefulness to them, he goes the way of his senior partner and dies of a broken heart. The thing is virtually and emblematically a suicide: the end of business, the vital activity, is the end of life for these people. The job in life is to stay ahead; the disgrace is in falling behind. Oppovich dies a superannuated man. But with another page to fill up after Oppovich's death and in line with his aesthetic, to give his readers "a laugh without much trouble for going in search of it," Lever brings matters to an optimistic conclusion by arranging for a marriage between his hero, who has just then come into his title and his fortune, and Oppovich's capable daughter, a girl who is transformed from a ruggedly unique Rebecca—a conceited and insolent female, with a head full of business facts and figures—into a merely conventional one, "a pale Jewish girl, silent and half sad-looking, but whose low soft voice still echoed in my heart." *Abie's Irish Rose,* more or less, with the sexes and nationalities transposed.[5] But in the story of old Ignaz Oppovich, Lever has written a pathetic, often touching, very slight, *Death of a Salesman.*

The likeness of the Nathanheimers to the Rothschilds differs from other Rothschild portraits in literature only in being more patent and literal than most. It must be remembered that in their portrayals of the great Jewish entrepreneurs, the bankers and philanthropists and big businessmen alike, the Victorian writers were largely drawing on historical models, who became blurred in the novelists' imaginations with the inherited stereotype of the Jew, so that it is often difficult, from the point of confluence, to track down the separate sources. How much of Trollope's Daubeny goes back to Shylock; and how much of him is Beaconsfield? What part of Melmotte comes out of Barabas; and what part of him is Gottheimer? By 1869, when Lever wrote about them, the Rothschilds alone could mean whatever the novelist (or anybody else) wanted them to mean. Disraeli and Balzac both wrote about them in the 'forties; to Disraeli, they meant Sidonia (or rather that part of Sidonia which Disraeli had not preempted for purposes of auto-mythology), champion and purifier of the race, lonely overlord of a fabulous family combine; to Balzac, they meant Nucingen, the big Alsatian manipulator with the vulgar accent, the degenerate Goriot's aggressive son-in-law. Dostoyevski and Trollope both wrote about the Rothschilds in the 1870's; for Dostoyevski, they furnished the Jews with a convenient blind ("wasn't the late James Rothschild of Paris a good man?") to the real fiasco, the Jews' "carnivorous craving for personal material welfare," the threat of "their complete reign," when "there would ensue such an era as could be compared not only with the era of serfdom but even with that of the Tartar yoke"; Trollope, writing about them in *The Eustace Diamonds* five years before Dostoyevski, sourly regards their installation in political life as a dreary *fait accompli,* not an apocalyptic probability: "all the Directors of the Bank of England were in the gallery of [the House of Lords], and every chairman of a great banking company, and every Baring and every Rothschild, if there be Barings and Rothschilds who have not been returned by constituencies, and have no seats in the House by right." And as late as 1893, Henry Adams pined for the day of wrath which should find him at the barricades, "helping the London mob pull up Harcourt and Rothschild on a lamppost in Piccadilly." In this, too, his education turned out, as regards himself, a thing of nought;

naturally the Rothschilds survived the holocausts and, for the purposes of literature, they were still in circulation at least as late as 1940, when Franz Werfel's Jacobowsky, expert in the techniques of flight, talked or bribed the Rothschild chauffeur into selling him the family limousine, the last operating motor-vehicle left in occupied Paris and the last means of escape from the current lamppost law.[6]

Family: Fathers, Sons, Lovers

The Jewish paragon, like the criminal, has some new features to register, though the animus behind his conception—to talk Shylock out of our system—has changed little. A few of his latter-day poses have already defined themselves in the foregoing remarks. He is a little more complicated than he used to be, which is to his credit. For example, he is no longer necessarily in business, though he still meets us in this guise three-fourths of the time. "It is just as well that some of our ability should show itself in other than business lines," one of Besant's Jewish characters remarks with a certain cynical satisfaction, speaking of his cousin, who is both a scientist of genius and a talented woodcarver. Whether he is nominally in business or not, the good Jew has been spiritualized in the past hundred years. Like Eliot's Daniel Deronda, Kingsley's Raphael, Besant's Emanuel Elveda, or Hale White's Baruch Cohen, he is often an essentially meditative human being, who has swapped the soul of a shopkeeper for the sensibilities of an artist, who feels himself doubly isolated in a nation—supposedly—of shopkeepers, and who thus points forward to the twentieth-century cliché of the Jew as well as back to the eighteenth-century stereotype. If he still sounds a little bombastic at times, at least he has stopped being the clown, the "little Jew" with the droll inflections, on whom Cumberland and his generation practiced their tolerance. He has grown in inches as well as inwardness; he is taller and deeper than his grandfathers were. The Jew's wisdom has always been the better part of his valor, but where his wisdom spent itself wickedly in necromancy, it now presumes a scrupulous and humane application to science and philosophy, religion, art, scholarship. Of the introspective middle-aged Baruch Cohen of *Clara Hopgood,* a mathematical instrument maker by profession, we are told that his features were Jewish, his thinking was Jewish, and he believed after a fashion in the Jewish sacred books, or, at any rate, read them continuously, although he had added to his armoury defensive weapons of another type. In nothing was he more Jewish than in a tendency to dwell upon the One, or what he called God, clinging still to the expression of his forefathers, although departing so widely from them. In his ethics and system of life, as well as in his religion, there was the same intolerance of multiplicity which was not reducible to unity. He seldom explained his theory, but everybody who knew him recognised the difference which it wrought between him and other men. There was a certain concord in everything he said and did, as if it were directed by some enthroned but secret principle.[7]

In a passage like this, one is struck by the apparent paradox that although the author goes out of his way to emphasize Cohen's typically Jewish qualities, the result is not really a type, and scarcely a stereotype at all, except in the limited sense that one is apt to find, after George Eliot, a tendency to identify the thoughful Jew with Spinoza, often physically as well as intellectually. Cohen's first name is pointedly the same as the philosopher's; his family is Dutch on the father's side; the father's break with orthodox Judaism suggests, of course, Spinoza's expulsion from the synagogue; and Cohen's own nominal half-Jewishness (the mother is a Gentile) symbolically recalls Spinoza's schismatic role, Talmudic and secular both. But all this really tells us more about Hale White's personal interest in Spinoza (whose *Ethics* he translated) than about anything "typed" in Cohen, who is, among other things, a substantial, serious, rather unhappy human being, whose problems connect up with the problems of other human beings, Gentile or Jew.

If the Jew has gained in spiritual depth, in "character," he has also become more public-minded. Often, as we saw, he has translated his grievances as a Jew and his defense of the Jew's private status in a hostile society into a positive creed for political action. Mordecai, Raphael, Daniel, Alroy, Sigismund Alvan, are exemplars of the Jewish activist who emerges in the course of the century as Zionist, socialist, or positivist, but always as a good soldier in the civil war of mankind. A figure like Alvan no longer practices charity privately and domestically, after the fashion of Sheva and Manasseh, doing good by stealth to a half-dozen near acquaintances, but performs on the public stage, doing good arrogantly and with a certain hard defiance. Meredith evidently enjoys the irony of a situation in which the world's great humanitarian tragically mismanages his private life by his overbearing egoism; but such a view itself suggests a degree of sophistication in the portrayal of the Jew which would have been inconceivable in Lessing's day.

The benevolent Jew, in short, has become both more extraverted and more introverted in the course of the century: the fact is that he has become some thirty years younger than we knew him to be. Down to about 1820, the paragon might have been mistaken from a distance for his cousin Shylock himself, since they were roughly contemporary—both in their fifties or sixties, say, bearded, and done up in the vestments of orthodoxy. Sheva and Isaac and the elderly cabbalistic gentlemen in Godwin and Maturin (I mean the "real" Jews who appear in their novels, not the Wandering) are well past the meridian of life, physically beyond the point where they can be expected to exert themselves aggressively *in coram publico*. Even someone like Mr. Montenero, who is still in his prime and cuts rather a dashing figure, seems to be comfortably ensconced in the part of elder statesman, not active politician. Near relations of Nathan the Wise, all of them, they are defined by their patriarchal qualities; they are fathers, not sons; widowers, not suitors. If they are all a little New Testamental in their meekness, they are at least gotten up to look like Abraham and Isaac, by whom they are always made to swear and after whom half of them are named.

By contrast, Disraeli's Alroy and Trollope's Trendelsshon, Besant's Elveda and Hale White's Cohen, Scott's Middlemas and Bulwer's Levy (these last-named bad Jews, however, not good), as well as the Jews in Eliot, Kingsley, and Meredith, are young enough to serve the purposes of romance. The interesting thing about all these figures is that each of them at some point during his courtship has to face the question of intermarriage—as if the author had a difficult time in conceiving anything romantic about intramural marriages among the Israelites, or could not expect the public to buy so dreary an article. The general idea is that if Jews can never be friends with Gentiles, the least they can do is to marry them. "Nina Balatka," Trollope opens his novel, "was a maiden of Prague, born of Christian parents, and herself a Christian—but she loved a Jew; and this is her story";

and by the time the story is over, young Trendelssohn has been allowed to keep both his girl and his Judaism. Daniel Deronda is, in a sense, "converted" to Judaism and alerted to an awareness of Mirah's availability by discovering that he is a Jew on prior grounds; Alvan and Alroy both, though for vastly different reasons, come to grief by seeking their partners among the Gentiles. In Besant's *Rebel Queen* and Hall Caine's *Scapegoat*—both products of the 'nineties—Jew is mated with Jewess, but the results do not warrant optimism: in Besant's novel, the marriage is dissolved almost immediately, and in Caine's novel the Jewess dies with similar promptitude, leaving the husband in charge of their sole daughter after the fashion of the earlier elderly paragon. In their sonship, almost all these figures revolt, tacitly or openly, against the parent: the emancipated Trendelssohn Junior against the stiff-necked Trendelssohn Senior; the pious scholar Mordecai against the pious fraud Lapidoth; the convert Daniel against the apostate Charisi; the enlightened Raphael-Aben-Ezra against the superstitious mother figure of Miriam; Alroy, conqueror and captive audience of the caliphs, against the parent-body of the rabbinate; Caine's Israel-ben-Oliel, the idealist, against Oliel the mercenary father, who enters on matrimony as on "another business transaction," and whose dying summons the son obeys "without a throb of filial affection," not because he is wicked but because the father has relinquished all claims to his affection.

In other words, the young Jew has taken on some of the plot-functions that it was customary heretofore to assign to his counterpart, the Jewess—though the Abigail-Jessica problem, in so far as it involves marrying outside the clan, continues at least to be touched on, in one form or another, in connection with the daughter. Thus we have the examples of Berenice Montenero (who providentially turns out not to be a Jewess); Mirah Lapidoth (whose boy friend providentially turns out to be a Jew); Sarah Oppovich (whose intermarriage proves little either way, since it seems not to have been foreseen by the author); Scott's Rebecca (who renounces the Gentile, and is renounced by him, as a matter of course and of historical necessity); Marie Melmotte and the title-heroine of Bulwer's *Leila* (both of whom aspire to the hand of the non-Jew and are punished for their efforts by the father, one by being "whipped within one inch of her life," the other by sacrificing that final inch as well); Sherrick's daughter in *The Newcomes* (who goes needlessly far afield by marrying a Protestant clergyman, an insufferable hypocrite, whose hypocrisy extends precisely to marrying a Jewess); and, finally, Leah Gibson in Du Maurier's last novel (the course of whose true love runs relatively smooth, though it takes a Martian resident to get it going to begin with).

Since he functions, within the tradition, as something of a daughter-surrogate, we must not be surprised to find the Jewish son frequently retaining a certain quantum of girlishness, often in conjunction with a lot of voluble and heroic derring-do. An idealist first and a realist second, in the course of the century he has shed some of the common sense that used to safeguard his purse-proud ancestors; he is definitely a third-generation Buddenbrook. "What with making their way and enjoying what they have won, heroes have no time to think. But the sons of heroes—ah, they have all the necessary leisure."[8] The romantic young Jew is still terribly involved in the ethics of an acquisitive society, but half the time in order to repudiate them: either endeavoring, like Raphael-Aben-Ezra, to find the *via media* between the meaningless dog-eat-dog materialism of the Hebraic, and the spineless abstract formalism of the Hellenic world; or, like Daniel and Mordecai, deliberately standing Shylock upside down. The second-generation Jews are not notably interested in making a fortune. Anton Trendelssohn, the hero of Trollope's *Nina Balatka,* is something of an exception—and even Trendelssohn, like a smaller and saner Sidonia, endows money with a certain liturgical quality by which it is brought into relation with his other articles of faith and ultimately divested of its purely commercial function:

> To go forth and be great in commerce by deserting his creed would have been nothing to him. His ambition did not desire wealth so much as the enjoyment of wealth in Jewish hands, without those restrictions upon its enjoyment to which Jews under his own eyes had ever been subjected. It would have delighted him to think that, by means of his work, there should no longer be a Jews' quarter in Prague, but that all Prague should be ennobled and civilised and made beautiful by the wealth of Jews.

There is something of the same detached quality in this as in Barabas's greed, but the argosies plainly sail in opposite directions: for Barabas the point is to have his infinite riches piled up in front of him, where he can see, smell and touch them in the manner of the old-fashioned miser; for Trendelssohn the idea of wealth is both deprived of its personal function and transformed to mean "Jewish wealth"—though without any of the obnoxious associations elsewhere attached to the phrase.

In the strictly practical aspects of the economy the young Jew is not vastly interested—but the young Jewess is, very much so. Some of the Rialto values, without the attendant brutality, have suddenly developed on the modern Jessica—without the attendant frivolity. It is not among people like Daniel and Raphael or even Anton that we may look for solid common sense, but among people like Marie Melmotte, educating herself to the world of stocks and bonds, or Sarah Oppovich, who replies to her lover's romantic effusions with a laconic business letter, full of freight rates, bank drafts, and discounts.

In rebelling against the parent, the Jewish son or daughter, of course, re-enacts an ancient literary ritual. Long before the Jews began to cut each others' throats commercially, conflicts within the family had become an essential feature of the myth. The economic rivalry among the Jews in literature is an emphatically Victorian phenomenon, but the clash between the generations is as old as Marlowe. In the Tudor prototypes, the daughter initiates at best a secondary conflict; and she provides the old Jew with the one foil from within the tribe—a notoriously stiff-necked and clannish community, in which such defections counted for a good deal. In the nineteenth century, the tensions between Barabas and Abigail no longer require the presence of Ferneze: what used to be sub-plot stands now on its own. By and large, the novelist continues to side with the younger generation against the old, with Abigail (or the male surrogate) against Barabas; but the alignment is not a rigid one, and occasionally the formula may be reversed. In *Clara Hopgood* and *The Rebel Queen,* for example, the fathers, Baruch and Emanuel, are sympathetically contrasted with the children, who are a little too ready to make snide comments about Jews; young Adolph Oppovich in Lever's story is simply a ne'er-do-well in a family that takes its civic and commercial responsibilities most seriously; and in a novel like Trollope's *Nina Balatka,* in which the conflict between the generations and the ancillary problem of intermarriage spell out the dominant themes of the book, the issue all but ends in a draw.

On the whole, Trollope is all with Anton Trendelssohn in his battle for emancipation, his struggle to break out of the bohemian ghetto environment in which he has been raised, to intermarry with a Catholic girl, and book passage on the next train heading west. "To crush the prejudice which had dealt so hardly with his people—to make a Jew equal in all things to a Christian—this was his desire; and how could this better be fulfilled than by his union with a Christian?" But Trendelssohn himself is presented as a terribly gloomy, sullen, and saturnine person, while the father, the orthodox ghetto-Jew, not only is free from any of the fanatic bigotry that marks his Catholic opposites, but faces the question of intermarriage with admirable restraint and common sense. By allying himself with a Christian, he cautions his son, Anton is simply going to create impossible social barriers for the girl as well as for himself. "'You will live to rue the day in which you first saw her,' said the elder Jew. 'She will be a bone of contention in your way that will separate you from all your friends. You will become neither Jew nor Christian, and will be odious alike to both. And she will be the same.'" Trollope's understanding, as evidenced in a passage like this, is remarkably in advance of his day (*Nina Balatka* was published in 1867); the viewpoint expressed here by the old ghetto-merchant is precisely that of Mr. Leonard March, the retired banker in C. P. Snow's novel ninety years later, and the conflict suggests something of the same inevitability in both books, though Trollope's is infinitely more trivial. Still, equivocal as he is in his presentation of Anton, Trollope ends by taking his stand with him, both because the attitude of the elders strikes him as reactionary and inhibiting, and because he seems to resent parental interference on principle—it will be remembered that in *The Way We Live Now* he flourishes Marie Melmotte's opposition to her parents and her insistence on marrying a Gentile as a point greatly in her favor.[9]

Considering some of the interesting moral implications Trollope has raised in that novel, it is a pity that *Nina Balatka* never rises much above the patronizing tone of its opening sentence. Trollope's latest interpreter, Bradford Booth, has called his characterization of Anton "a remarkably acute study in racial history":

> In a more ambitious and infinitely more difficult psychological portrait than he usually attempted, Trollope develops in Anton the disabling experiences of ghetto segregation and persecution. . . . In him Trollope traces the disintegration of European ghetto society and the emergence of a more self-reliant Jewish individualist who can escape environmental neuroses.[10]

And his treatment of Anton the lover is remarkably unromantic and balanced. Trollope shows him to be a fallible human being who, for all his idealism, retains a good many elements of the disreputable merchant. He does not look the part of a lover, really: "his eyes were somewhat too close together in his face, and the bridge of his aquiline nose was not sharply cut, as is mostly the case with such a nose on a Christian face. The olive oval face was without doubt the face of a Jew, and the mouth was greedy . . ." And if Anton is, at bottom, like Daniel Deronda after him, something of a visionary, going forth to forge in the West the uncreated conscience of his race, he does not talk about it like a promotional dust-jacket. The prophet is also a shrewd businessman.

The opening sentence of *Nina Balatka* states the theme of intermarriage, of Gentile versus Jew; the closing sentence resolves the conflict between parent and son, East and West, ghetto and freedom: "Early in the following year, while the ground was yet bound with frost, and the great plains of Bohemia were still covered with snow, a Jew and his wife took their leave of Prague, and started for one of the great cities of the West." Throughout the story proper, Anton remains safely insulated in Prague; and if one comes upon *Nina Balatka* after reading *The Way We Live Now,* one is apt to be nervous about Trendelssohn's reception in Paris or London. The uncomfortable suspicion urges itself that he will be as unwelcome to Trollope as Melmotte and Brehgert and Joseph Emilius and Daubeny and Cohenlupe. By ringing down the curtain the moment Trendelssohn's train crosses the border, Trollope avoids meeting head-on the problem of a Jew in his own backyard. While in Prague, Trendelssohn remains virtuous, because "contained"—a relatively complex bundle of loyalties and hostilities. In view of Trollope's effort to deepen for once the Semitic caricatures and gargoyles with which he peopled three or four very good novels afterward, it is doubly regrettable that *Nina Balatka* should be one of his worst—thin, humorless, badly underplotted, soap-opera in tone and incident, as though Trollope were bent on warning potentially anti-Semitic teen-agers to be guided by the sterling example of Nina Balatka, Maiden of Prague, who dared marry a Jew, got away with him, and lived happily ever after.

Race: Svengali Adler

Anton is an Easterner, an Ashkenazi among Jews—not, on the whole, the best sort of catch from the racial point of view, if one is to trust the evidence of Victorian fictionists; Nina Balatka could have done better. To a girl of marriageable age, Jewess or Gentile, who is desirous of finding a partner for life among the Jews, a member of the Sephardic race from the southern countries is to be most warmly recommended. She is likely to find him, in comparison with his English or Middle- and Eastern-European cousins, richer, better looking, more creative, more intelligent, and better groomed for society; and his pedigree stretches back (though uncertainly) to Solomon and his seven hundred concubines. He may well be an issue of some one of the seven hundred, considering the mysterious wealth of possibilities in which his antecedents remain poised, the genius he has for turning out to be somebody else's descendant than his or hers he has been tricked into believing himself. It is all part and parcel of his exotic make-up. The Sephardic Jew is to be found among the upper crust and he has an excellent chance of being famous. He has (ideally) wealth, knowledge, culture, leisure, and, though he may not wish to take advantage of it, the right of political power; he retains strong traces of his Spanish or Portuguese or Italian or Near-Eastern ancestry; and the very euphony of his name, with the romantic associations it evokes, serves as a certificate of moral beauty: Montenero, Elveda, Deronda, Sidonia, Mendoza, Moncada, Baroni, Baruch [Spinoza] Cohen, Alcharisi, Oriel-ben-Israel, Joshua Manasseh. Nina (or Mirah) ought to be cautioned, however, that the Sephardic Jew is also more apt than his Eastern relative to tax her patience by his bookishness, his bias toward cabbalistic hocus-pocus, his assumption that she would rather serve as a sounding board for his metaphysics than engage in gossip, and his tendency to brood about the nature of the world instead of scheming to get the better of it. But then there is an even chance of his having the better of it already by right of inheritance—assuming that his heredity has been established.

What does he look like? Well, like Daniel Deronda; like the youthful Emanuel Elveda. His features are not picturesque so much as they are evocative; what they add up to is less the portrait of an individual than the history of a race.

When in your walks abroad you pass such a young man . . . you begin to think of a street in a Spanish city—narrow, with lofty houses, windows with balconies, women leaning over the balconies, bits of bright people down below showing just such faces. Then the word Sephardim comes back to your memory. This face, you say, belongs to the Children of the Dispersion; they were in Spain long before the legions of Titus completed that Scattering; they are of the ancient people, whose lineage is so long that, compared with them, the Bourbons are mushrooms and the Hapsburgs are of yesterday.

In this face there was something of the eagle, the nose was narrow and slightly aquiline, the nostrils were finely cut and delicate, the eyes keen and clear, deep-set, under straight and well-marked eyebrows, and in color blue as the finest steel of Damascus; the lips were firm, the mouth finely curved; there was a rich, deep coloring of the cheek; the forehead was broad and white, the clustering hair was chestnut; the sun had touched that face with a glow which lingered on it. Surely the Rabbi Akiba, or Gamaliel, or even Onkelos himself, must have had such a face. Surely this was the face which belonged to the illustrious Maccabaean house. Surely this was the face at sight of which Joshua's enemies turned and fled. Such a face . . . may serve for [the portrait of] the Prophet Elisha when he was still young and had just received the cloak of his Master and Forerunner. Such a face . . . is always striking and always handsome.[11]

The homegrown what-have-you London Jew, as well as the Ashkenazi to the East—Oppovich, Trendelssohn, Brehgert, Lucas, Max Goesler, Melyius, Shedrick alias Shadrach—is not so distinguished as his southern relative in either his looks or his outlook. His outlook is businesslike, solidly or shadily. His face, too, is both plainer and less sunny than the Sephardic, identified in a glance and exhausted in a glance. It does not, like Elveda's, connect up with anything behind it; it suggests nothing except that the trunk which holds it up is a Jew's. But the trunk has no roots in Spain, let alone in Joshua's Lebanon; neither is it crowned by the crown of Akiba or Onkelos. The genealogy of Elveda's Eastern antitype is lost in the obscurity of the ghetto; he gives you the impression of having sprung directly from the gutters of the metropolis and gone on from there to bigger, if not better, things. His history is clinched in the notation that he has been spawned in some estaminet of Antwerp, blistered in Brussels, patched and peeled in London—patched by Old-Clothes Levi and peeled by Nathanheimer's London agent or by Melmotte, whose name is no more Melmotte than Gottheimer's is Grant. These last gentlemen notwithstanding, we may expect to see the Eastern- and Central-European Jew assigned to a relatively modest income-group, to the distinctly non-U middle classes made up of the shopkeeping and small trading interests, or he may even be dumped to the bottom layer of peddlers, fences, and thieves. His name (if he is middle-class) is apt to be nothing more exciting than Cohen (or Cohenlupe, Cohen in Wolf's Furs) or Levy or Levi—names which in effect reveal their bearers to be primates in the Jewish hierarchy, but which encourage the uninformed common reader to take a common view of them. But if the Jew is quite needy, the novelist thinks nothing of compounding his indigence by peeling him of his Christian name, too, and sending him out into the streets as Jacob or Isaac or Rachub or Fagin.

Since the Sephardic Jew tends to social exclusiveness within his own venerable community, encounters between him and the merchant-upstart are rare. Instead of consorting with Cohens and Levis, the ideally constructed Deronda talks only to Mordecai, and Mordecai talks only to God. When the mushroom-Cohen does find himself by the side of the Hidalgo, the contrast does not, as has been suggested, accrue to his advantage. In Meredith's *Tragic Comedians,* the Christian heroine, Clotilde von Ruediger, is about to meet the Jewish hero, Sigismund Alvan—factually a German Jew (the Lassalles were Silesians named Wolfssohn until the 1812 Emancipation Laws) but affectively the purest-bred Castilian. Clotilde knows that Alvan is a Jew but she has not seen him before. Meredith places her in a room with three men—her host, who looks "mildly Jewish"; a caricature of a Semite; and a tall demigod of a man—and puts her through a guessing game: which of the three Jews is Alvan? Naturally Clotilde, who has definite ideas about what definitive Jews look like, assumes him to be the caricature. (Naturally he turns out to be the demigod.) The passage, interesting for the contrast Meredith establishes by placing the two racial antitypes side by side, gains added interest from the character of Clotilde's preconceptions. Writing in 1880, Meredith already views the stereotype as an object for parody. The result is not so much a stereotyped Jew as a stereotyped Christian viewpoint. The three of them are as it were lined up for the guessing game like so many caskets labeled Gold, Silver, and Sampson Brass; to them, Portia.

They were indistinct; she could see that one of them was of good stature. One she knew; he was the master of the house, mildly Jewish. The third was distressingly branded with the slum and gutter signs of the Ahasuerus race. Three hats on his head could not have done it more effectively. The vindictive caricatures of the God Pan, executed by priests of the later religion burning to haunt him out of worship in the semblance of the hairy, hoofy, snouty Evil One, were not more loathsome. She sank on a sofa. That the man? Oh! Jew, and fifty times over Jew! nothing but Jew!

The three stepped into the long saloon, and she saw how veritably magnificent was the first whom she had noticed. . . . This man's face was the born orator's, with the light-giving eyes, the forward nose, the animated mouth, all stamped for speechfulness and enterprise, of Cicero's rival in the forum before he took the headship of armies and marched to empire. . . . Alas, he could not be other than Christian, so glorious was he in build! One could vision an eagle swooping to his helm by divine election. . . .

Then again, could that face be the face of a Jew? She feasted. It was a noble profile, an ivory skin, most lustrous eyes. Perchance a Jew of the Spanish branch of the exodus, not the Polish. There is the noble Jew as well as the bestial Gentile. . . . The noble Jew is grave in age, but in his youth he is the arrow to the bow of his fiery eastern blood, and in his manhood he is—ay, what you see there! a figure of easy and superb preponderance, whose fire has mounted to inspirit and been tempered by the intellect.[12]

It will be observed that the Italianate quality of the Jew, once so inseparably linked up with the Jew's fiendishness, has come to suggest three hundred years after Shakespeare an aura of good breeding, of social and intellectual unction, a relaxed sense of one's historical moorings, and an aristocratic view of one's wealth. Though the same quality also continues to throw into sharp relief the Jew's alien features, the important thing, after all, is that they are handsomely alien, issuing the good-natured reminder that it will never do to cry "Moneybags!" after someone, "compared with whom, the Bourbons are mushrooms and the Hapsburgs are of yesterday." The Italianate Jewish villain of the old school, who represents a direct sexual threat to the Gentiles, has to all intents gone the way of the religious ogre. He already looks a little threadbare by 1838, the year Fagin died, when Mrs. Trollope tried to give him another run in her slickly venial three-volume *A Romance of Vienna,* where he appears as Imla Balthazar, the repulsive castellan of a stout-hearted English girl, whom he feebly endeavors to ravish from time to time; and even Balthazar, though his tactics recall the prototypical Machiavel, is nominally a German Jew. Though Shylock's literary offspring has grown younger with the years, along with the antipode, the old Shylock remains more important than the son. Shylock Junior is far less dangerous than his parent used to be, and correspondingly more ludicrous. Since he is bound to fail in his one vital scheme, to seduce the Christian girl, he stands a much better chance of making a fool of himself than his father, whose failure to carry out his Oriental vengeance came so close to success as to excite terror; and besides he used to be a public menace, where the son is merely a domestic nuisance. Thanks to his Italianate coloring, the younger Shylock, like the younger Sheva, is defined more by his amorous desires (one cannot really call them erotic) than by his businesses, and as he has it not in him to be either a capable villain, like his father, or a capable hero, like his antipode, his importance for literature is relatively negligible. There is no wicked (or silly) young Jew in Victorian fiction comparable with the tame young lions in *Daniel Deronda, Hypatia, The Tragic Comedians.* He is a born minor character.

Shylock Junior may be recognized by his swarthy complexion, his oily black hair, which he is fond of wearing in curls and ringlets, his fleshy red lips and his flashy clothes, his name-dropping, and his maladroit efforts to look smooth. A portrait of Mrs. Trollope's man—Shylock at thirty-five—may be hung beside those of Trendelssohn and Elveda to complete the tryptich of racial types: solid middle-grade Eastern, top-grade Sephardic, low-grade Austrian, compounded of Eastern vulgarity and Italianate malice.

His person was . . . very short and plump; and his nether lip, too, was so untowardly large and thick-set, that, notwithstanding its being richly red, it could hardly escape being considered by most people, and by all Christian ladies in particular, as singularly disagreeable. . . . His nose was large, high and arched; and there are advocates for such noses who would have declared it a very handsome nose: but all who look at expression rather than outline in a face, must decidedly have voted against the nose as well as the lip; for, if the latter spoke of coarse and vulgar voluptuousness, the former . . . gave notice of a keen and wary spirit that might come in contact with many varieties of human acuteness, and delude them all. In complexion the gentleman was of a sallow white, and not a few deep marks of the small-pox were visible in various parts of his large face; though, perhaps, more still were concealed by the careful cultivation of his black favourites, which were trained and trimmed with such happy skill as to leave that portion of his visage between them very nearly of an oval form. . . . This personage extended a short-fingered thick white hand to lead the trembling Countess to a seat.[13]

Mrs. Trollope's laboriously burlesqued vocabulary makes it fairly plain that the Countess has nothing to fear from an Israelite who, as a specimen of comic horror, is three parts comedy to one part horror, and that if she nonetheless trembles, it is merely because that is what Countesses automatically do in the presence of Jews. But it is difficult to think Balthazar capable of rape, let alone slaughter, though Mrs. Trollope, whose perceptions are unbelievably crude and infantile, apparently meant him to be capable of both. Elsewhere the youthful Jew's basic harmlessness is underlined by droll externals. Occasionally (like Dickens's Barney) he lisps. At other times (like young Moss, Clive Newcome's companion) he speaks through his nose. Instead of saying "Step in, Mr. Newcome, any day you are passing down Wardour Street," he says, "Step id, Bister Doocob, ady day idto Vordor Street," which presents difficulties to the reader, who is thus apt to be more exasperated with Thackeray than with young Moss.[14] There is no physical menace in any of this. The hopeful seducer may get as far as the Gentile's drawing room, and usually he does, but it takes no great vigilance to keep him out of the bedroom—unless, like Joseph Emilius, he comes as father-confessor to Lady Eustace's bedside, reading her first a chapter from the Bible in his celestial capacity, and after that the first half of the fourth canto of *Childe Harold* in his terrestrial one. Balthazars and Baron Levys may ogle their Mary Ringolds and Nora Avenels all they want, but that is as far as they get. Brehgert could have Georgina Longestaffe if he wanted her, but the prospect of their union merely proves that the Genteel Tradition is about to declare its bankruptcy; and besides, Brehgert, though very greasy, is relatively sound. Of the remaining boudoir-Machiavels—the antitypes to Alvans and Derondas—Scott's Middlemas scores high as a seducer, but he is only half a Jew in fact and barely more than a quadroon to look at. Toward the end of the century, of course, there is Svengali, whose real name, however, is Adler, which is hardly better than Cohen.

It is in our own century rather than in the last that the Jew once more affronts us as an object of quasi-religious as well as sexual horror: he reappears, sponsored by T. S. Eliot and the protégés of Eliot, the by-product of an aesthetic impulse which has rejected, as being somehow too thin, the socio-economic basis of the nineteenth-century novel, and has propped it up with religious and mythological materials, and which has sacrificed realistic techniques of fiction to surreal and symbolistic ones. The ghastly figure of Clerk Simon in Charles Williams's eerie novel *All Hallows' Eve,* for example—a combination of Svengali, Black Priest, and Eternal Jew—is a creature at once so acutely horrible, so minutely and graphically defined, and at the same time so vastly distorted by the totemic and symbolic uses to which Williams puts him, that in reading the book one has the impression of dreaming the whole thing, an impression Williams controls by resorting to frequently monotonous and oddly mesmeric sentence rhythms.[15]

A creature who is at home among both the living and the dead, Simon Magus (to stay with the book for a moment) endeavors not simply to "murder Progress" in the slick sense in which an anti-Semitic crank of John Jay Chapman's ilk uses the phrase, but literally to remand the universe to its prerational phase, part *Urschleim* and part kingdom of the dead, to be dominated absolutely by his own sinister Messianic powers; his is going to be the "final miracle" of Kazanzakis's sentence, the miracle of turning civilized life back into a fairy tale. Before he walks into the story in person, his appearance is foreshadowed in the appropriate frame of a surreal painting, in which both his sacerdotal and primitivistic features define themselves:

The extended hand [of the priest] was no longer a motion of exposition or of convincing energy, holding the congregation attentive, but drawing the congregation after it, a summons and a physical enchantment. . . . A crowd of winged beetles, their wings yet folded but at the very instant of loosening, was about to rise into the air and disappear into that crevice and away down the prolonged corridor. And the staring emaciated face that looked out at them and over them was the face of an imbecile. . . . Blatant and blank in the gray twilight, where only a reflection of the sun shone from the beetles' coats, the face hung receding; blank and blatant, the thousand insects rose toward it.

When in England, Clerk Simon rents a meeting hall in Holborn, where he performs ghastly sexual rites, works at the manufacture of homunculi, and drains his auditors of all rational energies; the place furnishes the background for a periodical lecture in which the elements of a Black Mass are fused with those of a massive brainwashing:

The Clerk sat and spoke. His hands rested on the arms of his chair; his body was quite still; except that his head turned slightly as he surveyed the half-moon of his audience. The Jewish traits in his face were more marked. The language in which he spoke was ancient Hebrew, but he was pronouncing it in a way not common among men. . . . A curious flatness was in his voice. He was practicing and increasing this, denying accents and stresses to his speech. . . . The Clerk was going farther yet. He was removing meaning itself from the words. They fought against him; man's vocabulary fought against him. Man's art is perhaps worth little in the end, but it is at least worth its own present communication. . . . It was this that the Clerk was removing; he turned, or sought to turn, words into mere vibrations.

Simon, as Eliot notes in his introductory comments to the novel, "is defined by his function of representing the single-minded lust for unlawful and unlimited power"; and the attainment of power, on the theological level on which Simon seeks it, involves not only the denial of human freedom by the anaesthetizing of the will (of transforming men into vermin), but the Clerk's own withdrawal into a preconscious arena, sacramental and bestial, shrouded in secrecy and hemmed in by power taboos. In process of setting himself up as God-surrogate, for example, Simon begets a child who is eventually to negotiate his incursions into the Christian world; and the scene of begetting is itself dense with fear, a rite in which Simon reverts to the role of the Jew who is both demiurge and beast, Anti-Christ as well as satyr.

> He was standing between [the woman's] bed and the great mirror. They had had that mirror put there for exactly such operations, and however dark the room there always seemed to be a faint gray light within the mirror, so that when she saw him in it, it was as if he himself and no mere image lived and moved there. He had put off his clothes, and he stood looking into the mirror, and suddenly the light in it disappeared and she could see nothing. But she could hear a heavy breathing, almost a panting, and almost animal, had it not been so measured and at times changed in measure. It grew and deepened, and presently it became so low a moan that the sweat broke out on her forehead and she bit her hand as she lay. But even that moan was not so much of pain as of compulsion. The temperature of the room grew hotter; a uterine warmth oppressed her. She sighed and threw the blankets back. And she prayed—to God? not to God; to him? certainly to him. She had given herself to his will to be the mother of the instrument of his dominion; she prayed to him now to be successful in this other act.

In passages like these, Williams has recaptured some of the primitive sensations of religious fright that the Jew must have inspired in his early sub-literary manifestations, before he passed from the literal fact into the metaphorical extension, midway in his journey from the cave into the ghetto. Williams's appeal is direct, instinctive; the nineteenth century had nothing like it to offer. Svengali, compared with Simon Magus, is a silly man who plays the flageolet; even Fagin momentarily slides back into a relatively consoling perspective, from which it is possible to view him as the poor old Jew, the fence, a man who has his feet solidly on the ground, teaching little boys the useful craft of stealing watches and handkerchiefs. In the nineteenth-century portrayal of the Jew, sacerdotalism is likely to look for its priests among the multimillionaires; the high-priest is Melmotte, turning his banquets into affairs of liturgical magnificence in the absence of other powers and dominations.

History: Coleridge and Mrs. Disraeli

All the same, the nineteenth century, too, had its genuine Jewish Priests and Prophets—or had had them, rather, in the pluperfect, for they had passed from the scene of action so long ago that one could only toast them *in absentia,* sigh for their restoration, and—pending their return—put them to rhetorical uses, teaching aids by which to measure the distance between the Jewish ideality and the Jewish reality. Throughout the century we encounter this insistence on the ambivalent character of the Jew—the ambivalence Coleridge rhetorically formulated when he opposed the thunder of the Prophet Isaiah to the nasal twang of old Levi of Hollywell Street. Some years after Coleridge's pronouncement, the Baroness Lionel de Rothschild gave birth to a son and received a visit from Mary Anne Disraeli who, in her scatterbrained way, is supposed to have said to her: "My dear, that beautiful baby may be the future Messiah, whom we are led to expect. Who knows? And you will be the most favored of women!" A wife to Disraeli, with his singular ideas of the Jews' world mission, may be expected to mix up her mythologies and think of the Messiah as coming in a general Nativity setting, in a manger as it were, on Christmas, more or less immaculately conceived by the Baroness de Rothschild. But at any rate Mrs. Disraeli managed to reconcile the discrepant images of prophet and businessman which drew from Coleridge his pious disapproval. "For the Messiah to be the son of the world's wealthiest Jewish bankers," Cecil Roth annotates the story, "is a curiously nineteenth-century conception."[16] (Mrs. Disraeli, of course, may have remembered that the Merchant-Prophet already enjoyed literary currency in the superb Sidonia, an invention of her husband's, who combines the features of Disraeli's optimistic image of himself with traits taken from his friend Lionel, the parent of the future Messiah, God the Father of God the Son.)

But in this, as in most other matters, Disraeli remained the maverick; other writers subscribed to Coleridge's antithesis, opposing the prophet to the merchant, the visionary to the materialist, the ugly present to the glorious past; and more often than not Disraeli himself furnished them with a point of reference. "After reading his last work, *Tancred*"—a contributor to *Punch* maliciously formulated the contrast—"we took quite a fresh view of all the itinerant sons of Israel, whom we met in the streets of the great Metropolis. 'Look at that Old Clothes Man,' said we to ourselves. 'Who would think that the unmixed blood of the Caucasus runs through the veins of that individual who has just offered his nine-pence for our penultimate hat?' " The same juxtaposition (and rather the same malice) is at the bottom of countless parodies. There is Thomas Ingoldsby's vicious critique of *Alroy* under the title of *The Wondrous Tale of Ikey Solo-*

mons; the brief and witless take-off on *Tancred* which Trollope wrote into *Barchester Towers,* in which Bertie Stanhope, on a mission to convert the Jews, runs into "one of the family of Sidonia," "a dirty little man," who converts Stanhope to Judaism instead, robs him of his money, and installs himself indefinitely in the Stanhope villa; and there is Thackeray's famous parody of the same personage:

> The occupants of the London Ghetto sat at their porches basking in the summer sunshine. . . . Ringlets glossy, and curly, and jetty—midsummer night, when it lightens . . . every man or maiden, every babe or matron in that English Jewry bore in his countenance one or more of the characteristics of his peerless Arab race.
>
> "How beautiful they are!" mused Codlingsby, as he surveyed these placid groups calmly taking their pleasure in the sunset.
>
> "D'you vant to look at a nishe coat?" a voice said, which made him start.[17]

Naturally the lines between Alroy and Ikey, Coningsby and Codlingsby, are not quite so clear cut in the novel as Coleridge drew them in epigram or Thackeray in parody, so that we are apt to find among the Hollywell-Street Levis a few (Isaac Levi comes to mind, but Scott's Isaac, too) whose mercenary features shade off into a quality which, remotely and intermittently, betray the angry prophet in the cheap jack, in whose eyes the fire has not quite gone out, and whose wrath is as the wrath of Isaiah when it does not trail off into the empty fulminations of the ragman. All the same, Scott, Dickens, Eliot, Reade, Bulwer, get round sooner or later to the reflection that if the Jews are a race of hucksters now, at least they can console themselves with the knowledge of having once been a race of warrior-prophets. The *ubi sunt* motif haunts nineteenth-century literature about the Jew—*ubi sumus,* rather, since the point is always made by the Jews themselves, by Riah and Mirah and Mordecai. The dominant note is one of defeatism as much as defiance, of apology as well as accusation, as if they chiefly blamed themselves for having fallen so on evil days since the generations of Joshua and of David and of the Hasmoneans; and indeed the Dispersion is often experienced by the Jews as a just punishment for their ante-exilic crimes. Rebecca may be very resonant in telling the Templar "thou art the man," but behind the reproach one detects the sense of an historic self-destruction, a comprehensive national eclipse, in course of which Maccabaeus went underground and re-emerged two thousand years later, looking either like Lapidoth, the small-time thief, like Riah, the walking archaism, or like Mordecai, the consumptive. The *ubi-sumus* motif is always sounded by the sentimentally good Jews, never by the bad, for the wicked have no genealogy, and besides they never apologize; they merely say "I am not well"—not from a sense of their racial decline but from a sense of the opportunism of being unwell.

"In the meantime," writes Edmund Wilson, "for the Jew—or for many Jews—it must become almost as embarrassing to be taken for a Hebrew prophet on confidential terms with God as for a diabolical demiurge who is out to 'murder Progress' [in John Jay Chapman's phrase]." Wilson, to back this up, tells an amusing story about Dr. Paul Tillich: Dr. Tillich, the story goes, used to dislike the idea of Zionism on the grounds that the Jews as a group demonstrated the possibility of survival in the modern world by a common religious faith independent of patriotic ties. But it was then "pointed out to him by a Jewish friend that he was being quite unfair to the 'petty bourgeois Cohens and Levis,' who could hardly be expected to be Moseses and Isaiahs," and who, without a national homeland to fall back on, had no choice but to acquiesce in the role of aliens in countries to which they were not really assimilable. "Dr. Tillich was so struck by the justice of this that he at once joined a Zionist organization."[18] Disraeli would no doubt have ridden roughshod over this argument with one of his Arabian steeds and claimed that the burden of assimilating rested, not with the Jews, but with everybody else (I take this to be the point of Trollope's parody, in so far as it has a point); and George Eliot might have accepted it with some tentative reservations, either claiming the advent of an occasional Moses or Isaiah from "among the finer elements" of the bourgeois Cohens, "some men of instruction and ardent public spirit, some new Ezras, some modern Maccabees, who will know . . . how to triumph by heroic example over the indifference of their fellows"; or arguing that the bourgeois Cohens (as long as they did not become too depressingly bourgeois) could display their integrity just as well in the Diaspora as in Zion, and that Dr. Tillich should not have allowed himself to be outmaneuvered but stuck to his original proposition. For the majority of the novelists, however, the Jew remains a king of shreds and patches, a symbol of lost grandeur, who gave up his heroic status at about the time Judas rose to point the way toward a different iconography.

For the novelists who disliked either the Jewish reality around them or the dualism implied in the foregoing remarks, two solutions were possible. One has been mentioned: to idealize the contemporary Jew by exaggerating his Sephardic qualities. Someone like Walter Besant's hero in a way begins to reconcile (though inadequately) the extreme alternatives by evoking the memory of Kings and of Prophets in his own character and conduct, and thus establishing a direct link with the heroic past instead of merely making it an object of polemic (though he does that too). The second solution is to ignore the Jew's present vices and humiliations altogether, to turn one's back on the current Rialto-facts, and to deal with the Jew entirely in the context of an exotic and idealized past by writing historical romances about him. The logical answer to Ikey Alroy is David Alroy, Ikey's sponsor. This solution was offered by a number of famous novelists, whom I have neglected throughout this essay as being ancillary to Scott and the purveyors of the paragon, and whom I salute belatedly: the young Disraeli, Croly, Kingsley, Bulwer, and a dozen largely forgotten novelists in the 'nineties: Rider Haggard, Marie Corelli, Hall Caine, Charlotte Yonge.

Kingsley's *Hypatia,* much the most thoughtful of these novels, has been mentioned: it is set in fifth-century Alexandria and has for its hero a young Jewish intellectual who both observes and later on engages in the conflict between the expiring paganism of the Greeks and the growing spirit of Christianity. Dissatisfied with the doctrines prevailing among Hebraists and Hellenists alike, he converts to Christianity at the end of the novel.[19] Bulwer's *Leila, or the Siege of Granada* hinges on a similar question of conscience, presents a corresponding conflict, and urges a similar conclusion: the story, put in a nutshell, is about a Spanish Jewess who loved a Moor and became a Christian.[20] Leila the Jewess (*floruit* 1491) is not much more than a rather anemic and flattened-out combination of Rebecca (in her looks) and Abigail (in her plot-function), who moves a little dazedly between two worlds, both of them overfurnished with ottomans, lords, and liveries—between the "Egyptian gorgeousness" of her father's establishment and the "light pavilions of the graceful Moors." Before she has a chance to install herself in the mansions of Christ by way of logical compromise, her father Almamen, a hot-tempered Jew as well as a practicing sorcerer, settles the issue by stabbing her under the cool gaze of Torquemada, just as Leila is on the point of taking the veil. ("Thus—thus—thus—Almamen the Jew delivers the last of his house from the curse of the Galilee!") Bulwer pushes the issue beyond Scott back to Marlowe not only in allowing the girl to convert but in presenting her as a Christian affectively even before she turns into one factually: "Leila was a Christian, while she still believed herself a Jewess"; but that is old hat. The story is silly enough and not even Bulwer specialists like to talk about it; the conversation, measured even by Bulwer's dreary standards, is hopeless ("My soul wants a bath of music; these journeys into a pathless realm have wearied it, and the streams of sound supple and relax the travailed pilgrims"); and, boring as it is, the plot is wrapped up with unseemly haste; thus: "Book V, Chapter IV. The Return. The Riot. The Treachery. And the Death." But the novel derives a certain strategic usefulness from the figure of Almamen who stands before us, an amalgam of so many bromidic Jewish stock-traits, that he commands at least the secondary importance that attaches to a composite and exemplary cliché.

Leila appeared in the same year as *Oliver Twist* and Mrs. Trollope's light-weight triple-decker, and by then Bulwer already had enough models to be as eclectic as he liked. Almamen thus serves the purposes of autopsy. To anatomize him is to lay bare, for the last time, the separate mechanisms, the rusty and inelastic springs, that compelled the Jew in English literature to act the way he acted over a period of five centuries. What roles could he play? Seven or eight, hardly more, and he played those without finesse. But at least he knew the script by rote and could reel off his lines in his sleep. Almamen has his choice of sounding

(1) like Sheva:

". . . while my lord the king rejects the fanaticism of belief, doth he reject the fanaticism of persecution? You disbelieve the stories of the

Hebrews; yet you suffer the Hebrews themselves, that ancient and kindred . . . race, to be ground to the dust . . ."

(2) or like Isaac, with Sir Walter in the prompter's box:

"Your laws leave [the Jews] no ambition but that of avarice, and as the plant will crook and distort its trunk, to raise its head through every obstacle to the sun, so the mind of man twists and perverts itself, if legitimate openings are denied it, to find its natural element in the gale of power or the sunshine of esteem."

(3) He may look like Shylock in his Satanic role:

The dark face . . . became terrible in its wrath and passion: his brow and lip worked convulsively . . . Amidst the infidels . . . at a little distance he gazed for a few moments upon the fierce and relentless slaughter of Moor and Christian with a smile of stern and complacent delight . . .

(4) or in his parasitic role:

the art with which the Jews concealed their wealth, scattering it over various cities, had secured to Almamen the treasures the tyrant of Granada had failed to grasp . . .

(5) though the metaphor may also relate him to Fagin:

Serpent as he was, he cared not through what mire of treachery and fraud he trailed his baleful folds, so that at last he could spring upon his prey. . . . He had the crawl of the reptile,—he had also its poison and its fangs.

(6) He has his choice of playing the Wandering Jew in his harmless dromomaniac phase:

. . . the youth of that remarkable man had been spent, not in traffic and merchandise, but travel and study. . . . He had visited the greater part of the world then known; and resided for many years in the court of the sultan of that hoary Egypt which still retained its fame for abstruse science and magic lore . . .

(7) unless he prefers to feature himself as Black Magician:

A wonderful change had come over [Almamen]; he seemed to stand amongst [the Christians] literally wrapped in fire; flames burst from his lip, and played with his long locks, as, catching the glowing hue, they curled over his shoulders, like serpents of burning light. . . . He seemed indeed to verify all the superstitions of the time,—no longer the trembling, but the mighty demon or the terrible magician. . . . There was a dead silence, broken by a cry and groan; and when, after some minutes, the darkness gradually dispersed, Almamen was gone. One of the guards lay bathed in blood upon the ground . . .

(8) By concealing his wizard's costume, he may even revert to the role of the medieval Judas:

Ferdinand beheld opposite to him a strange form, that seemed . . . rather fiend than man; his raven hair and beard, clotted with blood, hung like snakes about a countenance whose features, naturally formed to give expression to the darkest passions, were distorted with the madness of despairing rage.

(9) If he plays the evil prophet among Moors and Christians, he sets himself up as the prophet militant among the "tribe of Moisa":

"What matters who the instrument that would have restored thee thy throne? Yes! I who have ruled thy councils, who have led thine armies, I am of the race of Joshua and of Samuel, and the Lord of Hosts is the God of Almamen!"

(10) And though he may bicker like Shylock, he barters like George Eliot:

"I demand for the people of Israel free leave to trade and abide within the city, and follow their callings subjected only to the same laws and the same imposts as the Christian population."

Almamen, in the course of the book, avails himself of all these roles. The result is neither depth nor complexity, but the exhaustion of banality, the complete coverage of the surface.

Shylock and Out

For this, surely, is the conclusion which urges itself upon us at the end of this study: that the image of the Jew in English literature has been a depressingly uniform and static phenomenon, and that the changes and variations which were struck upon it in the course of the centuries fade into relative insignificance in the face of its monumental durability. The obtrusive presence in literature of such a thing as a Jewish stereotype reduces such a conclusion to something of a tautology, for it is in the nature of stereotype to be an oversimplified and persistent image; it conforms to a fixed pattern, the reflection, in art or what passes for art, of a popular idée fixe. "A type," to return to the sentence by Praz that stands at the head of this study, "is like a neuralgic area. Some chronic ailment has created a zone of weakened resistance, and whenever an analogous phenomenon makes itself felt it immediately confines itself to this predisposed area, until the process becomes a matter of mechanical monotony." At the heart of the problem is the comic Shylock, not simply an Elizabethan stage-figure called "Shylock," but a figure who is, as it were congenitally, "*a* Shylock," the member of a species: a type. There are other comic types who are identified with a single literary referent—Pecksniffs, Tartuffes, Babbitts, Quixotes, Don Juans—but offhand I should say that the Jews are one of the few peoples on earth, in the recent history of culture, to have one all to themselves.

Of the two conventions I have tried to describe, the convention of the Jew-villain has no doubt been the more successful and the more persistent, and we have not seen the last of it yet. The benevolent Jew was perhaps too much the creature of a single historical impulse to survive the exhaustion of that impulse: a product of humanitarian and sentimental doctrines, he has little to say to an age which is not notably humanitarian and prides itself on being unsentimental. As to the deeper question, why the novelists failed on the whole to produce a decent Jew who had other claims on our attention than his decency, the answer has been suggested: he had only Shylock to fall back on. Sheva, like Shylock, ends by making one uncomfortable, not because he is so embarrassingly kind, but because he is so embarrassingly careful to be kind. His presence points at an element in our moral blood stream which is in its way as disturbing as the presence of his opposite number, though it will not lead to massacre. Both stereotypes are finally "inauthentic," but Sheva is inauthentic in the special modern sense of Sartre's "inauthentic Jews," who "have allowed themselves to be poisoned by the stereotype that others have of them and live in fear that their acts will correspond to this stereotype," whose conduct, like Sheva's, is "perpetually overdetermined from the inside," and whose generosity is vitiated "by the decision to be generous."[21] An earlier, more notorious philo-Semite assigned all absolutes to the domain of pathology, and the Sheva-type is no less suspect for posing as the absolute denial of an absolute. The generosity is too patent, and so is the self-consciousness, and behind the self-consciousness, the anger. Sheva, too, is one of our "terrible simplifiers." Indeed, his proper métier is not literature but journalism. He does not figure in sensational trials such as sent Shylock to the baptismal font and Fagin to the scaffold, but he may well be found in the gallery—among the sea of faces at which Fagin "wistfully" glanced from the dock—stoking up fuel for an editorial in the liberal press.

For there is, it seems to me, another way of looking at the caricature of the good Jew in English literature, the Fagin-view of Sheva, and it suggests some family likeness between them. Sheva's whole history in the literature of the West (it is his whole point) has been a history of martyrdom, an interminable atonement for the guilt of Judas, and there clings to him a vague and remote suggestion of horror of which not even his most enlightened interpreters—a Lessing or a George Eliot—quite succeed in depriving him. In this connection, another phrase of Nietzsche's comes to mind: that dreadful experiences suggest something dreadful in him who experiences them. There is a point at which figures like Riah and Mordecai and Isaac cease to be papier-mâché agents of pathos and turn under one's eyes into terrible grotesques, as though they were engaged in living down some primitive shock. They remind one of those types of lunacy with which Dickens peopled his world, harmless and engaging creatures, who received some fright in the past, in their anterior existence, before the curtain went up on the farce, which permanently stunted their growth and froze them in the role of eccentrics—benevolent and funny people, but mad. Their motions are a source of laughter, but their history—their case-history, abstracted from the absurd consequences—is instinct with anguish. Sometimes Dickens, with an astonishing sense of timing, rends the veil between past and present, and at those moments he reaches the heights of his genius: in the scene, for example, in which Copperfield's aunt, Betsey Trotwood, is startled out of her permanent amazement to confront, with sad and sudden insight, the whole meaning and ruin of her life. " 'Six-and-thirty years ago, this day, my dear,' said my aunt, as we walked back to the chariot, 'I was married. God forgive us all!' " And there comes a moment when even the most insipid Jew in fiction (and often precisely the most insipid) retraces this process—when he reveals himself, the more one looks at him, as some such monumental oddity, and one is made to feel that it cannot be for nothing he has turned out the way he has. At some point in the history of the race, he must have incurred some appalling affront, which paralyzed his reflexes and immobilized him in a single gesture, a monotonous refrain. Beneath the bleak pages of his Vindication of the Rights of Man there lies, like a palimpsest, the illustrated diary of his martyrdom. This kept him relatively infantile. He acted out his eccentricities with a certain strident aplomb. Like a child, he gave you the appearance of taking himself very seriously; but he was not serious. He must have looked with amazement at the "holy mirth" that inspired young Ben Disraeli to take the part of Gratiano, the Jew-baiter, in a schoolboy performance of *The Merchant of Venice.* It is recorded, however, that he played the part badly, and the chances are anyhow that the Shylock he scorned was already being played for all the sympathy one could put into him.[22]

Meanwhile old Shylock our Heavy Father lives, though nervously. In the verse of T. S. Eliot he continues to figure in the traditional images of the toad, squatting on the window-sill; of the vulture, murderously tearing at the grapes; of the rat beneath the piles; or in the image of the simian Bleistein: "a saggy bending of the knees / And elbows, with the palms turned out, / Chicago Semite Viennese." In the fiction of Evelyn Waugh we meet him as Augustus Fagan, Esquire, Ph.D., of *Decline and Fall,* director of a unique boys' academy, who combines the professional gesture of Augustus Melmotte ("his fingers crooked like claws") with the professional substance of his other namesake; in the greasy trader Youkoumian of *Black Mischief* and "Father Rothschild," S.J., the Jesuit impostor in the crazy society of *Vile Bodies.* In the novels of Graham Greene, the Jewish criminal persists in the functions of the mutilator, the alien upstart, and the usurer; he lives on in the gangster Colleoni of *Brighton Rock,* the small Jew with the neat round belly, who has swapped the old knife for a razor blade; in the vulgar parvenu Myatt of *Stamboul Train,* the little Jew in the big fur coat with "the too familiar features, the small eyes, the large nose, the black oiled hair"; or in the sinister magnate Sir Marcus of *This Gun for Hire,* whose "lip was like a badge of class—his great white open face was like a curtain on which you can throw grotesque images: a rabbit, a man with horns." To the Mrs. Davises, the position of a writer like Greene, who publicly defends the Jews in his radio broadcasts while peopling his novels with odious Jewish caricatures, may be dishonest or disgraceful—

doubly disgraceful in a writer who no longer has the excuse of writing down to the Victorians. But whether the nauseating figures and allusions which Greene or Waugh or Eliot have taken over from the old conventions are the hallmarks of the anti-Semite must remain for the moment a moot point; they prove chiefly a point about the old conventions.[23]

There are also in our own day the conscious anti-Semites, writers on the order of Lawrence, Wyndham Lewis, and Ezra Pound, whose versified insults of the Jews are confirmed by his extra-literary statements in prose. When, in *The Pisan Cantos,* Pound notes that "the goyim go to saleable slaughter" for "David rex the prime s.o.b.," it is evidently no longer possible to explain away Pound's lines exclusively on the grounds of literary convention, in view of his statements elsewhere that the Jews started the Second World War. The man who described Geneva as "the usurers' dunghill / Frogs, brits with a few dutch pimps"; who claims that "Pétain defended Verdun while Blum was defending a bidet," and jokingly refers to mass murder as "fresh meat on the Russian steppes" is clearly the same man who on the Rome radio approved the massacre of the Eastern European Jews and warned American Jews that it was their turn next. For writers like Eliot and Greene—this is the distinction to be made—the Jew operates as a metaphor, and it is with fictional metaphors that this study has concerned itself, with the "prosaic statement of a poetic truth" or a "poetic lie," not with statements of abuse. "Moving from the cliché to the theatrical personification," Harold Rosenberg notes, "art does no harm. What does the harm is the movement in the opposite direction, from the personification to the cliché. This second movement is made by the propagandist and the sociological critic. With these, the personifications made by artists for pleasure become descriptions of 'reality.' "[24]

Still, one cannot ignore the personification either, and in the long run the Fagin-issue ceases to be a literary sport and raises some serious problems in the modern world. The trouble is that the cliché is embarrassingly apt to create the "zone of weakened resistance" in which the play-figure secures and consolidates its hold on the public imagination. (To say, with Harold Rosenberg, that "Shylock is not my brother, but brother to those other Shakespearean pigstickers, Iago,

Claudius, Macbeth" on the grounds that "one is labeled a Jew, the others Italian, Dane, Scot," is not really meeting the issue head-on either, in so far as Iago, Claudius, and Macbeth have a good many more strings to their bows than their Italian, Danish, and Scottish strings, whereas Shylock is entirely the slave of his Jewishness.) Effects have a way of being anyhow confused with causes; and a literary stereotype, which is up to a point almost prescriptively a distortion, no matter how stupendous, of the observed reality, ends by persuading the superstitious mass of men to mistake the genuine article for the fabulous imitation. Such a state of affairs is an appalling convenience to propaganda machines the world over. From this point of view, the stereotype of the Jew is doubly vulnerable since it has been, from the first, a physically repulsive type, accessible to the crudest kind of caricature. In *My Life as German and Jew,* the novelist Wassermann, observing that as a child he escaped the customary brow-beating of Jews because of his un-Jewish features, writes:

> This argument sounds primitive; but people who have not had this experience cannot imagine how primitive non-Jews are in their estimation of what is Jewish or in their idea of Jewish characteristics. Their instinct is silent when it is not confronted by a caricature. I have always found that the race prejudice into which they talk themselves, or of which they let themselves be convinced, is fed by the most external things.[25]

For the gratification of the less primitive, the physical caricatures can be dressed up with sophistic race-theories; the cartoon can be filled in with pretentious pseudo-scientific jargon; and the mischief is done.

In the meantime, too, the myth of Shylock has, as it has once before, given rise to the countermyth: the myth of the Jew as artist, as aesthete, as hypersensitive and anxious man; and in this mask he has engaged the attention of the great novelists of our century. For the creators of Swann (but also Bloch), of Leopold Bloom, Joseph K, as well as the recreator of the Biblical Joseph, the Jew has come to reflect increasingly the problems and pressures of Western man. If he is still (or more than ever) the Outsider, he knows that he has been cast in a role that symbolically identifies him with a world of Ishmaels—viewed no longer from the historical perspective of a Scott, but solidly within the framework of his own generation. In the Age of Anxiety, as Leslie Fiedler has reminded us, the Jew as symbol in literature has moved from the periphery to the center—but by remaining, as ever, on the periphery of the active social and moral world. His weapon is no longer the aggressive cunning of a Machiavel but the melancholy cunning of the ironic man: the irony of Swann, who squints at the world by negotiating his view of it in quotation marks, as much as to say: I don't really mean it that way; of Joseph, the beautiful boy in the pit, supercessor of Hugh of Lincoln in his sewer, who needs to console himself with the quixotic reminder that he is only living in a story-world after all; of Joseph K, the *eiron* who submits to the knife which has been torn from his hands and who dies—*ganz wie ein Hund*. "Under our very eyes," Diana Trilling writes, "we see the Wandering Jew become wandering man, the alien Jew generalizing into the alienated human being. We would do well to transfer some of our anxiety about the anti-Jewish myth to all the anti-human myths which contemporary culture is so self-destructively bent upon creating.[26]

How, finally, is one to get around the stereotype—any stereotype? It is idle to pretend that, for the purposes of literature, Jews share all qualities with all men, and that therefore whatever is peculiar, eccentric, individual about them ought to be suppressed. Unless the Jew in fiction is in some sense recognizably Jewish (he need not either have a long nose or parade his cosmic fatigue), the writer ought not to have bothered to make him one. (I may as well confess that the Jewishness of Joyce's Bloom has always struck me as erring on this side of the picture. The intention is there; the symbolization points to the Jewish qualities; Bloom's reveries are there to confirm it all, but, substantial human being though he is, the Jewishness remains oddly extraneous, unassimilated, to be taken on faith and Joyce's say-so.) How is one to supersede intelligently the Meyer Wolfsheims and the Myatts, the Bleisteins and Youkoumians, short of waiting for them to die of attrition and short of coming up with merely another stereotype?

It is easier, after all, to answer with an example than a prescription. Such an example, it seems to me, and a very recent one, is provided by C. P. Snow's novel *The Conscience of the Rich*.[27] It deals with its Jewish characters in such a way that they are both unmistakable

Jews as well as ordinary sensual men, whose perplexities and well-being are at once rooted in their Jewish make-up and in the wider social context of their times. Sir Charles is too scrupulous a novelist simply to call his characters Jews and then deprive them of their Jewish qualities merely in order to repudiate an antique image, to take the sting out of Shylock. His Jews happen to be exceedingly rich; they gesticulate enormously; they frown on intermarriage; some of them are odiously confused in their politics; naturally they are very conscious of being Jews. But they are a good deal else; they suffer the domestic shocks and public calamities of other men; they go about their businesses; they know as well as most people that everything is necessary under the sun, and everything is dangerous. Since Sir Charles also treats them in the spirit of comedy and critique which have been the intellectual props of the novelist in all ages, one feels that justice has been done.

Appendixes and Notes

Appendixes

Appendix I is a bibliographical list, arranged chronologically, of English fiction on Jewish themes. The remaining appendixes consist of literary and historical documents bearing on the Jew in England from the days of Richard Lionheart to those of Victoria Regina. I have chosen to begin them with James Drummond's account of a ritual murder à la Chaucer, which falls midway between *The Merchant of Venice* and Cumberland's *The Jew.*

All my additions and explanations are in brackets except in Appendixes V and VI, which amount to essays rather than documents. The sources of the material cited are indicated in a general fashion by the appendix titles and subheadings; precise citations may be found in the Notes, p. 378.

I

ENGLISH FICTION ON JEWISH THEMES: 1594–1900

The following chronology lists the novels of non-Jewish writers only, an exception being made in the case of Disraeli; it excludes Jewish novelists on the order of Grace Aguilar, Farjeon, and Zangwill. More inclusive bibliographies of nineteenth-century novels of Jewish interest appear in the studies by Modder, pp. 412–26, and Calisch, pp. 199–265, and in Rebecca Schneider, *Bibliography of Jewish Life in the Fiction of America and England* (Albany, 1916), though all these sources omit a good many important titles which I have reinstated below. Where the appearance of the Jewish personnel is incidental to the novel, I cite the relevant chapter; where the Jewish matter is incidental but too diffused to be cited by chapter, the title is followed by the notation *passim.* My principle of selection has been to pay more attention to the importance of the writer than to the extensiveness in the treatment of the Jewish material, which may range from a few paragraphs (in *David Copperfield*) or half a dozen pages (*Gaston de Blondeville*) to the entire novel. The writers I have chosen are those who appear in the standard histories of the English novel, but for the sake of completeness I have drawn the line beneath, not above, famous third-raters like Corelli and Hall Caine. To round out the dossier, I include a number of interesting novellas, short stories, and eighteenth-century "characters," Thackeray's parodies, and Borrow's imaginative autobiography. Novels which deal with the legend of the Wandering Jew or in which that legend is used allusively are followed by the letters WJ.

1594. Thomas Nashe, *The Unfortunate Traveler, or The Life of Jack Wilton*
1724. Daniel Defoe, *The Unfortunate Mistress or . . . Roxana*
1748. Tobias Smollett, *The Adventures of Roderick Random,* chap. xi
1751. ———, *The Adventures of Peregrine Pickle,* chaps. liii–lvi, lxxix
1752. Samuel Johnson, "Rabbi Abraham Ben Hannasse," *The Rambler* (Feb. 11, 1752)
1753. Samuel Richardson, *Sir Charles Grandison,* I, letter xxxvi; II, x; IV, xli
Tobias Smollett, *The Adventures of Ferdinand Count Fathom*
1762. ———, *The Adventures of Sir Launcelot Greaves,* chap. ix.
1769. Laurence Sterne, *The Life and Opinions of Tristram Shandy,* IX, chaps. iv–vii
1770. Tobias Smollett, *The Expedition of Humphrey Clinker, passim*
1782. Fanny Burney, *Cecilia, or Memoirs of an Heiress,* III, i; IV, i; V, vii
1785. Richard Cumberland, "Abraham Abrahams," *Observer,* Nos. 38, 41–46
1790. ———, "Nicolas Pedrosa," *Observer,* Nos. 88–90
1794. Robert Bage, *Hermsprong, or Man as He Is Not,* chap. xxvi
1796. Matthew Gregory Lewis, *The Monk,* chap. iv (WJ)
George Walker, *Theodore Cyphon, or The Benevolent Jew*
1800. William Godwin, *St. Leon, A Tale of the Sixteenth Century* (WJ)
Maria Edgeworth, *Castle Rackrent*
1801. ———, *Moral Tales* ("The Good Aunt," "The Prussian Vase")
1803. Ann Radcliffe, *Gaston de Blondeville* (pub. 1826), II, 288–95
1804. Maria Edgeworth, *Popular Tales* ("Murad the Unlucky")
1811. Percy Bysshe Shelley, *St. Irvyne, or The Rosicrucians* (WJ)
1812. Maria Edgeworth, *The Absentee*
1817. ———, *Harrington*
1819. John Galt, *The Wandering Jew, or The Travels and Observations of Harreach the Prolonged* (WJ)
Sir Walter Scott, *Ivanhoe: A Romance*
1820. Charles Robert Maturin, *Melmoth the Wanderer* (WJ)
1824. John Galt, *Rothelan: A Romance of the English Histories*

1828. George Croly, *Salathiel the Immortal, or Tarry Till I Come* (WJ)
Sir Walter Scott, *The Surgeon's Daughter*
1833. Benjamin Disraeli, *David Alroy, A Tale of the Captivity*
1834. Capt. Frederick Marryat, *Peter Simple,* chap. xi
1836. ———, *Japhet in Search of a Father,* chaps. xxix–xxxii
Charles Dickens, *Sketches by Boz,* "Scenes," chaps. i, vi, xiii
1837. Capt. Frederick Marryat, *Snarleyyow, or The Dog-Fiend,* chap. xiii
Charles Dickens, *Posthumous Papers of the Pickwick Club,* chap. xv
1838. ———, *Oliver Twist, or The Parish Boy's Progress*
Edward Bulwer-Lytton, *Leila, or The Siege of Granada*
Thomas De Quincey, "The Avenger," *Blackwoods,* xliv (1838), 208–33 (Masson, *Tales and Romances,* xii, 234–85)
Frances Trollope, *A Romance of Vienna*
1840. William Harrison Ainsworth, *Jack Shephard*
1842. Edward Bulwer-Lytton, *Zanoni* (WJ)
1844. Benjamin Disraeli, *Coningsby, or The New Generation*
1847. W. M. Thackeray, "Codlingsby," *Notes by Eminent Hands,* chap. ii
Benjamin Disraeli, *Tancred, or The New Crusade*
1850. Charles Dickens, *David Copperfield,* chap. xiii
Charles Kingsley, *Alton Locke, Tailor and Poet, passim*
W. M. Thackeray, *Rebecca and Rowena: A Romance Upon a Romance*
1851. George Borrow, *Lavengro: The Scholar, The Gypsy, The Priest,* chaps. i, xxvi
1853. Edward Bulwer-Lytton, *My Novel, or Vanities of English Life*
Charles Kingsley, *Hypatia, or New Foes with an Old Face*
1855. W. M. Thackeray, *The Newcomes: Memoirs of a Most Respectable Family*
1856. Charles Reade, *It Is Never Too Late to Mend: A Matter-of-Fact Romance* (WJ)
1857. Anthony Trollope, *Barchester Towers,* chaps. ix, xix
1861. Charles Dickens, *Great Expectations,* chap. xx
1865. ———, *Our Mutual Friend*
1867. Anthony Trollope, *Nina Balatka: The Story of a Maiden of Prague*
1869. ———, *Phineas Finn: The Irish Member, passim*
Charles Lever, *That Boy of Norcott's*
1870. Benjamin Disraeli, *Lothair,* chap. xxix
1872. Anthony Trollope, *The Eustace Diamonds*

1873. ———, *Phineas Redux*
1875. ———, *The Way We Live Now*
1876. ———, *The Prime Minister, passim*
George Eliot, *Daniel Deronda*
1880. Benjamin Disraeli, *Endymion*
George Meredith, *The Tragic Comedians: A Study in a Well-Known Story*
1886. Sabine Baring-Gould, *Count Royal: A Story of Cross-Currents*
1888. Dorothea Gerard, *Orthodox*
1891. Hall Caine, *The Scapegoat*
Rider Haggard and Andrew Lang, *The World's Desire*
Rudyard Kipling, *Life's Handicap* ("The Wandering Jew," "Jews in Shushan")
1892. George Du Maurier, *Peter Ibbetson*
1893. Walter Besant, *The Rebel Queen* (WJ)
Marie Corelli, *Barabbas: A Dream of the World's Tragedy*
1894. George Du Maurier, *Trilby* (WJ)
1895. Sabine Baring-Gould, *Noémie: A Story of Rock-Dwellers*
1896. Mrs. Humphrey Ward, *Sir George Tressady,* chaps. ix, xiv
Mark Rutherford (William Hale White), *Clara Hopgood*
1897. George Du Maurier, *The Martian*
Olive Schreiner, *Trooper Peter Halkett*
Charlotte M. Yonge, *Pilgrimage of the Ben Beriah*
Mrs. Craigie (John Oliver Hobbes), *The School for Saints*
1898. Charlotte M. Yonge, *The Patriots of Palestine: A Story of the Maccabees*
1899. Mrs. Craigie, *Robert Orange*
1900. Anthony Hope, *Quisanté*

II

DEAD CENTER, 1694: A LITEL CLERGEON, SEVEN YEER OF AGE

[James Drummond, fourth Earl of Perth, Justice-General of Scotland, Chancellor of Scotland, and Sheriff principal of the county of Edinburgh; converted to the Roman Catholic faith on the accession of James II to the throne of England; imprisoned in 1688 by the followers of William & Mary; set free five years later on penalty of leaving the kingdom; afterwards recalled by James to the King's court-in-exile at St. Germain, and there created Duke of Perth and Knight of the Garter, First Lord of the

Bedchamber, Chamberlain to the Queen, and Governor to the Prince of Wales, wrote this letter to his sister, Lady Anna Drummond, Countess of Errol, from his travels in the Netherlands.]

Antwerp, 5th May, 1694

Dear Sister,

Although I wrote to you the 25th of last moneth, I cannot leave this place without taking leave of you, although my adieu will be long of reaching you. If I could express my affection for you and all your dear family you would be convinced that never brother loved a sister with more tenderness. But words are but wind. If ever I be able I will convince you of my faithful service by more substantiall proofs. Give my most humble service to dear Lord Hay, Lady Mary, Mr. James, and all your hopefull sweet babies. I cannot but still hope that God will give you and them the light of the true faith; all lyes in your will, which I pray our Lord to bend to a sweet complyance with his divine call, and then you will be as happy as I wish you, which is not a litle felicity.

For news we have none, but we have just now received an account of a very strange thing happened at Prague, the chief town of Bohemia, within these 6 weeks. The Prince of Nassau, who is Governor of Mastreicht, his son writes it to his father, as many merchants and religious men have done to their correspondents; it is thus: —

There was a Jew who had a very pretty sweet-natured witty child to his son, of about 8 years old; he used to be playing with Christian boys, who it seems were zealous enough to be endeavouring to gett him made Christian, and at last gott the boy to go to the Catechism with them at the Jesuits. He continued to go thus 3 whole years, untill he came to be well instructed, and then he beged to be baptized, and ever after he carryed his chaplet in his hand to prayers, kissing his cross and triumphing in his being a Catholick. His father strove to gett him perverted [reconverted], and begun to be harsh with him; the father who was his confessor, fearing they would be too cruel to the child, gott the Archbishop to remove him from his father; but the father dissembled his rage against his son so well that they let the boy return to him. So soon as they gott him, he put him to bread and water and twice a week he scourged him to that degree of cruelty that he bathed him in his own blood. But the poor child never uttered a word, but that he thanked our Lord he was a Catholick. His father, seeing he could not prevaill, took another Jew with him, and entered the cave or cellar where he had allways kept the child prisoner, and told him he was come to make his last essay to recover him to the religion of his fathers; if he would yield he should be made so rich that his life should be as pleasant as he pleased, but if not he would dye. The child said he was most willing to render up a life to Almighty God which he had only to use for his glory in what manner he pleased to call for it. That to shed his blood for his dear Lord, who had shed his precious blood for him, was the death he had ever wished. That he accepted it from his own father's hand as a favour, and that far greater than that of giveing him a temporal life; he was only sorry that the parricide must suffer for so great a crime. The father then and that cruell assistant threw down the child on his back. The father put his knees upon his breast and the other turned about his head to break his neck, while he cryed out, Jesus, Maria, sweet Jesus receive my soul, and accept my thanks for your dearest favours. They buried him in the cave. Six weeks after, when the child was missed, the Christians began to enquire after him. The father said he was dead and buried as the Jews use to bury their dead. I forgott to tell you that they had bruised his head too, that his brain had come out in several places.

The magistrates would needs raise the body, so the Jew must needs shew where it was; which he did. They found the body as fresh as if asleep; it bled, the brains were sweet, neither stink nor corruption, nor the blood so much as congealed in his veins. The father was immediately put in prison. The boy exposed three days in the cathedral. The father told all that had passed, and said that the accursed boy vexed him so with his chaplet, and the hated names of Jesus and Mary, that had he been the whole world in one person he had killed him. The Archbishop, magistrates, and great many people of quality, clad in red garments, went to the church, where the concourse was incredible. They sung a mass of thanksgiving, instead of one for the dead, and carryed the body of the holy child to its buriall under a cloath of red velvet fringed with gold, and glorified God who had supported the litle martyre in his passion. The Prince of Nassau says he was so hapy as to kiss his dear litle hand, which was as soft as if he had been alive, and his face had a sweetness in it which charmed him.

The relation is sent to Rome; what will be done upon it we know not; but I would not scruple to beg the Blessed saint's intercession. His father found a way to strangle himself in prison, and was found in such a posture that it is not doubted but that he who instigated him to committ the villany, helped him to his reward. The story makes much noise here, and I hope it may edifie you. Communicate it to my daughter Mareschall and to Anne, to both whom I give my blessing. Tell the whole house of Mareschall I'm their faithful servant. My Lord Mareschall's death was in the

Bruxelles Gazette yesterday. Tell my daughter I'll write her from Aix by first occasion. My wife gives to you and all yours and to all at Jenny's her faithful service. The weather here is excessive hott and dry, and pestilential fevers are very frequent. Troops arrive daily from England; but I find at Bruxelles they look for no great matters this campaign.

Adieu.

III

MARGINALIA TO IVANHOE: FROM HOLINSHED'S CHRONICLES (1577)

Coronation of Richard Lion-Heart

[An. Dom. 1189. An. Reg. 1]

Upon this daie of king Richards coronation, the Jewes that dwelt in London and in other parts of the realme, being there assembled, had but sorie hap, as it chanced. For they meaning to honour the same coronation with their presence, and to present to the king some honourable gift, whereby they might declare themselves glad for his advancement, and procure his freendship towards them, for the confirming of their privileges & liberties, according to the grants and charters made to them by the former kings: he of a zealous mind to Christes religion, abhorring their nation (and doubting some sorcerie by them to be practised) commanded that they should not come within the church when he should receive the crowne, nor within the palace whilest he was at dinner.

But at dinner time, among other that pressed in at the palace gate, diverse of the Jewes were about to thrust in, till one of them was striken by a christian, who alledging the kings commandement, kept them backe from comming within the palace. Which some of the unrulie people perceiving, and supposing it had beene doone by the kings commandement, tooke lightlie occasion thereof, and falling upon the Jewes with staves, bats and stones, beat them and chased them home to their houses and lodgings. Heerewith rose a rumor through the citie that the king had commanded the Jewes to be destroied, and thereupon came running togither, to assault them in their houses, which when they could not easilie breake up nor enter, by reason the same were strongly builded, they set fire on them, so that divers houses were consumed, not onelie of the Jewes, but also of their neighbours, so hideous was the rage of the fire. Here we see that

Regis ad exemplum totus componitur orbis.

The king being advertised of this riotous attempt of the outragious people, sent some of his councellours, as Ranulfe de Glanville lord justice, and other officers to appease the tumult: but their authoritie was nothing regarded, nor their persuasions any whit reverenced, but their thretnings rather brought themselves in danger of life among the rude sort of those that were about to spoile, rob, and sacke the houses of the Jewes: to the better accomplishment of which their unlawfull act, the light that the fire no small helpe and occasion of furtherance. The Jewes that were in those houses which were set on fire, were either smoldred and burned to death within, or else at their comming foorth most cruellie received upon the points of speares, billes, swords and gleaves of their adversaries that watched for them verie diligentlie.

This outrage of the furious and disordered people continued from the middest of the one day, till two of the clocke on the other; the commons all that while never ceassing their furie against that nation, but still killing them as they met with any of them, in most horrible, rash and unreasonable maner. At length, rather wearied with their cruell dooings, than satisfied with spoile, or mooved with respect of reason or reverence of their prince, they withdrew themselves from their riotous enterprise, after they had executed manie unlawful and horrible enormities. This great riot well deserved sore and greevous punishment, but yet it passed over without correction, in respect of the great number of the transgressors, and for that the most part of men for the hatred generallie conceived against the obstinate frowardnesse of the Jewes, liked the dooings hereof well inough, interpreting it to be a good token, that the joifull daie of the kings advancement to the crowne should be dolefull unto the Jewes, in bringing them to such slaughter and destruction. Finallie, after that the tumult was ceassed, the king commanded that no man should hurt or harme any of the Jewes, and so they were restored to peace, after they had susteined infinit damage.

The occasion of this tragedie and bloudie tumult (redounding to the Jewes great vexation and pitifull distresse, but to the satisfieng of the peoples furious and unbridled pronesse to crueltie) sprang principallie from the king, who if he had not so lightlie esteemed of the Jewes when they repaired unto him with their present, in signe of submission and hope of obteining their sute then purposed to be exhibited; this hurlie burlie had not insued. For it was a violent example & a mightie motive to the people to maligne the Jewes; as also a hart-greefe to them in respect of their rejection, when the prince gave them so discourteous a repulse. Here therefore is to be observed, that the people is the princes ape, as one verie well saith. For looke whereto he is inclined, note wherein he delighteth;

the same is the practise of the people: in consideration whereof the mightie ones of the world have speciall cause to have an eye to their course of life, & to set caveats before their actions, that the people may in them see none but good signes of commendable & vertuous imitation.

King John's Taxation of the Jews

[An. Dom. 1210. An. Reg. 11]

. . . about the same time the king taxed the Jewes, and greevouslie tormented and emprisoned them, bicause divers of them would not willinglie pay the summes that they were taxed at. Amongst other, there was one of them at Bristow, which would not consent to give anie fine for his deliverance: wherefore by the kings commandement he was put unto this penance, that everie daie, till he would agree to give to the king those ten thousand marks that he was seized at, he should have one of his teeth plucked out of his head. By the space of seaven daies togither he stood stedfast, loosing everie of those daies a tooth, but on the eight day, when he shuld come to have the eight tooth and the last (for he had but eight in all) drawne out, he paid the monie to save that one, who with more wisedome and lesse paine might have doone so before, and have saved his seaven teeth, which he lost with such torments, for these homelie toothdrawers used no great cunning in plucking them foorth (as may be coniectured).

Expulsion of the Jews under Edward the First

[An. Dom. 1290. An. Reg. 18]

In the eighteenth yeare of his reigne, the king married two of his daughters, that is to saie, Joane de Acres unto Gilbert de Clare earle of Glocester, and the ladie Margaret unto the lord John sonne to the duke of Brabant. The king ordeined, that all the wooll, which should be sold unto strangers, should be brought unto Sandwich, where the staple thereof was kept long time after. In the same yeare was a parlement holden at Westminster, wherein the statutes of Westminster the third were ordeined. It was also decreed, that all the Jewes should avoid out of the land, in consideration whereof, a fifteenth was granted to the king, and so heerupon were the Jewes banished out of all the kings dominions, and never since could they obteine any privilege to returne hither againe. All their goods not mooveable were confiscated, with their taillies and obligations; but all other their goods that were mooveable, togither with their coine of gold and silver, the king licenced them to have and convey with them. A sort of the richest of them, being shipped with their treasure in a mightie tall ship which they had hired, when the same was under saile, and got downe the Thames towards the mouth of the river beyond Quinborowe, the maister mariner bethought him of a wile, and caused his men to cast anchor, and so rode at the same, till the ship by ebbing of the streame remained on the drie sands. The maister herewith entised the Jewes to walke out with him on land for recreation. And at length, when he understood the tide to be comming in, he got him backe to the ship, whither he was drawne up by a cord. The Jewes made not so much hast as he did, bicause they were not ware of the danger. But when they perceived how the matter stood, they cried to him for helpe: howbeit he told them, that they ought to crie rather unto Moses, by whose conduct their fathers passed through the red sea, and therefore, if they would call to him for helpe, he was able inough to helpe them out of those raging flouds, which now came in upon them: they cried indeed, but no succour appeared and so they were swallowed up in water. The maister returned with the ship, and told the king how he had used the matter, and had both thanks and reward, as some have written. But others affirme, (and more truelie as should seeme) that diverse of those mariners, which dealt so wickedlie against the Jewes, were hanged for their wicked practise, and so received a just reward of their fraudulent and mischeevous dealing. But now to the purpose.

In the foresaid parlement, the king demanded an aid of monie of the spiritualtie, etc. etc.

IV

READMISSION OF THE JEWS TO ENGLAND

The Petition to Cromwell

To His Highnesse Oliver Lord Protector of the Comonwelth of England, Scotland and Ireland & the Dominions thereof. The Humble Petition of the Hebrews, at Present Residing in this city of London whose names ar underwritten Humbly Sheweth, That Acknolledging The Manyfold favours and Protection yor Highnesse hath bin pleased to grant us in order that wee may with security meete privately in owr particular house to our Devosions, And being desirous to be favoured more by yor Highnesse wee pray with all Humblenesse yt by the best meanes which may be such Protection may be graunted us in Writing as that we may herewith meete at owr said private devosions in owr Particular houses without feere of Molestation either to owr persons famillys or estates, owr desires Being to

Live Peacebly under yor Highnes Governement, And being wee ar all mortall wee allsoe Humbly pray yor Highnesse to graunt us License that those which may dey of owr nation may be burued in such place out of the cittye as wee shal thincke convenient with the Proprietors Leave in whose Land this place shall be, and soe wee shall as well in owr Lifetyme, as at owr death be highly favoured by yor Highnesse for whose Long Lyfe and Prosperity wee shall continually pray To the Almighty God etc. Menasseh ben Israel, David Abrabanel, Abraham Israel Caruajal, Abraham Coen Gonzales, Jahacob De Caceres, Abraham Israel De Brito, Isak Lopes Chillon.

[Cromwell's Acknowledgement]: Oliver P. Wee doe referr this peticon to the Consideracon of or Councill. March ye 24th 1655–6.

Cromwell in Council

[Rev. Joseph Spence, born 1699, died 1768; critic and collector of anecdotes; friend of Pope and recorder of the conversations of Pope and his circle, wrote this account some ninety years after the event.]

The Jews offered my Lord Godolphin to pay five hundred thousand pounds (and they would have made it a million), if the government would allow them to purchase the town of Brentford, with leave of settling there entirely, with full privileges of trade, &c. The agent from the Jews said, that the affair was already concerted with the chiefs of their brethren abroad; that it would bring the richest of their merchants hither, and of course an addition of above twenty millions of money to circulate in the nation. Lord Molesworth was in the room with Lord Godolphin, when this proposal was made, and as soon as the agent was gone, pressed him to close in with it. Lord Godolphin was not of his opinion. He foresaw, that it would provoke two of the most powerful bodies in the nation, the clergy and the merchants; he gave other reasons too against it, and in fine it was dropped.

The Jews had better success with Oliver Cromwell, when they desired leave to have a synagogue in London. They offered him, when Protector, sixty thousand pounds for that privilege. Cromwell appointed them a day, for his giving them an answer. He then sent to some of the most powerful among the clergy, and some of the chief merchants in the city, to be present at their meeting. It was in the long gallery at Whitehall. Sir Paul Rycaut, who was then a young man, pressed in among the crowd, and said he never heard a man speak so well in his life, as Cromwell did on this occasion. When they were all met, he ordered the Jews to speak for themselves. After that he turned to the clergy, who inveighed much against the Jews, as a cruel and cursed people. Cromwell in his answer to the clergy called them "Men of God;" and desired to be informed by them whether it was not their opinion, that the Jews were one day to be called into the church? He then desired to know, whether it was not every Christian man's duty to forward that good end all he could? Then he flourished a good deal on the religion prevailing in this nation, the only place in the world where religion was taught in its full purity: was it not then our duty, in particular, to encourage them to settle here, where alone they could be taught the truth; and not to exclude them from the sight, and leave them among idolaters? This silenced the clergy. He then turned to the merchants, who spoke much of [the Jews'] falseness and meanness, and that they would get their trade from them. " 'Tis true," says Cromwell, "they are the meanest and most despised of all people."— He then fell into abusing the Jews most heartily, and after he had said every thing that was contemptible and low of them: "Can you really be afraid," said he, "that this mean despised people, should be able to prevail in trade and credit over the merchants of England, the noblest and most esteemed merchants of the whole world!" — Thus he went on, till he had silenced them too; and so was at liberty to grant what he desired to the Jews.—*L[ockier, Dean of Peterborough]* (*Who had this from Sir P. Ricaut himself; as he had the former from Lord Molesworth*).

V

"AROMATIZED BY CONVERSION": SIR THOMAS BROWNE'S MEDICAL TESTIMONY

"That an unsavoury odour is gentilitious or national unto the Jews, if rightly understood, we cannot well concede; nor will the information of reason or sence induce it." Browne's refutation of the vulgar error "That Jews Stink," an early specimen of sympathetic racism, appears in Bk. IV, chap. x of his *Pseudodoxia Epidemica* (1646) and is conducted with his customary mixture of scientific zeal and eclectic learnedness. The arguments which he marshals in support of his view may be considered under five heads.

1. "Upon consult of reason, there will be found no easie assurance to fasten a material or temporal propriety upon any nation; there being scarce any condition (but what depends upon clime) which is not exhausted or obscured from the commixture of introvenient nations either by commerce or conquest; much more will it be difficult to make out this affection in the Jews; whose race however pretended to be pure, must needs

have suffered inseparable commixtures with nations of all sorts; not only in regard of their proselytes, but their universal dispersion; some being posted from several parts of the earth, others quite lost, and swallowed up in those nations where they planted." Browne then traces the intricate movements of the various Biblical tribes, concluding that naturally Jews "are not exempted from the common contagion of Venery contracted first from Christians."

2. At the time Browne wrote his treatise, the Jews had not, of course, been officially readmitted to England. But, as Browne very well knew, it was a matter for boastfulness among continental Jews that thousands of their coreligionists managed to survive *incognito* in countries—like England—from which they had been publicly banished for centuries. If Jews can be recognized by their distinctive odour, Browne ironically asks, how is it that these crypto-Jews have not been "smelled out" by the authorities, when their discovery evidently "would much advantage, not only the Church of Christ, but also the coffers of Princes?" Browne finds the entire charge anyhow vitiated by its partiality to unbaptized Jews, while "unto converted Jews who are of the same seed, no Man imputeth this unsavoury odour; as though Aromatized by their conversion, they lost their scent with their Religion."

3. "Again, if we concede a National unsavouriness in any people, yet shall we find the Jews less subject hereto than any": i.e., of all races the Jews are the most temperate in their dietary and sexual habits, "seldom offending in ebriety or excess of drink, nor erring in gulosity or superfluity of meats; whereby they prevent indigestion and crudities, and consequently putrescence of humors." Browne's famous "quaintness" is never more evident than in itemizing the Jews' dietary laws:

"That Animal, Propter convivia natum, they touch not, nor any of its preparations, or parts so much in respect at Roman Tables, nor admit they unto their board, Hares, Conies, Herons, Plovers, or Swans. Of Fishes they only tast of such as have both fins and scales; which are comparatively but few in number, such only, saith Aristotle, whose Egg or spawn is arenaceous; whereby are excluded all cetacious and cartilagineous Fishes; many pectinal, whose ribs are rectilineal; many costal, which have their ribs embowed; all spinal, or such as have no ribs, but only a back bone, or somewhat analogous thereto, as Eels, Congers, Lampries; all that are testaceous, as Oysters, Cocles, Wilks, Scollops, Muscles; and likewise all crustaceous, as Crabs, Shrimps, and Lobsters," etc. "As for [the Jews'] generations and conceptions (which are the purer from good diet) . . . they severely observe the times of Purification, and avoid all copulation, either in the uncleanness of themselves, or impurity of their Women. A Rule, I fear, not so well observed by Christians."

4. Moreover, Browne regards the whole proposition as an instance of linguistic confusion, the literalizing of what was originally meant to be simply a metaphor expressive of corruption or guilt: "the ground that begat or propagated this assertion, might be the distasteful aversness of the Christian from the Jew, upon the villany of that fact, which made them abominable and stink in the nostrils of all Men. Which real practise, and metaphorical expression, did after proceed into a literal construction; but was a fraudulent illation; for such an evil savour their father Jacob acknowledged in himself, when he said, his sons had made him stink in the land."

5. As a physician Browne finds himself out of all patience with the argument from "miracle," the "cause . . . urged by Campegius, and much received by Christians, that this ill savour is a curse derived upon them by Christ, and stands, as a badge or brand of a generation that crucified their Salvator." He dismisses this with contempt as the last refuge of the uninquiring mind, "a conceit without all warrant; and an easie way to take off dispute in what points of obscurity soever. A method of many Writers, which much depreciates the esteem and value of miracles; that is, therewith to salve not only real verities, but also nonexistencies."

VI

PERPETUAL MOTION: HEROD IN JUDEA; PEPYS IN SYNAGOGUE

"O, it offends me to the soul to hear a robustious periwig-pated fellow tear a passion to tatters, to very rags, to split the ears of the groundlings, who for the most part are capable of nothing but inexplicable dumb shows and noise. I would have such a fellow whipped for o'erdoing Termagant. It out-herods Herod. Pray you avoid it."

The frantic bodily gestures associated with the Jewish bogeys in the mystery plays have been largely derived from the New Testament account of Herod, king of Judea, whom the magi kept in a perpetual state of anxiety: first, by reporting the birth of Jesus, king of the Jews, in fulfillment of the prophecy in Micah 5: 2; afterwards, by ignoring Herod's orders to fetch the Jesus-child to Jerusalem where he proposed to have him killed. The magi, it will be remembered, are sent to Bethlehem to spy out the scene of the nativity and they remain to worship, thus giving the Holy Family the necessary breathing space to escape to Egypt. The results are given in Matt. 2: 16. Herod, when he discovered that he had been duped by the magi, flew into a rage, sent for all male children up to the age of two in and around Bethlehem, and ordered the slaughter known as the Massacre of the Innocents. (The Hebrew verb *y'cherad* [agitated] has been interpreted as a pun on the royal name.) Medieval writers, shopping about for a religiously accredited prototype of the Jew, found a serviceable model in Herod, whom the Gospelist taxes with every imaginable vice. The compact account in Matt. 2 alone presents him as a ferocious blusterer, a butcher, a frightened knave on whom the tables are turned, and a monstrous hypocrite, who in appointing the magi as his deputies, pretends to be actuated by all the proper motives.

But it is as a byword for bodily rage that Herod comes into English drama and figures in Hamlet's often-cited remark. Herod's blustering and the excitable motions of the Jewish extras in the mystery plays served evident comic ends, like Mammon's nose or the Sancho-Panza figure of Vice. Even when it no longer served the direct purpose of farce, the Jew's physical mobility, with its suggestions of the absurd and the diabolic (i.e., the possessed), remained an essential feature of the stereotype: Shylock, Fagin, Scott's Isaac and Reade's, Cumberland's agitated Little Jews, are obvious examples. Since the Jew's excitability has come down the ages as one of his chief properties in literary portraiture, I append the following "exhibits," the first two taken from fictional sources, the others from extra-fictional accounts.

The revolting Rumpelstiltskin figures who bestride excerpts (1) and (2) appear respectively in Grimm's *Household Tales* (the *"Kinder"* in *Kinder- und Hausmaerchen* is always kept out of the English translations) and in Defoe's *Roxana.* Since it lends itself to ghoulish distortions, the Jew's physical turbulence (with Satan, the angry man within, egging him on) is especially useful to the writers of fairy tales, who build on primitive materials. The Jew in Grimm's piece, who is forced by a strolling fiddler to perform lunatic jumps in time to the music until, at the point of exhaustion, he begs the fiddler to rob him and go away, is made of crudely the same stuff as the Jew who leaps madly around the Cross during the comic intermezzo in one of the Towneley mysteries. At the end of the story, Grimm's Jew gets his "halter gratis," of course, the implication being that cosmic justice has once more had a narrow escape. Defoe's Jew is identically spasmodic, and less primitive than Grimm's only because he runs a relatively complex commercial network and is thus presented under a minimally sophisticated aspect. Apart from this, he commands a certain historical interest as the first Jewish caricature in English fiction after Nashe: the first Jew in the "modern" English novel, the first who is meant to be viewed in something like a "realistic" and contemporary perspective—prototype of Melmotte as well as Fagin. But the results, of course, are not realistic.

(*1*) *Grimm's Household Tales:* "The Jew in the Thornbush"

"When [the Jew] was stuck fast among the thorns, the good lad's whim got the better of him, and he took up his fiddle and began to play. And straightaway the Jew's legs began to move and to jump into the air; and the faster the servant fiddled the better went the dance. But the thorns tore the Jew's shabby frock and combed his goat's-beard for him and pricked and scratched him all over the body. 'Oh my,' cried the Jew, 'what do I want him befiddling me! leave go of your fiddle, master, I want not your fiddling, I desire not to dance!' But the servant paid no heed and he thought: you've fleeced enough folks in your time; now let the thorns fleece you for a change; and up he started again, that the Jew jumped higher and higher and scraps of his frock came off on the thorns. 'Oh woe is me!' cried the Jew, 'leave go of your fiddle, I'll give the gentleman whatever he asks, a purse full of gold I'll give the gentleman!' 'Well,' said the servant, 'if you're that minded, why, I suppose I'll have to stop playing. But I'll have to say this for you: you dance that it's an art to see it'; and then he took the Jew's purse and went his way.

"Stockstill stood the Jew and gazed after him, and quiet he remained until the fiddler-lad was out of sight and far away, and then he shrieked with all his might: 'Oh, you miserable musicus! Oh, you lousy beer-hall fiddler! wait till I catch you alone! I'll run you down till the soles of your boots fall off: oh, you ragamuffin! just you stop up your mouth with a dollar-piece and you'll be worth a penny if you're lucky,' and he kept muttering and abusing the fellow as fast as the words came out. And as soon as he had relieved himself a little in this wise, he ran into town to the judge. 'Lord Judge, oh woe is me, oh my! See how the godless knave pilfered my moneys and besoiled my body! A stone on the ground should have pity on me! My suit in tatters! My body pricked and run through! My piddling moneys stolen, and the purse stolen too! Fine ducats, Lord Judge, one piece finer than the one before' " etc., etc.

(*2*) *Daniel Defoe,* The Fortunate Mistress or . . . Roxana (*1724*)

"As soon as the *Jew* saw the Jewels, he falls a-jabbering in *Dutch,* or *Portugeuse,* to the Merchant, and I could presently perceive that they were in some great Surprize, both of them; the *Jew* held up his Hands, look'd at me with some Horror, then talk'd *Dutch* again, and putting himself into a thousand Shapes, twisting his Body, and wringing up his Face this way, and that Way, in his Discourse, stamping with his Feet, and throwing abroad his Hands, as if he was not in a Rage only, but in a meer Fury; then he wou'd turn, and give a Look at me, like the Devil; I thought I never saw anything so frightful in my Life."

The remaining excerpts are reportage, not fiction, and they have a slightly different application; I subjoin them not by way of irrelevant physiological documentation, but to compare the fantastic distortion with the fanciful observation. None of the four authorities is free from prejudice, given the time and the place. The locale in each case is a synagogue, so that an element of purely religious bias gets into all their accounts. The tourist reports given in excerpts (3) and (4) date back to the first decades under the Stuarts and describe Jewish services in Jerusalem and Constantinople; (5) and (6) record the impressions with which the chief seventeenth-century diarists came away from visits to synagogues in London and Rome. What strikes all these writers as ludicrous or shocking is the fidgetiness which Jews manifest at their devotionals. The Herod motif appears again in Southey's malicious account which heads Appendix VII, where it is joined to a more general view of English Jewry at the beginning of the nineteenth century.

(*3*) *George Sandys,* A Relation of a Journey begunne Anno Dom. 1610 . . .

"They [the Jews] reade in savage Tones, and sing in Tunes that have no affinitie with Musicke: joyning voyces at the severall closes. But their fantasticall gestures exceed all Barbarisme, continually weaving with their bodies, and often jumping upright (as in the manner in Dances) by them esteemed an action of zeale, and figure of spirituall elevation. They pray silently, with ridiculous and continuall noddings of their heads, not to be seene and not laught at."

(*4*) *Thomas Coryat,* Master Thomas Coryates travels to, and Observations in, Constantinople, etc. (*1613*)

"When they sat at their devotion they used a most ridiculous and unseemly gesture; for they alwayes mooved their bodies up and downe very strangely, the head being in a continuall motion without cessation. After that they moove their right side, then their left and lastly their forepart forward; which kind of wagging of their bodies by interchangeable turnes they use during the whole time of their service."

(5) *John Evelyn's* Diary (*January 7, 1645*)

"A sermon was preach'd to the Jewes, at Ponte Sisto, who are constrain'd to sit till the houre is don; but it is with so much malice in their countenances, spitting, hum'ing, coughing, and motion, that it is almost impossible they should heare a word from the preacher. A conversion is very rare."

(6) *Samuel Pepys's* Diary (*October 14, 1663*)

". . . after dinner my wife and I, by Mr. Rawlinson's conduct, to the Jewish Synagogue: where the men and boys in their vayles, and the women behind a lattice out of sight; and some things stand up, which I believe is their Law, in a press to which all coming in do bow; and at the putting on their vayles do say something, to which others that hear him do cry Amen, and the party do kiss his vayle. Their service all in a singing way, and in Hebrew. . . . And in the end they had a prayer for the King, which they pronounced his name in Portugall; but the prayer, like the rest, in Hebrew. But, Lord! to see the disorder, laughing, sporting, and no attention, but confusion in all their service, more like brutes than people knowing the true God, would make a man forswear ever seeing them more: and indeed I never did see so much, or could have imagined there had been any religion in the whole world, so absurdly performed as this. Away thence with my mind strongly disturbed with them, by coach and set down my wife in Westminster Hall . . ."

It has since been suggested that Pepys chose a singularly bad day for his visit, which happened to coincide with the Feast of Tabernacles, when Jewish services are conducted with even greater gusto than they are ordinarily. I note in parenthesis that the same holiday upset a writer as garrulous as Pepys exactly a hundred years later: on October 3, 1763, Horace Walpole writes to George Montague: "I have given my assembly to show my gallery; and it was glorious; but happening to pitch upon the feast of tabernacles, none of my Jews could come, though Mrs. Clive proposed to them to change their religion. So I am forced to exhibit once more."

VII

JEWS IN ENGLAND, 1807: ROBERT SOUTHEY ROUNDS UP THE NEWS

I went yesterday evening to the Synagogue. Never did I see a place of worship in which there was so little appearance of devotion. The women were in a gallery by themselves, the men sate below, keeping their hats on, as they would have done in the street. During the service they took from behind their altar, if that word may be thus applied without profanation, certain silver—utensils they cannot be called, as they appeared to be of no possible use,—silver ornaments rather, hung with small rattle bells, and these they jingled as they carried them round the room, then replaced them in the receptacle. This was the only ceremony. It is impossible to describe the strange and uncouth tone in which the priest sung out a portion of the Pentateuch, from a long roll. The language was so intolerably harsh, and the manner in which it was chaunted so abominably discordant, that they suited each other to a miracle; and the larynx of the Rabbi seemed to have been made expressly to give both their full effect. . . .

During the last reign an attempt was made to naturalize [the Jews], in a body; and the measure would have been effected had it not been for the indignant outcry of the people, who very properly regarded it as an act of defiance, or at least of opposition, to the express language of prophecy. But this feeling has abated, and were the attempt to be renewed it would meet with little opposition. In Catholic countries our pictures and crucifixes perpetually set before the Christian's eyes the sufferings of his Redeemer, and there is no possibility of his forgetting the history of his religion. Even the most trifling ceremony is of use. At one of the public schools here, the boys on Easter Sunday rush out of the chapel after prayers, singing

He is risen, he is risen,
All the Jews must go to prison.

This custom is certainly very old, though I cannot learn that it was ever usual to imprison this wretched people upon this festival. Some of these boys cut the straps of a Jew's box one day, and all his ginger-bread nuts fell into the street. Complaint was made to the master; and when he questioned the culprits what they could say in their defence, one of them stepped forward and said, "Why, sir, did not they crucify our Lord!" Without admitting the plea in excuse, it may be remarked that if the boy had not remembered his Easter rhymes, he would have been as indifferent to the crime of the Jews as the rest of his countrymen. . . .

In Rome these misbelievers are obliged to hear a sermon once a week; here a sermon attracts them as a novelty. One of the Methodist itinerants, some few years ago, fancying that, like St. Vicente Ferrer, he had a special gift for converting this stiff-necked generation, undertook to confute their errors, and invited them to attend his preaching. The place appointed was the great Methodist Chapel in Tottenham Court Road; and they assembled in such crowds as to fill the chapel and the court in which it is built. One of the windows was taken out, and the orator taking his stand in the opening addressed the congregation both within and without at the same time. There can be no reason to suppose that they came with hearts more accessible to conviction than usual; but, had it been the case, the method which this fanatic took was little likely to be successful; for he began by telling them that he was not yet twenty years old, that he had no human learning whatever, and that for all he was about to say to them he trusted to the immediate impulse of the Lord. The rest of his discourse was in character with the beginning, and the Jews returned, the greater number ridiculing his folly, the more thoughtful remembering their own law against him who presumes to speak in the name of the Lord, what the Lord hath not commanded him to speak. . . .

The English church has no zeal for souls. At the beginning of the last century the daughter of a rich Jew, by name Jacob Mendes de Breta, was at her own instance publicly baptized. The father ran into the church like a madman, charged the officiating clergyman to desist, and, when he perceived that this was in vain, cursed his child with the bitterest imprecations, and prayed to his God that the church might fall in, and crush all who were concerned in the ceremony. After this he utterly disowned her:—the law had made no provision for such cases, and the parish were obliged to support her; which, to their honour, they did in a manner suitable to her former situation in life. At their petition, however, a bill was enacted compelling the Jews to provide decently for their converted children. Thus much was done upon the emergency of the case, and nothing more. Not the slightest effort is made for their conversion, nor the slightest impediment opposed to the public celebration of ceremonies, which the Gospel has expressly abrogated. The Jews have nothing to complain of, except that they pay tithes to the clergy, and that they are liable to the trouble of parish offices—the law even allowing them to be made churchwardens. Any person may be excused from serving this office if he chooses to pay a fine amounting to about ten pieces of eight: it is not long since a parish in London nominated a Jew for the sake of getting this money; he, however, was determined to disappoint them by taking the situation;—the profanation was theirs, not his;—and accordingly the church affairs for the year were actually managed by this son of the Synagogue.

It may well be supposed that when Bonaparte was in Syria, his movements were anxiously watched by the Jews. There was a great stir among them, and it is probable that if he had invited them by proclamation, and promised to give them Palestine, armies would have been raised to take and keep possession of that Holy Land, to which they look, individually and collectively, as their destined gathering place. Individually, I say, because it is taught by many Rabbis, that the children of Israel, wherever buried, can rise again at the coming of the Messiah, nowhere except in the Promised Land; and they, therefore, who are interred in any other part of the world, will have to make their way there through the caverns of the earth; a long and painful journey, the difficulty and fatigue of which are equivalent to purgatory. I know not whether this is believed by the English Rabbis . . .

No particular dress is enjoined them by law, nor indeed is any such mark of distinction necessary: they are sufficiently distinguished by a cast of complexion and features, which, with leave of our neighbors, I will call a Portugueze look.—Some of the lowest order let their beards grow, and wear a sort of black tunic with a girdle; the chief ostensible trade of this class is in old clothes, but they deal also in stolen goods, and not unfrequently in coining. A race of Hebrew lads who infest you in the streets with oranges and red slippers, or tempt school-boys to dip in a bag for gingerbread nuts, are the great agents in uttering base silver; when it is worn too bare to circulate any longer they buy it up at a low price, whiten the brass again, and again send it abroad. You meet Jew pedlars every where, travelling with boxes of haberdashery at their backs, cuckoo clocks, sealing wax, quills, weather glasses, green spectacles, clumsy figures in plaister of Paris, which you see over the chimney of an alehouse parlour in the country, or miserable prints of the king and queen, the four seasons, the cardinal virtues, the last naval victory, the prodigal son, and such like subjects, even the Nativity and the Crucifixion; but when they meet with a likely chapman, they produce others of the most obscene and mischievous kind. Any thing for money, in contempt of their own law as well as of the law of the country;—the pork-butchers are commonly Jews. All these low classes have a shibboleth of their own, as remarkable as their physiognomy; and in some parts of the city they are so numerous, that when I strayed into their precincts one day, and saw so many Hebrew inscriptions in the shop windows, and so many long beards in the streets, I began to fancy that I had discovered the ten tribes. . . .

England has been called the hell of horses, the purgatory of servants, and the paradise of women: it may be added that it is the heaven of the Jews—alas, they have no other heaven to expect!

VIII

"THE SPIDER OF THE MIND": HAZLITT ON JEWISH EMANCIPATION (1831)

The Emancipation of the Jews is but a natural step in the progress of civilization. Laws and institutions are positive things: opinions and sentiments are variable; and it is in conforming the stubbornness and perversity of the former to the freedom and boldness of the latter, that the harmony and beauty of the social order consists. But it is said, "The Jews at present have few grievances to complain of; they are well off, and should be thankful for the indulgence they receive." It is true, we no longer burn them at a stake, or plunder them of their goods: why then continue to insult and fix an idle stigma on them? At Rome, a few years ago, they made the Jews run races (naked) in the Corso on Good Friday. At present, they only oblige them to provide asses to run races on the same day for the amusement of the populace, and to keep up the spirit of the good old custom, though by altering it they confess that the custom was wrong, and that they are ashamed of it. They also shut up the Jews in a particular quarter of the city (called Il Ghetto Judaico) and at the same time will not suffer the English as heretics to be buried within the walls of Rome. An Englishman smiles or is scandalized at both these instances of bigotry; but if he is asked, "Why then do you not yourselves emancipate the Catholics and the Jews?" he may answer, "We *have* emancipated the one." And why not the other? "Because we are intolerant." This, and this alone, is the reason.

We throw in the teeth of the Jews, that they are prone to certain sordid vices. If they are vicious, it is we who have made them so. Shut out any class of people from the path to fair fame, and you reduce them to grovel in the pursuit of riches and the means to live. A man has long been in dread of insult for no just cause, and you complain that he grows reserved and suspicious. You treat him with obloquy and contempt, and wonder that he does not walk by you with an erect and open brow.

We also object to their trades and modes of life; that is, we shut people up in close confinement, and complain that they do not live in the open air. The Jews barter and sell commodities, instead of raising or manufacturing them. But this is the necessary traditional consequence of their former persecution and pillage by all nations. They could not set up a trade when they were hunted every moment from place to place, and while they could count nothing their own but what they could carry with them. They could not devote themselves to the pursuit of agriculture, when they were not allowed to possess a foot of land. You tear people up by the roots, and trample on them like noxious weeds, and then make an outcry that they do not take root in the soil like wholesome plants. You drive them like a pest from city to city, from kingdom to kingdom, and then call them vagabonds and aliens.

When reason fails, the Christian religion, is, as usual, called in aid of persecution. The admission of the Jews, it is said, to any place of trust or emolument in the State ought not to be sanctioned, because they expect the coming of the Messiah, and their restoration, one day or other, to their own country: and Christianity, it is said, is part of the law of the land.

As to their exclusion because they expect the coming of the Messiah, and their restoration, one day or other, to their own country, a few words will be sufficient. Even if it is too much for a people, with this reversion in the promised land, to have a "stake in the country" added to it; and the offer of a seat in the House of Commons is too much for any one who looks forward to a throne in the *New Jerusalem*; this objection comes with but an ill grace from the followers of him who has declared, "My kingdom is not of this world;" and who on that plea profess to keep all the power and authority in their own hands. Suppose an attempt were made to exclude Christians from serving the office of constable, juryman, or knight of the shire, as expressly contrary to the great principle of their religion, which inculcates an entire contempt for the things of this life, and a constant preparation for a better. Would not this be considered as an irony, and not a very civil one? Yet it is the precise counterpart of this argument. The restoration of the Jews to their own country, however firmly believed in as an article of faith, has been delayed eighteen hundred years, and may be delayed eighteen hundred more. Are they to remain indifferent to the good or evil, to the respectability or odium that may attach to them all this while? . . . Suppose a Jew to have amassed a large fortune in the last war, and to have laid by money in the funds, and built himself a handsome house in the neighbourhood of the metropolis; would he be more likely by his vote in the House of Commons to promote a revolution, so as to cause a general bankruptcy; or to encourage the mob to pull down his house, or root up his favourite walks, because after all, at the end of several centuries, he and the rest of his nation indulge in the prospect of returning to their own country? The most clear-sighted John Bull patriotism hardly reaches beyond ourselves and our heirs. . . .

The proposal to admit Jews to a seat in Parliament in this country is treated as an irony or a burlesque on the Catholic question. At the same time, it is said to be very proper and rational in France and America, Denmark and the Netherlands; because there, though they are nominally admitted, court influence excludes them in the one, and popular opinion in the other, so that the law is of no avail; that is, in other words, in England as there is neither court-influence nor popular prejudice, and as everything in this country is done by money alone, the Stock Exchange would soon buy up the House of Commons; and if a single Jew were admitted, the whole would shortly be a perfect Sanhedrin. This is a pleasant account of the spirit of English patriotism, and the texture of the House of Commons. All the wealth of the Jews cannot buy them a single seat there; but if a certain formal restriction were taken off, Jewish gold would buy up the fee simple of the consciences, prejudices and interests of the country, and turn the kingdom *topsy-turvy*. Thus the bedrid imagination of prejudice sees some dreadful catastrophe in every improvement, and no longer feeling the ground of custom under its feet, fancies itself on an abyss of ruin and lawless change. How truly has it been said of prejudice, "that it has the singular ability of accommodating itself to all the possible varieties of the human mind. Some passions and vices are but thinly scattered among mankind, and find only here and there a fitness of reception. But prejudice, like the spider, makes everywhere its home. It has neither taste nor choice of place, and all that it requires is room. There is scarcely a situation, except fire and water, in which a spider will not live. So let the mind be as naked as the walls of an empty and forsaken tenement, gloomy as a dungeon, or ornamented with the richest abilities of thinking; let it be hot, cold, dark or light, lonely or inhabited, still prejudice, if undisturbed, will fill it with cobwebs, and live like the spider, where there seems nothing to live on. If the one prepares her food by poisoning it to her palate and her use, the other does the same; and as several of our passions are strongly characterised by the animal world, prejudice may be denominated the spider of the mind."

Three hundred years ago all this was natural and in order, because it accorded with the prejudices of the time: now it is absurd and Gothic, because it is contrary to men's reason and feelings. Hatred is the food and growth of ignorance. While we know nothing but ourselves and our own notions, we can conceive of nothing else as possible; and every deviation from our practice or opinions gives a shock to our faith that nothing can expiate but blows. Those who differ from us in the smallest particular are considered as of a different species, and we treat them accordingly. But this barrier of prejudice, which is founded on ignorance, is thrown down by the diffusion of light and knowledge; nor can any thing build it up again. In the good old times, a Jew was regarded by the vulgar and their betters as a sort of monster, a *lusus naturae,* whose existence they could not account for, and would not tolerate. The only way to get rid of the obnoxious opinion was to destroy the *man.* Besides, in those dark ages, they wanted some object of natural antipathy, as in country places they get a strange dog or an ideot to hunt down and be the bugbear of the village. But it is the test of reason and refinement to be able to subsist without bugbears. While it was supposed that "the Jews eat little children," it was proper to take precautions against them. But why keep up ill names and the ill odour of a prejudice, when the prejudice has ceased to exist? It has long ceased amongst the reflecting part of the community; and, although the oldest prejudices are, it is to be lamented, preserved longest in the highest places, and governments to have been slow to learn good manners, we cannot but be conscious that these days are passing away. We begin to see, if we do not fully see, that we have no superiority to boast of but reason and philosophy, and that it is well to get rid of vulgar prejudices and nominal distinctions as fast as possible.

IX

MACAULAY'S "CIVIL DISABILITIES OF THE JEWS" (1831)

The distinguished member of the House of Commons, who, towards the close of the late Parliament, brought forward a proposition for the relief of the Jews, has given notice of his intention to renew it. The force of reason, last session, carried it through one stage, in spite of the opposition of power. Reason and power are now on the same side; and we have little doubt that they will conjointly achieve a decisive victory. In order to contribute our share to the success of just principles, we propose to pass in review, as rapidly as possible, some of the arguments, which have been employed to vindicate a system full of absurdity and injustice.

[1] The constitution—it is said—is essentially Christian; and therefore to admit Jews to office, is to destroy the constitution. Nor is the Jew injured by being excluded from political power. For no man has any right to power. A man has a right to his property;—a man has a right to be protected from personal injury. These rights the law allows to the Jew, and with these rights it would be atrocious to interfere. But it is a mere matter of favour to admit any man to political power; and no man can justly complain that he is shut out from it. . . .

The strange argument which we are considering would prove too much even for those who advance it. If no man has a right to political power, then neither Jew nor Christian has such a right. The whole foundation of government is taken away. But if government be taken away, the property and the persons of men are insecure, and it is acknowledged that men have a right to their property and to personal security. If it be right that the property of men should be protected, and if this can only be done by means of government, then it must be right that government should exist. Now, there cannot be government unless some person or persons possess political power. Therefore it is right that some person or persons should possess political power. . . .

It is because men are not in the habit of considering what the end of government is, that Catholic disabilities and Jewish disabilities have been suffered to exist so long. We hear of essentially Protestant governments and essentially Christian governments—words which mean just as much as essentially Protestant cookery, or essentially Christian horsemanship. Government exists for the purpose of keeping the peace,—for the purpose of compelling us to settle our disputes by arbitration, instead of settling them by blows,—for the purpose of compelling us to supply our wants by industry, instead of supplying them by rapine. This is the only operation for which the machinery of government is fit, the only operation which wise governments ever attempt to perform. If there is any class of people who are not interested, or who do not think themselves interested, in the security of property and the maintenance of order, that class ought to have no share of the powers which exist for the purpose of securing property and maintaining order. But why a man should be less fit to exercise that power because he wears a beard, because he does not eat ham, because he goes to the synagogue on Saturdays instead of going to the church on Sundays, we cannot conceive.

The points of difference between Christianity and Judaism have very much to do with a man's fitness to be a bishop or a rabbi. But they have no more to do with his fitness to be a magistrate, a legislator, or a minister of finance, than with his fitness to be a cobbler. Nobody has ever thought of compelling cobblers to make any declaration on the true faith of a Christian. Any man would rather have his shoes mended by a heretical cobbler, than by a person who had subscribed all the thirty-nine articles, but had never handled an awl. Men act thus, not because they are indifferent to religion, but because they do not see what religion has to do with the mending of shoes. Yet religion has as much to do with the mending of shoes, as with the budget and the army estimates. We have surely had two signal proofs within the last twenty years, that a very good Christian may be a very bad Chancellor of the Exchequer.

[2] But it would be monstrous, say the persecutors, that a Jew should legislate for a Christian community. This is a palpable misrepresentation. What is proposed is not that Jews should legislate for a Christian community, but that a legislature composed of Christians and Jews, should legislate for a community composed of Christians and Jews. On nine hundred and ninety-nine questions out of a thousand,—on all questions of police, of finance, of civil and criminal law, of foreign policy, the Jew, as a Jew, has no interest hostile to that of the Christian, or even of the Churchman. . . .

In fact, the Jews are not now excluded from political power. They possess it; and as long as they are allowed to accumulate property, they must possess it. The distinction which is sometimes made between civil privileges and political power, is a distinction without a difference. Privileges are power. Civil and political are synonymous words,—the one derived from the Latin, the other from the Greek. Nor is this mere verbal quibbling. If we look for a moment at the facts of the case, we shall see that the things are inseparable, or rather identical.

That a Jew should be a judge in a Christian country, would be most shocking. But he may be a juryman. He may try issues of fact; and no harm is done. But if he should be suffered to try issues of law, there is an end of the constitution. He may sit in a box plainly dressed, and return verdicts. But that he should sit on the bench in a black gown and white wig, and grant new trials, would be an abomination not to be thought of among baptized people. The distinction is certainly most philosophical. . . . It would be impious to let a Jew sit in Parliament. But a Jew may make money, and money may make members of Parliament. Gatton and Old Sarum may be the property of a Hebrew. An elector of Penrhyn will take ten pounds from Shylock rather than nine pounds nineteen shillings and eleven pence three farthings from Antonio. To this no objection is made. That a Jew should possess the substance of legislative power, that he should command eight votes on every division, as if he were the great Duke of Newcastle himself, is exactly as it should be. But that he should pass the bar, and sit down on those mysterious cushions of green leather; that he should cry 'hear' and 'order,' and talk about being on his legs, and being, for one, free to say this, and to say that, would be a profanation sufficient to bring ruin on the country. . . .

If it is our duty as Christians to exclude the Jews from political power, it must be our duty to treat them as our ancestors treated them—to murder them, and banish them, and rob them. For in that way, and in that way alone, can we really deprive them of political power. If we do not adopt this course, we may take away the shadow, but we must leave them the substance. We may do enough to pain and irritate them; but we shall not do enough to secure ourselves from danger, if danger really exists. Where wealth is, there power must inevitably be.

[3] The English Jews, we are told, are not Englishmen. They are a separate people, living locally in this island, but living morally and politically in communion with their brethren, who are scattered over all the world. An English Jew looks on a Dutch or a Portuguese Jew as his countryman, and on an English Christian as a stranger. This want of patriotic feeling, it is said, renders a Jew unfit to exercise political functions.

The argument has in it something plausible: but a close examination shows it to be quite unsound. Even if the alleged facts are admitted, still the Jews are not the only people who have preferred their sect to their country. The feeling of patriotism, when society is in a healthful state, springs up, by a natural and inevitable association, in the minds of citizens who know that they owe all their comforts and pleasures to the bond which unites them in one community. But under partial and oppressive governments, these associations cannot acquire that strength which they have in a better state of things. Men are compelled to seek from their party that protection which they ought to receive from their country, and they, by a natural consequence, transfer to their party that affection which they would otherwise have felt for their country. . . .

It has always been the trick of bigots to make their subjects miserable at home, and then complain that they look for relief abroad;—to divide society, and to wonder that it is not united;—to govern as if a section of the state were the whole, and to censure the other sections of the state for their want of patriotic spirit. If the Jews have not felt towards England like children, it is because she has treated them like a step-mother. There is no feeling which more certainly developes itself in the minds of men living under tolerably good government, than the feeling of patriotism. Since the beginning of the world, there never was any nation, or any large portion of any nation, not cruelly oppressed, which was wholly destitute of that feeling. To make it therefore ground of accusation against a class of men, that they are not patriotic, is the most vulgar legerdemain of sophistry. It is the logic which the wolf employs against the lamb. It is to accuse the mouth of the stream of poisoning the source. It is to put the effect before the cause. It is to vindicate oppression, by pointing at the depravation which oppression has produced.

If the English Jews really felt a deadly hatred to England—if the weekly prayer of their synagogues were, that all the curses denounced by Ezekiel on Tyre and Egypt, might fall on London;—if, in their solemn feasts, they called down blessings on those who should dash our children to pieces on the stones, still, we say, their hatred to their countrymen would not be more intense than that which sects of Christians have often borne to each other. But, in fact, the feeling of the Jews is not such. It is precisely what, in the situation in which they are placed, we should expect it to be. . . . They are not so well treated as the dissenting sects of Christians are now treated in England; and on this account, and, we firmly believe, on this account alone, they have a more exclusive spirit. Till we have carried the experiment farther, we are not entitled to conclude that they cannot be made Englishmen altogether. The tyrant who punished their fathers for not making bricks without straw, was not more unreasonable than the statesmen who treat them as aliens, and abuse them for not entertaining all the feelings of natives.

Rulers must not be suffered thus to absolve themselves of their solemn responsibility. It does not lie in their mouths to say that a sect is not patriotic:—it is their business to make it patriotic. History and reason clearly indicate the means. The English Jews are, as far as we can see, precisely what our government has made them. They are precisely what any sect,—what any class of men selected on any principle from the community, and treated as they have been treated,—would have been. If all the red-haired people in Europe had, for centuries, been outraged and oppressed, banished from this place, imprisoned in that, deprived of their money, deprived of their teeth, convicted of the most improbable crimes on the feeblest evidence, dragged at horses' tails, hanged, tortured, burned alive,—if, when manners became milder, they had still remained subject to debasing restrictions, and exposed to vulgar insults, locked up in particular streets in some countries, pelted and ducked by the rabble in others, excluded everywhere from magistracies and honours—what would be the patriotism of gentlemen with red hair? . . .

[4] But, it is said, the Scriptures declare that the Jews are to be restored to their own country; and the whole nation looks forward to that restoration. They are, therefore, not so deeply interested as others in the prosperity of England. It is not their home, but merely the place of their sojourn,—the house of their bondage. This argument first appeared, we think, in the *Times* newspaper, and has attracted a degree of attention proportioned rather to the general talent with which that journal is conducted, than to its own intrinsic force. It belongs to a class of sophisms, by which the most hateful persecutions may easily be justified. To charge men with practical consequences which they themselves deny, is disingenuous in controversy,—it is atrocious in government. . . .

It is altogether impossible to reason from the opinions which a man professes, to his feelings and his actions; and, in fact, no person is ever such a fool as to reason thus, except when he wants a pretext for persecuting his neighbours. A Christian is commanded, under the strongest sanctions, to do as he would be done by. Yet to how many of the twenty millions of professing Christians in these islands would any man in his senses lend a thousand pounds without security? A man who should act, for one day, on the supposition that all the people about him were influenced by the religion which they professed, would find himself ruined before night: and no man ever does act on that supposition, in any of the ordinary concerns of life, in borrowing, in lending, in buying, or in selling. But when any of our fellow-creatures are to be oppressed, the case is different. Then we represent those motives which we know to be so feeble for good, as omnipotent for evil. Then we lay to the charge of our victims all the vices and follies to which their doctrines, however remotely, seem to tend. We forget that the same weakness, the same laxity, the same disposition to prefer the present to the future, which make men worse than a good religion, make them better than a bad one. . . .

People are now reasoning about the Jews, as our fathers reasoned about the Papists. The law which is inscribed on the walls of the synagogues prohibits covetousness. But if we were to say that a Jew mortgagee would not foreclose, because God had commanded him not to covet his neighbour's house, every body would think us out of our wits. Yet it passes for an argument, to say, that a Jew will take no interest in the prosperity of the country in which he lives, that he will not care how bad its laws and police may be—how heavily it may be taxed—how often it may be conquered and given up to spoil,—because God has pronounced that by some unknown means, and at some undetermined time, perhaps a thousand years hence, the Jews shall migrate to Palestine. Is not this the most profound ignorance of human nature? Do we not know, that what is remote and indefinite, affects men far less than what is near and certain? Besides, the argument applies to Christians as strongly as to Jews. The Christian believes, as well as the Jew, that at some future period the present order of things will come to an end. Nay, many Christians believe that the Messiah will shortly establish a kingdom on the earth, and reign visibly over all its inhabitants. . . . Now, wherein does this doctrine differ, as far as its political tendency is concerned, from the doctrine of the Jews? If a Jew is unfit to legislate for us, because he believes that he or his remote descendants will be removed to Palestine, can we safely open the House of Commons to a fifth-monarchy-man, who expects that, before this generation shall pass away, all the kingdoms of the earth will be swallowed up in one divine empire? . . .

[5] There is another argument which we would not willingly treat with levity, and which yet we scarcely know how to treat seriously. The Scriptures, it is said, are full of terrible denunciations against the Jews. It is foretold that they are to be wanderers. Is it then right to give them a home? It is foretold that they are to be oppressed. Can we with propriety suffer them to be rulers? To admit them to the rights of citizens, is manifestly to insult the Divine oracles.

We allow, that to falsify a prophecy inspired by Divine Wisdom, would be a most atrocious crime. It is, therefore, a happy circumstance for our frail species, that it is a crime which no man can possibly commit. If we admit the Jews to seats in Parliament, we shall, by so doing, prove that the prophecies in question, whatever they may mean, do not mean that the Jews shall be excluded from Parliament.

In fact, it is already clear, that the prophecies do not bear the meaning put upon them by the respectable persons whom we are now answering. In France, and in the United States, the Jews are already admitted to all the rights of citizens. A prophecy, therefore, which should mean that the Jews would never, during the course of their wanderings, be admitted to all the rights of citizens in the places of their sojourn, would be a false prophecy. This, therefore, is not the meaning of the prophecies of Scripture.

But we protest altogether against the practice of confounding prophecy with precept,—of setting up predictions which are often obscure, against a morality which is always clear. If actions are to be considered as just and good, merely because they have been predicted, what action was ever more laudable than that crime which our bigots are now, at the end of eighteen centuries, urging us to avenge on the Jews,—that crime which made the earth shake, and blotted out the sun from heaven? The same reasoning which is now employed to vindicate the disabilities imposed on our Hebrew countrymen, will equally vindicate the kiss of Judas and the judgement of Pilate. "The Son of man goeth, as it is written of him; but woe to that man by whom the Son of man is betrayed." And woe to those who, in any age or in any country, disobey his benevolent commands under pretence of accomplishing his predictions. If this argument justifies the laws now existing against the Jews, it justifies equally all the cruelties which have ever been committed against them,—the sweeping edicts of banishment and confiscation, the dungeon, the rack, and the slow fire.

X

THE SUEZ CANAL PURCHASE: THREE LETTERS

Disraeli to Queen Victoria

2, Whitehall Gardens, Nov. 24, 1875. Mr. Disraeli with his humble duty to your Majesty:

It is just settled: you have it, Madam. The French Government has been out-generaled. They tried too much, offering loans at an usurious rate, and with conditions, which would have virtually given them the government of Egypt.

The Khedive, in despair and disgust, offered your Majesty's Government to purchase his shares outright. He never would listen to such a proposition before.

Four millions sterling! and almost immediately. There was only one firm that could do it—Rothschilds. They behaved admirably; advanced the money at a low rate, and the entire interest of the Khedive is now yours, Madam.

Yesterday the Cabinet sate four hours and more on this, and Mr. Disraeli has not had one moment's rest to-day; therefore this despatch must be pardoned, as his head is rather weak. He will tell the whole wondrous tale to-morrow.

He was in Cabinet to-day, when your Majesty's second telegram arrived, which must be his excuse for his brief and stupid answer: but it was 'the crisis.'

The Government and Rothschilds agreed to keep it secret, but there is little doubt it will be known to-morrow from Cairo.

Queen Victoria to Disraeli

Windsor Castle, Nov. 25, '75.—This is indeed a great and important event, which, when known, will, the Queen feels sure, be most popular in the country. The great sum is the only disadvantage.

The Queen will be curious to hear all about it from Mr. Disraeli, when she sees him to-day.

Disraeli to Lady Bradford

Windsor Castle, Nov. 26, 1875.—A most hurried line to tell you that nothing cd. be more successful—I might say triumphant—than my visit. The Faery [i.e., Victoria] was most excited about Suez, said 'what she liked most was, it was a blow at Bismarck,' referring, I apprehend, to his insolent declaration that England had ceased to be a political power.

This remark she frequently made, showing it was the leading idea of her mind.

I got here at 1/4 to 6, and was summoned to the presence exactly at 6. . . . When I cd. get to general business, tho' I had an awful catalogue of demands and suggestions, they were comparatively soon exhausted: no difficulties made, everything granted, nothing but smiles and infinite *agaceries*. . . .

There were only courtiers at dinner. After din., altho' I had been in audience till 1/2 pt. 7, the Faery came up to me again, and was not only most gracious, but most interesting and amusing: all about domestic affairs. She shewed me, by the bye, at dinner, a couple of tels. she had received that morning from P[rince] of W[ales], and she wished me to write to him about Suez and all that. 'I wish it,' she sd., 'because he likes you.'

Lady Biddulph said after dinner she shd. resign if the Primo dined often there, as she cd. not stand while the Faery was talking to me. . . .

The Times has only got half the news, and very inaccurate, but it is evidently staggered. I believe the whole country will be with me. The Faery thinks so. . . .

XI

THE BALFOUR DECLARATION: A FOOTNOTE TO DANIEL DERONDA

The Foreign Secretary to Lionel Walter Rothschild

Foreign Office
2nd November 1917

Dear Lord Rothschild,

I have much pleasure in conveying to you, on behalf of His Majesty's Government, the following declaration of sympathy with Jewish Zionist aspirations which has been submitted to, and approved by, the Cabinet:—

> "His Majesty's Government view with favour the establishment in Palestine of a national home for the Jewish people, and will use their best endeavours to facilitate the achievement of this object, it being clearly understood that nothing shall be done which may prejudice the civil and religious rights of existing non-Jewish communities in Palestine, or the rights and political status enjoyed by Jews in any other country."

I should be grateful if you would bring this declaration to the knowledge of the Zionist Federation,

Yours sincerely,
Arthur James Balfour

Notes

NOTES TO CHAPTER ONE

1. Walter Allen, *The English Novel* (New York, 1957), p. 168.

2. F. R. Leavis, *The Great Tradition* (London, 1948), p. 10 n. For Trollope's comment, see *The Autobiography of Anthony Trollope* (World's Classics, London, 1928), pp. 235–37.

3. Helene von Racowitza, *Meine Beziehungen zu Ferdinand Lassalle* (Breslau, 1879). A more tepid version of the incident, written by the Princess von Racowitza at a much later date, is available in English: *An Autobiography,* trans. Cecil Mar (New York, 1910), pp. 67–180. The literature on the Lassalle-Doenniges episode is considerable; *vide* esp. Elizabeth E. Evans, *Ferdinand Lassalle and Helene von Doenniges* (London, 1897); George Brandes, *Ferdinand Lassalle* (New York, 1911), pp. 200–14; Arno Schirokauer, *Lassalle,* trans. Eden and Cedar Paul (New York, 1932), pp. 288–98; Edmund Wilson, *To the Finland Station* (New York, 1940), pp. 249 ff.; David Footman, *The Primrose Path* (London, 1946), pp. 209–39; and H. W. Haeusermann, *The Genevese Background* (London, 1952), pp. 182–98. Ina Britschgi-Schimmer, *Lassalles Letzte Tage* (Berlin, 1925), provides letters and documents relating to the affair; Erwin Kohn, *Lassalle der Fuehrer, Imago IX* (Leipzig, 1926), 50–70, treats it from the psychoanalytic standpoint; and H. W. Hewett-Thayer, "Ferdinand Lassalle in the Novels of Spielhagen and Meredith," *Germanic Review,* XIX (1944), discusses its reflection in nineteenth-century fiction.

4. Montagu F. Modder, *The Jew in the Literature of England* (Philadelphia, 1944), p. vii. The full-length studies on which I draw include David Philipson, *The Jew in English Fiction* (Cincinnati, 1889); Edward N. Calisch, *The Jew in English Literature as Author and Subject* (Richmond, 1909); Gerald Friedlander, *Shakespeare and the Jew* (London, 1921); J. L. Cardozo, *The Contemporary Jew in Elizabethan Drama* (Amsterdam, 1925); M. J. Landa, *The Jew in Drama* (London, 1926); Hijman Michelson, *The Jew in Early English Literature* (Amsterdam, 1926); and H. R. S. Van Der Veen, *Jewish Characters in Eighteenth Century English Fiction and Drama* (Groningen, 1935).

5. *The Jews* (Boston, 1922), p. 135. The same conclusion is urged by Lauriat Lane, Jr., who has written much the best recent essay on Fagin ("Dickens' Archetypal Jews," *PMLA,* LXXXIII [1957], 95–100). Lane locates the problem not in *Oliver Twist* but in *Our Mutual Friend,* the novel about the pious Riah, of whom he observes that Dickens took all the wind out of him by

placing beside him a set of characters (the Veneerings, Lammles, and their sort) who are unmistakably odious Jews, though Dickens, having Riah there as explicit apologist, refrains from calling them Jews: "unwitting and deeply held bias and prejudice," writes Lane, "have run directly counter to what the author conceived his conscious intention to be." *Vide* also Lane's "*Oliver Twist*: A Revision," *Times Literary Supplement,* July 20, 1951, p. 460, which provoked Roth's rejoinder, below.

6. "Dickens: The Two Scrooges," in *The Wound and the Bow: Seven Studies in Literature* (Boston, 1941), p. 64.

7. *Dickens, Dali and Others* (New York, 1946), p. 78. The sentence has been cited approvingly by almost every writer on the subject, but now Cecil Roth has rightly alerted us to its defectiveness by submitting ("Oliver Twist," *Times Literary Supplement,* August 3, 1951, p. 485) that while there were plenty of Jewish fences in Dickens's day, he had yet to discover the Jewish prototype of "Fagin's educational institution." And until that is found, Dickens's portrayal of Fagin will have to be accepted as surpassing the limits of verisimilitude, and his explanation for Fagin will be received with skepticism.

8. "Dickens, Fagin, and Mr. Riah," *Commentary,* IX (1950), 47–50; *vide* also Dickens, *Letters,* Nonesuch Dickens (London, 1937–38), XII, 357. The Dickens-Davis correspondence has been reprinted in full in Cecil Roth, *Anglo-Jewish Letters* (London, 1938), pp. 304–9.

9. *The Jew in English Literature,* p. 23.

10. *The Jew in Drama,* pp. 170 ff.

11. Kronenberger in "The Jewish Writer and the English Literary Tradition: A Symposium," *Commentary,* VIII (1949), 212; Calisch, *The Jew in English Literature,* pp. 64 and 75; Philipson, *The Jew in English Fiction,* p. 19.

NOTES TO CHAPTER TWO

1. A. W. Pollard, *English Miracle Plays* (Oxford, 1909), p. xxxiii. *Vide* also Katherine Lee Bates, *The English Religious Drama* (New York, 1895), pp. 241–54, and M. J. Landa, *The Jew in Drama,* pp. 36–46.

2. Quoted in E. E. Stoll, "Shylock," *Shakespeare Studies* (New York, 1927), p. 255. Landa, *The Jew in Drama,* p. 11, notes that the stage-Jew "forms an absolute link between the profane drama that was 'sacred' and the secular plays that were soon to be dubbed profane by the Puritans. Barabas, in presentation at any rate, was but Judas in a different setting, and so was Shylock for a century and a half after his creation."

3. The first reference to Jews in England occurs in Bede, in connection with the paschal practice of the Jews; *vide Ecclesiastical History* (Loeb Classical Library, London, 1930), I, 345. Although Jews are mentioned in the ecclesiastical laws of both Theodore of Canterbury and Ecgberth, which forbade Christians to have intercourse with Jews, E. A. Freeman, in his *History of the Norman Conquest* (New York, 1876), p. 547, suggests that these canons are copied from the decrees of ancient councils and cannot be taken as proving the presence of Jews at the time of promulgation. G. M. Trevelyan, *History of England* (London, 1929), p. 187, maintains that whether they were present or not, the Jews could scarcely have been active as money-lenders before William

had provided the necessary legal and administrative groundwork. For thorough discussions of the Jews in England from the Conquest to their expulsion in 1290, *vide* Heinrich Graetz, *History of the Jews* (Philadelphia, 1891–92), III, 400 ff., and Joseph Jacobs, *Jews of Angevin England* (London, 1893).

4. John Speed, *History of Great Britaine,* 3d ed. (London, 1650), p. 483, as quoted in Calisch, *The Jew in English Literature,* p. 22. Holinshed's oddly sympathetic account of the coronation-day disaster is transcribed in Appendix III.

5. Geoffrey Chaucer, *The Canterbury Tales,* in *Works,* ed. W. W. Skeat (Oxford, 1900), IV, 182, 184. A full study of the Hugh of Lincoln incident is given in Joseph Jacobs, *Jewish Ideals and Other Essays* (London, 1896), pp. 192–224. Carleton Brown, "Chaucer's *Prioresses Tale* and Its Analogues," *PMLA,* XXI (1906), 486–518, lists some fifteen analogues of Chaucer's tale, a number of which antedate the affair at Lincoln, each of the stories centering on "the murder of a boy by the Jews because he sang an anthem in praise of the Virgin, and the miracles wrought in his case." Earlier ritual murders were reported at Gloucester in 1160 and at Bury St. Edmunds in 1162.

6. Quoted in Michelson, *The Jew in Early English Literature,* p. 22.

7. "The Ballad of Gernutus" is reprinted in the New Arden edition of *The Merchant of Venice,* ed. John Russell Brown (London, 1955), pp. 153–55.

8. A. E. H. Swaen has edited Robert Daborne's *A Christian Turn'd Turk,* see *Anglia,* XX (1898). Daborne's play is incidentally interesting as the earliest extant English drama to present a receiver of stolen goods. Cardozo, *The Contemporary Jew in the Elizabethan Drama,* pp. 141–78, thoroughly discusses this and other proto-Shylock plays. For sources and analogues of the flesh-penalty story, *vide* Cardozo, pp. 235–95, and the same author's "The Background of Shakespeare's *Merchant of Venice,*" *English Studies,* XIV (1932), 177–86; also S. A. Small, "'The Jew,'" *Modern Language Review,* XXVI (1931), 281–87; E. A. J. Honigmann, "Shakespeare's Lost Source-Plays," *Modern Language Review,* XLIX (1954), 293–307; and Heinrich Graetz, *Shylock in der Sage, im Drama und in der Geschichte* (Krotoschin, 1889), the last-named discussing English and German analogues of the flesh-bond story in medieval and Renaissance literature. The standard background work, which takes the above studies into account, is Geoffrey Bullough, *Narrative and Dramatic Sources of Shakespeare* (London, 1957), I, 445–514.

9. Christopher Marlowe, *The Jew of Malta,* V, i, 81–82; III, iv, 91–101. All references are by act, scene, and lines to the Case Marlowe, ed. H. S. Bennett (New York, 1931). In my comments here and below I am indebted to Harry Levin, *The Overreacher: A Study of Christopher Marlowe* (Cambridge, Mass., 1952), pp. 55–80.

10. John Marston, *The Malcontent,* V, ii, 226–27; in *Works,* ed. A. H. Bullen (London, 1887), I, 305.

11. John Webster, *The Devil's Law-Case,* III, ii, 7–11; in *Complete Works,* ed. F. L. Lucas (London, 1927), II, 270.

12. James Howell, *Epistolae,* ed. Joseph Jacobs (London, 1890), p. 313.

13. *Jew of Malta,* II, iii, 191–99.

14. A. B. Stonex, "The Usurer in Elizabethan Drama," *PMLA,* XXXI (1916), 191. On the subject of the usurer in Shakespeare and his contemporaries, *vide ibid.,* pp. 190–210; Stoll, *Shakespeare Studies,* pp. 255–336; Celeste Turner Wright, "Some Conventions Regarding the Usurer in Elizabethan Literature,"

Studies in Philology, XXXI (1934), 176–97; E. C. Pettet, "*The Merchant of Venice* and the Problem of Usury," *Essays and Studies,* XXXI (1945), 19–33. Thomas Wilson's *A Discourse Upon Usury,* ed. R. H. Tawney (London, 1925), presents the Elizabethan point of view on the subject. *Vide* also Cecil Roth, "The Background of Shylock," *Review of English Studies,* IX (1933), 148–56. The following pages are heavily indebted to the articles by Pettet, Stonex, and Wright, which admirably complement each other, Pettet providing the historical background to the usury problem, Stonex tracing the dramatic plot-conventions of the usurer-plays, and Wright analyzing the psychological traits which have been traditionally foisted on the figure of the stage money-lender.

15. It must be remembered that only about a dozen Elizabethan and Jacobean dramas prominently deal with Jews, compared with the sixty-odd plays dealing with usurers. The chief Jew-plays are Robert Wilson's *Three Ladies of London* (1583); Marlowe's *Jew of Malta* (?1589); Greene's *Selimus* (1594); Shakespeare's *Merchant of Venice* (1596); *The Travails of Three Brothers* by Day, Rowley, and Wilkins (1607); Daborne's *A Christian Turn'd Turk* (1610); Fletcher's *Custom of the Country* (1622); and Thomas Goffe's *The Raging Turk* (1627). *Vide* Cardozo, *The Contemporary Jew in Elizabethan Drama,* pp. 141–78; Michelson, *The Jew in Early English Literature,* pp. 66–96; and Landa, *The Jew in Drama,* pp. 36–55, 86–104.

16. In *Essays and Studies,* XXXI, 25.

17. Stoll, *Shakespeare Studies,* pp. 289–93, discusses the patristic attitude toward Jewry. Benevenutoa Imola's remarks on the subject are cited by Arthur Quiller-Couch, "Introduction," *Merchant of Venice,* New Cambridge Shakespeare (Cambridge, 1926), p. xiv; and the pertinent passage in Dante's *Inferno* appears in Canto XIV, ll. 37–39. R. H. Tawney, *Religion and the Rise of Capitalism,* remains one of the standard works on the subject of usury from the general economic point of view.

18. Pettet, in *Essays and Studies,* XXXI, 20.

19. Wright, in *Studies in Philology,* XXXI, 190.

20. Sir Israel Gollancz, *Allegory and Mysticism in Shakespeare: A Medievalist on 'The Merchant of Venice'* (London, 1931), proposes an almost purely allegorical interpretation of the play, Portia figuring variously as Mercy, Salvation, *Grâce Dieu,* and the Church. The basic situation in *The Merchant,* in Gollancz's reading, suggests that a medieval homilist may have combined a number of Scriptural texts and woven them into exemplary stories—e.g., the texts "Greater love hath no man than this, that he should lay down his life for his friend"; and "Christ also loved the Church and gave Himself for it." Citing the passage from the *Ancrene Riwle* which deals with the wooing of Christ as an intermediate analogue, Gollancz thinks that Bassanio may be engaged on a pilgrimage to liberate and woo the Lady, and that "in his quest for Portia, [he] has points of contact with Spenser's Red Cross Knight in search of Una" (p. 56).

21. In *Essays and Studies,* XXXI, 27–29.

22. *Jew of Malta,* I, i, 104–5; II, ii, 54; *The Merchant of Venice,* II, viii, 15. All references are by act, scene, and lines to the New Arden edition, ed. John Russell Brown (London, 1955).

23. *Jew of Malta,* IV, i, 370–73; *Merchant of Venice,* IV, i, 370–73; II, vii, 61–69. Naturally Barabas and Shylock differ somewhat in their attitude

toward money, in proportion as their characters are conceived on a different scale. Harry Levin, *The Overreacher,* p. 72, notes that "Legalism both narrows and humanizes Shylock, in contradistinction to Barabas, who for the most part lives outside the law and does not clamor for it until it has overtaken him" (p. 72). Cf. also Philip Henderson, *Christopher Marlowe* (Bibliographical Series, London, 1956), p. 23: "The assuaging element of humanity is quite absent from [*The Jew of Malta*], which is nearer in spirit to Jonson's *Volpone* than Shakespeare's *Merchant of Venice.*"

24. *Merchant of Venice,* IV, i, 3–5.

25. Jeremy Bentham, "Defense of Usury," in *Works,* ed. John Bowring (London, 1838–43), III, 17.

26. In *Studies in Philology,* XXXI, 178.

27. *Jew of Malta,* III, iii, 125–26; *Merchant of Venice,* II, ii, 107–8; Ben Jonson, *Staple of News,* V, ii, in *Works,* eds. C. H. Herford, Percy and Evelyn Simpson (Oxford, 1925–52), VI, 371.

28. Stonex, in *PMLA,* XXXI, 197.

29. *Ibid.,* p. 198.

30. *Vide* Beatrix D. Brown, "Medieval Prototypes of Lorenzo and Jessica," *Modern Language Notes,* XLIV (1929), 227–32, and James L. Wilson, "Another Medieval Parallel to the Jessica and Lorenzo Story," *Shakespeare Association Bulletin,* XXXIII (1948), pp. 20–23.

31. By Nevill Coghill, "The Governing Idea," *Shakespeare Quarterly,* I (1948), 9–17.

32. Wright, in *Studies in Philology,* XXXI, 190.

33. *Ibid.,* pp. 192–94. Examples of death by hanging occur in Robert Wilson's *Three Ladies of London,* Haughton's *Englishmen for My Money,* Brome's *English Moor,* and Middleton's *Trick to Catch the Old One.*

34. *Ibid.,* p. 196.

35. *Jew of Malta,* IV, iv, 167–68.

36. E.g., *Splendeurs et misères; La maison Tellier; Mademoiselle Fifi; A Rebours; Paris; Du côté de Guermantes.*

37. *Prioress's Tale,* ll. 181–82; *Confessio Amantis,* bk. VII, 3207 ff.; *Jew of Malta,* V, v, 65–89; *Merchant of Venice,* IV, 1; *Oliver Twist,* chap. lii.

38. Stoll, *Shakespeare Studies*: "Shylock's being unwell is received as would be a similar plea from a bully at school, just worsted in a fight" (p. 322).

NOTES TO CHAPTER THREE

1. Richard Cumberland, *The Jew: A Comedy,* 4th ed. (London, 1795), p. 75. Full-length treatments of Richard Cumberland's life and work are by Stanley T. Williams, *Richard Cumberland* (New Haven, 1917), and Kurt Fehler, *Richard Cumberlands Leben und dramatische Werke* (Erlangen, 1911), the latter containing elaborate synopses of Cumberland's major comedies. More recent discussions of Cumberland's contributions to the mythology of the Jew may be found in Landa, *The Jew in Drama,* pp. 128–42, and H. R. S. Van der Veen, *Jewish Characters,* pp. 219–40. For Cumberland's position in literary history, *vide* esp. Ernest Bernbaum, *The Drama of Sensibility* (Cambridge, 1925), pp. 237–41, and Landa, "The Grandfather of Melodrama," *Cornhill Magazine,* N. S. LIX (1925), 476–84.

2. *Vide* Herbert Carrington, *Die Figur des Juden in der dramatischen Literatur des XVIII. Jahrhunderts* (Heidelberg, 1897), pp. 31 ff.

3. *Memoirs of Richard Cumberland, Written by Himself With Illustrative Notes by Henry Flanders* (Philadelphia, 1856), p. 141. Hereafter cited as *Memoirs.*

4. Landa, *Cornhill Magazine,* N.S. LIX, 477 ff., submits that Cumberland understood the principles of melodrama and practiced the genre some thirty years before Holcroft, whose *Tale of Mystery,* produced in 1802, is usually cited as the first melodrama to be staged in England. For a thorough discussion of the element of contrast as it provides the basis of melodramatic fiction, *vide* Walter C. Phillips, *Dickens, Reade, and Collins: Sensation Novelists* (New York, 1919), pp. 130 ff.

5. Bernbaum, *The Drama of Sensibility,* p. 238.

6. *Ibid.*

7. *Memoirs,* pp. 141–42.

8. *Ibid.,* p. 122. The pertinent characters and dramas are Major O'Flaherty in Cumberland's *The West Indian* (1771); Foigard in Farquhar's *The Beaux' Stratagem* (1707); the Irish and Scottish apprentices in Murphy's *The Apprentice* (1756); Captain O'Cutter in Colman's *The Jealous Wife* (1761); Sir Peter Pepperpot in Foote's *The Patron* (1764). *Vide* Bernbaum, *The Drama of Sensibility,* pp. 239–41 and 239 n. An extensive discussion of *The West Indian* is given in Fehler, *Richard Cumberlands Leben,* pp. 101–7.

9. *Memoirs,* p. 175. On Cumberland's early comedies, including *The Fashionable Lover, vide* Stanley T. Williams, "The Early Sentimental Dramas of Richard Cumberland," *Modern Language Notes,* XXXVI (1921), 160–65.

10. *The Fashionable Lover: A Comedy* (London, 1772), p. 42.

11. *The British Essayists,* ed. James Ferguson (London, 1819), XXXIX, 254–76. The Pedrosa papers are discussed in Louis I. Newman, *Richard Cumberland: Critic and Friend of the Jews* (New York, 1919), pp. 20 ff. Van der Veen, *Jewish Characters,* pp. 65–69, deals with Cumberland's extra-dramatic contributions to the humanitarian movement.

12. *British Essayists,* XXXVIII, 273–321.

13. Landa, *The Jew in Drama,* p. 31, suggests that Cumberland was forced to hide behind the *nom de plume* because he could not, in his own name, impute to his fellow-playwrights an offense of which he himself had been guilty in *The Fashionable Lover.*

14. Sheva's historical and literary prototypes have been variously identified as Abraham Goldsmid, the English financier and philanthropist (by Newman, *Richard Cumberland,* pp. 46–50); Baron Ephraim Lopez Pereira d'Aguilar, a benevolent Jewish eccentric (by Landa, *The Jew in Drama,* p. 138); the character of Joshua Manasseh in Smollett's *Ferdinand Count Fathom,* the first sympathetic Jew in English fiction (by Van der Veen, *Jewish Characters,* pp. 235–36). Van der Veen suggests as a further indirect source the portrayal of a kindly Polish Jew in Christian Gellert's novel *Life of the Swedish Countess de G***,* published in 1746 and translated into English one year before the appearance of Smollett's novel. Edward D. Coleman, "Jewish Prototypes in American and English *Romans* and *Drames à Clef,*" *Publications of the American Jewish Historical Society,* No. 35 (1939), 234–35, summarizes the conjectural sources of Sheva.

15. Carrington, *Die Figur des Juden,* p. 47, notes that in a German adaptation of *The Jew* undertaken in 1798, Sheva's miserly traits have been softened to lend the Jew a greater degree of dignity. "Wo Cumberlands Schewa . . den Entschluss aeussert, an dem Dampf von der Kueche eines Aldermans sich satt zu essen, sagt Moses (so heisst der Jude in der Bearbeitung), er muesse seine Ausgaben fuer sich noch sparsamer einrichten." Jabal's role (*infra*) is correspondingly attenuated: "Auch nehmen die komischen Bemerkungen des hungrigen Dieners des Juden keinen so breiten Raum in der deutschen Bearbeitung ein, wie im Englischen." Responsible for the serious conception of the German stage-Jew was, no doubt, Lessing's *Nathan* (1779), which was of a far more consistently didactic and philosophical order than anything the English dramatists, with their long-standing tradition of buffoonery, had to offer. Lessing's youthful *Die Juden* (1754) retained some of the comic features familiar to the English playgoer. *Vide* Paul Philemon Kies, "Lessing's Relation to Early English Sentimental Comedy," *PMLA,* XLVII (1932), 807–26, in which Cibber, Steele, and Edward Moore are cited as sources for Lessing's early one-acters. *Vide* also the same author's "The Source of Lessing's *Die Juden,*" *Philological Quarterly,* VI (1927), 406–10, relating Lessing's early dramatic techniques to Vanbrugh's in *The Relapse* and Farquhar's in *The Beaux' Stratagem.* Conversely, Lessing's critical influence in England is treated in Curtis C. D. Vail, *Lessing's Relation to the English Language and Literature,* Columbia University Germanic Studies, No. 3 (1936). The study fails to take account of Cumberland's play, however.

16. *Jewish Characters,* p. 233.

17. But, as pointed out in Newman, *Richard Cumberland,* pp. 26–27, *The Jew of Mogadore* also bears several striking points of resemblance to *Nathan.* Both plays are set in the Orient and emphasize the confluence of the three great monotheistic religions: Moslem, Jewish, and Christian. In his parable of the three rings, Nadab, like Nathan, poses as a rational universalist who discovers the same source behind all religions and finds them on that account equally justified. For discussions of *The Jew of Mogadore, vide* Stanley T. Williams, *Richard Cumberland,* pp. 265–66; Newman, *Richard Cumberland,* pp. 22–28. A consideration of Lessing falls beyond the limits of this study, but the following materials may be consulted in the context of the Jew-question. On the Jewish sources and prototypes of *Nathan*: August Wuensche, "Der Ursprung der Parabel von den drei Ringen," *Lessing-Mendelssohn-Gedenkbuch* (Leipzig, 1879), pp. 325–49; Kuno Fischer, *Lessing als Reformator der deutschen Literatur* (Stuttgart, 1881); David Friedrich Strauss, *Lessings Nathan der Weise* (Berlin, 1864). M. Kayserling, *Moses Mendelssohn,* 2d ed. (Leipzig, 1888), pp. 338–52, and Fr. Albrecht, *Moses Mendelssohn als Urbild von Lessings Nathan dem Weisen* (Ulm, 1864), discuss the Jewish philosopher's claim to be the prototype of Nathan. Heinrich Duentzer, *Lessings Nathan der Weise* (Leipzig, 1894), provides a textual analysis. Adolf Bartels's *Lessing und die Juden,* 2d ed. (Dresden, 1934), has an adventitious documentary interest as giving a proto-Fascist view of Lessing's relation to the Jews.

18. *Jewish Characters,* p. 236. Fehler, *Richard Cumberlands Leben,* p. 112, dismisses Sheva as "ein Paradoxon." Williams, *Richard Cumberland,* p. 235, notes that "to the modern reader Sheva can seem only ludicrous."

19. *Memoirs,* pp. 340, 304.

20. Dickens, *Our Mutual Friend,* The Nonesuch Dickens, ed. Arthur Waugh *et al.* (London, 1937–38), IX, 819.

21. *The Jew in English Fiction,* p. 96.

22. *Infra,* Chap. IV.

23. W. H. G. Armytage, "Little Woman: Maria Edgeworth," *Queen's Quarterly,* LVI (1949), 251. Serious critical material on Maria Edgeworth is extremely inadequate and her treatment of Jews has never, so far as I know, been systematically explored. Augustus J. C. Hare, *The Life and Letters of Maria Edgeworth* (Boston, 1895), is a standard source of subsequent studies. Three full-length discussions of her work are by Emily Lawless, *Maria Edgeworth* (English Men of Letters, London, 1904); Grace A. Oliver, *A Study of Maria Edgeworth, with Notices of Her Father and Friends* (Boston, 1892); and Helen Zimmern, *Maria Edgeworth* (Boston, 1883). More useful is the brief recent study by P. H. Newby, *Maria Edgeworth* (English Novelists, London, 1950). Theodore Goodman's *Maria Edgeworth: Novelist of Reason* (New York, 1936) has been unavailable to me. The following pages are indebted to Newby and the relatively summarial treatment found in Modder, *The Jew in the Literature of England,* pp. 132 ff.

24. Quoted in Newby, *Maria Edgeworth,* pp. 73, 6.

25. Maria Edgeworth, *Tales of Fashionable Life* (London, 1815), I, v. An entertaining sketch of Richard Lovell Edgeworth is contained in Virginia Woolf, "Lives of the Obscure: Taylors and Edgeworths," *The Common Reader* (London, 1929), pp. 146–60. *Vide* also Lawless, *Maria Edgeworth,* pp. 16–30; Newby, *Maria Edgeworth,* pp. 10–20; and Oliver, *A Study of Maria Edgeworth,* pp. 1–89 and *passim.* The best study on the didactic and sentimental vogue in fiction at the turn of the century remains J. M. S. Tompkins, *The Popular Novel in England: 1770 to 1800* (London, 1932).

26. Edgeworth, "The Good Aunt," in *Tales and Novels* (London, 1832), II, 217–33.

27. Norman A. Jeffares, "Introduction," *Castle Rackrent and Other Stories* (London, 1953), p. xv.

28. "The Prussian Vase," in *Tales and Novels,* II, 168–215.

29. *The Jew in the Literature of England,* p. 132.

30. For example: Cumberland's *Fashionable Lover*; Edgeworth's "The Good Aunt" (*infra*); *Oliver Twist*; Kingsley's *Alton Locke*. Edgeworth draws attention to this paradox in *Harrington.*

31. *Maria Edgeworth,* p. 86.

32. *Jewish Characters,* p. 34n.

33. "Murad the Unlucky," in *Tales and Novels,* V, 1–52.

34. *The Jew in the Literature of England,* p. 132.

35. Edgeworth, *The Absentee,* in *Tales of Fashionable Life,* IV.

36. Edgeworth, *Castle Rackrent and Other Stories* (London, 1953).

37. Newby, *Maria Edgeworth,* p. 39. The new interest in regional fiction is discussed in Tompkins, *The Popular Novel in England,* pp. 187 ff.

38. Edgeworth, *Harrington,* Vol. I of *Harrington and Ormond: Tales* (London, 1817).

39. The "extremely well written" plea came in 1816 from a Miss Rachel Mordechai, later Mrs. Lazarus, of Virginia, and initiated a correspondence that was to cover twenty-three years. Edgeworth to Mrs. Lazarus under date of April 9, 1824: "I forget whether in any of your letters you ever mentioned to me a novel of Sir W. Scott's (*Ivanhoe*) in which there is a charming Jewess Rebecca. . . ." *Vide* Harriet J. Butler and Harold Edgeworth Butler, "Sir Walter Scott and Maria Edgeworth: Some Unpublished Letters," *Modern Language Review,* XXIII (1928), 296 ff. On the origin of *Harrington,* see also Hare, *The Life and Letters of Maria Edgeworth,* I, 250.

40. *The Jew in the Literature of England,* pp. 136–37. Similarly Zimmern, *Maria Edgeworth,* p. 168: "Miss Edgeworth had set herself to work out a moral, this time an apology for Jews. It was written to suggestion, and was on a theme that lay entirely outside the domain of her experience. . . . her zeal outran her judgment; her elaborate apology is feeble; and if the Jews needed vindication they could hardly be flattered by one of this nature." Other critics slight the book even more: Newby, *Maria Edgeworth,* p. 71, dismisses it in half a sentence as "not a novel to take very seriously"; Lawless, in one of the standard studies on Edgeworth, makes no mention of the novel at all.

41. On the historical background to the Jewish Naturalization Bill, *vide* Sir Walter Besant, *History of the Eighteenth Century* (London, 1902), pp. 177–80; Van der Veen, *Jewish Characters,* pp. 43–45. An interesting opinion on the repeal of the Jew Bill is registered by the Earl of Chesterfield, who writes under date of November 26, 1753: "The Ministers here, intimidated by the absurd and groundless clamours of the mob, have, very weakly, in my opinion, repealed this session the Bill which they had passed the last, for rendering Jews capable of being naturalized, by subsequent Acts of Parliament. . . . Wise and honest governors will never, if they can help it, give the people just cause to complain; but then, on the other hand, they will firmly withstand groundless clamour. Besides that, this noise against the Jew Bill proceeds from the narrow mob-spirit of intoleration in religious, and inhospitality in civil matters, both which all wise governments should oppose." *Letters* (London, 1892), II, 591. The Gordon Riots are described in chap. xv of *Harrington* and chaps. xlviii ff. of *Barnaby Rudge*. *Vide* also Israel Solomons, "Lord George Gordon and Judaism," *Journal of the Jewish Historical Society of England,* VII (1911), 222–71.

42. Macklin's revolutionary interpretation of Shylock as a pathetic figure, which supposedly led Pope to extemporize "This is the Jew / which Shakespeare drew," dates from 1741. For a discussion of Macklin's Jew, *vide* W. Cooke, *Memoirs of Charles Macklin, Comedian* (London, 1804), pp. 91 ff.; Landa, *The Jew in Drama,* pp. 111–14; Van der Veen, *Jewish Characters,* pp. 134 ff.

43. On Abraham Goldsmid, consult Newman, *Richard Cumberland,* p. 48. On Sir Sampson Gideon, see Modder, *The Jew in the Literature of England,* pp. 47–48; Landa, *The Jew in Drama,* pp. 122–23. Horace Walpole amusingly relates Gideon's conversion in a letter to Bentley, July 9, 1754. A good account of Smollett's Jews is given in Van der Veen, *Jewish Characters,* pp. 37–50. For the sake of completeness, mention ought to be made of a good Jew chronologically halfway between Smollett and Edgeworth, who appears in a now forgotten novel of 1796, George Walker's *Theodore Cyphon, or the Benevolent*

Jew. The book is briefly alluded to by Tompkins, *The Popular Novel in England,* p. 180 n, and Modder, p. 148. I depend on these sources for my information of the novel, which is not available to me. According to Tompkins, the Jew, who seems to be modeled on Sheva, has no dramatic function in the novel; he merely acts as the protagonist's confidant "and satisfies the public taste for the sympathetic portraiture of outcasts." Modder cites a parallel to *Ivanhoe*; like Isaac, the Benevolent Jew has a daughter who nurses the Christian hero. The novel was successfully reissued in 1823, riding the wave of *Ivanhoe*'s popularity.

44. *The Jew in the Literature of England,* p. 136.

45. "The Birthday Present" and "Waste Not, Want Not" appear in Edgeworth's first collection, *The Parent's Assistant* (1796), in *Tales and Novels,* I.

46. Hare, *The Life and Letters of Maria Edgeworth,* I, 255.

47. Calisch, *The Jew in English Literature,* p. 128; Philipson, *The Jew in English Fiction,* p. 102. *Vide* also *infra,* Chap. X.

48. This view is urged in Maude Frank, "The Jew in English Fiction," *Critic,* XXXIX (1901), 79–81.

49. *Infra,* Chap. VI.

50. Compare *All the Year Round,* XVI (1867), 31: "The Character of the Jews has too long been wronged by Christian communities. We take old-clothes men and thieves—there being none such among Christians of course—as the types of an ancient, refined, and charitable people." See Philipp Aronstein, "Dickens' religioese Ansichten," *Anglia,* N.S. VI (1896), 222–47.

NOTES TO CHAPTER FOUR

1. Wilmon Brewer, *Shakespeare's Influence on Sir Walter Scott* (Boston, 1925), p. 300.

2. Jeffrey, "Ivanhoe, A Romance," *Edinburgh Review,* XXXIII (1820), 53.

3. *The Jew in English Fiction,* p. 76.

4. How great an impression the Jewish group made on the contemporary public can be judged from the titles of the adaptations and sequels. Thomas Seccombe, " 'Ivanhoe,' " *Times Literary Supplement,* December 18, 1919, writes: "Few titles in the English Catalogue have attracted such a tail of parasitic publications, abbreviations, illustrations, school classics, shorthand editions, Famous books and Hundred Books issues, American versions, translations and adaptations, almost without number, such as *The Jew of York, The Jew and his Daughter, The Knight Templar, Rebecca the Jewess, The Templar and the Jewess, The Return from the Crusade in 1194, The Black Knight, . . . The Maid of Judah, Il Templario, The Hebrew, Les Normands*—not to speak of *Rebecca and Rowena.*"

5. Scott's ignorance of the Middle Ages has been questioned by Edith Batho, "Scott as a Medievalist," *Sir Walter Scott Today: Some Retrospective Essays and Studies,* ed. H. J. C. Grierson (London, 1932), pp. 133–57, and by Hugh Walpole, "The Historical Novel in England Since Sir Walter Scott," *Sir Walter Scott Today,* pp. 164–65. Una Pope-Hennessy, *Sir Walter Scott* (English Novelists, London, 1948), pp. 69–74, argues that Scott's familiarity with Catholic practices deepened in the course of his career: "The uncertainty displayed in [his early approach] is very different from the assurance manifested in *Ivanhoe.*"

For the majority speaks Sir Herbert Grierson, *Sir Walter Scott, Bart.* (New York, 1938), p. 199: "Scott had got outside his own range of historical understanding. The Middle Ages were for him the Ages of Chivalry. Their animating spirit, that of the Catholic Church, he understood too little to modify the conventional Protestant conviction, in which he had grown up, that it was 'a degrading superstition.' "

6. Walter Bagehot, "The Waverley Novels," in *Works and Life,* ed. Mrs. Russell Barrington (London, 1915), III, 57.

7. Allen, "Sir Walter Scott," *Six Great Novelists* (London, 1955), p. 83; Buchan, *Sir Walter Scott* (London, 1932), p. 198; Cecil, *Sir Walter Scott* (London, 1933), p. 51; Daiches, "Scott's Achievement as a Novelist," *Nineteenth-Century Fiction,* VI (1951), 166.

8. Bagehot, in *Works and Life,* III, 58; Grierson, *Sir Walter Scott, Bart.,* p. 182; Pope-Hennessy, *Sir Walter Scott,* p. 93. The general animosity against *Ivanhoe,* the suspicion that all this noisy braggadocio will not do, is nothing positively startling. Even Ruskin, it may be remembered, who singled out Scott as the one clear mirror of fair fictionists in a century distinguished for its sordor and disease, found *Ivanhoe* "deeply wounded through all its bright panoply," addressed, he thought, to the same depraved reading public which sought its likeness in the dirty sweepings from the Pentonville bus-lines. *Vide* "Fiction Fair and Foul," in *Works,* Library Edition, eds. E. T. Cook and Alexander Wedderburn (London, 1903–12), XXXIV, 291: "The public has . . . foolishly praised the horrors of *Ravenswood* and the nonsense of *Ivanhoe*; because the modern public finds in the torture and adventures of these the kind of excitement which it seeks in an opera." It may be remarked that Coleridge, too, lumped *Ivanhoe* together with the "Bride of Ravensmuir, or whatever its name may be"—"two wretched abortions." Quoted in Edward Wagenknecht, *Cavalcade of the English Novel* (New York, 1954), p. 157.

9. In *Nineteenth-Century Fiction,* VI, 58, 94.

10. "We should be . . . inclined to describe a romance as 'a fictitious narrative in prose or verse; the interest of which turns upon marvellous and uncommon incidents'; being thus opposed to the kindred term Novel, which Johnson has described as a 'smooth tale, generally of love'; but which we would rather define as a fictitious narrative, differing from the romance, because the events are accommodated to the ordinary trains of human events, and the modern state of society." Scott, "On Romance," *Essays on Chivalry, Romance and the Drama* (London, n.d.), p. 226.

11. I am indebted for the following remarks to the article by Daiches, in *Nineteenth-Century Fiction,* VI, 81–95 and 153–73, and to Joseph E. Duncan, "The Anti-Romantic in *'Ivanhoe,'*" *Nineteenth-Century Fiction,* IX (1955), 293–300.

12. Quoted in R. H. Gordon, "Scott and the 'Comédie Humaine,'" *Sir Walter Scott Today,* p. 59.

13. All quotations are from the two-volume *Ivanhoe* in the Border Edition of the Waverley Novels, ed. Andrew Lang (London, 1892–94), vols. XVI–XVII.

14. In *Edinburgh Review,* XXXI, 27.

15. See Jared Wenger, "Character-Types of Scott, Balzac, Dickens, Zola," *PMLA,* LXII (1947), 213–32.

16. In *The Betrothed,* in which the same tensions between Saxons and Normans are presented, Scott creates a female counterpart to Cedric in Lady Ermengarde, who "looked with contempt and hatred on all innovations that had been introduced since the battle of Hastings." *Vide* Sir John Marriott, *English History in English Fiction* (London, 1940), pp. 51–52.

17. In *Nineteenth-Century Fiction,* IX, 295.

18. For the structural function of Scott's historic figures, *vide* Georg Lukacs, *Der Historische Roman* (Berlin, 1955), pp. 32–33. Compare Scott's essay "On Romance," in *Essays on Chivalry,* p. 246: "The sentiments of chivalry . . . were founded on the most pure and honourable principles, but unfortunately carried into hyperbole and extravagance; until their religion approached to fanaticism, valour to frenzy, their ideas of honour to absurdity, their spirit of enterprize to extravagance, and their respect for the female sex to a sort of idolatry."

19. "[Scott's heroes] are not heroes in the ordinary sense but symbolic observers. Their love affairs are of no significance whatsoever except to indicate the nature of the observer's final withdrawal from the seductive scenes of heroic, nationalistic passion" (Daiches, in *Nineteenth-Century Fiction,* VI, 86). Lukacs, *Der Historische Roman,* p. 30, sees the hero in the role of active (though strictly mediocre) negotiator between the contending parties, whose task it is to mediate the extreme alternatives and provide the means by which two impersonal historical forces can be brought into human contact with one another.

20. In *Nineteenth-Century Fiction,* IX, 298.

21. "Ivanhoe," *Blackwood's Edinburgh Magazine,* VI (1819), p. 263.

22. Jeffrey, "Ivanhoe," *Edinburgh Review,* XXXIII, 32, Maynadier, "*Ivanhoe* and Its Literary Consequences," *Essays in Memory of Barrett Wendell* (Cambridge, Mass., 1926), p. 223; Seccombe, in *Times Literary Supplement* (1919); Grierson, *Sir Walter Scott,* p. 182.

23. It may be noted that the whole picture of the exotic medieval Jewess remains, from the sartorial point of view, suspect. Israel Abrahams reminds us that "Jewish moralists and preachers shouted themselves hoarse in exhortation towards greater moderation [in dress]" and that "the wearing of gold embroidery was regarded as a token of pride." See his *Jewish Life in the Middle Ages,* ed. Cecil Roth (London, 1932), pp. 313–15.

24. " 'Suppose Sir Walter,' Mark Twain writes in *A Yankee at the Court of King Arthur,* 'instead of putting the conversations in the mouths of his characters, had allowed the characters to speak for themselves, we should have had talk from Rachel [he means Rebecca] and Ivanhoe and the soft Lady Rowena which would embarrass a tramp in our day. However, to the unconsciously indelicate all things are delicate.' " Quoted in Alfred Tressider Sheppard, *The Art and Practice of Historical Fiction* (London, 1932), p. 217. For a stylistic analysis of the dialogue in *Ivanhoe, vide* Sheppard, pp. 214–19.

25. On the personal prototypes of the Jewish group, *vide* J. G. Lockhart, *Memoirs of Sir Walter Scott* (London, 1914), III, 355–56: "The introduction of the charming Jewess and her father originated, I find, in a conversation that Scott held with his friend Skene during the severest season of his bodily suffer-

ings in the early part of this year. 'Mr. Skene,' says that gentleman's wife, 'sitting by his bedside, and trying to amuse him as well as he could in the intervals of pain, happened to get on the subject of the Jews, as he had observed them when he spent some time in Germany in his youth. Their situation had naturally made a strong impression; for in those days they retained their own dress and manners entire, and were treated with considerable austerity by their Christian neighbours, being still locked up at night in their own quarter by great gates; and Mr. Skene, partly in seriousness, but partly from the mere wish to turn his mind at the moment upon something that might occupy and divert it, suggested that a group of Jews would be an interesting feature if he could contrive to bring them into his next novel.' "

26. Thus Abrahams compares her importance for literary history to Nathan's: "Lessing's Nathan was as original on the male side as was Scott's Rebecca on the female." ("The Original of Scott's Rebecca," *Times Literary Supplement,* January 1, 1920, p. 9.) Perhaps such an estimate obscures the probability that Nathan spawned a whole tradition of exemplary Jews, while Rebecca, as Abrahams recognizes in his article, is already preceded by a good many distinguished literary Jewesses.

27. "Shakespeare and Scott," *Times Literary Supplement,* July 7, 1921, p. 426.

28. "It is obvious enough that Scott's sources for the Jewish group in 'Ivanhoe' were literary . . . I was long ago put on the right track by the extraordinary names chosen by Scott for some of his Jewish characters. He calls one of them Zareth, another Kirjath Jairam. These, however, are confused forms of Hebrew place-names; they are not the names of persons. What was the cause of Scott's slip? He took the names straight out of Marlowe's *Jew of Malta.* The motive of the love of the Jewess and Gentile was also literary. . . . Scott here, too, was influenced less by Shakespeare than by Marlowe. Abigail . . . has with the Gentile, Don Mathias, a love affair as hopeless as that between Rebecca and Ivanhoe. . . . Abigail becomes a Christian and enters a nunnery. Is it not obvious that Scott had this termination clearly in mind when he wrote the pathetic scene between Rebecca and Rowena towards the end of his tale? Rowena urges Rebecca to become a Christian. She refuses. 'Have you then convents to one of which you mean to retire?' asks Rowena. . . . Here then we see distinct traces of the influence of Marlowe, though Scott treats the idea in a spirit far other than that of his predecessors." Abrahams, in *Times Literary Supplement,* p. 9.

29. In *Illusions perdues,* D'Arthez exhorts Lucien Chardon: " 'Walter Scott is without passion; it is unknown to him, or perhaps it was forbidden him by the hypocritical morals of his country. For him woman is duty incarnate. With rare exceptions his heroines are absolutely alike. . . . They all come from Clarissa Harlowe. Paint then the passions, and you will have the immense resources of which this great genius deprived himself in order that he might be read in all the households of prudish England.' " Quoted in Gordon, in *Sir Walter Scott Today,* pp. 103–4. The same view is elaborated by Balzac in the "Avant-Propos."

30. Quoted in Roland Abramczyk, *Ueber die Quellen zu Walter Scotts Roman 'Ivanhoe'* (Halle, 1903), p. 152.

31. *Ibid.,* p. 153: "Clementina della Poveretta, die bleiche, stille Italienerin, die schwaermerische Katholikin im Sir Charles Grandison, muss in ihrer jungen

Seele einen gleichen Roman wie Rebecca erleben." Scott may also have drawn on Monk Lewis's *Castle Spectre* for the scene in which Bois-Guilbert endeavors to blackmail Rebecca into bed by threatening to have either her body or Ivanhoe's life. Rebecca's war bulletins to Ivanhoe during the seige of Torquilstone have been variously referred to Schiller's *Jungfrau von Orleans* and Goethe's *Goetz.* Van der Veen, *Jewish Characters,* pp. 79–80, cites verbal and substantive parallels between Rebecca and Edgeworth's Berenice Montenero.

32. Quoted by Andrew Lang, "Editor's Introduction," *Ivanhoe,* I, xxiii.

33. *The Jew in English Fiction,* p. 84. But *vide* Abrahams, *Jewish Life,* pp. 423–26, on the friendly personal relations between Jews and Christians. Abrahams blames the repressive anti-Semitic movements almost entirely on the clergy and nobility, and denies them any spontaneous support from the broad base of the population: the classes, not the masses are to blame. The contrary view is argued by Barnett Lionel Abrahams, *The Expulsion of the Jews from England in 1290* (Oxford, 1895), esp. pp. 73–77: "From the moment of their arrival in England [the Jews] had been hated by the common people." "Bradiers and hosiers, bakers and shoemakers, tailors and coopers, priests and Oxford scholars were all ready to take part in the looting of a Jewry." Where I. Abrahams attributes the Expulsion to Edward's policy of centralization, B. L. Abrahams contends that the Jews were expelled by popular demand, Edward acting as broker in a transaction sanctioned by the popular will.

34. *Nineteenth-Century Fiction,* IX, 298.

35. *Ivanhoe,* XVII, 95–97.

36. Trollope, for whom Thackeray could do no wrong, called *Rebecca and Rowena* "of all prose parodies . . . perhaps the best in the language." See his *Thackeray* (English Men of Letters, London, 1925), p. 195.

37. Which would run counter to the principles of Scott the historian. Or would it? "A certain monk of the [Cistercian] order, or rather a certain demoniac in our own times, being as it were tired of the Catholic faith and worn out with the sweet and light burden of Christ's yoke, and scorning, at the instigation of the devil any longer to walk in the way of salvation . . . as if phrenetic and mad, and truly turned to insanity, [fled] to the synagogue of Satan. And to cut short the whole wretched story which we have dilated upon at great length to show our detestation, at last he caused himself to be circumcised with the Jewish rite, and as a most vile apostate joined himself to his damnation to the enemies of the cross of Christ." Thus Giraldus Cambrensis, reporting on conversions to Judaism before 1200. *Vide* Joseph Jacobs, *The Jews of Angevin England: Documents and Records* (New York, 1893), p. 283. Similarly, I. Abrahams, *Jewish Life,* p. 435, records that "In 1222 a Christian deacon was executed at Oxford for . . . his apostasy to Judaism."

38. Scott, "Richard Cumberland," *Lives of the Novelists,* ed. Austin Dobson (World's Classics, London, 1906), p. 291.

39. I have promised in the Introduction to say as little as possible about the private prejudice of the authors for or against the Jews, but the pertinent comments may be crowded into a footnote. What Scott has to say of the Jews in private urges the conclusion that he thought them, on the whole, a race of scoundrels. We read in the Diary entry for November 25, 1825: "After all, it is

hard that the vagabond stock-jobbing Jews should, for their own purposes, make such a stroke of credit as now exists in London, and menace the credit of men trading on sure funds like Hurst and Robinson. It is just like a set of pickpockets, who raise a mob, in which honest folks are knocked down and plundered, that they may pillage safely in the midst of the confusion they have excited." Lockhart, *Memoirs,* IV, 364. Scott seems actually to have fallen into the clutches of money-lenders, for the entry for October 9, 1826, acknowledges "A gracious letter from Messrs. Abud and Son, bill brokers, etc.; assure my trustees that they will institute no legal proceedings against me for four or five weeks. And so I am permitted to spend my money and my time to improve the means of paying them their debts, for that is the only use of this journey. They are Jews: I suppose the devil baits for Jews with a pork griskin. Were I not to exert myself, I wonder where their money is to come from." *Ibid.,* V, 38–39. His correspondence discloses a similarly melancholy opinion: "One does not naturally and easily combine with [the Jews'] habits and pursuits any great liberality of principle, although certainly it may, and I believe, does, exist in many individual instances. They are money-lenders and money-brokers by profession, and it is a trade which narrows the mind." *Familiar Letters of Sir Walter Scott,* ed. D. Douglas (1894), I, 435.

40. *Charles Dickens* (English Novelists Series, London, 1951), pp. 69–70.

41. Compulsory Jewish badges and garments were not instituted until 1215, some twenty years after the events described in *Ivanhoe,* when Innocent III turned the Fourth Lateran Council into a sort of medieval *Reichsparteitag.* Sharon Turner, to whose *History of the Anglo-Saxons* (London, 1801) Abramczyk thinks Scott had access, notes (II, 94) that the Jews "were ordered to have two woollen tablets, of different colours, two fingers broad and four fingers long, to be sewn on their exterior garments, that they might be known from the Christians." The *Judenhut,* which Isaac is prematurely forced to wear, seems to have been more prevalent in Italy and the Germanic countries than in England, and its introduction is likely to date from an even later period than the introduction of the compulsory woollen patches. As to the motives for inflicting these sartorial stigmas, I. Abrahams, *Jewish Life,* p. 318, cites Innocent's allegation "that the measure was imperative if intermarriage or concubinage was to be prevented between Christians and non-believers." The whole subject of compulsory Jewish wardrobe in the Middle Ages has been treated exhaustively in Ulysse Robert, *Les Signes d'Infamie au Moyen Age: Juifs, Sarrasins, Hérétiques, Lépreux, Cagots et Filles Publiques* (Paris, 1891), pp. 1–113; the reader will remark the parallel categories that bestride Robert's subtitle. According to Robert, Jewish badges were generalized in England, by order of Stephen Langton, Archbishop of Canterbury, as late as 1222. *Vide* also Hermann Weiss, *Kostuemkunde: Geschichte der Tracht und des Geraeths im Mittelalter vom 4. bis zum. 14. Jahrhundert* (Stuttgart, 1883), II, 374–75, and I. Abrahams, *Jewish Life,* pp. 313–28. Rev. Dr. A. Cohen, speaking *en psychologue* in *An Anglo-Saxon Scrapbook, 1600 to 1840: The Jew Through English Eyes* (London, 1943), pp. 253–54, remarks on the tendency among early Jews to wear distinctively Jewish garments voluntarily.

On the more general anachronisms involved in the portrayal of the Jewish group in *Ivanhoe,* see Jacobs, *Jews of Angevin England,* p. 395: "Scott was unfortunate in naming his chief Jewish character Isaac of York, as at the time at which he places the novel, viz.: in 1194, the date of Richard's return, there were no Jews at York, owing to the scare caused by the massacre of 1190. . . . Rebecca also was a name unknown among English Jewesses of the twelfth century." Records relating to the York massacre as they appear in William of Newbury's *Historia Rerum Anglicanarum* and Ralph de Diceto's *Imagines Historiarum* may be found in Jacobs, pp. 112–30; see also Jacobs's own comments, "The York Riot," pp. 385–92. Specific errors in the depiction of Jewish practices in *Ivanhoe* are cited by Solomon Hurwitz, "Jews and Jewesses in English Literature," *Jewish Forum,* V (1922), 243 ff.

42. Scott's metaphor would be still more impressive were it not, presumably, straight out of Smollett. Of Isaac Rapine, Smollett notes that "he supported himself on an ivory-headed cane and his whole figure was a just emblem of winter, famine, and avarice." (*Roderick Random,* I, 69.) The echo may, of course, be an unconscious one. In his essay on Smollett, in *Lives of the Novelists,* pp. 29–72, Scott praises his precursor for making "the first candid attempt to do justice to a calumniated race [in *Count Fathom*]."

43. Dumas père has described the effect of this scene upon him: ". . . when the author introduced me to the old Saxon's romantic dining hall, when I had seen the fire on the hearth fed by a whole oak tree, with its light sparkling on the monk and on the dress of the unknown pilgrim; when I saw the Jew Isaac in his yellow cap and his daughter Rebecca in her gold corselet; when the tourney at Ashby had given me a foretaste of the powerful sword-shakes and lance thrusts, that I should come across again in Froissart, oh! then, little by little, the clouds that had veiled my sight began to lift, I saw open before me more extended horizons than any that had appeared to me." Quoted in Sheppard, *Art and Practice of Historical Fiction,* p. 52.

44. E. M. Forster, *Aspects of the Novel* (New York, 1927), p. 69.

45. Although it is generally agreed that Scott's sources for the Jewish group are almost wholly literary, he may have obtained the outlines for Isaac's character from the historical figure of Aaron of York. It may be noted that a similar prototype, Aaron of Lincoln, a wealthy money-lender at the court of Henry II, plays a minor role in Anne Radcliffe's *Gaston de Blondeville* (1803), where he appears at the court at Kenilworth to give evidence against a Christian merchant. Radcliffe's novel is touched on in Modder, *The Jew in the Literature of England,* pp. 127–28. *Vide* Joseph Jacobs, "Aaron of Lincoln," *Transactions of the Jewish Historical Society,* III, 157 ff.

46. The point is made by Abramczyk, *Ueber die Quellen zu . . . Ivanhoe,* pp. 146–47, who lumps the three Jews together on these grounds. Brewer, *Shakespeare's Influence on Scott,* pp. 298–99, dissents. "Shakespeare wrote in accord with the tolerance that Lessing had preached in *Nathan the Wise* and the lovable figure of Riah that Dickens was to paint in *Our Mutual Friend.* . . . Marlowe's play has nothing in common with *Ivanhoe.*" But see I. Abrahams's careful identification, *supra,* n.28.

47. E.g., I. Abrahams, *Jewish Life,* pp. 256–64. "The whole policy of the Church . . . forced the Jews to become money-lenders. . . . Even in Spain Jews were forbidden to act as physicians, as bakers, millers; they were prohib-

ited from selling bread, wine, flour, oil, or butter in the markets; no Jew might be a smith, carpenter, tailor, shoemaker, currier, or clothier, for Christians; he might not sell them shoes, doublets, or any other article of clothing; he might not be a carrier nor employ or be employed by Christians in any profession or trade whatsoever. . . . In England money-lending was absolutely the only profession open to the Jew." On the more general problem of the medieval usurer, *vide supra,* Chap. II; Tawney, *Religion and the Rise of Capitalism*; and the essays on usury by Bentham and Wilson, *supra,* Chap. II.

48. Michelet, *Histoire de France* (Paris, 1880), VII, has described these domiciles in a fine imaginative passage: "Ces mystérieuses maisons, si on eut pu les bien voir, eussent rehabilité dans le cœur du peuple ceux qu'ils haïssait à l'aveugle. La famille y était sérieuse, unie, serrée. . . . Rien n'égalait l'excellence de la femme juive, la pureté de la jeune fille juive, transparente et lumineuse en sa céleste beauté! La garde de cette perle d'orient était le plus grand souci de la famille." *Vide* Maurice Bloch, "La femme juive dans le roman et au théâtre," *Revue des études juives,* XXIII (1891), xlviii–xlix. Jewish residences are described in Jacobs, *Jews of Angevin England,* pp. 383–85. For comments on Jewish medical practice, see I. Abrahams, *Jewish Life,* pp. 254–56.

49. *Works and Life,* III, 48. Bagehot's view is elaborated in Max Korn, "Sir Walter Scott und die Geschichte," *Anglia,* LXI (1937), 416–41. See especially Korn's comments on Scott's *Life of Napoleon,* pp. 425–26 of his article.

50. On the sociological meaning of deviants such as Robin Hood, *vide* Leo Lowenthal, *Literature and the Image of Man* (Boston, 1957), pp. 40–45.

51. Isaac's and Rebecca's departure from England anticipates the Expulsion by almost precisely a hundred years. In 1283 all synagogues were ordered closed by the Bishop of London; in 1287 the London Jews were summarily imprisoned; the Expulsion took place in October 1290. See B. L. Abrahams, *The Expulsion of the Jews from England in 1290.* For a graphic reconstruction of London on the eve of the deportation, *vide* Joseph Jacobs, "The London Jewry, 1290," *Jewish Ideals and Other Essays* (London, 1896), pp. 162–91.

52. All quotations are from the text in the Border Edition of the Waverley Novels, Vol. XLVI, 223–483.

53. More precisely, latter half of the eighteenth century. But the material is treated as though it were contemporary, without conscious recourse to historical perspective. Only in the last—the Indian—portions of the novel does Scott write historical fiction, and then only in the sense of alluding to historical events and of assigning walk-on roles to Hyder Ali and Tippoo. On the historical background, *vide* L. B. Bowring, *Haidar Ali and Tipu Sultan* (Rulers of India Series, London, 1893).

54. Van der Veen, *Jewish Characters,* p. 37n., has traced the phrase about "the Pope, the Devil, and the Pretender" to *Roderick Random,* chap. xlii: ". . . so that I defy the Pope, the Devil and the Pretender; and hope to be saved as well as another." This does not, of course, preclude the likelihood that both novelists drew on a contemporary commonplace.

55. The novel has provoked next to no critical comment; what there is of it stresses the fraudulence of the Indian section. Lang, in the "Editor's Introduction," p. 226, writes: "The picture of life in the little Scotch town is . . . excellent. For the Indian part, which Lockhart thought rather incongruous,

Scott lacked . . . personal knowledge, and personal knowledge of localities was always, to him, very necessary." Lockhart's opinion appears in his *Memoirs,* V, 153. George Saintsbury, *Sir Walter Scott* (Edinburgh, 1897), p. 124, dismisses the novel in a phrase, noting that it "deals with Indian scenes, of which Scott had no direct knowledge, and in connection with which there was no interesting literature to inspire him. It appears to me almost totally uninteresting." Other biographical and critical studies of Scott avoid allusions to the book. The present excursus constitutes, as far as I know, the first such discussion in the past years.

56. Isaac, with more devotion to her person than to Hebrew word-formations, likewise calls Rebecca his *benoni,* the name given by the Biblical Rachel to Benjamin and inapplicable to females. *Vide* Hurwitz, in *Jewish Forum,* V (1922), 244.

57. For a definition of her type, *vide* Jared Wenger, "Character Types," in *PMLA,* LXII, 223: "Scott placed in almost every novel an Amazonian woman whom he could admire . . ." Wenger, who sees in this a "little boy" attitude, instances Rebecca, Flora, Mrs. Rob Roy, Lady Hautlieu, Brenhild, Mme de Montreville, Anne of Geierstein, and Fenella. It is no coincidence that Montreville first appears in a riding habit: as Pope-Hennessy, *Sir Walter Scott* (pp. 53–54, 58), reminds us, all Scott's superior women have a way of looking their best on a horse.

58. Brewer, *Shakespeare's Influence on Sir Walter Scott,* p. 302 n. In fairness to Brewer, his own qualification must be cited: "[Richard] can hardly be said to derive his vices from [his Jewish mother] . . . on the contrary, he appears to have been guided by unworthy Christian companions in his boyhood. Under these peculiar circumstances the depravity of Middlemas can hardly be held an aspersion of his race."

NOTES TO CHAPTER FIVE

1. Important studies of Fagin to which I am indebted are the following: Lauriat Lane, Jr., "Dickens' Archetypal Jews," *PMLA*, LXXIII (1958), 94–100; the same author's "The Devil in Oliver Twist," *Dickensian,* LII (1956), 132–36; and Harry Stone, "From Fagin to Riah: Jews and the Victorian Novel," *Midstream,* VI (1960), 21–37. Stone's heavily documented version of the same piece (in *Victorian Studies,* II) takes issue, point for point, with Lane's study in *PMLA.*

2. We remember that in his letter to Mrs. Davis, Dickens averred that Fagin had been described as a Jew "because it unfortunately was true of the time to which that story refers, that that class of criminal almost invariably was a Jew." For a thorough discussion of the Davis correspondence, *vide* Edgar Johnson, "Dickens, Fagin, and Mr. Riah," *Commentary,* IX (1950), 47–50.

3. Modder, *The Jew in the Literature of England,* p. 218: "As a Jew [Fagin] lacks actuality. He has so completely broken with his people and their ways that he possesses scarcely a trace of their peculiar diction and manners." Landa, *The Jew in Drama,* p. 164, modifies this view: "The term 'Jew' has become a damnation rather than a definition. This is shown in Dickens's remark—jejune under the circumstances—that the rest of the wicked characters

in the story are all Christians." Dickens's religious views are discussed in Philipp Aronstein, "Dickens' religioese Ansichten," *Anglia,* N.S. VI (1896), 224–47, and George Gissing, *Charles Dickens: A Critical Study* (New York, 1898), pp. 262–63.

4. *Vide* Lauriat Lane, Jr., "Oliver Twist: A Revision," *Times Literary Supplement,* July 20, 1951, p. 460; and *infra.*

5. *The Adventures of Oliver Twist, or The Parish Boy's Progress,* p. 410. All quotations are from the Nonesuch Dickens, ed. Arthur Waugh *et al.* (London, 1937–38), in which *Oliver Twist* is Vol. XVIII.

6. Greene, "The Young Dickens," in *The Lost Childhood and Other Essays* (New York, 1952), pp. 56–57.

7. Edmund Wilson, "Dickens: The Two Scrooges," in *The Wound and the Bow: Seven Studies in Literature* (Boston, 1941), p. 8. Wilson's essay has been of decisive influence on subsequent Dickens criticism. See Fred W. Boege, "Recent Criticism of Dickens," *Nineteenth-Century Fiction,* VIII (1953), 187.

8. "Night Walks," reprinted in *The Uncommercial Traveller, Works,* Universal Edition (London, 1914), XXII, 106. The remarks in *The Chimes* are quoted in Warrington Winters, "Dickens and the Psychology of Dreams," *PMLA,* LXIII (1948), 988 n.

9. John Forster, *The Life of Charles Dickens,* ed. J. W. T. Ley (London, 1928), pp. 25, 30.

10. Ernest Boll, "Charles Dickens in *Oliver Twist,*" *The Psychoanalytic Review,* XXVII (1940), 135.

11. Gissing, *Charles Dickens,* p. 274: "His saviour of society was a man of heavy purse and large heart, who did the utmost possible good in his own particular sphere. . . . At one with Carlyle in scorning the theory that 'cash was the sole nexus' between human beings, Dickens would have viewed uneasily any project for doing away with the nexus altogether; which would mean the abolition of a form of beneficence in which he delighted."

12. Symons, *Charles Dickens* (London, 1951), p. 47.

13. Quoted in *ibid.*

14. G. K. Chesterton, *Criticisms and Appreciations of the Works of Charles Dickens* (London, 1911), pp. 198–99: "The heroic modern hero, this demi-god in a top-hat, may be said to reach his supreme moment and typical example about the time when Dickens was writing . . . the scene where Nicholas [Nickleby] hopelessly denounces the atrocious Gride in his hour of grinning triumph, and a thud upon the floor above tells them that the heroine's tyrannical father has died just in time to set her free. . . . Most of Pip's actions are meant to show that he is not heroic."

15. Hippolyte Taine, *History of English Literature,* trans. H. van Laun (New York, 1908), II, 153–54. Oliver's nurse harbors "a green glass bottle, the contents of which she had been tasting in the corner with evident satisfaction"; the "medical gentleman" who presides at Oliver's birth prescribes "a little gruel" for the infant in one paragraph and deliberately "walked away to dinner" in the next; Mr. Bumble is introduced as "a fat man, and a choleric"; the master who orders Oliver whipped in the famous scene in which the boy, "desperate with hunger, and reckless with misery," asks for more, has the consolation of being himself "a fat, healthy man"; the Board before which Oliver is brought

to hear his future decided consists of "eight or ten fat gentlemen," presided over by "a particularly fat gentleman with a very round, red face." Apprenticed to an undertaker Oliver is treated to "a plateful of coarse broken victuals" which the Sowerberry dog has disdained to touch, and which Oliver "tore . . . asunder with all the ferocity of famine"; shortly afterwards he rebels for the first time against his persecutors and is accordingly regarded as insane by his employer's wife. " 'It's not Madness, ma'am,' replied Mr. Bumble, after a few moments of deep meditation. 'It's Meat.' " When they are not specifically defined by their gluttony, Oliver's early instructors are petty tyrants like Sowerberry's wife, or pretentious and cowardly bullies like Noah Claypole, "a large-headed, small-eyed youth," red-nosed and pimply, who "could trace his genealogy all the way back to his parents" and who "now that fortune had cast in his way a shameless orphan" pounces on his sudden prey.

16. Johnson, *Charles Dickens,* I, 276–77: ". . . it is specifically the harshness and the starvation regimen of the new [Poor Law system] that Dickens lashes with all his fury. Bumble illustrates . . . the stupidity of employing the old officers for its administration; but Mrs. Corney symbolizes the frigid brutality of an economic system that condemned the ill, the aged, and helpless children to misery in the name of destroying temptations to idleness." For a discussion of the Poor Law of 1834, *vide* Humphry House, *The Dickens World* (Oxford, 1941), pp. 197–98, and Monroe Engel, *The Maturity of Dickens* (Cambridge, Mass., 1959).

17. In several of his later novels, particularly in *Bleak House, Little Dorrit,* and *Our Mutual Friend,* Dickens displays an ability to handle such contrasts more meaningfully by relating the child's stuntedness to the whole social complex of industrialized England. Note, for example, the aged features of the idiot girl Maggie; the adult responsibilities taken on by Jenny Wren; the ironic contrast between Caddy Jellyby's stunted baby, who is born old, and the irresponsible infantilism of Harold Skimpole, who refers to himself as "the child," etc.

18. With respect to Fagin's physiognomy, Edgar Johnson, in *Commentary,* IX, 48–49, offers the interesting opinion that Fagin has very little of the conventional stage-Jew about him. "Fagin is given none of the usual earmarks of caricature. . . . He has no monstrous bulge of nose, no weird or frenzied gestures, no strange Hebrew idioms, not even the lisp or accent of the stage Jew." Our notions of Fagin have no doubt been largely colored by Cruikshank; but hear Johnson: "Curiously enough, Fagin actually resembles nobody so much as Cruikshank himself; and the artist told Horace Mayhew that the famous plate of Fagin awaiting his death in Newgate was inspired by a glimpse he caught of himself in the mirror, biting his fingernails in anxiety over his difficulties in conceiving the picture" (*ibid.*).

19. "Whereas the distorted form given to comic characters like Pecksniff and Mrs. Gamp and young Bailey becomes an artistic virtue, the distorted form given to the serious characters appears to act the other way, so that wicked people like Jonas or merely . . . good people like the Pinches are just vessels for sentimentality." R. C. Churchill, "Dickens, Drama, and Tradition," *Scrutiny,* X (1942), 360.

20. Pugh, *The Charles Dickens Originals* (New York, 1912), p. 251. Johnson's description recalls a similar, though widely repudiated, interpretation of

Marlowe's Jew, whom T. S. Eliot assigns to "the terribly serious, even savage comic humour . . . which spent its last breath in the decadent genius of Dickens." *Vide Elizabethan Essays* (London, 1942), p. 28.

21. *The Charles Dickens Originals,* p. 249. Marie Hamilton Law, "The Indebtedness of Oliver Twist to Defoe's *History of the Devil,*" *PMLA,* XL (1925), 892–97, alleges that Dickens read Defoe's *History* while writing *Oliver Twist.* But see Lane's corrections in *Dickensian,* LII, 132.

22. *Criticisms and Appreciations,* p. 40.

23. Greene, in *The Lost Childhood,* p. 55.

24. In *PMLA,* LXIII, 984–1006.

25. "Point of View in Dickens," *PMLA,* LXV (1950), 90–105.

26. *Letters,* XI, 624, as quoted in Boege, p. 91 n. Dickens's editorial activities and the literary principles which they reflect have been investigated thoroughly in a series of articles by Gerald Grubb; *vide* esp. his "Dickens' Editorial Methods," *Studies in Philology,* XL (1943), 79–100, and "The Editorial Policies of Charles Dickens," *PMLA,* LVIII (1943), 1110–24.

27. Boege, p. 101.

28. That in the case of "Fagin's Last Night Alive" the humanizing touches were deliberately added many years later happens to be verifiable. In the version as Dickens originally wrote it, Fagin remains consistently sensational to the end. Dickens rewrote the chapter for the 1867 edition of his works, and the revised rather than the original version has become the accepted one. Lane, "Oliver Twist: A Revision," thinks that Dickens may have been moved to tone down Fagin for the same reason which impelled him to manufacture the good Jew Riah: in order to make *amende honorable* for the earlier Fagin and propitiate his outraged Jewish readers (*Times Literary Supplement,* July 20, 1951).

29. Trollope, *The Autobiography of Anthony Trollope* (World's Classics, London, 1928), p. 226.

30. I am greatly indebted for the following remarks to Pugh, *The Charles Dickens Originals,* pp. 240–51, and Landa, *The Jew in Drama,* pp. 159–69. An amusing account of the Victorian theater is given in R. C. Cruikshank, *Charles Dickens and Early Victorian England* (London, 1949), pp. 221–43. Dramatic adaptations of Dickens's novels are discussed in S. J. Adair Fitzgerald, *Dickens and the Drama* (London, 1910), and T. Edgar Pemberton, *Dickens and the Stage: A Record* (London, 1888).

31. *The Charles Dickens Originals,* pp. 241–42.

32. Landa, *The Jew in Drama,* p. 161.

33. *The Charles Dickens Originals,* p. 246.

34. *Charles Dickens,* p. 54. Phillips, *Dickens, Reade and Collins,* pp. 14–17, analyzes *Oliver Twist* from the point of view of its sensation-elements.

35. Wilkie Collins, *Basil* (New York, 1893), pp. vi–vii.

36. *Vide* Malcolm Morley, "Early Dramas of Oliver Twist," *Dickensian,* XLIII (1947), 74–79.

37. Quoted in Pemberton, *Dickens and the Stage,* pp. 161–62.

38. Quoted in John Harrison Stonehouse, "Introduction," *Sikes and Nancy: A Reading by Charles Dickens* (London, 1921), pp. vi–vii.

39. Ralph Straus, *Charles Dickens: A Biography from New Sources* (New York, 1928), p. 328.

NOTES TO CHAPTER SIX

1. *The Jew in the Literature of England,* pp. 351–52.

2. The most eminent of Jewish financiers, the Rothschilds settled in Frankfort about 1530; the house from which they took their name, "Zum roten Schild," was erected in 1567. As an active banking concern, the firm dates from 1760, its founding father being Mayer Amschel (or Anselm) Rothschild (1743?–1812). The gigantic expansion of the firm was undertaken by Mayer Anselm's five sons, who directed their operations respectively from Frankfort, Vienna, London, Naples, and Paris. Among the founder's sons, the third, Nathan Meyer (1777–1830), the head of the London branch, was regarded as the financial genius of the family; it was he who speculated on the defeat of Napoleon, risking the family fortune on the event. James, the director of the Parisian concern, patronized Balzac and Heine. The London business passed from Nathan Meyer to Lionel (1808–79), a close friend of Disraeli's, and the guarantor in the purchase of the Suez Canal. Elected to Parliament as Member for London in 1847, he remained unseated until the act of 1858 removed the last bars to his admission. Lionel's son Nathaniel Meyer (1840–1915) was the first English Jew to be raised to the peerage. Since their record for religious piety has been good, the Rothschilds have for more than a century figured as the lay leaders of the English Jewish community; it was to Lionel Walter (1868–1937), a distinguished naturalist, that the Balfour Declaration of 1917 was officially addressed. The standard work on the subject is Egon Caesar Conte Corti, *Der Aufstieg des Hauses Rothschild: 1770–1830* (Leipzig, 1927), and its sequel, *Das Haus Rothschild in der Zeit Seiner Bluete: 1830–1871* (Leipzig, 1928). For a detailed account of the London branch to the end of the nineteenth century, *vide* Ignac Balla, *Die Rothschilds* (Berlin, 1912), pp. 75–140.

3. Trollope, *The Way We Live Now* (London, 1875).

4. Allen, *The English Novel: A Short Critical History* (New York, 1955), pp. 238–39.

5. A number of prototypes, other than Rothschild, have been alleged. S. Baring Gould, *Early Reminiscences* (London, 1923), pp. 52–53, is of opinion that Trollope found the model for Melmotte in the German-Jewish company promoter and speculator Albert Gottheim, who received the patent of nobility for obscure services to the Austrian Court and, as Baron Grant, became Member for Kidderminster. G. M. Young, *Victorian England: Portrait of an Age,* 2d ed. (London, 1953), p. 219 n, writes: "There had been bursts of company promoting before, in the twenties, forties, and sixties. But the first man to appreciate the unlimited possibilities of limited liability was Albert Gottheim . . . towards whose great house on the outskirts of Kensington Palace a trustful public had contributed, it was reckoned, some twenty million pounds." Michael Sadleir, *Trollope: A Commentary* (New York, 1947), pp. 399–400, notes that "Trollope was . . . accused of having copied Melmotte from Merdle in *Little Dorrit,* but he asserted that he first read that novel in 1878."

6. Sadleir, *Trollope,* pp. 426–28, has printed Trollope's "Advance Lay-Out for *The Way We Live Now.*" Melmotte barely figures in Trollope's annotated projected cast of characters; "it is clear," Sadleir remarks, "that Melmotte was not in the author's intention so important an element in the book as in performance he turned out to be."

7. Trollope, *Autobiography,* p. 324.

8. "The accusations are exaggerated. The vices are coloured, so as to make effect rather than to represent truth" (*ibid.*).

9. *Trollope,* pp. 400–401.

10. Or, for that matter, Frances Trollope. *Vide* Lucy Poate Stebbins and Richard Poate Stebbins, *The Trollopes: The Chronicle of a Writing Family* (New York, 1945), p. 291.

11. A comment by the Stebbinses, *The Trollopes,* p. 270, helps to explain Marie's ethical function: "Trollope's reverence for the institutions of the past was always at odds with his resentment against family and social interference in human action; such mischief was the theme of *Rachel Ray, Linda Tressel,* and *Nina Balatka.* . . . In *Linda Tressel,* where its result was most nearly tragic, he exclaimed 'Are we to believe that the very soul of the offspring is to be at the disposition of the parent?'"

12. *Autobiography,* p. 228.

13. *Vide* the standard critical biography, The Earl of Lytton, *The Life of Edward Bulwer, First Lord Lytton* (London, 1913), II, 104: "*The Caxtons* and *My Novel* represent the most mature work of Bulwer-Lytton's genius." Similarly extravagant claims are implicit in T. H. S. Escott, *Edward Bulwer, First Baron Lytton of Knebworth* (London, 1910), p. 299.

14. Entertaining critiques of Bulwer's taffeta art are Edmund Gosse, "Edward Bulwer-Lytton," *Fortnightly Review,* C (1913), 1033–46; Walter Frewen Lord, "Lord Lytton's Novels," *Nineteenth Century,* L (1901), 449–58, and the same author's "The Wand of Prospero," *Nineteenth Century,* XCV 1924), 59–68. For a defense of Bulwer's extravagances, *vide* Desmond MacCarthy, "The Padded Man," *Experience* (New York, 1935), pp. 59–63.

15. Edward Bulwer-Lytton, Lord Lytton, *My Novel, by Pisistratus Caxton.* All quotations are from the Knebworth Edition (London, 1875), of which *My Novel* are Vols. XVII–XVIII.

16. *Edward Bulwer,* pp. 299–300.

17. "A bookmarker is advisable, with a careful list of the people of the story, accompanied by an abstract of their mental endowments and mutual relations. . . . Towards the end of the eleventh book of *My Novel* we discover a story: the characters become agitated, things happen, and the fate of the characters is briefly summarised in about 10,000 well-chosen words." Lord, in *Nineteenth Century,* XCV, 65.

18. Bulwer's own loyalties are explained in Escott, *Edward Bulwer,* p. 299: "To strengthen the old English cordial feeling, to bind together those classes which the Manchester school are always trying to separate and the French school would plunge in the fusing-pot:—such in his own words was the purpose with which Bulwer wrote *My Novel.*"

19. Trollope, *Autobiography,* p. 228.

20. C. P. Snow, *The Conscience of the Rich* (New York, 1958), pp. 47–48.

NOTES TO CHAPTER SEVEN

1. All quotations are from the Rosehill Limited Edition (Boston, 1893–95), in which *Daniel Deronda* are Vols. XI–XIII.

2. *Vide* James, "Daniel Deronda: A Conversation" (1876), in *Partial Por-*

traits (London, 1888), p. 73; Bennett, *George Eliot: Her Mind and Her Art* (Cambridge, 1948), p. 182; Bullett, *George Eliot: Her Life and Her Books* (London, 1947), p. 205; Lawrence and Elisabeth Hanson, *Marian Evans and George Eliot: A Biography* (London, 1952), p. 296; F. R. Leavis, *The Great Tradition: A Study of the English Novel* (London, 1948), p. 102.

3. Robert Speaight, *George Eliot* (London, 1954), p. 110. Eliot herself protested the tendency to cut up the novel into disconnected halves. "I have had some very interesting letters both from Jews and Christians about *Deronda.* . . . a Christian . . . thanks me for embodying the principles by which Christ wrought and will conquer. This is better than the laudation of readers who cut the book up into scraps, and talk of nothing in it but Gwendolen. I meant everything in the book to be related to everything else there." *The George Eliot Letters,* ed. Gordon S. Haight (New Haven, 1954–55), VI, 290. Highly favorable verdicts on *Daniel Deronda* have been registered by Oscar Browning, *Life of George Eliot* (London, 1890), p. 144; Edward Dowden, " 'Middlemarch' and 'Daniel Deronda,' " *Contemporary Review,* XXIX (1877), 348–69; and Sidney Lanier, *The English Novel,* in *Works,* ed. Charles R. Anderson (Baltimore, 1945), IV, 217 ff.

4. Quoted in Samuel Blum, "As Great Christian Writers Saw the Jews," *Jewish Tribune,* XCIV (1929), 16.

5. In *Partial Portraits,* p. 84.

6. Sol Liptzin, "Daniel Deronda," *Jewish Book Annual,* X (1951–52), 43–44.

7. *George Eliot,* p. 110.

8. In short, one does not have the impression that issues are being met head on. Cf. Claude T. Bissell, "Social Analysis in the Novels of George Eliot," *Journal of English Literary History,* XVIII (1951), 221–22: "The political situation from which Felix Holt emerged was, at least, specific and real, but the hapless Daniel moves in a mist of sentimental idealism in which at times one can vaguely recognize sympathy for nationalistic aspirations, belief in the power of heredity, and in racial solidarity and tempered interest in the programme of Zionism. The political section of the novel provides a catalogue of almost all the vices to which the novelist can succumb." For a hostile stylistic analysis of the book, *vide* notably Sidney Colvin, "Daniel Deronda," *Fortnightly Review,* N.S. XX (1876), 610–13.

9. Woolf, "George Eliot," *The Common Reader* (London, 1925), pp. 216–17.

10. *Daniel Deronda,* III, 341–43.

11. *The Jew in English Fiction,* p. 128.

12. *The Jew in English Literature,* p. 133: "The word 'Klesmer' is the Yiddish . . . for musicians. In reality, in pure Hebrew, it means 'instruments of music,' but by an unconscious metonomy it was used popularly to denote the musicians themselves." On the Klesmer-Liszt parallel, *vide* Speaight, *George Eliot,* p. 21.

13. "One of her friends . . . says that she gathered strength to write on the Crucifixion [in her translation of Strauss] by gazing on the crucifix, and we may infer from this remark that some confusion of thought prevailed at Coventry." Lord Acton, "George Eliot's Life," *Historical Essays and Studies* (London, 1908), p. 280.

14. Disraeli, *Tancred,* in *Novels and Tales of Benjamin Disraeli,* Bradenham Edition (London, 1926–27), X, 394–95.

15. "Daniel Deronda," *Edinburgh Review,* CXLIV (1876), 468.

16. Gobineau's *Essai sur l'inégalité des races humaines* appeared in 1853–55. The essence of Gobineau's doctrine, which is the foundation of twentieth-century race theories, insists that the human race consists of irreconcilably unequal races, of which the nobler is destined to dominate the lower. It has been the tragedy of the white race (which Gobineau designates the noble) that it has been forced to mix with the lower races and thus brought on itself the seeds of its own decay. The Jews, "the most astonishing example of race consistency that history has ever provided," are especially to blame for the decline of the white race since they appear to be an immutably destructive element in modern society. Gobineau was a friend of Richard Wagner's, whose *Aufklaerungen ueber das Judentum in der Musik,* reflecting a similar bias, preceded Gobineau's work by three years. The appearance of Houston Stewart Chamberlain's now discredited *Grundlagen des 19. Jahrhunderts* dates from 1899. I am not familiar at first hand with Gobineau's treatise, but useful shortcuts are Ernest Seillière, *Le Comte de Gobineau et l'aryanisme* (Paris, 1903), and J. M. Hone, "Count Arthur de Gobineau: Race Mystic," *Contemporary Review,* CIV (1913), 94–103.

17. George Meredith, *The Tragic Comedians: A Study in a Well-Known Story,* in *Works of George Meredith,* Standard Edition (London, 1914–16), XVII, 78.

18. *The English Novel,* p. 175.

19. Disraeli, *Coningsby, or The New Generation,* in *Novels and Tales,* VIII, 231–32, 263.

20. *Tancred,* in *Novels and Tales,* X, 153, 154, 270.

21. *Vide* Philip Rieff, "Disraeli: The Chosen of History," *Commentary,* XIII (1952), 22–33.

22. Eliot, *Letters,* I, 246–47. To John Blackwood she wrote under date of February 25, 1876: "Doubtless the wider public of novel-readers must feel more interest in Sidonia than in Mordecai. But then, I was not born to paint Sidonia" (VI, 223).

23. Eliot, *Letters,* VI, 301–2. *Vide* also her letter to David Kaufmann, *ibid.,* pp. 378–80.

24. *The Jew in English Fiction,* p. 137.

25. *George Eliot* (English Men of Letters, London, 1926), pp. 187–88.

26. *Ibid.,* p. 165.

27. "Daniel Deronda," *Edinburgh Review,* CXLIV, 459; Leavis, *The Great Tradition,* p. 107.

28. James, in *Partial Portraits,* p. 65.

29. Liptzin, in *Jewish Book Annual,* X, 46. Solomon Hurwitz, "George Eliot's Jewish Characters," *Jewish Forum,* V (1922), 369, writes: "Four years after the book appeared, a new school of theorists, Peretz, Gordon, Smolensky and Lilienblum, had arisen in Russia; men who, having started life by teaching their coreligionists the doctrines of assimilation, saw themselves in 1880 plunged into the horrors of persecution and massacre, and to them the national-political restoration at once became the only road to human salvation. These writers at once made 'Daniel Deronda' their own; translated it into Hebrew; and supplemented it by their own views on the re-colonization of Palestine. These books

went through several successive editions and were greedily absorbed by the bulk of Jewish thinkers."

NOTES TO CHAPTER EIGHT

1. My chief authority throughout has been Werner Zirus, *Der ewige Jude in der Dichtung, vornehmlich in der englischen und deutschen* (Leipzig, 1928). I am indebted to Zirus for my opening remarks on the origins of the legend, and the job of gathering the seventeenth-century versions of the legend would have been vastly complicated without recourse to his work. Moncure Daniel Conway, *The Wandering Jew* (London, 1881), elaborates on the mythological foundations of the legend and deals extensively with analogues other than those to be found in the literature of the West. Eino Railo's section on "The Wandering Jew and the Problem of Never-Ending Life," in *The Haunted Castle: A Study of the Elements of English Romanticism* (London, 1927), pp. 191–215, remains, I believe, the best short discussion of the subject, valuable chiefly for its treatment of the romantic versions of the legend in eighteenth- and nineteenth-century English poetry and fiction. *Vide* also Alice M. Killen, "L'évolution de la légende du juif errant," *Revue de littérature comparée,* V (1925), 5–36.

2. *Vide* Conway, *The Wandering Jew*, pp. 1–3.

3. Roger of Wendover, *Flowers of History,* trans. J. A. Giles (London, 1849), II, 512–14; Matthew Paris, *English History from the Year 1235 to 1273,* trans. J. A. Giles (London, 1889), II, 542.

4. Railo, in *The Haunted Castle,* pp. 191–93, cites Scriptural sources.

5. Buttadeus offers some interest in that he seems to be the first extant type within the legend whose immortality is joined to an eternal restlessness; he is thus, properly speaking, the first "wandering" Jew in Western literature. Killen, in *Revue de littérature comparée,* V, 14–15, notes: "Une expression . . . que nous trouvons chez Guido Bonatti (que Dante place au huitième cercle de l'Enfer) ferait croire qu'il a déjà paru sous cet aspect [de voyageur]. Parlant de 'Johannes Buttadeus,' qui repoussa le Seigneur lorsqu'il allait au supplice et à qui celui-ci dit: 'Tu attendras que je vienne,' il continue: 'Ce Giovanni passa par Forli en 1267.' Il est déjà en marche." Buttadeus foreshadows the figure popularized in the *Volksbuch* (*infra*) three hundred years later, that of the Wandering Jew whose passage through specific European localities becomes a staple of superstitious rumor.

6. Chaucer, in *Works,* IV, 312–13. Nelson Sherwin Bushnell, "The Wandering Jew and *The Pardoner's Tale,*" *Studies in Philology,* XXVIII (1931), 450–60, discusses sources and analogues and offers various interpretations as to the meaning of Chaucer's old man; *vide* also George Lyman Kittredge, *Chaucer and His Poetry* (Cambridge, 1915), p. 215.

7. Quoted in Zirus, pp. 8–9. Translation mine. For my discussion of the *Volksbuch* I have had to rely on such summaries as are given in Albert Soergel, *Ahasver-Dichtungen seit Goethe* (Leipzig, 1905), pp. 12–16, Zirus, pp. 8–14, and Conway, *The Wandering Jew,* pp. 5–10.

8. *The Wandering Jew,* p. 109.

9. *The Haunted Castle,* p. 193. Killen, *Revue de littérature comparée,* V, 21,

assigns definite anti-Semitic motives to the translation of the Roman into the Jew.

10. Conway, *The Wandering Jew,* pp. 11–27, records the alleged appearances of the Wandering Jew to 1650.

11. Thomas Percy, *Reliques of Ancient English Poetry,* ed. Rev. George Gilfillian (Edinburgh, 1858), II, 236. For a discussion of the poem, *vide* Zirus, pp. 15–20.

12. *The Roxburghe Ballads,* ed. W. Chapell (Hertford, 1871–97), VI, 693.

13. Zirus, p. 19.

14. *Ibid.,* pp. 20–22.

15. Killen, in *Revue de littérature comparée,* V, 6: "Chaque siècle et chaque peuple a pu l'interpréter [le juif errant] à sa guise, a pu y voir le reflet de ses propres croyances, de ses propres superstitions, de sa propre imagination. Elle faisait appel au goût du merveilleux, et aux âmes naïves et croyantes de jadis elle offrait un témoignage vivant de la foi chrétienne et de la justice divine."

16. In *The Haunted Castle,* p. 195.

17. "Wild und laut, prahlerisch und sentimental . . ." "Nachwort," in *Schubart: Dokumente Seines Lebens,* eds. Hermann Hesse and Karl Isenberg (Berlin, 1926), p. 184.

18. Christian Daniel Schubart, "Schubarts Leben und Gesinnungen von ihm selbst im Kerker aufgesetzt," in *Schubart: Dokumente,* pp. 9–121.

19. Zirus, p. 34. In the Appendix to his *Life of Schiller,* Carlyle amusingly describes Schubart's project. "The idea of making old *Joannes a temporibus,* the 'Wandering,' or as Schubart's countrymen denominate him, the 'Eternal Jew,' into a novel hero, was a mighty favorite with him. In this antique cordwainer, as on a raft at anchor in the stream of time, he would survey the changes and wonders of two thousand years: the Roman and the Arab were to figure there; the Crusader and the Circumnavigator, the Eremite of the Thebaid and the Pope of Rome. Joannes himself, the Man existing out of Time and Space, Joannes the unresting and undying, was to be a deeply tragic personnage. Schubart warmed himself with this idea; and talked about it in his cups, to the astonishment of simple souls. He even wrote a certain rhapsody connected with it, which is published in his poems." *The Works of Thomas Carlyle,* Centenary Edition (New York, 1896–1901), XXV, 299–300.

20. Schubart, "Der Ewige Jude: Eine lyrische Rhapsodie, 1783," *Saemmtliche Gedichte* (Frankfort, 1825), II, 62. An English prose translation, with minor misconstructions—the text, in fact, from which Shelley worked—may be found in that poet's "Notes to *Queen Mab,*" in *Complete Poetical Works,* ed. George Edward Woodberry (Boston, 1892), I, 371–73.

21. Schubart, "Der Ewige Jude," in *Saemmtliche Gedichte,* II, 64.

22. Albrecht Waechter, *Ueber Robert Southeys Orientalische Epen* (Halle, 1890), p. 20, discusses Southey's Oriental sources.

23. Robert Southey, *The Curse of Kehama,* in *Poems of Robert Southey,* ed. Maurice H. Fitzgerald (London, 1909), p. 126.

24. Edward Dowden, *Southey* (English Men of Letters, London, 1909), p. 191, notes: "In *Kehama* . . . the chivalric ardour of [Southey's] earlier heroes is transformed into the sterner virtue of fortitude and an almost despair-

ing constance. The power of evil as conceived by the poet, has grown more despotic."

25. Southey, in *Poems of Robert Southey*, pp. 117, 183.

26. Newman Ivey White, *Shelley* (New York, 1940), I, 653 n: "'The Wandering Jew's Soliloquy' . . . infuses the orthodox horrors of Schubart's poem with a definitely Shelleyan hatred of the Author of his hero's sufferings." The poem has been ignored by most commentators. A brief analysis is given in Zirus, pp. 57–58.

27. Shelley, "The Wandering Jew's Soliloquy," in *Complete Poetical Works*, IV, 336.

28. "Ahasuerus, in spite of his particularized name and his associations with Shelley's juvenile writing, is the spiritual essence of all those infidels who have been crushed under the heel of the Christian Church." Carlos Baker, *Shelley's Major Poetry: The Fabric of a Vision* (Princeton, 1948), p. 24.

29. Shelley, *Queen Mab: A Philosophical Poem*, in *Complete Poetical Works*, I, 58–59.

30. *Ibid.*, pp. 59–62. On Shelley's anti-clerical views, *vide* Baker, *Shelley's Major Poetry*, pp. 28–32.

31. In *Complete Poetical Works*, I, 62–63.

32. Baker, *Shelley's Major Poetry*, p. 182, specifies three aims of the poem: "The first is fundamentally political: to celebrate the Greek War against the Turks 'as a portion of the cause of civilization and moral improvement.' The second is ethical: to hold up as an *exemplum* for the modern world the wonderful achievements of Athens in the fifth century B.C., and to envision, as a lofty ideal towards which the world ought to move, a new Athens, conceived in liberty and dedicated to the spread of brotherly love. The third is metaphysical: to assert that thought is the sole reality and that all else in the world is a shadow and dream."

33. Shelley, *Hellas, A Lyrical Drama*, in *Complete Poetical Works*, III, 117.

34. *Ibid.*, p. 142. Douglas Bush, *Mythology and the Romantic Tradition in Poetry* (Cambridge, 1937), p. 164, designates Ahasuerus as "a mystic who reutter's Prospero's speech in the spirit of Berkeley."

NOTES TO CHAPTER NINE

1. Quotations are from Matthew Gregory Lewis, *The Monk: A Romance* [1795], ed. E. A. Baker (London, 1929). The most thorough discussion of the Wandering Jew as he appears during the period covered in this chapter is to be found in Eino Railo, *The Haunted Castle*, pp. 191–215. Montague Summers, *The Gothic Quest: A History of the Gothic Novel* (London, 1938), pp. 202–308, contains amply documented biographical material on Lewis, as well as a comprehensive discussion of the sources, influences, and critical reception of *The Monk*. For my general assumptions on the Gothic novel, I have drawn on Summers, *passim*; Edith Birkhead, *The Tale of Terror: A Study of the Gothic Romance* (New York, 1920); H. P. Lovecraft, *Supernatural Horror in Literature* (New York, 1927); J. M. S. Tompkins, *The Popular Novel in England*, pp. 243–95; and Ernest A. Baker, *History of the English Novel* (London, 1924–39), V, 205–11.

2. "This scandalous book is pervaded by a sort of excitable heat" (Tompkins, *The Popular Novel in England,* p. 278). Similarly Baker, *History of the English Novel,* p. 207: "Lewis betrays the perverted lusts of a sadist." Summers, *The Gothic Quest,* pp. 222–23, defends Lewis on the grounds that "his pictures of voluptuous passion are necessary to the narrative; the violence of the orgasm but serves to balance and throw in high relief the charnel horrors." It may be noted that even a hardened libertine like Byron, who was personally fond of Lewis, has nothing good to say about Lewis's novel. He notes in his Journal, under date of December 6, 1818: "I looked yesterday at the worst parts of the *Monk*. These descriptions ought to have been written by Tiberius at Caprea—they are forced—the *philtered* ideas of a jaded voluptuary. It is to me inconceivable how they could have been composed by a man of only twenty. . . . They have no nature—all the sour cream of cantharides. I should have suspected Buffon of writing them on the death-bed of his detestable dotage." *Works of Lord Byron, Letters and Journals,* ed. Rowland E. Prothero (London, 1898–1901), II, 368.

3. Summers, *The Gothic Quest,* p. 220.

4. It has been generally alleged that Lewis plagiarized the whole incident of the Bleeding Nun from a German *Volksmaerchen,* J. K. A. Musaeus's "Die Entfuehrung" (1787). This view has been recently challenged by Louis F. Peck, "*The Monk* and Musaeus' 'Die Entfuehrung,'" *Philological Quarterly,* XXXII (1953), 346–48. Tompkins, p. 245 n., has more sweepingly charged Lewis with wholesale theft; "two-thirds of [*The Monk*] are taken almost word for word from a German romance, *Die Blutende Gestalt mit Dolch und Lampe, oder die Beschwoerung im Schlosse Stern bei Prag,* in which the two themes of the devil's compact and the spectral nun are already united, though the hero of the former is an old nobleman, not a monk."

5. Compare Shelley's debt in "The Wandering Jew, or the Victim of the Eternal Avenger," in *Poetical Works,* IV, 354:

"Rosa, wilt thou then be mine?
Ever fairest, I am thine."

6. I omit *St. Irvyne* [1811] from discussion, less for its obtrusive badness than for the fact that it provides at best an *omnium gatherum* of various facets of the legend which are explored more intelligently in Godwin and Bulwer, and adds few or none of its own. The novel fragment may be read in *The Prose Works of Percy Bysshe Shelley,* ed. Richard Herne Shepherd (London, 1888), I, 113–220. Its interest in the framework of this study derives chiefly from two aspects: it continues that part of the myth, referable to Godwin's *St. Leon* (*infra*), by which the Ahasuerus-figure appoints a legatee who is to inherit the Jew's magic talents at the price of assuming his immortality; secondly, Ginotti's hynotic powers are, for the first time in the development of the legend, the alpha and omega of his supernatural strength. "From the gaze of Ginotti Wolfstein's soul shrank, enhorrored, in confessed inferiority: he . . . started from Ginotti's eye-beam as from the emanation of some superior and preter-human being" (p. 140). "It was Ginotti, of whose strangely and fearfully gleaming eyeball Wolfstein endeavoured to evade the fascination in vain. His eyes, resistlessly attracted to the sphere of chill horror that played around Ginotti's glance, in vain were fixed on vacuity" (p. 148). "The eyes of Ginotti,

glaring with demoniacal scintillations, spoke tenfold terror to the soul of Wolfstein" (p. 187). "On a sudden Ginotti's frame mouldered to a gigantic skeleton, yet two pale and ghastly flames glared in his eyeless sockets" (p. 219). Shelley to Godwin: "To you I owe the inestimable boon of granted power, of arising from the state of intellectual sickliness and lethargy into which I was plunged two years ago, and of which *St. Irvyne* and *Zastrozzi* were the distempered, although unoriginal visions." In *Complete Works of Percy Bysshe Shelley*, eds. Roger Ingpen and W. E. Peck (London, 1926–30), VIII, 287. *Vide* also John Addington Symonds, *Shelley* (English Men of Letters, London, 1929), p. 21: "A certain interest attaches to [*St. Irvyne*] as the first known link between Shelley and William Godwin, for it was composed under the influence of the latter's novel, *St. Leon*." Other sources for Shelley's fragment are cited in Newman Ivey White, *Shelley*, I, 90, and in Birkhead, *The Tale of Terror*, pp. 123–24.

7. *The Haunted Castle*, pp. 198–99.

8. *The Popular Novel in England*, pp. 245–46.

9. Quotations are from William Godwin, *St. Leon: A Tale of the Sixteenth Century* (London, 1816).

10. It has not always seemed so. H. N. Brailsford, *Shelley, Godwin and Their Circle* (New York, 1913), pp. 172–73, reminds us that Godwin's "contemporary fame chiefly rested [on his novels], and publishers paid for them high though diminishing prices . . . the radical critics of the day, including Hazlitt, tried hard to convince themselves that Godwin was a greater novelist than the Tory, Scott." Holcroft, writing to Godwin, September 9, 1800, delivers himself of the ultimate criticism of *St. Leon* in a phrase which is not meant to be interpreted the way it sounds "Men must have arrived at an uncommon degree of general wisdom, when 'St. Leon' shall no longer be read." *Vide* Kegan Paul, *William Godwin: His Friends and Contemporaries* (Boston, 1876), II, 25.

11. Holcroft, in *ibid.*: "I always felt the insurmountable defect of the work and the strained if not improbable incidents that must be invented to exhibit a miserable man who had every means of enjoyment in his power. You have repeated to me times almost innumerable the necessity of keeping characters in action, and never suffering them to sermonize, yet of this fault 'St. Leon' is particularly found guilty by all whom I have heard speak of the work, with whom my feelings coincide." Similarly, Birkhead, *The Tale of Terror*, pp. 104–5: "Godwin . . . first constructs his machinery, and afterwards, with laborious effort, carves the figures who are to be attached to his words. . . . Godwin's point of view was not that of an artist but of a scientist, who, after patiently investigating and analysing mental and emotional phenomena, chose to embody his results in the form of a novel."

12. For the ideas in *Political Justice*, *vide* Brailsford, *Shelley, Godwin and Their Circle*, pp. 94–114.

13. Later commentators have interpreted the theme of *St. Leon* in the light of Godwin's *avant-propos*, with minor modifications. D. H. Monro, *Godwin's Moral Philosophy: An Interpretation of William Godwin* (London, 1953), p. 67, has noted that "there is a single theme in all of Godwin's novels: the tragedy of loneliness and misunderstanding." A similar purpose is discovered by David Fleischer, *William Godwin: A Study in Liberalism* (London, 1951), pp. 36–37: "Godwin's novel . . . took for its major theme one of the minor

themes of *Caleb Williams.* The hardest thing that Caleb had to bear from the persecution of Falkland was that, destroying as it did his good name in whatever circle he endeavoured to establish himself, he was virtually cut off from human society." Rather more perverse, perhaps, is the meaning at which George Woodcock arrives in *William Godwin: A Biographical Study* (London, 1946), p. 159, that "a man who attains wisdom and wishes to use it for the general good must expect and be willing to forego the ordinary comforts of life, and the benefits of domestic affection and even friendship in the course of his efforts." Woodcock's reading, as Monro, pp. 88–98, correctly annotates it, would be more convincing "if St. Leon's efforts for the general good had been more successful; but in fact they made himself and everyone else miserable."

14. Monro, *Godwin's Moral Philosophy,* p. 67.

15. Godwin's remark is quoted in Paul, *William Godwin,* I, 330; the *Review* critic in Tompkins, *The Popular Novel in England,* p. 213. Birkhead, *The Tale of Terror,* p. 112, writes: "The phrase, 'mixing human feelings,' betrays in a flash Godwin's mechanical way of constructing a story. He makes no pretense that *St. Leon* grew naturally as a work of art. He imposed upon himself an unsuitable task, and, though he doggedly accomplished it, the result is dull and laboured."

16. Beverly Sprague Allen, "William Godwin as a Sentimentalist," *PMLA,* XXXII (1918), 1–29.

17. We are plainly back in the world of Maria Edgeworth's homiletic juvenilia, the world of "Waste not, Want not," in which children are as pitilessly recruited to inculcate our daily lessons as the professional gradgrinds and gerund-grinders. It is not surprising to find that Godwin's novel appeared in the same year as Edgeworth's *Moral Tales.*

18. As an historical novel, *St. Leon* may be considered an egregious anachronism from beginning to end. "Godwin is wholly indifferent to historical accuracy," writes Birkhead, *The Tale of Terror,* p. 115, "and fails to transport us back far beyond the end of the 18th century. Rousseau's theories were apparently disseminated widely in 1525." There is thus some point in the title of a travesty which appeared the year after the novel: *St. Godwin: A Tale of the 16th, 17th, and 18th Century.*

19. Edward Bulwer-Lytton, Lord Lytton, *Zanoni,* p. 218. All quotations are from the Knebworth Edition of Lord Lytton's Novels, Vol. XXII. Cited hereafter by title.

20. Monro, *Godwin's Moral Philosophy,* p. 101: "A second main theme of *St. Leon* is the futility of indirect philanthropy. St. Leon is compelled to use devious means and never to be completely frank; hence he is invariably misunderstood and his plans miscarry. . . . This is, of course, the favourite Godwin theme of the need for sincerity."

21. Niilo Idman, *Charles Robert Maturin: His Life and Works* (London, 1932), p. 196.

22. C. Nelson Stewart, *Bulwer-Lytton as Occultist* (London, 1927), p. 1.

NOTES TO CHAPTER TEN

1. Biographical information is contained in Daphne Du Maurier, *The Du Mauriers* (New York, 1937), and the same author's *Gerald: A Portrait* (Garden

City, 1934). Miss Du Maurier has also edited a volume of letters: *The Young George Du Maurier: Letters, 1860–67* (London, 1951). E. V. Lucas has reprinted extracts from Du Maurier's diary in "George Du Maurier at Thirty-three," *Cornhill Magazine,* CL (1934), 385–410. For a useful assessment of Du Maurier's fiction, see Martin T. Wood, *George Du Maurier: The Satirist of the Victorians* (London, 1913), pp. 87–118.

2. Henry James, "George Du Maurier," in *Partial Portraits* (London, 1888), pp. 327–72, discusses Du Maurier's contributions to *Punch*. For a discussion of Du Maurier's craftsmanship, *vide* Derek Pepys Whiteley, *George Du Maurier: His Life and Art* (English Masters of Black and White, London, 1948).

3. Among the qualified admirers there is Bernard Shaw. "I have read 'Trilby' and enjoyed it greatly. It is no mere novel with illustrations; it is a homogeneous work of art in which the master, like a composer who sets his own poem to music, shows us his people by the art of the draughtsman, and tells us their story by the art of the fabulist. What Thackeray, with his enslaved mind and clumsy hand, tried to do in vain, is here brought happily off by the pleasantest of free-thinkers and the most charming of artists. Oddy enough, the successful artist has taken the unsuccessful one for his model, greatly improving on him in every respect save one: to wit, honesty. Thackeray saved his reputation and forced his oppressive books like sentences of penal servitude on the reading public by telling the truth in spite of himself. . . . If I want to respect Thackeray, I must think of his veracity and forget his workmanship; if I would respect Mr. Du Maurier, I must think of his workmanship and forget his veracity." "Trilby and 'L'Ami des Femmes,'" in *Dramatic Opinions and Essays* (New York, 1922), I, 228–29.

4. Writing to Tom Armstrong, Du Maurier notes: "I'm glad you approve of my literary style. I took pains, of course . . . and now see that I should have taken more. It all came too easily, and I found it far more difficult to illustrate than to write!" (Quoted in Daphne Du Maurier, *Gerald,* p. 48).

5. Quotations are from *Trilby* (New York, 1895).

6. Maurice Lanoire, "Un Anglo-Français, Georges Du Maurier," *Revue de Paris,* XLVII (1940), 263–81, gives a somewhat different interpretation of Du Maurier's subject matter: "Ce qui est . . . curieux, c'est la persistance du motif qui chante dans ces trois romans et fait d'eux une sort de mélancolique mélodie. Ce motif, c'est la nécessité de fuir la réalité dans le rêve, en attendant la mort" (p. 278).

7. The incident, minus the supernatural matter, is heavily autobiographical. While at work in an Antwerp studio, Du Maurier began to lose the sight in his left eye. Similarly, Barty's collapse is based on Du Maurier's near breakdown. See *The Du Mauriers,* pp. 296–97.

8. It need not be, of course. One can see that the subject matter of Peter Ibbetson might have attracted writers as different as Pirandello and the Balzac of *Ursule Mirouët.* Little Billee's passage from bohemian carefreeness to artistic maturity, via "Kunstekel" and acedia, suggests Mann's recurrent themes. The Martian religion of vital intelligence, down to the spoof of having Martia reenact the processes of conception and birth, recalls Shaw's metabiological pentateuch. These analogies themselves suggest that Du Maurier might have been a

gifted writer, had he only known how to write, and that very proviso is perhaps enough to distinguish him from the thousand practicing disciples of Bradbury.

9. Lanoire, "Un Anglo-Français," p. 280: "Il s'agit donc d'esquiver la vie, mauvaise ou médiocre. Le refuge se trouve tantôt dans le temps retrouvé, tantôt dans l'hypnose, l'alliance avec les esprits, l'anticipation de notre vie future."

10. Quotations are from *Peter Ibbetson* [1891], Modern Library (New York, 1932).

11. *The Haunted Castle,* p. 216.

12. The phrase is John Masefield's, who well defines Du Maurier's theme as recording "the influence of mind upon mind, of sympathy in its extreme between two spirits; of memory, unconsciously recorded, and of racial or familial memory in mysterious ways transmitted." See his "Introduction to *Peter Ibbetson* and *Trilby,*" *The Novels of George Du Maurier* (London, 1947), p. ix.

13. Anthony Powell finds the common literary ancestor of Taffy and the Laird in the hero of G. A. Lawrence's *Guy Livingstone* (1859), the prototype of the muscular man-about-town. "He can be dimly recognized even so far afield as 'Taffy-the-Laird' in *Trilby,* for, as The Yellow Dwarf remarked in his review of that book, Taffy and the Laird are indistinguishable." *Vide* "Introduction," *Novels of High Society from the Victorian Age* (London, 1947), p. x.

14. It is scarcely surprising, in the light of the foregoing plot summary, that *Trilby* enjoyed a tremendous vogue on the English and American stage in the 'nineties. A contemporary review of the stage adaptation, attributed by Wood to Justin Huntly Macarthy, can be applied verbatim to the novel. "In *Trilby* we get back, as it were to Humpty-Dumpty—to its simplicity at least, if not to its pitch of art. The strong man and the odd man and the boy man, brothers in Bohemianism, brothers in art, brothers in love for youth and beauty; the girl, the fair, the kind, the for-ever-desirable, pure in impurity, and sacred even in shame; the dingy evil genius who gibbers in Yiddish to the God he denies; the hopeless, devoted musician, whose spirit in a previous existence answered to the name of Bowes [Gecko]; the mother who makes the appeal that so many parents have made on behalf of their sons to fair sinners since the days when Duval the Elder interviewed Marguerite Gauthier; all this company of puppets please in their familiarity, their straight-forwardness, their undefeated obviousness, very much as a game of bowls on a village green with decent rustics . . . might please after a supper with Nana or an evening with the Theosophists." Quoted in Wood, *George Du Maurier,* pp. 100–101. It is only fair to add that Du Maurier himself regarded *Trilby* with derision. "He felt it was all rather vulgar, and he knew in his heart . . . that *Peter Ibbetson,* written with the spirit and not with an eye to the public taste, was by far the better book." *Vide* Daphne Du Maurier, *Gerald,* p. 49.

15. Railo, *The Haunted Castle,* p. 194, cites a comedy by Le Sage, *Le Diable boiteux,* in which a playwright markets his manuscript *The Wandering Jew* to three different publishers; the summary alone suggests that the legend is used as nothing more than an arbitrary point of reference. *Vide* also Zirus, *Der Ewige Jude,* pp. 39–40, for a discussion of Andrew Franklin's comedy *The Wandering Jew, or Love's Masquerade.*

16. Examples occur in *Tristram Shandy,* Bk. 2, chap. xxi; *Pickwick Papers,* chap. xxxix; and *Sartor Resartus,* Bk. 2, chap. vi.

17. It must not be thought that Svengali is made out to be either completely ludicrous or completely horrid, however. Occasionally Du Maurier reminds us that he is capable of kindly impulses. A good case for Svengali's basic decency is put forward in Alfred Welch, *Extracts from the Diary of Moritz Svengali* (New York, 1897), pp. 85–89. *Vide* also the comments by Shaw and Wilson, *infra.*

18. Wilson, "The Jews," in *A Piece of My Mind: Reflections at Sixty* (Garden City, 1958), p. 101.

19. *Dramatic Opinions and Essays,* I, 231–32.

20. *A Piece of My Mind,* pp. 81–104.

21. *Ibid.,* pp. 101–2.

22. Again, it is fair to add that Du Maurier seems to have been on excellent terms with Jews in his private life. His fellow artist Felix Moscheles has left a record of their close friendship in a volume of reminiscences, *In Bohemia with Du Maurier* (London, 1898). Du Maurier's correspondence in *The Young George Du Maurier* cites the artist family of Abraham and Simeon Solomon among his close companions; and finally it should be noted that the Jewess Leah Gibson is almost certainly an idealized portrayal of Du Maurier's wife, Emma Wightwick. See *The Young George Du Maurier,* pp. 294–95.

23. Writing from the retrospect of the twentieth century, with its bulky literature correlating art and disease, one may be tempted to assume that Svengali's profession tells us as much about his vital deficiencies as does his Jewish blood. Against such an impression speak not only the half-dozen "strong, sturdy, irrepressible, indomitable" artists in Du Maurier's novels who are not Jews, but the author's specific sideswipe at Max Nordau's theory on the degeneracy of artists. The allusion to Nordau is no less pointed for being phrased in Du Maurier's most offensive sophomoric strain: "According to the amiable, modest, polite, delicately humorous, and even tolerant and considerate Professor Max Nordau, this perfection of the olfactory sense proclaims poor Barty a degenerate! I only wish there were a few more like him, and that I were a little more like him myself!" (*The Martian,* p. 37.)

24. "And to whom but Barty Josselin do we owe it that our race is on an average already from four to six inches taller than it was thirty years ago, men and women alike; that strength and beauty are rapidly becoming the rule among us, and weakness and ugliness the exception?" (*The Martian,* p. 375.) Daphne Du Maurier, "Introduction," *The Martian, The Novels of George Du Maurier,* p. xv, sees a large element of wish-fulfillment in all this. "Barty Josselin . . . is the man that George Du Maurier, in his secret heart, longed to have been. Kicky [i.e., Du Maurier] was small of stature, brown-haired, and unremarkable; Barty Josselin was a broad-shouldered giant . . . a golden-haired god. Kicky came of bourgeois parentage; Barty Josselin was the illicit offspring of a passionate love affair between an English Duke and a beautiful French maiden."

25. Taylor, "Introduction," *Peter Ibbetson,* p. ix.

26. Du Maurier has a kidding reference to his obsession for tall women in *The Martian,* p. 339: writing in the *persona* of Du Maurier the famous illustrator to Barty's biographer, the narrator of the novel who has asked him to

supply the drawings for his biography, Du Maurier notes: "I remember the beautiful Miss Royce they were all so mad about, and also Miss Gibson, whom I admired much the more of the two, although she wasn't quite so tall—you know my craze for lovely giantesses."

27. Gerald Du Maurier, "Preface," *Trilby,* Everyman (London, 1931), p. viii.

NOTES TO CHAPTER ELEVEN

1. *Saint Joan,* iv.

2. *It Is Never Too Late to Mend: A Matter-of-Fact Romance* [1856], Library Ed. (London, 1913). Modder's discussion of Reade (*The Jew in the Literature of England,* pp. 229–31) presents Levi virtually as another paragon, a bias similarly apparent in his comments on Borrow, Lever, Caine, and others. Hilaire Belloc's sour remark that "with writers as different as Charles Reade and George Eliot we reach a time when the Jew is impeccable" (*The Jews,* p. 225) is nonsense not only with respect to Reade. A brief, perceptive critique of Reade by the late George Orwell may be found in "Books in General," *New Statesman,* Aug. 17, 1940; Reade's literary technique is comprehensively analyzed in Walter C. Phillips, *Dickens, Reade and Collins: Sensation Novelists* (New York, 1919).

3. In Caine's novel, the antagonists of the Jewish hero are described almost as though they were a Shylock-collective, who propose not only to rob the leader of the tribe but to exercise something very like ritual murder on him. Similar displays of fanaticism within the tribe can be found, earlier in the century, in Croly's Wandering-Jew romance *Salathiel,* in which the hero keeps running up against the contrast between Hebrew feuding and Christian forbearance, until he gets the point and flirts with the prospect of converting. See Hall Caine, *The Scapegoat* [1891, 1899], Manx Ed. (New York, 1899); and Rev. George Croly, *Salathiel: A Story of the Past, the Present and the Future* (New York, 1828). The author of *Ben-Hur* has cited *Salathiel* as "one of the six greatest novels ever written," an opinion to be seriously credited by readers who agree with him on any one of the other five.

4. *That Boy of Norcott's* [1869], Copyright Ed. (London, 1897–99), XXXV, 1–222. Shaw's debt is recorded in the Preface to *Major Barbara.*

5. In the Palliser novels, Trollope handles the same relationship—Irish lover, continental Jewess—with incomparably greater sophistication and insight in describing the amour between Phineas and "Madame Max," the widow of a German banker. It may be noted that in *Phineas Redux,* Trollope plays the same game of mixed doubles with his Jews and Jewesses that he repeats in *The Way We Live Now*: A courtship involving a Jew (Emilius-Lizzie, Brehgert-Longstaffe) is played off against one involving a Jewess (Madame Max–Phineas, Marie Melmotte–Felix). Naturally, the rules are flexible. Besant, for example, sets up two parallel romances—Gentile lovers, Jewish girls—and achieves his contrast in other ways: one of the Jewesses turns down a Gentile who is much too good for her; the other runs after a Gentile who is a cad and an imbecile. In Snow's *Conscience of the Rich* we get still another configuration: Leonard March's daughter intermarries with a Gentile whereas his son marries a Jewess. The permanent breach, however, is not with the daughter for marrying the

Gentile (much as this revolts the father *prima facie*) but with the son for marrying a Jewess whose political radicalism undermines the stability of the March family a lot more than a good middle-class intermarriage does.

6. Dostoyevski, "The Jewish Question," *Diary of a Writer* [1873–80] (New York, 1949), II, 637–53; Trollope, *The Eustace Diamonds* [1872], Oxford Trollope (London, 1950), II, 130; Henry Adams, *Letters* (Boston, 1938), II, 33 (to Elizabeth Cameron, Aug. 8, 1893); Werfel, *Jacobowsky and the Colonel* (New York, 1944). Disraeli drew on the Rothschilds both for his portrayal of Sidonia and for his group picture of the Neufchatels in *Endymion* [1880]; and Sidonia himself, it has been suggested, derives from two separate Rothschilds: Alfred, the head of the Neapolitan branch, who furnished the prototype for the Sidonia of *Coningsby,* and Lionel, who figures as Sidonia in *Tancred.* Balzac's De Nucingen, modeled on the Parisian principal James R., turns up throughout the *Comédie. La maison de Nucingen* [1838] describes his financial ascendancy; *Splendeurs et misères des courtisanes* [1838–47] his erotomania for Esther Gobseck; but he may also be tracked down to *Le père Goriot* [1835], *César Birotteau* [1837], *Un grand homme de province* [1839], *Pierrette* [1840], and *La cousine Bette* [1847].

7. *Clara Hopgood* [1896] (London, 1923). Rutherford's debt to Spinoza is intensively analyzed in the standard work on the subject: Wilfred Stone, *Religion and Art of William Hale White* (Stanford, 1954), pp. 101–21; *vide* also Basil Willey, *More Nineteenth Century Studies* (London, 1956), pp. 186–247. For a discussion of *Clara Hopgood,* see pp. 159–73 of the study by Stone, who elaborates the parallel of Spinoza and Baruch Cohen, pp. 161–64. White, like Eliot, translated Spinoza's *Ethics.*

8. Aldous Huxley, *Vulgarity in Literature* (London, 1930), p. 10.

9. *Nina Balatka: The Story of a Maiden of Prague* [1867] (Edinburgh, 1879). L. P. and R. P. Stebbins, *The Trollopes,* p. 270, discuss Trollope's views on parental interventionism; see *supra,* Chap. VI.

10. Bradford A. Booth, *Anthony Trollope: Aspects of His Life and Art* (Bloomington, 1958), pp. 30–31. Booth's critical work, the finest book on Trollope since Sadleir's biography, is also the one which analyzes Trollope's portrayals of Jews most astutely and thoroughly.

11. Walter Besant, *The Rebel Queen* (New York, 1893).

12. *The Tragic Comedians: A Study in a Well-Known Story,* Memorial Ed. (1909–12), XV. For the prototypes of these people, see the works listed *supra,* Chap. I, n.3.

13. *A Romance of Vienna* (London, 1838), I, 96–98. Mrs. Trollope heads this "A Portrait from the Life." Her novel may be read as a counterirritant to *Salathiel* as one of the six worst novels ever written. Mrs. Trollope's primitive attitude toward Jews supposedly stemmed in part from her contact with them in Vienna, where she spent some months of social-climbing in 1836, getting as high up as the Metternichs, who dined and entertained her. In her book of travels *Vienna and the Austrians* (London, 1838), which came out the same year as the *Romance* and forms a companion volume to it, she writes: "The love of this stiff-necked race for gold is so well known and so universally acknowledged in every land into which their active service has found entrance, that it will appear little better than a paradox to say that it is the excess of this

eagerly-sought gold which generates the canker so evidently destroying the heart's ease of all the Israelitish tribes in Vienna. . . . Do not believe that these observations arise from intolerance; they arise solely from observation" (II, 5). Eileen Bigland, *The Indomitable Mrs. Trollope* (London, 1953), pp. 176–88, deals with Mrs. T.'s Austrian experiences.

14. *The Newcomes: Memoirs of a Most Respectable Family* [1855] (London, 1911), XII–XIII; XII, 231.

15. *All Hallows' Eve* (New York, 1948).

16. Roth, *Benjamin Disraeli, Earl of Beaconsfield* (New York, 1951), p. 83. The other way of reconciling the discrepancy is James Russell Lowell's. In his review of *Tancred* in the *North American Review* (LXV [1847], 201–24), Lowell wrote: "Seldom has the inner life been so aptly symbolized in the outward as in the case of the Jews. That the idolaters of ceremony and tradition should become the venders of old clothes, that the descendants of those who, within earshot of the thunders of Sinai, could kneel before the golden calf, should be the money-changers of Europe, has in it something of syllogistic completeness. The work by which the elder D'Israeli will be remembered is the old curiosity shop of literature. He is merely a cast-off-clothes-dealer in an aesthetic sense. The son, with his trumpery of the past, is clearly a vender of the same wares, and an offshoot from the same stock."

17. The lines from *Punch* are cited by Modder, p. 209; on Ingoldsby's "Ikey Solomons," which came out in *Blackwood's* in 1832, see Philip Rieff, "Disraeli: The Chosen of History," p. 29. Trollope's Sidonia appears in Chaps. IX and XIX of *Barchester Towers* [1857]; Trollope also uses the name in a kidding allusion to Disraeli's politics in *Framley Parsonage* [1861]. Thackeray's burlesque, of course, is "Codlingsby," second in the book *Notes by Eminent Hands* [1847], in *Works,* VI, 478–88. Disraeli returned the favor by caricaturing Thackeray as the envious and conceited minor novelist St. Barbe in *Endymion.* Two notes by C. L. Cline clarify these little literary feuds: "Disraeli and Thackeray," *Review of English Studies,* XIX (1943), 404–8, and "'Coningsby' and Three Victorian Novelists," *Notes and Queries,* CLXXXVI (1944), 41–42.

Rather more amiable fictional versions of Disraeli are found in Anthony Hope's *Quisanté* [1900] and in two novels by Mrs. Craigie: *The School for Saints* [1897] and its sequel *Robert Orange* [1899]. In *School for Saints,* Disraeli merely has a walk-on part, but in the later novels Mrs. Craigie uses the Disraeli-myth for all she can get out of it: Orange, himself an idealized portrait of Disraeli, at the same time functions as a political adherent of the historical one, with the result that Disraeli, on one level of reality, walks into the novel every so often to encounter himself on another level, and $Disraeli_1$ finds himself writing letters to $Disraeli_2$. This is quixotic but humorless. Cf. the author's comments in *The Life of John Oliver Hobbes ("Mrs. Craigie")* (London, 1911), pp. 107 ff. Roland Grey, "Disraeli in Fancy Street," *Cornhill,* LXVI (1929), 102–10, gives a run-down of Disraeli portrayals in English fiction and drama.

18. *A Piece of My Mind,* pp. 102–3.

19. *Hypatia, or New Foes with an Old Face* [1852], Westminster Ed. (New York, 1899). Discussions of the novel and its Jewish characters appear in W. F. Lord, "The Kingsley Novels," *Nineteenth Century,* LV (1904), 996–1004; Stanley E. Baldwin, *Charles Kingsley* (Ithaca, 1934), pp. 126–34; Margaret Far-

rand Thorp, *Charles Kingsley* (Princeton, 1937), pp. 108–16; W. M. Conacher, "Charles Kingsley," *Queens Quarterly,* XLV (1938), 503–11; and Una Pope-Hennessy, *Canon Charles Kingsley* (London, 1948).

20. *Leila, or The Siege of Granada,* Knebworth Limited Ed. (Boston, 1891–92), XXI, 1–175.

21. *Anti-Semite and Jew* (New York, 1948), pp. 95–96.

22. W. F. Monypenny and G. E. Buckle, *Life of Benjamin Disraeli,* rev. ed. (New York, 1929), I, 24.

23. The foregoing summary comes out of Leslie Fiedler's brilliant piece, "What Can We Do About Fagin?" *Commentary,* VII (1949), 411–18. His article should be read in conjunction with the symposium in *Commentary* which it provoked: "The Jewish Writer and the English Literary Tradition," VIII, 209–19 and 361–70, with contributions by David Daiches, Alfred Kazin, Harry Levin, Lionel Trilling, *et al.*; and Milton Hindus, "F. Scott Fitzgerald and Literary Anti-Semitism," *Commentary,* III (1947), 508–16, which contains pertinent material on Eliot. Josef Rischik, *Graham Greene und sein Werk* (Berne, 1951), pp. 84–87, reviews Greene's Jewish personnel. The dates of Greene's novels are: *Stamboul Train,* 1932; *This Gun for Hire,* 1936; and *Brighton Rock,* 1938; Waugh's appeared as follows: *Decline and Fall,* 1928; *Vile Bodies,* 1930; *Black Mischief,* 1932. The usual unflattering allusions to "the whores and the Jews" and to the young girls who deserve something better in life than "a Jew called Furstein who kept a girl in Shepherd's Market" may be spotted in Greene's *It's a Battlefield* [1934] and *The Confidential Agent* [1939]. To Waugh's gallery of miniature monsters should be added his portrait of Ambrose Silk, the half-Jewish homosexual littérateur of *Put Out More Flags* [1942], editor of the aesthetic journal *The Ivory Tower,* who sits out the Second World War in the Ministry of Information (Department of Religion, Desk: Atheism) and ends up in Ireland as Fr. Flanagan, S.J.: a combination of Fr. Rothschild and Youkoumian, the squalid Financial Secretary to the Azanian Minister of Modernization.

24. "The Jewish Writer and the English Literary Tradition," p. 218. On Pound, see Peter Viereck, "Pure Poetry, Impure Politics, and Ezra Pound," *Commentary,* XI (1951), 340–46, to which I am indebted for the quoted matter from the *Pisan Cantos.* To restore the balance, see Archibald MacLeish, *Poetry and Opinion* (Urbana, 1950). William Van O'Connor and Edward Stone have put the much publicized Bollingen Award to pedagogic uses in freshman themes by anthologizing the pertinent journalistic, critical, and legal documents in *A Casebook on Ezra Pound* (New York, 1959), including reprinted pieces by George Orwell, Dwight Macdonald, and others. Eliot's position cannot perhaps be so neatly divorced from Pound's as the above remarks suggest, in so far as his cultural program calls for a certain amount of religious discrimination which gets itself into his polemical utterances. (Conversely, one often hears it alleged that Pound is the one who speaks in symbol and metaphor, who, when he says "Jew," means USURA, whether he says it in verse or in prose.) The text which it is customary to cite against Eliot is: *After Strange Gods* (New York, 1934), page 20: "reasons of race and religion combine to make any large number of free-thinking Jews undesirable." But that was in 1934. Hindus ("Literary Anti-Semitism," p. 518) draws the line by noting that anti-Semitism is "central,

philosophical, obsessive" for Pound (or Céline, whose *Trifles for a Massacre* struck Gide as so vehemently exaggerated that, in his review, he mistook it for a satire on anti-Semitism) and "decorative, fashionable, literary," for Eliot (or Gide), whose anti-Jewishness, on the level of explicit prose statement, "as its explosive social qualities were revealed was completely and silently dropped."

25. *My Life as German and Jew* (New York, 1933), pp. 11–12.

26. "The Jewish Writer and the English Literary Tradition," p. 216.

27. *The Conscience of the Rich* (New York, 1958). Snow's novel is the latest in the sequence collectively entitled *Strangers and Brothers.* The structure of this work and Snow's literary techniques generally have been analyzed by Pamela Hansford Johnson, "Three Novelists and the Drawing of Character," *Essays and Studies,* N.S. III (1950), 82–99, and, most recently, by William Cooper, *C. P. Snow,* "Bibliographical Series" (London, 1959), pp. 15–29.

SOURCES OF MATERIAL CITED IN THE APPENDIXES

Appendix II. *Letters from James Earl of Perth . . . to His Sister the Countess of Erroll, and Other Members of His Family,* ed. William Jerdan (London, 1845), pp. 20–23.

Appendix III. *Holinshed's Chronicles of England, Scotland, and Ireland* (London, 1807), II, 205, 301, 492.

Appendix IV. The petition to Cromwell from E. N. Calisch, *The Jew in English Literature* (Richmond, 1909), p. 45. Cromwell in council from *Rev. Joseph Spence, Anecdotes, Observations, and Characters of Books and Men* [1728–44], ed. S. W. Singer (London, 1820), pp. 77–79.

Appendix V. *Works of Sir Thomas Browne,* ed. Geoffrey Keynes (London, 1928), III, 42–48.

Appendix VI. (1) Grimm, *Maerchen* (Leipzig, 1937, translation mine); (2) Defoe, *The Fortunate Mistress or . . . Roxana* (Oxford, 1927), I, 130; (3) Sandys, in *Hakluytus Posthumus, or Purchas His Pilgrimes* (Glasgow, 1905), VIII, 172; (4) Coryat, in *Hakluytus Posthumus,* X, 433; (5) Evelyn, *Diary and Correspondence,* ed. William Bray (London, 1906), I, 160; (6) Pepys, *Diary of Samuel Pepys,* ed. Henry B. Wheatly (London, 1929), III, 303, and Walpole, *Letters of Horace Walpole,* ed. Paget Toynbee (Oxford, 1902–5), V, 375.

Appendix VII. Robert Southey, *Letters from England* [1907], ed. Jack Simmons (London, 1951), pp. 392–98.

Appendix VIII. *The Tatler,* March 28, 1831.

Appendix IX. *The Edinburgh Review,* January 1831.

Appendix X. Monypenny and Buckle, *Life of Benjamin Disraeli* (New York, 1920), V, 448–50.

Appendix XI. The London *Times,* November 9, 1917.

Index